SITUATING ENVIRONMENTAL HISTORY

Situating Environmental History

Edited by

RANJAN CHAKRABARTI

MANOHAR
2026

First published 2007
Second edition 2021

Reprinted 2026

ISBN 978-81-7304-683-4

Published by

Ajay Kumar Jain for
Manohar Publishers & Distributors
4753/23 Ansari Road, Daryaganj
New Delhi 110 002

Printed at

Replika Press Pvt. Ltd.

Contents

SECTION III: COLONIALISM, POST-COLONIALISM, THE STATE AND THE MANAGEMENT OF NATURE

SECTION IV: BEYOND INDIA

Preface to the New Edition

The present collection of essays was first published more than thirteen years ago. The work, I believe, did raise certain new questions relevant to the, then, emerging frontier of environmental history. More than a decade has passed since then, but the book is still widely used by the students and researchers across the world as the reading lists of university courses available in the websites would testify. In view of the popularity and extensive appreciation of the book, both Mr Ramesh Jain of Manohar Publishers and myself felt the need of a revised edition. As I learn from the available feedbacks about the book in general, and the editorial essay, in particular, the volume still generates some interest among the students and scholars, who found it to be a starting point for the study of global environmental history and environmental history of South Asia. Though a new generation of scholars is already looking at this frontier of historical knowledge with new materials and questions, yet, the major arguments of the introductory chapter that appeared in the first edition still hold ground, and in view of this I decided not to disrupt the major framework of the text of the introductory essay. The first edition was primarily geared to situate environmental history which was then in an embryonic form in South Asia. One of the objectives of this revised edition is to further explain the relevance of environmental history against the backdrop of the growing literature on the subject and to ascertain with clarity what environmental history teaches us.

I also take this opportunity to profoundly thank Mr Ramesh Jain and his team at Manohar Publishers for bringing out the revised new edition of the book within a very short time.

I hope that this edition of the book will receive more appreciation than the preceding one.

6 February 2021 RANJAN CHAKRABARTI

Preface

In the course of preparing this volume, I have accumulated a great many debts of gratitude, which it is my duty and pleasure to acknowledge. I would like to thank the University Grants Commission of India for identifying the Department of History of Jadavpur University as a potential centre for the study of environmental history under the UGC's Special Assistance Programme. It is in this programme that most of the essays compiled here have their root. Some of the essays that feature in this anthology were presented at the international seminar held at Jadavpur University (3-5 March 2005) on the 'Situating Environmental History' which brought together scholars from across the world. I would like to acknowledge my debt to all the contributors for their continued assistance and cooperation. They were always very prompt with their replies to all my editorial queries.

My sincere thanks to all my colleagues in the History Faculty at Jadavpur University. They were my companions in daily discussions and debates. I also take this opportunity to acknowledge my sense of gratitude to Kaushik Chakraborty, Subhosree Chaudhuri, Prianka Ghosh and Md. Sohrabuddin for various help. A special note of thanks to Professor Deepak Kumar for offering many helpful comments. My special thanks are due to Mili Ghose for all necessary cooperation. My dear friend Larry was also a great source of inspiration.

I also take this opportunity to express my sense of gratitude to Mr Ramesh Jain of Manohar for undertaking the publication of the book. Mr Siddharth Chowdhury and his team at Manohar saved me from many errors by their excellent editorial skills.

The responsibility for all lapses, if any, are mine alone.

RANJAN CHAKRABARTI

Introduction

Ranjan Chakrabarti

The study of environmental history in today's world has become important as a natural and inevitable result of a perceived 'environmental crisis'. This perception has resulted in the development of a broad area called Environmental Studies. However, in view of the important role of scientists in the emergence of Environmental Studies – and the subsequent contribution of scholars from diverse disciplinary backgrounds to this field – it has remained an open-ended subject. Within the field, 'environmental history' remains universally acknowledged as a critically important area of inquiry, but without well-defined disciplinary canons and methodological guidelines. It is strongly felt that only professional historians with the requisite methodological training will be able to (1) develop and define the agenda and disciplinary canons of this field of inquiry, and (2) historicise present-day concerns and anxieties in the broad area of Environmental Studies. Unfortunately, professional historians in India and abroad appear to be reluctant to undertake this task in a concerted and coordinated manner. This is the vacuum that this volume in general, and this editorial in particular, seeks to fill. I confess that I have not been able to make an exhaustive survey of the fast expanding literature on environmental history and the present essay is based on a limited sampling of the recent scholarship in this field. As the work progressed, I was particularly amazed by the richness of this literature and embarrassed by my ignorance of it. The historiography of environmental history has multiplied more than a hundred times over the last two decades.

It is well known that history is essentially a continuous dialogue between the past and the present. Historians give voice to the silences of the archives. The pattern of historical research changes frequently and there is no doubt that it has changed substantially in recent times. It seems that under the forceful impact of postmodernism today we are hearing the voice of alternative histories instead of a simple single track. I am not a post-modernist because I do not understand post-modernism very well. But I agree with Dr Sekhar Bandopadhyay that history has survived the onslaught of post-modernism[1]. The present volume throws light on one of the emerging frontiers of historical research. One significant area where the recent approach of historians has yielded result is what has come to be called 'history of the environment'. The purpose of the present essay, apart from offering a brief editorial note on the other essays that feature in this book, is to raise three important questions that scholars interested in this particular branch of history might wish to ask.

These questions are:

(1) Is environmental history a separate sub-discipline under the discipline of history or is it just a recent offshoot of social history/cultural history/intellectual history/economic history/history from below/tribal history/history of peasant resistance/history of socio-political crime?
(2) What is the present state of scholarship in this field and what is the shape of the historiography of the subject at present?
(3) What could be the strategy or methodology to be pursued by scholars practising this genre of history?

The present discussion will cater to the needs of those who have only a hazy notion of this particular branch of history. It may be of limited help to introduce the snooping passers-by and helpless beginners to the new frontier of environmental history. Let us now attempt to answer the questions I have already raised.

Defining the Territory

Is environmental history a separate sub-discipline under the discipline of history or is it just a recent offshoot of social history/cultural history/economic history/history from below/tribal history/history of peasant resistance/history of socio-political crime?

This is a question my colleagues and professional friends across the world who are not directly engaged in environmental history, have been asking me over the last two years. There is no simple answer. The origins of environmental history are firmly rooted in social, cultural or economic history, history of science and technology, history of health or beyond. It still shares a very porous border with economic and social histories and even with various other disciplines. Such mechanical branding of histories like 'social history' or 'cultural history' or 'environmental history' may not always convey the essence. To answer this critical question one needs a commendable knowledge of the philosophy of history and a great deal of skill to map out the ongoing changes in the philosophy of history. I do not qualify on either ground. But it does not require much sophistication to understand the fact that environmental history has stemmed from the recent concern for environmental or ecological changes. The historiography of environmental history has been expanding at such a remarkable pace in recent years that it is humanly impossible to keep pace with it. It has indeed emerged as a separate sub-discipline within the historical discipline in a number of countries. Initially, it appeared to be a device to arouse public consciousness to the environmental crisis the scientists, engaged in various branches of biology and ecology, had identified. However, it is increasingly being acknowledged now that the recent environmental crisis calls for an active and independent role of historians to develop a new paradigm for the future.

Concern for the environment in human society has always been there. Of all the decisions human society takes, perhaps the most crucial ones have always been related to the natural world. One of the flash points in the inner conflicts within human societies of the past was fuelled by the continuous effort to resolve the question of the legitimate use of the natural world. As human settlements spread across the earth and technology advanced, the urge to resolve this fundamental question relating to the legitimate use of the natural world increased. With the passage of time the urgent need of resolving this unresolved question has been increasingly felt everywhere. It may be possible to explain many relations in the language of power. The human encounter with the natural world, too, can be explained in the language of power. Environment is one of those spaces where we see the most intense form of demonstration of power. Nature may be seen as a parallel category with race, class, gender, ethnicity or nationalism – that is, as categories deployed to reveal power relationships in societies. The rapid unfolding of power relations, the random misuse of the natural world, the rise of new technology to exploit nature, and the growing resource crunch have made this age-old debate complex and intense as never before. It is a question central and global to the entire human civilization. The more human society progresses and prospers, the greater is the longing to resolve the problem. Writers, philosophers, historians, lawmakers, administrators, and thinkers through the ages have been wrestling to settle this unresolved question. The method of addressing this crucial question has attained a refinement over the last two decades and one important manifestation of this can be found in the rise of a new field of knowledge, i.e. environmental history.

How did it all begin? I have already mentioned that concern for nature did exist in the past. Historians and philosophers of the past were aware that the natural environment plays an important role in how humans behave, relate to one another, and organize themselves. Historians since Herodotus and Thucydides have understood the value of geography and the environment in the understanding of human societies. Thucydides' description of the plague and its origins may be a starting point. Environmental history seems to have a much longer and richer pedigree than is often supposed. W.G. Palmer has opined that the works of Braudel, Bodin, Montesquieu, and Machiavelli may be connected and seen as constituting the foundations of environmental history. He cites More's *Utopia*, Bacon's *New Atlantis* and other works to argue that the earth's decay is a sign of the Second Coming and Winstanley's view of the world as a treasure house for mankind.[2]

South Asia is no exception in this line. In ancient India, forests were regarded as abodes of spiritual solace and the concept preserving forests and wildlife developed around the *ashrams* sages. These forest-based *ashrams* propagated *aranya sanskriti* or a forest culture and human understanding of the fundamental ecological utility of forest ecosystems and their economic importance, which led to trees and animals being treated with veneration.[3] Ancient texts like the *Ramayana* give clues to such sensibilities. When Rama, the prince of Ayodhya, is about to set out on his long exile in the forests south of the Gangetic plains, his mother Kaushalya expresses fears about his safety: 'May the huge elephants not harm you, my dear son', she says, 'nor the lions, tigers, bears, boars or ferocious horned buffalo'. Rama himself, in a bid to dissuade his wife Sita from following him to the woods, paints a similar portrait of the forest as a place of hidden menace. In fact, the word *vana* or forest was only given to lands where pleasure gave way to hardship. But it is also a place that is beautiful. The twin themes of the forest as a place of dangers to be confronted and of beauty to be enjoyed run like a thread through the epic.[4]

The protection of elephants had become serious business by the time of the Mauryas. The *Arthasastra* mentions rules for protecting elephant forests. Apart from elephant forests there were other forests where the aim was to secure timber and tiger and lion skins. The protector of the forest worked to eliminate thieves, tigers, and other predators from the woods to make them safe for cattle herders. The same tenor of concern for the wilderness runs through the medieval period. Babur, a keen observer of wildlife, gives interesting information about it in his memoir.

Interestingly, everywhere the conservationist urge became more pronounced after the industrial revolution that transformed the rural and urban landscapes of Europe. The loss of woodlands and changing landscape created space for ideas of the romantic world of nature. The romantic writings, which were in some ways also a critique of the industrial revolution, celebrated lost nature. It encouraged a 'back-to-the-land' movement. William Wordsworth, John Ruskin, and William Morris were some of the leading literary figures who contributed to this movement and to the setting up of environmental societies in Europe. The rapid disappearance of forests in Europe and America also gave birth to the idea of wilderness, which combined elements of morality, science and aesthetics.[5]

The United States is very rich in environmental history as a separate sub-discipline. It was here that self-conscious environmental history first began to take shape. Environmental history in the US grew out of the history of conservation as an ideal and as a social movement and drew its stimulus from a tradition. The origins of this tradition may be traced to the works of scholars like George Perkins Marsh and Frederick Jackson

Turner. Marsh was the American minister to Turkey during the Crimean War and later to the Kingdom of Italy between 1861 and 1882. The environmental conditions he experienced abroad left a permanent imprint on his mind. What intrigued him was the receding forest cover in the Mediterranean basin. In *Man and Nature*, published in 1864, he linked the large-scale deforestation of the Mediterranean basin to the decline of the Romans and the Western European civilization in a cause-effect relationship. He went on to argue that the region's deforested land had experienced erosion, desertification and eventually ecological collapse.

Marsh, arguably the first environmental historian of the world, warned that the environmental disaster that had once devastated the Old World might well threaten the New World.[6] He singled out the urgent need of protecting the Adirondack mountains, which contain the headwaters of several of New York's most important rivers, including the Hudson.

Additional stimuli for US environmental history came from the frontier history of Frederick Jackson Turner. Turner's is a spatial explanation of history. He discussed in detail the significance of space or wilderness in the formation of American character and culture.[7] Walter Prescott Webb, too, wrote about the American frontier and attached importance to the vast wilderness.[8] In the United States, environmental history has a historiographical canon largely rooted in the American scene. This is simply because environmental history, as distinct from the practice of conservation, first made its appearance in the US. But one serious problem in American environmental historiography is the lack of enthusiasm to face American engagement with the rest of the world. However, American historians are now making a sincere attempt to come out of their shell of insularity.[9]

Such direct concern for the environment or its impact on human societies was, however, rare among professional historians until the 1970s. Barring a few exceptions, until the mid-1970s, historians have, by and large, indirectly addressed various environmental or ecological issues while writing economic, social and cultural histories of various types. So, various environmental issues actually remain scattered in the history of peasant resistance or history from below, agrarian history, tribal history, social and cultural history, history of ideas, and so on. It is true that such histories concentrated primarily on the arable parts of the landscape with some minor exceptions. This meant that non-arable forests, pastoral lands, mountains and marshes were, on the whole, ignored by the practitioners of the discipline. Sir Jadunath Sarkar, who focused primarily on the political history of the Mughal Empire, writes about the impact on the environment of Mughal military expeditions to the Indian deep south. But here, as anywhere else, references to environmental degradation are made occasionally and rarely. Only in the history of medicine and public health do environmental issues acquire real prominence in the historical scholarship before 1970. Some environmental issues do feature in themes like history of crime, conflict over forest laws, movements for folk justice, and microscopic studies of popular culture.[10]

Broadly speaking there are four categories of environmental history: (1) environment-oriented environmental history, (2) cultural or intellectual environmental history, (3) environmental history that uses environment as a site for the exercise of power, and (4) environmental histories that run through all three. Environment-oriented environmental history is primarily preoccupied with changes in biological or physical environments and how these changes affect human beings or how human actions affect the physical environment. Cultural and intellectual environmental history is very rich and is concerned with representations of images of nature in ideas, arts, and letters. It traces the shifts in these representations and what light they throw on the societies that produced them. The third variety uses environment as a site for the exercise of various types of power. It includes ideas, law, and state policy in relation to the natural world. It attempts to make systematic studies of how State power approached and used nature and how different interest groups struggled over it. The final variety of environmental history moves around with one or more of the issues stated above. It is essentially ragbag in character, yet very absorbing.

Professional historians were initially cynical about environmental history and the response it generated within the profession was not very encouraging. Mainstream history has always been very conservative and suspicious about new frontiers of historical research.[11] The pattern of reception of environmental history by historians, however, varies. The history of the American West has been well received. The same is true about Chinese,

South Asian and African environmental histories. A favourable reception of any brand of history often depends on the skill and ability of scholars to package and shape the problems they are probing. This is equally true about environmental history.[12]

The lack of appreciation for environmental history is more prominent in the academic job market, even in those countries where this sub-field is fairly well established. Under the circumstances, young and promising environmental historians are frequently forced to market themselves as practitioners of the conventional discipline of history. One serious charge against environmental history is that it leaves out people and focuses more on climate, vegetation, wildlife, viruses, or technology. Forrest Mcdonald, one of the most accomplished historians of the American South, writes in the opening page of his autobiography:

> The objects of historical thinking are varied, and people are often ambiguous as to what they mean by the term history. Always it refers to events that took place in the past, but never to all events. The evolution of the animal kingdom, changes in climate, and the alterations of the surface of earth, for example, took place in the past and constitute what is sometimes called natural history, but these are outside the purview of conventional history, whose content is human affairs.[13]

I will argue that environmental historians do not always deliberately push human agency to the sideline; it depends more on the strategy and methodology the historian pursues. Micro-level environmental history, like social history, may be written with the human agency in the forefront but macro-scale environmental history would inevitably tend to underline the long *duree* forces, both cultural and natural rather than human beings as the key players.[14] Another criticism of environmental history is that it is, in most cases, packed with narratives of environmental destruction and dislocation with a sprinkling of romanticism or nostalgia. This is but natural given the fact that environmental history seeks to take lessons from the past interactions of humankind with the natural world. Such lessons may help us to make the future worth living. Again, all environmental histories are not pale and grim. Those dealing with the condition of fresh drinking water and sanitation and health and medicine of the modern period depict a joyous story of progress and not of decadence. Certain types of environmental history, especially those that derived their strength from environmental activism, express a clear political prejudice and make common cause with various interest groups struggling to establish control over the natural resources. A substantial fraction of South Asian environmental history which stemmed from grassroots protests against India's aborted Forest Bill of 1982 did demonstrate a political bias. In recent years, however, Indian environmental history has become more academic and less partisan in character.[15]

We are aware of the turns in the pattern of mainstream historical research in modern times. Environmental history has benefited in recent years from these recent shifts in history writing. The quest for alternative voices in history has exerted a sobering influence on the subject itself and made conservative historians tolerant to ongoing swings within the discipline. The steady expansion of environmental history has given it a separate identity as a sub-discipline. There has been a tendency to play down the importance of the subject and see it as an integral part of the currently emerging frontier of Environmental Studies. Historians of environment, I will argue, have the responsibility to retain the methodology of their own discipline in their own way. In the process, historians will be better able to contribute to the broader framework of Environmental Studies. History is a discipline which does not need rigorous theories. Historians are helpless without facts and facts are meaningless without historians.[16] My friends in various social science faculties often consider this as a drawback of the discipline and many of them believe that post-modernist history may help the historians elevate the status of the subject. I do not think that historians or environmental historians are expected to push forward the cause of social theory. Historians are required to stick to documents and the corroboration and interpretation of those documents rather than construction of theories. History as a discipline has survived the onslaught of post-modernism, but it is still necessary to defend the discipline. We shall return to this point later while discussing the third important question relating to this particular branch of history, i.e. methodology.

Environmental history has survived the initial unfriendliness it met from the mainstream discipline. But this attitude to environmental history has undergone a qualitative change in recent years. The sub-field is now growing and it is being treated with respect and admiration not only by historians but also by scholars belonging to other disciplines. There are several indications of the growing impact of environmental history in India and the wider world. A number of universities in the United States, the UK, Switzerland, Sweden, Germany, Australia, and New Zealand have been either developing research centres or offering formal programmes in environmental history. In this connection mention may be made of the centres of environmental history located in several US universities in California, Wisconsin and Kansas, the Australian National University in Canberra, the Centre for World Environmental History in Sussex, St. Andrews and Stirling in Scotland, Gottingen in Germany, Vienna in Austria, and Otago in New Zealand. It can be presumed that more such centres of environmental history are being developed. A number of universities in India have followed suit. The revision of the history syllabi in several Indian universities, under the guidance of the University Grants Commission (UGC), points to the increasing institutionalization of the sub-discipline of environmental history.[17]

The UGC has identified the Department of History at Jadavpur University in Kolkata, as a potential centre for pursuing research and teaching in the Environmental History of India for a period of five years under its Special Assistance Programme. The community of environmental historians is much more organized today than it had been a couple of decades earlier. The American Society for Environmental History was founded in 1976 and a European equivalent was born in 1999.[18] At present there are two main journals[19] in the English language on environmental history: *Environmental History*, published in the USA and *Environment and History*, published in the UK since 1995.[20] According to one estimate, at least 50 other history journals published environmental history articles in the years 1999-2003. *History and Theory*, published in the United States, chose Environment and History as one of its theme issues in 2003 (theme issue 42). A journal of South Asian environmental history, given the robustness of South Asian environmental history, is long overdue. The number of books, conferences, and websites dealing with environmental history has multiplied in recent years. These are some of the important signs of the currently shifting attitude to environmental history.[21]

Brief Historiography

This brings us to the second question I raised at the starting of the present article:

What is the present state of scholarship in this field and what is the shape of the historiography of the subject at present?

We have already noted that environmental history as a separate subject actually arose in the Euro-American world as an offshoot of the post-War wave of environmentalism. Interestingly the subject was first dragged into the academic arena by natural scientists, who recognized the political and historical significance of their subject, rather than by historians. The work that set a global agenda for environmental history was the 1967 book *Traces on the Rhodian Shore* by Clarence Glacken. Glacken was a geographer and not a historian. Quite a number of scholars, following in Glacken's footsteps, made environmental history intellectually acceptable in the United States. A major English contribution was *Man and the Natural World* by Keith Thomas (1983). With the publication of Alfred Crosby's *Ecological Imperialism* in 1986, the subject reached another landmark. However, the continents of Asia and Africa did not properly feature in any of these works.[22]

Environmental history in Asia and Africa initially derived its strength from the upsurge of the history from below, pioneered by Peter Burke and E.P. Thompson, and from the increasing interest in material culture so vividly portrayed in the work of Braudel. In fact, the *Annales* School (association of scholars like Marc Bloch, Braudel, and Ladurie) had been nurturing the seeds of environmental history since the 1970s though in a different way. These scholars understood that the human experience was the composite result of the interaction of many things, many of which were either autonomous or only partially subject to human volition. They inherited from Durkheim the notion that the individual could only be comprehended within his social context. They thought that the external context could be understood by the same kind of logic as that employed by natural science. This total history was, therefore, a history which sought a synthesis of all the material, physical, and mental forces that had shaped the life of men in the past.[23] Thus, to the scholars of the *Annales* School, the natural environment, too, among other things, appeared to be an important consideration in the understanding of the structures of the past. Fernand Braudel could discern in the Mediterranean world a powerful influence of geography, but he saw it as a static force. Ladurie, however, brought to light the point of environmental change in some of his major works. The *Annales* historians, however, did not consider themselves as environmental historians and they did not use the phrase until 1974. Nevertheless, the *Annales* School served as a great source of inspiration to the environmental historians of the future.[24]

In South Asia, environmental history began to emerge in the late 1980s. A series of books and articles brought forth this new quest for an environmental history of South Asia. Two of the earliest articles were written by North Americans, Robert K. Winters, a professional forester, the other a radical Indianist and political historian, Richard Tucker. Tucker aimed at drawing a link between nationalist protest and the colonial forest policy in Western India.[25] With his article the whole pace of work changed and in the early 1980s writers from a variety of disciplines started to construct a coherent agenda in the environmental history of South and South-East Asia. From this time onwards, environmental history and the forest history of India in particular became intensely politicized. The process of politicization had begun with the rise of the Chipko movement in northern India. In the 1980s and 1990s two important questions kept the environmental historians on their toes:

(1) What was the real history of protest against State forestry in India and in what ways was it connected to the broad history of nationalist protest?
(2) What was the ideological history of the State agency that was threatening the ecology of India?

The debate that took off regarding a fresh forest act in 1980 freed the historians from their earlier indifference to the subject. A number of scholars stationed in India, the Duke University, and Oxford approached the subject from different directions. While the Duke project concentrated more on agrarian changes and land use in the tropics and its impact on environment, researchers in India concentrated on the history of resistance to colonial forest policy and the ideological content of that policy.[26]

Ramachandra Guha in his articles and subsequently in his books asserted that in the pre-British period there was little or no interference with the customary use of forest and forest produce. Thus, Guha views colonial forest policy and conservation as primarily driven by materialistic considerations – that of serving the strategic and revenue interest of the British Empire. In opposition to the argument propounded by Gadgil and Guha, that imperial needs for timber and shipbuilding propelled scientific forestry with its associated bureaucracy, Richard Grove argues that colonial conservationism was based on humanist concerns motivated by growing deforestation and drought. Grove opines that it was desiccationism that promoted the idea of forest conservancy in the colonies. Desiccationism draws on the connection between deforestation and drought, shrinking water resources, soil erosion, and productivity.[27] Officials of the European trading companies were able to take note of them.

These people systematically developed desiccationist discourses and sought State intervention in the protection of forests. In the process, Grove plays down the importance of imperialist or capitalist greed behind the forest policy and focuses on other considerations, which were more humane.[28] Mahesh Rangarajan does not see simple polarities between the two sets of ideas and suggests that a convergence of ideas was indeed the case. He argues that the desiccationist fear had only a limited impact and was only one of the influences that shaped the course of the early nineteenth-century Indian forestry.[29] Ajay Skaria views forest conservancy which emerged out of the desiccationist discourses also as a part of the broader 'civilising mission' of imperialism. Skaria disagrees with Grove and says that the agenda of forest conservancy was not 'innocent of colonial domination'.[30] D.D. Dangwal followed up the view of Skaria and showed how desiccationism was frequently used by the State to extend control over the central Himalayan forests (Uttarakhand).[31]

I see the problem as essentially an integral part of a broader strategy of power which was geared primarily to ensure the domination of the Indian colony by its white rulers. To the British rulers, the colonization of India seemed to be incomplete without the pacification of the jungle. To them the Indian jungle alone had the wilderness to match the valour of the masculine occident.

The Forest Acts, in a single stroke, made government's claim over the forest legitimate, and hunting, food gathering, or cutting trees became illegitimate. The main group of offences was that of hunting, wounding or stealing of animals, and poaching or fishing. In this manner was created a whole new legal category of forest crimes. There was progressive criminalization of varied forms of human activity within the Indian forests which were previously not under the purview of the State. Legislators throughout the colonial period were constantly extending the boundaries of forest crimes, though the popular perception of what constituted 'forest crime' still remained very fluid. The government's claim over the forest was displayed as just and legitimate. The new forest policy was geared to generate a new sensibility as to the use of forests. There is no disagreement on the point that the forests were destroyed due to the policy of ruthless commercial exploitation adopted by the colonial government. The British first destroyed the forests and then became the self-styled protectors of the same forests. I have argued elsewhere that the English were the real poachers but they used the game law to brand the indigenous forest people, who earned their livelihood from the forest, as 'poachers'. The indigenous people, being deprived of their age-old forest rights, often refused to recognize the validity of government's claims and continued to cultivate at will, cut trees, and burn the forest floors as they had been doing since time immemorial. Thus, having destroyed the animals the European hunters later emerged as self-styled conservationists and went flat out to romanticize the tropical rain forest and its animals.[32]

Grove rejects the Guha thesis as 'a golden age' approach to South Asian environmental history and questions the assumptions about the existence of pre-colonial common property and communal customary forest use. The recent research of Rangarajan, Skaria, Damodaran, and others certainly takes some of its cues from the early works of Tucker and the subalternists. But it has been also influenced by the globalist approach of Alfred Crosby[33] and the revisionism of Christopher Bayly.[34] Bayly has encouraged environmental historians to treat colonial rule not as a watershed but as a period in which continuities with the pre-colonial period were to be regarded as important. Grove also sees the bias in South Asian environmental history caused by an overemphasis on the post-1857 period. Both Rangarajan and Grove rightly point to the significance of the forest policies pursued by the successor states to the Mughals. Grove in particular draws our attention to the need of a comprehensive history of drought, famine, and climatic changes. In considering the impact of climatic changes on the history of this region we have advanced very little so far. It is perhaps in this area of research that we can expect to see most movement in the environmental history of South Asia in the coming years. This inclination has already surfaced in some of the essays in the volume edited by Grove and others.[35] South Asian environmental history sees the coming of colonialism as an environmental watershed and its legacy as the key agent of all environmental problems. There is a clear emphasis on the negative impact of the interventionist role of colonial and post-colonial states in the degradation of human ecologies. Fresh turns in this historiography will help to rejuvenate it. I will comment further on this point below.

METHODOLOGY

What could be the strategy or methodology to be pursued by scholars practising this genre of history?

Knowledge is considered as knowledge only when it is methodologically obtained; history is a piece of knowledge as it is obtained through a definite methodology. The practitioners of the discipline are expected to practise the discipline according to certain methods. Like any other history, here too it is for the historian necessary to concentrate on the collection of primary and secondary sources and the selection and interpretation of such sources. As to the choice of subjects, historians are usually attracted by silences or slippages in the writing of history. Environmental history is a new area and here such slippages and silences are understandably many. They now await their historians. I will argue that environmental history does not call for any separate methodology; the basic tenets of the discipline remain very much valid in this sub-discipline. It might, however, require specific strategies, tactics and some preliminary knowledge of environmental sciences on the part of the historian to negotiate particular issues depending on the subject or the nature of his or her research.

I have mentioned earlier that there has been a tendency to down-play the importance of the subject and see it as an integral part of the currently emerging frontier of Environmental Studies. There are certain misconceptions as to the respective territories of history of the environment and Environmental Studies. It is important to clear these misconceptions to foster historical researches in this field. There is also a general misconception that natural scientists are better equipped than historians to contribute to this particular branch of knowledge. It has to be admitted that the roots of this misconception can be attributed to the initial indifference of historians to the subject. We have seen that the historians of an earlier generation considered environmental subjects to be of dubious value. This is precisely why historians themselves could not contribute much to this new frontier of Environmental Studies in the beginning. Interestingly enough, environmental history was first forced into the academic arena by natural scientists who recognized the political and historical significance of their subject. To make matters worse, the agenda of environmental history was actually drawn up by scholars from various disciplines and not by historians. The methodological uncertainty of the history of the environment has stemmed from this initial inertia of historians. The problem has, in the course of time, triggered off another misconception that – environmental history has to be necessarily interdisciplinary in nature. Even historians engaged in environmental history are not completely free from this misconception. It is true that these historians should have a rudimentary knowledge of such basic concepts like ecosystem, atmosphere, hydrosphere, lithosphere, biosphere, epidemic diseases, medical science, forestry, climate, soil, vegetation, fauna, and so on, but such borrowing of knowledge from other disciplines does not necessarily make environmental history an interdisciplinary field. When the methodologies of two or more disciplines combine to produce a fresh methodology, only then can we call it an interdisciplinary study. The notion that experts from the natural sciences are better placed to pursue environmental history, history of medicine, or history of science has little substance. Such notions actually are the result of the absolute lack of historical sense from which many scientists unfortunately suffer. I have heard an eminent scientist saying at a seminar, 'you have to be a scientist to write history of science'. According to this logic, one has to be a peasant to write peasant history or a criminal to pursue the history of crime. Little do such scientists realize that history too has its methodology and one needs some training in that discipline to become a historian. This is why in most cases what they produce at the end of the road is nothing more than mere chronicles or mere stories of scientific inventions. Historians of the environment, I will therefore, argue, have the responsibility to retain the methodology of their own discipline in their own way. In the process, historians will be better able to contribute to the broader framework of Environmental Studies.

Environmental history shares a very messy border with economic and social histories, history of science and technology, disease history, and even with various other disciplines. It shares a lengthy border with historical geography and historical ecology. Roughly speaking, environmental historians, historical geographers, and historical ecologists try to answer similar sorts of questions though their methodologies vary. For example, historical ecologists are usually trained in anthropology or archaeology and their work is collaborative in nature. Environmental historians, on the other hand, are expected to work alone. Climate history, too, shares a porous border with environmental history. Climate historians who work on textual sources are very similar to environmental historians. In the United States, however, climate history relies heavily on the natural sciences due to poor textual documentation.[36]

The appellations of all the various branches of history are labels of convenience rather than names of essences. The phrase 'environmental history' is no exception. Environment is a broad term which encompasses all that surrounds us, both the natural world in which we live as well as the technology of production and things produced by us. In this sense all histories can be viewed as environmental history. However, in actual fact we make a distinction between environmental history and other histories. The historiography of the history of environment shows that in environmental history there is an emphasis on various ecological factors and their impact on the history of a particular region. An external force, substance or condition that surrounds and affects the life of an organism in any way becomes a factor of its environment and is called an environmental or ecological issue. Historians might be of some help in mapping out the social, economic, and cultural impact of the changes in the ecosystem. An ecosystem can be defined as the grouping of various kinds of plants, animals, and micro-organisms interacting with each other and with their environment. Thus an ecosystem consists of living organisms and the physical environment in which they live. A grassland, a forest, a pond, or a lake may be considered an ecosystem. A historical study of an ecosystem is ecological history or environmental history. It is important for the environmental historian to remember that unlike other branches of history it may not remain confined to a strictly guarded chronological framework; shorter periods may not be ideal for ecological histories; on the contrary, the emphasis here is on the *longue durée*. I have already said that in a sense all histories can be viewed as environmental history. Environment is a broad term which encompasses all that surrounds us. Environmental history is pregnant with immense possibilities. There is a wonderful opportunity to undertake various social, economic, cultural, and intellectual histories under the umbrella of environmental history and explore such themes like race, ethnicity, class, community, gender, power, and knowledge. One could see, for example, how the *jungle* or the Indian forest became an important site for the interplay of various forces like racism, colonialism, nationalism, and struggle for equality during British colonialism in India. It is understandable that the forest became one of the important social sites for the exercise of colonial power and for the domination and inferiorization of the 'Indian other'. I have argued elsewhere that it is possible to comprehend the implication of the exercise of power in various social and cultural sites or spaces when social construction of space is viewed historically.[37] The historical transformation of space as a container of power can only be identified when we study discourses in their dialectical interaction with the dynamic of human agency or producers or architects of such discourses. I have shown in one of my articles how in the course of the nineteenth century the forest turned into an important venue where the 'Euro-American Selves' and the 'Indian Others' started interacting.[38]

The choice of the subject of research is indeed the unique autonomy of the historian.[39] But here for the sake of discussion I can suggest certain gateways for environmental histories. I do not intend to say these gateways are ideal or that these are the only methods that have to be necessarily followed. This is only a tentative set of options, which may help to open up this particular frontier. The themes mentioned here are all interlinked and overlapping:

(1) Social, economic, cultural and intellectual histories under the umbrella of environmental history and study of themes like race, ethnicity, class, community, gender, power, knowledge, etc. Richard Grove documents the profound dependence of western ideas about the natural world upon the knowledge of people living in the colonial periphery, showing especially how 'the seeds of modern conservation developed as an integral part of the European encounter with the tropics and with local classifications and interpretation of the natural world and its symbolisms'.[40]

(2) Forest, deforestation, soil erosion, resistance, politics of environment, subsistence, the animal and the insect worlds in tropical forests, hunting or *shikar*, poaching, forest crime, smuggling, etc., the recent approach to hunting provides an important theme in history. The killing of animals is associated with ideological overtones and both text and pictorial art have tended to emphasize the mystic, courtly, and martial rather than the purely narrative side of the chase. European hunters of the nineteenth and twentieth centuries were aware of this rich tradition and turned hunting into a symbolic activity within the study of natural history, a central area of scientific debate in the period. Hunting had its assigned place in the social and economic system. It was subject to complex legislation and was much influenced by technical developments in firearms.

If we look at the development of human society we find three different typologies in hunting: (1) subsistence hunting, (2) defence hunting, and (3) hunting as sport or pleasure.[41] Subsistence hunting was an important economic activity among primitive men who lived primarily on a food-gathering-hunting economy. Even among those communities who were peasantised and all set for settled agriculture, hunting offered a subsidiary economic activity. Many primitive or tribal communities in India, who are peasantized, still depend on hunting to a considerable extent. Again, hunting for meat interestingly coexisted with relatively advanced stages of production, and to a limited extent, the practice survives even today.

Defence hunting means killing or trapping of animals (deer, wild boar, monkey, elephant, bison, tiger, etc.) for the protection of crops and human lives. Defence hunting, understandably, occupied a greater part of human activity when larger areas were under forests, and technology, particularly weaponry, was at a primitive stage. In some areas, however, protection of crops or human lives still remains one of the major problems for the local people and forest officials in India and elsewhere in South Asia.[42]

Hunting as pleasure or sport acquired importance in the relatively advanced stages of civilization and continues in some form or other to the present day, despite the fact that legislators in recent times have been continuously expanding the frontier of law to ensure conservation and the scientific management of forests all over the world. A study of the animal world too can give important clues to sensibilities. I have tried to unveil the amazing fact of how the colonial authorities and the Bengal tiger seemed to be locked in a conflict for command of the Sundarbans. Thus the big cat turned into a victim for the demonstration of colonial power.

(3) Climate, impact of climatic changes on history, demography, natural calamities like earthquakes, cyclonic storms, hurricanes, tornadoes, floods, rainfall, tsunamis, volcanic eruptions, mudslides and forest fires.[43]
(4) Air and water pollution, history of sound and smell.[44]
(5) History of public health, epidemics, medicine.

There are hundreds of other themes in environmental history that await their historians. I predict vigorous activity in these areas in the near future.

Editorial Notes

As the editor of the present compilation it would be pertinent to say a few things about the essays that feature in the volume. The present volume is partly based on the proceedings of the three-day international seminar on 'Situating Environmental History' held between 3 and 5 March 2005 under the UGC-DRS Programme of the Department of History, Jadavpur University, Kolkata. The seminar brought together about 30 leading scholars sharing a common interest in the environmental history of South Asia. The volume will address some of the probable themes (though not all) of environmental history discussed there. The essays that feature in this volume have been grouped under four different themes: (1) Situating Environmental History; (2) Communities on the Margin; (3) Colonialism, Post-colonialism, the State and Management of Nature; and (4) Beyond India. The four essays in the opening section contribute to our understanding of environmentalism, different perceptions of environment and nature, historiography of environmental history, the role of state legislation and popular responses to those legislations. Notions discussed in this section will help to develop and define the agenda and disciplinary canons of the history of environment.

In the opening essay, Karl Jacoby stresses the need for a smarter and significant dialogue between social and environmental histories 'Classifying Nature: In Search of a Common Ground Between Social and Environmental History' in the North American context. Jacoby's attempt is indeed significant and laudable in view of the fact that integration of cultural and social history is apparent in many recent works. There are many overlappings between environmental and social history. In many cases environmental history plays an umbrella-type role which incorporates the role of specific human societies and their relationships with nature, environmental policy and politics. Alok Kumar Ghosh's article 'State Versus People: The Indian Experience of Environmentalism', locates some very pertinent questions and brings to light the various structural anomalies in

Indian environmentalism. Ghosh argues that environmentalism is not only movements for nature, but also a fight for the people, their survival and rights to mutual interaction with nature. He sees two clear divisions, one above and the other at the bottom.

Arun Bandopadhyay in 'Forest, Land Use and Water in Colonial South Asia: Issues from Agrarian and Environmental History' addresses certain crucial issues relating to the methodological uncertainties of the environmental history of colonial and post-colonial South Asia. Archana Prasad's 'Marginal People and Politics of Anti-Modern Development: Revisiting the Indian Environmental Movement in India' traces the rise of environmental and tribal movements in colonial South Asia.

The second section focuses on different communities in the periphery lying outside the supposed 'mainstream' and their fight for their own perceptions of 'justice' and 'legitimate claims'. Vinita Damodaran in 'Tribes in Indian History' raises significant questions regarding the revisionist argument and shows how the colonial accounts led many of the revisionist critics to conclude (often despite very clear linguistic evidence) that distinct tribes never existed, and that the claims of the indigenous people for autonomy must have no theoretical legitimacy or historical validity. She argues here that earlier generations of ethnographers did very often understand the complexities of ethnic identity and cultural dynamics. Ritajyoti Bandyopadhyay in 'Role of Women in the Joint Forest Management Programme in West Bengal: Case Studies of Two Forest Villages of West Bengal' makes a modest attempt to revisit the process of democratization through community involvement and its much problematized 'gender' dimension. Identifying a slippage between 'involving women' and 'addressing gender', it ventures to make participatory development in general, and Joint Forest Management in particular, more gender sensitive. The author's endeavour is commendable in view of the fact that it is based on extensive fieldwork and survey of government documents.

The third section looks at the evolution of state policy on environmental questions through different periods of Indian history. It examines how state power identified and shaped various environment-related issues including the diverse problems relating to the management and conservation of natural resources and crises concerning epidemic diseases, mortality, health and sanitation. Kaushik Roy in 'Managing the Environment: Disease, Sanitation and the Army in British India, 1859-1913' gives a blow-by-blow account of how the Raj in general and the British Indian Army in particular attempted to manage the environment in order to protect the vulnerable military manpower from the ravages of 'oriental' diseases. This is a creditable attempt to analyse the army's response to improve sanitation and the hygiene of the soldiery with special reference to climate and the natural setting. Arabinda Samanta's paper 'Plague and Prophylactics: Ecological Construction of an Epidemic in Colonial Eastern India' explores the epidemic plague in colonial Eastern India in the nineteenth century. Plague, Samanta demonstrates, was represented in the colonial official literature as a disease emanating from dirt and filth. The author makes a sincere attempt to identify the multiple sites that tended to underpin the digital divide between plague and prophylactic, and environment and disease. In the next article, 'Industrial Workers, Their Environmental Crises and Empire: Perspectives on Colonial Bengal', Amal Das endeavours to make a number of significant observations about the attitudes of the Empire with regard to public health, sanitation, and environment. Sahara Ahmed's 'Conflicting Claims, The Colonial Forest and Forest Dwellers in the Jalpaiguri District, 1869-1947' explicates the historical determinants of imperial intervention and ecological change in a single colonial district and gives an account of the connection between the issues related to conservation and the ongoing process of state formation. Jagdish N. Sinha in 'Congress and Conservation: A Look at the NPC Reports' examines the Indian National Congress', concern for conservation and environment with particular reference to the endeavours of its National Planning Committee in the final decade of colonial rule in India. In 'Genetic Change and Colonial Cotton Improvement in Nineteenth and Twentieth Century India', Sumit Guha traces the genetic transformation of cotton in colonial India and thus questions the image of 'traditional' Indian farming as a practice that evolved centuries ago and has existed unchanged ever since.

The final section of this volume focuses on a number of environmental issues in the countries beyond India. Rita

Pemberton's paper 'Shaping the Caribbean Environment: The Impact of India' discusses India's contribution to Carribbean development during the eighteenth and nineteenth centuries by an examination of plants introduced during this period. It also brings to light India's role in the conservation efforts of the late nineteenth and early twentieth centuries. This article, which focuses on Trinidad and Tobago, argues that India has shaped the Caribbean environment in two noteworthy ways. It is from India that the mango plant, an essential part of Caribbean culture, came to the West Indies. Secondly, the forest programmes that were launched in the twentieth century were based on the Indian experience and it was from India that the forest experts came. Pemberton's argument substantiates the 'empire forestry' thesis and the origins of modern environmentalism put forward by Gregory A. Barton. Lawrence G. Gundersen's essay 'West Tennessee, Cotton Cultivation and the Environment, 1820-1860' is an interesting study of cotton cultivation in West Tennessee (USA) with detailed references to environmentally-friendly ways of conducting cotton cultivation. Finally, Tridib Chakrabarti's 'Fire, Fume and Haze: Environmental Disorder in South-East Asia' examines the epidemic outbreak of smoke pollution due to forest fires in parts of South-East Asia in 1997 and narrates how the incident has emerged as a major issue in the ongoing environmental debate and politics of environment in recent times.

South Asian environmental history, which focuses on the Indian subcontinent in particular, has been increasingly acknowledged by the non-South Asian environmental historians in recent years as one of the most developed. Basically, the core component of this historiography is forest history, though issues like irrigation, water management, public health, and epidemics also feature. It sees the coming of colonialism as an environmental watershed and its legacy as the key agent for determining social and economic relations in colonial and post-colonial South Asia. This history is preoccupied with the discussion of the importation of a scientific model of forest conservation, the dislocation of a complex structure of localized forest uses, the degradation of peasants, and a series of conflicts with the interventionist colonial State. South Asian environmental history is more favourably inclined to the social consequences than the ecological consequences of that change. A number of essays which feature in the present volume too, demonstrate these trends in South Asian environmental history. In an article in *Environmental History*, Paul Sutter has drawn the attention of US environmental historians to the lessons that can be learnt from South Asian history. One lesson, he says, can be drawn from the 'subaltern' voices that have expressed opposition not only to the environmental costs of capitalist expansion but also the social costs of state conservation. In fact, US environmental historians like Mark Spence, Karl Jacoby, Louis Warren, and others have already done this to good effect.[45] Gunderson's essay in the present volume is a laudable attempt to relate cotton cultivation to the environment. Such studies remind us of the need for comparative studies of the origins of environmentalism and environmental history in the United States and South Asia. But it has to be borne in mind that there are fundamental differences between the US and South Asian landscapes. The roots of environmentalism in the two regions will show that unlike South Asia, in the US the scale of popular traditions of environmental protests is much less significant. Native Americans are perhaps the closest that the United States comes to a peasant tradition. Paul Sutter argues that the Native Americans offer to the American environmental historians an agrarian tradition worthy of intensive study 'not because they were the "original ecologists" but because they have inhabited a position on the political and environmental margins whose study will continue to diversify US environmental historiography'.[46] Several other marginal groups may also fit into this model. But an imitation of the South Asian model will not take the American environmental historians very far as environmental politics in the US is not conditioned by a persistent conflict between the agrarian population and the State. Here, wilderness advocates are the major opponents of technocratic State conservation.

Comparative environmental history on a global scale would be an interesting and absorbing field to pursue. For many sorts of histories, including environmental history, the nation state may not be the ideal geographical unit to explore. Ecological changes take place overlapping man-made national frontiers. Few professional historians have attempted to write environmental history on a global scale.[47] However, for the study of certain types of political history and policy history, the nation state paradigm holds ground. Gregory A. Barton's recent work is an important contribution in this direction. It may open up fresh frontiers of research in environmental history.[48] Barton has harped upon the origins and the global scale dissemination of the idea of environmentalism. What we know as environmentalism began with a series of legislations in British India. Imperial foresters warned of impending catastrophe and global climate change if deforestation continued. This particular concern later reverberated through Africa, Australia, New Zealand, Canada, and then the United States. Forest administrators in India were the first to link forest cover to climate. As early as the 1850s, it was acknowledged by the British forest officials that the existence or non-existence of large well-wooded areas in a country affects its climate to a very marked degree. Thus, precipitation depended upon wooded areas as well as the evaporation of water from the oceans of the world. Gregory A. Barton traces the international trail of environmentalism from colonial India to the British colonies in Africa, Australia, New Zealand, and finally, Canada, United States, and other parts of the globe. Environmental historians in the United States drew impetus initially from the history of conservation as an ideal and a social movement. American environmental historians recognize that the foresters from the German and French traditions trained Gifford Pinchot, the swashbuckler in the history of US conservation. But adequate attention has not been paid to the fact that most of Pinchot's mentors got their practical knowledge of forestry in British India. The export of forestry ideals and methods from the British Indian empire to other British colonies was a fascinating process and it is in this area of global, comparative history that we may expect to see significant movements in the near future. It is all the more fascinating because Britain's own forests were in private hands and State-sponsored forestry did not begin in the UK until the Second World War.

To return to the point of South Asian environmental history, there is a clear emphasis on the negative impact of the interventionist role of colonial and post-colonial states in the degradation of human ecologies. But this bias seems to be the natural outcome of empirical research based on the interpretations of archival documents. There is little disagreement on the point that colonial forest policy was not geared to bring welfare to the colonized people. 'Scientific forestry' never appeared to be fruitful in the colonial context. The legacy of failure in the domain of forest policy continues unabated in the post-colonial period too. The ideology of State-managed conservation is facing a crisis in today's India. Smugglers and poachers, supported by political and business interests and sheltered by local communities, raid the protected forests for valuable exports, killing elephants for their tusks and tigers for their skins. Scientific forestry has alienated the indigenous population settled near the forest zones, who are hostile to the idea of conservation. This is precisely why smugglers and poachers are able to operate at ease. They can, if necessary, slip into the fold of popular concealment and resentment of decades enables them to evade the law. The official forest policy has excluded the local people from protected areas; it has deprived them of the right to use the forest and it has preserved the forest only for the animals. To ensure success of the project, it is necessary to integrate the local people in the project of conservation. Local knowledge and resources can be used only through a participatory policy involving the people. The inability of the Forest Department to improve the condition of forests has forced it to opt for participatory management – Joint Forest Management or JFM. Under JFM the Forest Department involves village communities in forest management. Village forest committees have been formed under JFM. This is yielding positive results in some regions. But the domination of the official foresters stays. The forest should not be looked upon as merely a source of various products or as an object of protection. Nature lovers continue to visit national parks, hoping to see tigers in Ranthambhor or rare birds in Bharatpur. Forest officials congratulate themselves on the rapid population increase of many threatened species. It is necessary to humanize the forests and adopt a more humane approach to the people and their way of life. To achieve success, a utilitarian approach would be more effective.

Conclusion

Nature is one of those spaces where we observe the most intense form of class struggle and power politics. Those who are more privileged control the bulk of the natural resources across the world, including the developed nations. Thus, it has to be appreciated that the history of environment would serve as one of the important gateways to knowledge in general, and Environmental Studies in particular. It will lead historians to areas hitherto unexplored, raise questions hitherto unasked, penetrate into the mysterious world of the common people and disclose how attitudes to the environment change in keeping with the changing structure of culture and ideology. The history of the environment, therefore, does matter. Environmental history would continue to use the past as a prologue to give new choices for the future. There still remains some confusion regarding the territory of the historians of environment. This problem would automatically recede to the background with further progress of this sub-discipline. I would prefer to define the sub-discipline in simple terms: it is the history of mutual relations between human beings and the rest of nature. Human beings have established their control over nature. They have exerted a marked influence on earthly ecosystems. The Enlightenment thinkers of the eighteenth century introduced new ideas about nature. In addition to the already existing notion that climate affected human beings and the human societies, some thinkers argued for the first time that human actions affected climate.[49] But this new understanding did not immediately influence environmentalism or trigger off environmental history. When history became an academic discipline in the nineteenth century, its vital inspirations were German philosophers like Kant and Hegel who believed in the power of ideas and who regularly denigrated the influence of geography.[50] Hegel credited geography with some role in the formation of a spirit but the working of that spirit was a matter of its internal logic to which geography and environment were of no value.[51] However, the ontological doubts expressed by Kant and Hegel have not dashed out teleology from the modern understanding of nature. They have simply shifted the emphasis to the 'idea of progress'.

The idea of progress did not rule out the idea of a designed earth, but it did emphasize optimism that human beings may manage their environment so that they materially improve their happiness. Cutting of trees or destruction of wildlife may contribute to their happiness, but the 'idea of progress' implies a broad-based and purposeful management of nature.

There seems to be a global realization (not resolution) that in the greater interest of humankind there should be a 'proper balance' between humans and the natural world. Modern environmentalism is in search of a clear definition of this 'proper balance'. Environmental history is rooted in environmentalism and historians have now joined this grand quest for a resolution as to the use of nature. Environmental historians are more concerned with the mistakes of the past; they have respect for the physical sciences and unbounded optimism for the capabilities of man.[52] One serious charge against environmental historians is that they are too oriented to advocacy. They must be aware of this because it might be dangerous.[53] Environmental history certainly poses a challenge for mainstream history. It has already started to influence the broader discipline and young historians are showing interest in this new sub-discipline.[54]

It is in this area of environmental history that we may expect to see intense activity in the near future. I have no doubt that environmental history shall continue to thrive uninterrupted because interest in this history does not depend on any contemporary or immediate social problem. The grand quest for a resolution of the legitimate use of nature, I believe, would continue to dominate the discipline of history in particular and the rest of human history in general. It is less narrow and political now than it was in the early stages. This sub-discipline will thrive because the seeds of a new social and cultural history are firmly embedded in it. This new social history will be free from the riddles of the so-called 'post-modernist' exercises of recent times and will be rich and readable.

NOTES

1. Sekhar Bandyopadhyay (ed.), *Bengal: Rethinking History – Essays in Historiography*, Delhi: Manohar, International Centre for Bengal Studies, 2001, pp. 12-16.
2. W.G. Palmer, 'Environment in Utopia: History, Climate and Time in Renaissance Environmental Thought', *Environmental Review*, vol. 8, no. 2, Summer 1984, pp. 162-78.
3. A.S. Rawat (ed.), *A History of Forestry in India*, New Delhi: Indus Publishing Company, 1991, p. 130.
4. R.P. Goldman (ed.), *The Ramayana of Valmiki: An Epic of Ancient India*, vol. II: *The Ayodhyakanda*, tr. Sheldon I. Pollock, Princeton: Princeton University Press, 1986, pp. 131-6.

5. Madhav Gadgil and Ramachandra Guha, *This Fissured Land: An Ecological History of India*, Delhi: Oxford University Press, 1992, passim; also Ramachandra Guha and Madhav Gadgil, 'State Forestry and Social Conflict in British India', *Past and Present*, no. 123, May 1989, pp. 141-77, and David Hardiman (ed.), *Peasant Resistance in India 1858-1914*, Delhi, 1993, pp. 259-95.
6. George Perkins Marsh, *Man and Nature*, 1864, reprint, Cambridge: Harvard University Press, 1965, pp. 42-3.
7. Frederick Jackson Turner, 'The Significance of the Frontier in American History', *Annual Report of the American Historical Association for the Year 1893*, Washington: Government Printing Office, 1894, pp. 197-227.
8. Walter Prescott Webb, *The Great Plains*, Boston: Ginn and Company, 1931; also *The Great Frontier*, Boston: Houghton Mifflin Company, 1952.
9. Paul Sutter, 'Reflections: What Can U.S. Environmental Historians Learn from Non-U.S. Environmental Historiography?', *Environmental History*, vol. 8, no. 1, January 2003, pp. 109-29.
10. Cf. E.J.E. Hobsbawm, *Primitive Rebels: Studies in Archaic Forms of Social Movement in the 19th and 20th Centuries*, Manchester: Manchester University Press, 1959; *Bandits*, New York: Pantheon Books, 1981, revd. edn.; E.P. Thompson, *Whigs and Hunters: The Origin of the Black Act*, New York: Pantheon Books, 1975, and Douglas Hay, Peter Linebaugh, John G. Rule, E.P. Thompson and Cal Winslow (eds.), *Albion's Fatal Tree: Crime and Society in Eighteenth Century England,* London: Allen Lane, 1975; James C. Scott, *The Moral Economy of the Peasant: Rebellion and Subsistence in Southeast Asia,* New Haven and London: Yale University Press, 1976.
11. I myself have encountered this antipathy to environmental history several times during interactive sessions in seminars and workshops. To cite an instance, during the workshop at Visva Bharati University, 'New Directions in History' (2004), held in the Department of History, where I had the opportunity to deliver a lecture on this emerging frontier of environmental history, Professors Barun De and B.B. Chaudhuri, two most revered senior practitioners of my discipline and co-speakers in the said seminar, could not hide their doubts about the usefulness of this particular branch of history during the interactive session that followed my lecture.
12. J.R. McNeill, 'Observations on the Nature and Culture of Environmental History', *History and Theory* (*Theme Issue: Environment and History*), vol. 42, no. 4, December 2003, p. 13.
13. Forrest McDonald, *Recovering the Past: A Historian's Memoir*, Lawrence: University Press of Kansas, 2004, p. 1. Having said this he adds in the footnote: 'The new field of environmental history has not

yet shown that it is history rather than reinvigorated natural history, geology, paleontology, or expanded archaeology.'

14. As McNeill asserts, 'we ought to accept that we are only one species among many, and should gracefully share top billing at times with bison, tsetse flies, and El Nino', McNeill, op. cit., p. 36.
15. Ramachandra Guha, *Unquiet Woods: Ecological Change and Peasant Resistance in the Himalaya*, Delhi: Oxford University Press, 1989, passim.
16. E.H. Carr, *What is History?*, New York: Vintage Books, 1961, pp. 34-5.
17. In the model curriculum circulated by the UGC in 2001, there is a clear indication that environmental history has to be taught at both undergraduate and postgraduate levels (see 'UGC Model Curriculum', New Delhi, 2001, p. 123). Jadavpur and Calcutta Universities have already introduced environmental history or environmental studies related courses at the undergraduate level (see 'History Extra Departmental Semester Courses', Kolkata, 2003). Semester courses on environmental history also feature in the current syllabi of both Jawaharlal Nehru University, Jadavpur University, Vidyasagar University, Banaras Hindu University, University of Hyderabad and many other leading universities in India.
18. Recent trends suggest that a Latin American Association for Environmental History and an Indian Association of Environmental Historians may soon be born.
19. At present there are three journals on environmental history. *Global Environment: A Journal of Transdisciplinary History* with a base in Italy made its appearance in the year 2008. At present it is regularly published by the White Horse Press (UK).
20. The *Environmental Review* began as a scholarly journal in 1976 in the United States, changed its name to the *Environmental History Review* in the mid-1980s and eventually became *Environmental History* in 1996; environmental history articles regularly feature in the *Pacific Historical Review* too.
21. The literature on environmental history is fast expanding. Among the publishers who are regularly publishing books on environmental history, mention may be made of Cambridge University Press, Texas University Press, University of Washington Press, Ohio University Press, Arizona University Press, Columbia University Press, White Horse Press and University of California Press. Among the Indian publishers Oxford (India), Indus, Manohar, Sage, Routledge, Springer, etc., are showing interest in environmental history. A large number of conferences and seminars on environmental history are held all over the world every year. India, too, is not lagging behind. One of these conferences, 'Environmental History of Asia', was held in Jawaharlal Nehru University, between 4th and 7th December 2002. This conference

had about 65 papers spread over 20 sessions and covered a dozen sub-themes ranging from forest history to water, irrigation, land management, health, sanitation, wildlife, and so on. One of the major international seminars, 'Situating Environmental History' was held in the Department of History, Jadavpur University, between 3rd and 5th March 2005. This three-day international conference had about 21 papers spreading over 12 sessions. The present edited volume grew out of this Jadavpur conference. The theme of the last major international seminar in Jadavpur History Department was 'History of Waters in South Asia' held in 3-4 March 2006.

Websites are another major index of academic viability and internet resources are plenty: http://www.carsoncenter.uni-muenchen.de/index.html; https://foresthistory.org; www.eh-resources.org; www.h-net.org; www.h-net.org; https://www.sciencedirect.com.

22. Richard H Grove, Vinita Damodaran and Satpal Sangwan (eds.), *Nature and the Orient: The Environmental History of South and South East Asia*, Delhi: Oxford University Press, 1998.
23. Ranjan Chakrabarti, 'Foucault and the New Social History', *Journal of History* (Jadavpur University), vol. XI, 1990, pp.1-22; Jacques Le Goff and P. Nora (eds.), *Constructing the Past: Essays in Historical Methodology*, Cambridge: Cambridge University Press, 1985.
24. Fernand Braudel, *The Mediterranean and the Mediterranean World in the Age of Philip II*, 2 vols., New York: Harper and Row, 1972, 1973; Emmanuel Le Roy Ladurie, *Times of Feast, Times of Famine, A History of Climate Since the Year 1000*, tr. Barbara Bray, New York: Doubleday, Garden City, 1971
25. Richard Tucker, 'Forest Management and Imperial Politics: Thane District, Bombay, 1823-1887', *The Indian Economic and Social History Review*, vol. 16, no. 3, 1979, pp. 273-300.
26. Richard Grove et al. (eds.), *Nature and the Orient*, op. cit., p. 16.
27. Richard Grove, op. cit.; See also *Green Imperialism: Colonial Expansion, Tropical Island Edens and the Origins of Environmentalism, 1600-1800*, Cambridge: Cambridge University Press, 1995; *Ecology, Climate and Empire: Colonialism and Global Environmental History, 1400-1940*, Cambridge: White Horse Press, 1997.
28. Ibid. Deepak Kumar,Vinita Damodaran and Rohan D'Souza (eds.), *The British Empire and the Natural World: Environmental Encounters in South Asia*, Delhi: Oxford University Press, 2011 is a follow-up account of the 1998 book titled Nature and the Orient (1998) edited by Richard Grove et. al. which collected several dozen essays on the various aspects of environmental history of South Asia and for many years it helped scholars to open up new research frontiers. As such, it served a number of purposes and presented a broad overview of the historiography of environmental history of the region, to develop further on the research programme laid out by Grove especially the ecological impact of

colonialism and the of colonial environmental knowledge systems , and, more broadly, to publicise the necessity of taking the empire as a useful scale of analysis in environmental history between the constraints of the local and the global histories. The volume emphasizes the empire-wide interconnections that fashioned South Asian environmental history from the eighteenth century onwards. It does this by classifying the subject into five cardinal themes, most of which were crucial to Grove's vision of the environmental history of South Asia. Richard Grove possessed the rare skill to draw these kinds of global linkages, and the editors overtly acknowledge that the collection reproduces only fragments of his broader vision.

29. Mahesh Rangarajan, *Fencing the Forest: Conservation and Ecological Change in India's Central Provinces, 1860-1914*, New York: Oxford University Press, 1996.
30. Ajay Skaria, *Hybrid Histories: Forests, Frontiers and Wilderness in Western India*, New Delhi: Oxford University Press, 1999.
31. D.D. Dangwal, 'Scientific Forestry and Forest Management in Colonial and Post-Colonial India', *Contemporary India*, vol. I, issue 1, 2002, pp. 153-69.
32. Ranjan Chakrabarti, 'The Jungle, the Imperial Hunt and British Imperialism 1800-1947', in C. Palit and A. Bhattacharyya (eds.), *Science, Technology, Medicine and Environment in India: Historical Perspectives*, Kolkata: Bibhasa, 1998; 'Colonising the Forest 1800-1900', in Sukumar Bhattacharyya (ed.), *Mountains and Forests in Indian History*, Kolkata: Institute of Historical Studies, 2004; 'Tiger and the Raj: Ordering the Maneater of the Sundarbans 1800-1947', in Ranjan Chakrabarti (ed.), *Space and Power in History: Images, Ideologies, Myths and Moralities*, Kolkata: Penman, 2001.
33. Alfred W. Crosby, *Ecological Imperialism: The Biological Expansion of Europe, 900-1900*, Cambridge: Cambridge University Press, 2004 (new edn.).
34. Christopher and Susan Bayly, 'Eighteenth-century State Forms and the Economy', C.J. Dewey (ed.), *Arrested Development in India: The Historical Dimension*, New Delhi: Manohar, 1988, pp. 66-92.
35. Richard Grove (ed.), *Nature and the Orient*, op. cit.
36. J.R. Mcneill, op. cit., p. 10. Climate history may be particularly useful in understanding drought, famine, bad harvest, price rise and mortality; see C.E.P. Brooks, *Climate Through the Ages: A Study of the Climatic Factors and Their Variations*, London: Ernest Benn, 1926; Emmanuel Le Roy Ladurie, op. cit., 1971; Neville Brown, *History and Climate Change: A Eurocentric Perspective*, New York: Routledge, 2001. An important area that attracts historians now is the El Nino episodes.
37. Ranjan Chakrabarti (ed.), *Space and Power in History*, op. cit.
38. Ibid.
39. E.H. Carr, *What is History*, op. cit., pp. 51-5.

40. Richard Grove, *Green Imperialism*, op. cit.
41. J.M. Mackenzie, *The Empire of Nature: Hunting, Conservation and British Imperialism*, Manchester and New York: Manchester University Press, 1988, passim.
42. J.K. Anderson, *Hunting in the Ancient World*, Berkeley: University of California Press, 1985, pp. 1-16.
43. Interestingly, climate history is emerging as a crucial component of global environmental history. Climate history calls for an in-depth understanding of the inter connection between water resources on the one hand and deforestation, rainfall, soil erosion, climatic change, global warming, drought, famine, and various natural calamities on the other. Another stimulating subfield relating to climate and political unrest has been opened up by scholars like Sam White and Zheng Jingyun and others, See Sam White, *The Climate of Rebellion in the Early Modern Ottoman Empire*, Cambridge: Cambridge University Press, 2011, Zheng Jingyun et al., How Climate Change Impacted the Collapse of the Ming Dynasty, *Climatic Change* (New York: Springer) November 2014, 127(2), pp. 169-182, Climate has also made its way into another important sub-theme of environmental history in recent years, namely, health and epidemics. To cite just one example from the recent publications, Anthony McMichael et.al., *Climate Change and the Health of Nations: Famines, Fevers, and the Fate of Populations,* Oxford: Oxford University Press, 2017.
44. Alain Corbin, *The Foul and the Fragrant: Odor and the French Social Imagination*, Cambridge: Harvard University Press, 1986.
45. Paul Sutter, 'Reflections: What can U.S. Environmental Historians Learn from Non-U.S. Environmental Historiography?', *Environmental History*, vol. 8, no. 1, January 2003, p. 112.
46. Ibid., p. 114.
47. They were mostly geographers. I have mentioned earlier that geographers and scientists first brought environmental history to the academic arena and not the historians.
48. Gregory A. Barton, *Empire Forestry and the Origins of Environmentalism*, Cambridge: Cambridge University Press, 2002.
49. Ibid., p. 16.
50. Ibid.
51. J.R. McNeill, 'Observations on the Nature and Culture of Environmental History', op. cit., p. 14.
52. The very idea of an orderly and designed earth has been questioned and criticized by many.
53. William Cronon, 'The Uses of Environmental History', *Environmental History Review*, vol. 17, no. 3, Autumn 1993, pp. 1-22.
54. This is already evident in the recent syllabi adopted by various social science faculties in India and the wider world.

SECTION I
Understanding Environmental History

1. Classifying Nature: In Search of a Common Ground between Social and Environmental History

Karl Jacoby

Over the past few decades, environmental historians have written numerous works that, by placing nature in history, present the past in a fresh and revealing light. Less clear in this burgeoning literature, however, has been the extent to which environmental history intersects other ways of understanding the past. For some North American environmental historians, this state of affairs seems to represent one of the chief virtues of their field. To such practitioners, environmental history's distance from other historical methodologies appears to promise a more unified vision of the past, one grounded in a single, tangible ecological reality. Donald Worster, for example, has celebrated environmental history for its ability to avoid the 'downward spiral that social history has taken toward fragmentation and a paralyzing fear of all generalization.'[1]

Other practitioners of environmental history, however, have expressed concern about the field's tendency towards holism, a quality that, in William Cronon's words, 'discourages us from looking as much as we should at conflict and difference *within* groups of people.'[2] Indeed, at a time when most historians seem intent on elucidating ever more fully such categories of social difference as ethnicity, gender, class, and sexuality, environmental history, for all its interpretive innovation, can appear somewhat contrarian, with little to offer scholars of other, more human-centred subjects. As Richard White observed, 'Other historians still do not have to read environmental history in the way that they have to read literature on slavery, colonial history, the South, and even the West in order to claim a basic historical literacy.

There are few strong central claims that other historians have to engage, whether they agree with them or disagree with them.'[3]

White's comments would seem to be borne out by a preliminary overview of recent synthetic work on the North American past. Ted Steinberg's *Down to Earth,* perhaps the first effort to integrate the environmental history of North America into a single readable volume, contains elegant discussions on urban sanitation, the near extinction of the buffalo, and other subjects integral to environmental history. But topics familiar to most standard textbooks of American history—the American Revolution, the First and Second Great Awakenings and other religious revivals, the Civil Rights movement—receive scarcely a mention in *Down to Earth*'s 285 pages.[4] Similarly, most mainstream textbooks of American history tend to adopt a political or social history approach that, for whatever reason, sees little need to engage with subjects of interest to environmental historians. The two standard exceptions to this trend—the 'Columbian exchange' of plants, animals, and diseases from the 'New World' to the 'Old World' set in motion by European contact, and the rise of conservation during the Progressive Era—only underscore the relative absence of attention to environmental matters elsewhere, even on subjects such as the fur trade or farm policy, for which there exists a well-developed body of environmental history scholarship.[5]

At first glance, there would seem to be little reason for this enduring estrangement between environmental history and social history. After all, the great narrative engine that drives so many foundational works of social history—the rise of capitalist economic relations across the globe—is one that many environmental histories share. As a result, similar themes, as a number of scholars have noted, run through much of environmental history and social history. Gunther Peck has described how environmental history and labour history alike stress the penetration of market relations, the changes in material conditions wrought by capitalism, and the creation of new forms of alienation. In an insightful article in *Environmental History,* Alan Taylor observed that social historians and environmental historians have a common concern with enlisting new sorts of sources and with recapturing the perspectives of the subaltern and exploited. As a result, Taylor concluded, 'social and environmental history are fundamentally compatible and mutually reinforcing.'[6]

Yet, for all this seeming congruence between the two fields, the long-foretold synthesis of social and environmental history has often proven elusive. In spite of their shared interest in charting the effects of capitalism, for instance, environmental historians and social historians continue to emphasize different aspects of capitalist relations. If most social historians are concerned about the alienation of labour created by capitalist conditions, most environmental historians emphasize instead the alienation from nature that, to their eyes, takes place under capitalist relations. Likewise, to most labour historians, the salient characteristic of capitalism is the social division of labour in the production process into distinct classes. By contrast, for environmental historians, the defining feature of capitalism has typically been trade and the process of capital accumulation. Thus, although labour historians and environmental historians both explore capitalist relations, they remain focused on relatively distinct manifestations of them.

One can trace this peculiar state of affairs back to some of the earliest and most influential works on the environmental history of North America. While the path-breaking studies of Donald Worster and William Cronon brilliantly demonstrated the ways in which capitalism reduced complex natural ecosystems into discrete bundles of commodities, the human beings engaged in 'changing the land'—transforming nature into marketable natural resources—usually appeared as a relatively uniform group, unmarked by clear class divisions. Whether landless or the owners of vast estates, independent farmers, agricultural labourers, or indentured servants, the European colonists in Cronon's path-breaking study all manifest similar responses to the New England landscape.[7]

Even the promising recent work on the 'environmental justice' movement has not been entirely successful in bridging the divide between environmental history and social history. To its credit, by illuminating the efforts of workers and others to protect their homes and workplaces from toxins, scholarship on environmental justice has included working-class voices to a much greater extent than most other environmental histories. Furthermore, by focusing on the concerns of workers and peoples of colour with the fates of urban neighbourhoods and industrial landscapes, the literature on environmental justice has expanded our notions of the environment and of environmental struggles beyond the usual rural and wilderness areas in extremely useful ways. Yet this scholarship does not entirely escape the impression that it remains most able to deal with workers when they act like environmentalists and express a concern with environmental degradation (albeit one defined in a new, more expansive way). Furthermore, it remains uncertain how one might extend the work on twentieth-century struggles over toxins, that have been the predominant focus of most environmental justice studies, to earlier time periods and less urban settings.[8]

The conceptual issues that lead to this frequent estrangement between North American social history and environmental historians are, of course, far too complex to solve in a single essay. But I want to argue in the limited space available to me here that as a first step towards a more productive exchange between social history and environmental history, historians in both camps might profit by revisiting a figure who has been pivotal for many social historians, whose early work touched on such familiar environmental subjects as forests and forestry, and who, to judge by the regularity with which he appears in the epigraphs of such landmark works as William Cronon's *Changes in the Land* and Alfred Crosby's *Ecological Imperialism,* has at least a nodding acquaintance with several leading environmental historians. The scholar in question is the young Karl Marx.[9]

In 1842, shortly after receiving his Ph.D., Marx published his first essays: a series of articles that decried the widespread prosecution of German peasants for the theft of wood from local forests. Although Marx would later recall this investigation into the forest practices of the German peasantry as a turning point in his thinking, many scholars have dismissed these early essays, composed before Marx arrived at the grand theories of class and capitalism that animated his later (and far more famous) work, as little more than preliminary exercises, a juvenilia of sorts. If carefully revisited, however, they offer a number of promising new points of departure for environmental historians and social historians alike.[10]

The event that prompted Marx's early essays was the legal transformation of Germany's forests into private property in the early nineteenth century—a shift connected, in part, to the developing science of forestry and new notions of what was healthiest for the forest ecology. Marx wrote to defend those peasants who, despite the new forest laws, continued to assert their customary rights to fallen wood. Labeling such products the '*alms of nature*', Marx contended that the German State should protect, not undermine, the peasantry's access to forest resources. Once Marx began to work on *Capital,* however, his early essays on the German forests lingered in obscurity. Not until 1976 did the labour historian Peter Linebaugh revisit them and add a crucial insight. One of the central reasons why customary rights to the forest emerged as so hotly contested an issue in the early nineteenth century, Linebaugh noted, was that peasants hoped to use fallen wood and other forest products to distance themselves from another transformation sweeping Germany during this era: the rise of the factory system and the industrial workplace. If peasants were a potential reserve labour force for German capitalists, the forests were for German peasants a potential reserve of a different sort—a place where they might find the means to supplement or even stave off wage work in the new mills and mines arising in their homeland.[11]

Reread in this light, young Karl Marx's account of the German forests allows one to link together several key historical phenomena: the material conditions of the natural world; the differing conceptualizations of the forest held by subalterns and elites; and the process of class formation. Indeed, Marx's early work on German forests suggests that one of the central concerns of environmental history—the contest of human populations for control over the landscape—is intimately intertwined with one of the central concerns of social and labour history: the formation of the working class.

My own research into the effects of conservation on North American rural communities in the late nineteenth and early twentieth centuries provides a number of illustrations of the complex and enduring interplay between resource use and class formation. At the turn of the century, for example, one witnesses Native Americans, Chicanos, and other rural people who, as they lost their lands to outsiders as a result of the rise of protected forest reserves or due to declining soil fertility, cultivated subsistence farms part of the year and joined the migrant labour force the other part of the year. One also finds repeated references to heightened reliance on hunting, fishing, and foraging by workers during strikes and depressions, by workers injured in industrial accidents or blacklisted for union activities, and even by a few would-be workers who, much like their German predecessors, hoped to use the gathering of natural resources to avoid altogether the dependency and labour discipline of the workplace. After one encounters turn-of-the-century accounts from poachers in Wyoming, boasting that they hunted illegally because it 'was foolish to work for wages', or letters from other Wyoming residents, grumbling that there were two distinct 'classes' in their communities, one that sought to improve their homesteads and another 'who have . . . no property' and who 'kill game . . . [so as to] make a partial living without work', it becomes difficult to conceive of an environmental history that does not take into account labour conditions or the cultural meanings that different human groups assigned to work.[12]

Such events not only constitute evidence for environmental historians of the ways in which class relations are intimately connected to the decisions that humans make about how to use nature; they also represent a challenge to labour historians to venture farther into the countryside than most have at present. Currently, the bulk of North American labour history focuses on class relations as expressed on the shop floor and in the taverns, tenements, streets, union halls, and shops frequented by urban workers. The result, however, has been a somewhat lopsided understanding of the past. As Hal Barron observed over two decades ago: 'The majority of people in nineteenth-century America lived in rural communities, but most of the social history of nineteenth-century America is not about them.'[13]

If one is interested in creating a complete portrait of how class was lived in the United States in the nineteenth century, one needs to investigate the rural settings in which class was expressed and reformulated. In so doing, labour historians would find themselves engaging with questions that are also of interest to environmental historians. What, for example, were the ecological factors that propelled rural folk into the labour market in the nineteenth and early twentieth centuries? (Here we might extend the term rural folk to include not only the inhabitants of the American countryside but the many immigrants to the United States from Europe, Mexico, Asia, and elsewhere who were often completing a transnational rural to urban migration during this era.) What forms of resource use did country people adopt in an attempt to moderate or avoid their entry into the workforce? Did they, for example, intensify the sale of natural resources so as to avoid having to sell their labour? And did such strategies lead to the over-exploitation of certain resources? Certainly this last point was an accusation lodged in numerous American communities against some of the most aggressive game poachers in their midst—that they were placing increased demands on resources on which all rural inhabitants had traditionally depended.[14]

For their part, environmental historians might adopt from labour historians a more sophisticated understanding of the competing crosscurrents that exist within class as a category of analysis. While members of the working class often differed in perspective from elites, they also frequently possessed distinct perspectives from one another. In the Adirondacks of upstate New York in the closing decades of the nineteenth century, for instance, one finds, unsurprisingly, that many of the region's working-class inhabitants disagreed sharply with upper-class conservationists over natural resource policy. While conservationists tended to view nature in the Adirondacks as 'wild' and endeavoured to remove its trees and game from local access, many Adirondackers asserted that the forests around their home were part of a thoroughly human landscape.

Residents thus contested conservationists' claims on multiple levels. Not only did they emphasize their prior use of the region's woodlands, they also asserted a natural right to subsistence and therefore a natural right to hunt, fish, and forage in local forests. This set of beliefs was reinforced by a still vital Republican tradition, which held that in the United States, unlike aristocratic

Europe, all classes had the right to hunt, especially since supporting oneself by the chase helped to ensure the independent citizens so prized in a Republican society. The combination of these ideas led residents of the Adirondacks to contend that the conservationists' new game and forest laws were unnatural and 'unAmerican'. 'The deer were given to us as food', asserted one inhabitant. 'It matters not how we kill them.'[15] 'I dunno what we're a-comin' to in this free country,' stated another. '[I]n them days nobody said a word if a poor man wanted a little meat an' killed it, but now . . . they'd put me in jail ef [*sic*] I killed a deer when I needed meat.'[16]

If such comments demonstrate the strikingly different conceptualizations of nature held by conservationists and locals at the turn of the century, closer examination reveals that not all of the region's residents were in accord as to the precise contours of this natural right to subsistence. Some contended that hunting, fishing, or cutting timber in violation of New York's conservation laws was morally legitimate only so long as one used the resources directly to feed or shelter one's own family and did not sell them to someone else. Others, taking note of the expanding commercial economy of the late nineteenth century, concluded that it should be legitimate to harvest natural resources in violation of New York's conservation laws *and* to market them for the cash necessary to purchase staples for one's family—a view that their local opponents considered the opening wedge to an environmentally destructive market engagement.

These different responses sparked frequent, heated, and sometimes even violent debates within Adirondacks communities at the turn of the century. Adding to the furore was the fact that the wage work available to the region's residents in the latter half of the nineteenth century could take quite different forms. While some locals worked in New York's lumber industry, others found employment as guides for visiting tourists. The members of this latter group even formed a union, which advocated several measures limiting the timber industry, thus placing workers from different sectors of the local economy on a collision course with one another and illustrating the difficulty of generalizing a single, working-class way of interacting with the environment.[17]

As one confronts the sometimes-conflicting agendas of

working-class people, it becomes apparent that perhaps the most important question that a heightened dialogue between social historians and environmental historians might address is the relationship between social and environmental justice. Environmental historians writing on the responses of the working class and communities of colour to the spread of urban toxins in the twentieth century have asserted a clear congruence between social justice and environmental justice. Robert Bullard, for example, has argued that the efforts by communities of colour to protect themselves from toxic pollution 'are not unlike the civil rights battles waged to dismantle the legacy of Jim Crow.' Andrew Szasz coined the term 'ecopopulism' to describe what he sees as an emerging social movement in which environmental issues are connected to the 'struggle of small people against big government and big business.'[18]

When one looks at the environmental history and labour history of the nineteenth- and early twentieth-century United States, however, the relationship between environmental justice and social justice appears much more murky. Many of the institutions created during this period and commonly perceived to represent environmental triumphs—national parks and forests, state nature preserves, game laws, and so on—have frequently involved social injustices. As environmental historians such as Louis Warren, Mark Spence, and Benjamin Johnson have all demonstrated, the burden of protecting the environment during this era often fell heaviest on the most marginal members of society: American Indians, immigrants, and the poor.[19] At the same time, recent research in labour history has documented how workers during this era avidly embraced roles as consumers *and* as producers—a development that led, in turn, to increased consumption and heightened demands for natural resources.[20] Over time, these resources came increasingly to be drawn from beyond the borders of the United States, distancing, both literally and figuratively, many American workers/consumers from the negative effects that their expanded consumption patterns were having on the planet's environment.[21]

One might counter that these dilemmas are not as extreme as they appear at first glance. The work of Nancy Langston, Alston Chase, and others, for example, has demonstrated that parks and national forests were not always ecological triumphs. In fact they often suffered serious declines under the policies of 'state simplication' imposed by supposedly expert foresters and park superintendents. Other scholars, such as Lizabeth Cohen and Timothy Breen, have taken pains to suggest how heightened consumption did not necessarily have a tranquilizing effect on workers and others but in fact made new forms of social mobilization, from union activism to political revolution, possible. But the larger fact remains: the connection between social justice and environmental justice is undertheorized at present. All too often, the linkages between the two have been asserted rather than investigated.[22]

It is with this point in mind that we might explore again the potential points of departure that Marx's early essays on the German forests offer. As useful as they may be, Marx's articles have little to say about the ecological health of the German forests or the agency of nature. Gathering fallen wood and other 'alms of nature' may have helped nineteenth-century German peasants economically. But did the heightened use that peasants made of forests during this time have negative repercussions for the ecology of German woodlands? Similarly, we tend to see the creation of the working class during this time as the result of purely human decisions. To what extent, however, did factors such as climate change or the introduction of new tree species drive peasants into the labour market?

Beyond these specific questions lurk even larger ones. For reaching an understanding of the rise of mass cities and of an urban working class of producers *and* consumers—a phenomena that has arisen across the planet in the last few centuries—is virtually impossible if one does not take into account both the city *and* the changes in the countryside, both social and environmental, that gave birth to these processes. Filling in such gaps is a project that ought to draw environmental historians and social historians alike into a much deeper dialogue than the limited exchange that they have engaged in so far. In the final analysis, after all, both social historians and environmental historians share with Marx a certain utopian vision of history, in which the past is measured against a potentially better future. It is time for environmental historians and social historians to examine whether their histories point in different directions or whether they have been describing a similar destination all along.[23]

Notes

1. Donald Worster, 'Transformations of the Earth: Toward an Agroecological Prospective in History', *Journal of American History*, 76, March 1990, pp. 1087-1106.
2. William Cronon, 'Modes of Prophecy and Production: Placing Nature in History', *Journal of American History,* 76, 1990, pp. 1128-9.
3. Richard White, 'Environmental History: Watching a Field Mature', *Pacific Historical Review,* 70:1, February 2001, p. 110.
4. Ted Steinberg, *Down to Earth: Nature's Role in American History,* New York, 2002. It should be noted that because this work is a synthesis of the current literature in North American environmental history, the lacunas in Steinberg's study reflect larger gaps in the field as a whole rather than any intellectual liabilities of the author himself.
5. These conclusions are based on an examination of John Mack Faragher et al., *Out of Many: A History of the American People,* 4th edition, NJ, 2005; John M. Murrin et al., *Liberty, Equality, Power: A History of the American People.* 4th edition, Belmont, CA, 2005; Mary Beth Norton et al., *A People and a Nation,* 7th edition, Boston, 2005; Eric Foner, *Give Me Liberty: An American History,* New York, 2005; and Jeanne Boydston et al., *Making a Nation: The United States and its People*, NJ, 2002.
6. Gunther Peck, 'The Nature of Labor: Fault Lines and Common Ground between Labor and Environmental History' (paper in possession of author); Alan Taylor, 'Unnatural Inequalities: Social and Environmental Histories', *Environmental History*, 1, October 1996, p. 9.
7. Note, for instance, Worster's definition of capitalism in *Dust Bowl,* which mentions only nature's role as capital, not capitalism's social divisions. Donald Worster, *Dust Bowl: The Southern Plains in the 1930s*, New York, 1979, p. 6. See also William Cronon, *Changes in the Land: Indians, Colonists, and the Ecology of New England*, New York, 1983; and William Cronon, *Nature's Metropolis: Chicago and the Great West*, New York, 1991.
8. For examples of recent work on environmental justice, see Robert D. Bullard, *Dumping in Dixie: Race, Class, and Environmental Quality*, Boulder, CO, 1990); Robert D. Bullard (ed.), *Confronting Environmental Racism: Voices from the Grassroots*, Boston, 1993; Dan McGovern, *The Campo Indian Landfill War: The Fight for Gold in California's Garbage*, Norman, 1995; Andrew Szasz, *EcoPopulism: Toxic Waste and the Movement for Environmental Justice*, Minneapolis, 1994; Robert Gottlieb, *Forcing the Spring: The Transformation of the American*

Environmental Movement, Washington, D.C., 1993; and Laura Pulido, *Environmentalism and Economic Justice: Two Chicano Struggles in the Southwest* Tucson, 1996.

9. Alfred Crosby, *Ecological Imperialism: The Biological Expansion of Europe, 900-1900*, New York, 1986, p. vii; Cronon, *Changes in the Land*, pp. xiii and 170. In the latter section, Cronon suggests a way of recasting Marxist notions of alienation. Several other leading environmental historians have included aspects of Marxist thought. See, for instance, Carolyn Merchant, *Ecological Revolutions: Nature, Gender, and Science in New England*, Chapel Hill, 1989, pp. 3-4, 172-3, 223; and Donald Worster, 'Transformations of the Earth: Toward an Agroecological Perspective in History', *Journal of American History*, 76, March 1990, pp. 1087-1106. Worster's ideal approach for environmental history owes much to Marxist notions of base, structure, and superstructure.
10. 'Debates on the Law on Thefts of Wood', in Karl Marx and Frederick Engels, *Collected Works*, New York, 1975, 1, pp. xxx, 224-63. At the time Marx wrote his essay, the theft of wood was by far the most prevalent form of crime in Prussia, constituting three-quarters of all the penal proceedings in 1836. See Franz Mehring, *Karl Marx: The Story of his Life*, trans. Edward Fitzgerald, New York, 1935, pp. 65-71.
11. Marx, 'Debates on the Law on Thefts of Wood', p. 234 (emphasis in the original); Peter Linebaugh, 'Karl Marx, the Theft of Wood, and Working Class Composition: A Contribution to the Current Debate', *Crime and Social Justice*, 6, Fall-Winter 1976, pp. 5-16.
12. Karl Jacoby, *Crimes against Nature: Squatters, Poachers, Thieves, and the Hidden History of American Conservation*, Berkeley, 2001, pp. 121-46, 164, 187-91 (the quoted material at the end of the paragraph is from pages 136 and 138). For more on workers turning to hunting and foraging during strikes and when blacklisted, see Benjamin Johnson, 'Conservation, Subsistence, and Class at the Birth of Superior National Forest', *Environmental History*, 4, January 1999, pp. 80-99; for more on the melding of subsistence agriculture and migrant wage labour by Chicano villagers at this time, see Sarah Deutsch, *No Separate Refuge: Culture, Class, and Gender on an Anglo-Hispanic Frontier in the American Southwest, 1880-1940*, New York, 1987.
13. Hal Barron, *Those Who Stayed Behind: Rural Society in Nineteenth-Century New England*, New York, 1984, p. xi.
14. Jacoby, pp. 138-9. A number of works are suggestive of ways in which the social history of rural America might fruitfully connect with environmental history. See Steven Hahn, *The Roots of Southern Populism: Yeoman Farmers and the Transformation of the Georgia Upcountry, 1850-1890*, New York: Oxford University Press, 1983; John

Mack Faragher, *Sugar Creek: Life on the Illinois Prairie*, New Haven, 1986; Allan Kulikoff, *The Agrarian Origins of American Capitalism*, Charlottesville, 1992; and Christopher Clark, *The Roots of Rural Capitalism: Western Massachusetts, 1780-1860*, Ithaca, 1990.

15. Quoted in Philip Terrie, *Wildlife and Wilderness: A History of Adirondack Mammals*, Fleischmanns, NY, 1993, p. 70. For more on the natural rights doctrine among Adirondacks residents, see Jacoby, pp. 48-78.
16. *Boonville (N.Y.) Herald*, 15 April 1897.
17. Jacoby, pp. 48-78. A description of the guides' unions and their advocacy of conservation measures can be found on pp. 67-72.
18. Bullard, *Dumping in Dixie*, p. xiii; Szasz, 81.
19. For more on the class and ethnic biases in early conservation, see Mark Spence, *Dispossessing the Wilderness: Indian Removal and the Making of the National Parks*, New York: Oxford University Press, 1999; Louis Warren, *The Hunter's Game: Poachers and Conservationists in Twentieth-Century America*, New Haven, 1997; and Carl Jacoby, *Crimes against Nature.*
20. For more on workers' embrace of consumerism, see Neil McKendrick, John Brewer, and J.H. Plumb (eds.), *The Birth of Consumer Society: The Commercialization of Eighteenth-Century England*, Bloomington, 1982; Lizabeth Cohen, *Making a New Deal: Industrial Workers in Chicago, 1919-1939*, New York, 1990; George J. Sánchez, *Becoming Mexican American: Ethnicity, Culture, and Identity in Chicano Los Angeles, 1900-1945*, New York, 1993, pp. 171-206; William R. Leach, *Land of Desire: Merchants, Power, and the Rise of a New American Culture*, New York, 1993; Meg Jacobs, *Pocketbook Politics: Economic Citizenship in Twentieth-Century America*, Princeton, 2005; and William Cronon's discussion of increasing consumption among farm families in *Nature's Metropolis*, pp. 333-40.
21. William Cronon discusses the role of the market in obscuring changes in the natural environment in *Nature's Metropolis*.
22. For works that problematize the claim that conservationism necessarily equates with the wise management of the environment, see Nancy Langston, *Forest Dreams, Forest Nightmares: The Paradox of Old Growth in the Inland* West, Seattle, 1995 and *Where Land and Water Meet: A Western Landscape Transformed*, Seattle, 2003; Alston Chase, *Playing God in Yellowstone: The Destruction of America's First National Park*, Boston, 1986; and the first chapter of James Scott, *Seeing Like a State: How Certain Schemes to Improve the Human Condition have Failed*, New Haven, 1998. For works that argue that consumerism under certain circumstances enabled activism, see Cohen, *Making a New Deal*; and T.H. Breen, *The Marketplace of Revolution: How Consumer Politics Shaped American Independence*, New York, 2004.

23. Alan Taylor notes the shared sense of moral engagement and utopian possibility between social historians and environmental historians in 'Unnatural Inequalities', pp. 8-9. Ramachandra Guha limns both the activist nature of environmental history and its need to further explore the landscape of the city in Guha, 'Movement Scholarship', *Environmental History*, 10, January 2005, pp. 40-1.

2. State *Versus* People: The Indian Experience of Environmentalism

Alok Kumar Ghosh

INTRODUCTION

Environmentalism is traditionally explained in India in terms of non-materialist social and religious values. Sometimes it looks into essentialist identification of human society with nature. The non-materialist approach has two lines of thinking. One is close to the Western back-to-land philosophy advocated by Romantic poets like Blake and Wordsworth, for whom 'the dark satanic mills of the industrial age threatened to obliterate for ever their green and pleasant land', or by the novelists like Charles Dickens who could not tolerate 'inhuman working and living conditions, the bleak homes and the dark, damp, polluting factories'. The other is found in the ideas of M.K. Gandhi who combined a 'moral critique with a simple lifestyle, living gently on the earth while deploring the multiplication of wants that modern civilization had brought about'.[1] In sharp contrast to these two non-materialist approaches, the colonial experience has triggered off among some of our leading political modernists a materialist voice that refuses to accept unlimited economic growth at the cost of nature and claims to follow the model of western environmentalism. It is obvious that the state in post-colonial India is in the hands of these materialists.

Indian environmentalism has, therefore, two clear divisions, one above, i.e. based on the materialist approach, the State, and the other at the bottom, i.e. the people. State environmentalism, is meant for development with the declared objective of scientific conservation. People mostly side with the ethical or non-materialist Gandhian idea of survival of the community. The dichotomy is, of course, the legacy of India's colonial past. The present essay is an attempt to analyse Indian environmentalism against the backdrop of colonial developments involving two major issues, one being the variable meaning of Nature in the eyes of authoritarian centre and subaltern periphery, the other being the ever growing binarity of post-colonial Indian society affecting the state of nature.

THE CONSTRUCTION

Generally speaking, environment is an intellectual construction,[2] an umbrella term aggregating different socio-economic spaces and political manoeuvres. Environmentalism emerges from a discourse on how a society transforms nature into environment and what the consequences are. As such environmentalism is, in the Barthian sense, a 'myth' which is both unreal and true.[3] It is unreal when it tries to naturalize the society, thus representing the paradox of culturalization or politicization and turning to be the case of inversion. It is true when it looks, in both the regional and global contexts, into centre-periphery relationship expressed through the media of academics, politics or economics of the powerful and the powerless. The powerful centre exploits the periphery and categorizes it according to its own need to dominate. Of course, the periphery obstructs, as the Indian peripheral societies did in the colonial period. The Chuars in 1799, Santals in 1855 and Mundas in 1890 resorted to revolts to resist colonial centre's intervention into their economy, law and culture.

THE COLONIAL APPROACH

Colonial intervention in India was motivated to some extent by what may be called 'social Darwinism'. Richard Grove has wrongly linked Darwin's thesis, along with those of David Corneille, Alexander Anderson, William Burchell, W.H. Webster, Joseph Hooker and Hugh Strickland, to a growing awareness of extinction processes contributing to environmental discourses. In fact, Darwin's thesis strengthened the Europeans' belief that extinction of barbarian tribes and communities through natural selection in the form of their clash with advanced technological societies was an inevitability. So was the surrender of barbarian nature of the East to Western industrial agencies. The statement in the chapter 'Genesis' of the Bible that by Order of the God Christians must dominate the nature of the whole world gave this idea a religious flavour. The domination was made possible by the technological revolution. Technology alienated the eco-system people from the production-structure and environmental degradation started in the West. Eco-system people one those who have traditionally or historically become a constituent part of a given eco-system. Scholars who wanted to study nature had now to look for their fields either in Africa or in India. William Jones wrote in 1784:

> When I was at sea last August on my voyage to this country (India) – I found – that India lay before us, and Persia on our left, whilst a breeze from Arabia blew – on our stern – It gave me inexpressible pleasure to find myself in the midst of so noble an amphitheatre – I could not help remarking, how important and extensive a field was yet unexplored. It is your design (the Court of Directors of the East India Company) – to take an ample space for your learned investigations, bounding them only by the geographical limits of Asia – (if asked) what are the intended objects of our inquiries within these spacious limits we answer Man and Nature. . . .[5]

Asiatic studies of the *sahibs*, however, strengthened Christian Humanism and upheld the Enlightenment philosophy: 'It is for him (man) that the sun rises, it is for him that the stars shine.[6] Nature was dominated by the Europeans and humans were exploited victimized by the humans.[7] In the world view of the 'enlightened Europeans' the East was the land of snake-charmers, rope-trickers and sex-monsters; Africa and America were infested with cannibals, who were not able to dominate stretches of forests, rivers and uncultivated land and were sinners against the Heaven, and also against Christian religiosity. They were thus destined to be enslaved by the white people who were entitled to hold their lands for the sake of civilization. No wonder that Morris Kingo, in an article published in the *Lancet*, argued that black children may sacrifice themselves for the interest of white children because the latter are superior to the former and have the natural right to survive.[8]

Indian jungles were an important venue for the Europeans to perform their sacred duties of ruling the nature. By the time they established themselves in this country, wildlife in England had almost vanished.[9] Hunting in the eastern *jungles* was now an important and entertaining power game in which both beasts and natives could be killed to exhibit the valour of the 'masculine occident'.[10] Even the weakest partners of nature were not spared by the European 'heroes'. In Bharatpur in 1916, 4,206 birds were killed in a single day to celebrate the visit of Lord Chelmsford; in 1938, 4,273 birds were killed in 'honour' of Lord Linlithgow.[11]

THE INDIAN SHOCK

Long before these bird killings, the Indian periphery had started experiencing 'centre's' gaze, particularly from the late eighteenth century. It was from this time that the native concept of natural space, designated as 'their idea', came into conflict with the European 'ours'. Historically, man-nature relationship in India was always thought to be one of two-way cooperation. Since the Vedic times people had developed religious devotion to trees, groves and ponds.[12] *Vrksayurveda*, one of the sixty-four *kala*s (arts) of traditional learning, informed people of the merits of gardening; classified trees, soil, manure and other 'botanical marvels'; diagnosed diseases; explored water and minerals; and discussed pest management based on sound ecological principles.[13] A study of medieval Indian literature such as Kalhana's *Rajtarangini*,[14] Maladhar Basu's *Srikrishnavijaya*,[15] or the *Mongal Kavyas*[16] reveals that the people of the land 'learnt through experience the wise principle of adjustment and accommodation' with nature and that the country was gifted with a definite Asiatic environmental management system constituted by social and cultural institutions regulating utilization of natural resources. The colonialists destroyed this system by asserting European domination over Indian nature, monopolizing resources of the land with absolute denial of traditional popular rights over soil, forests and rivers, and by rejecting the notion of development entertained by the dominated.

In the European 'centre's' view, subsistence, survival and development were possible not by gentle coexistence with nature, but by colonizing it through advanced technological applications. Use of forest resources for subsistence and survival by Indian peripheral people was synonymous to them with deforestation. Their Asiatic studies, while justifying colonial hegemony in terms of white superiority, appreciated the Aryanization of ancient India, which meant expansion of agriculture with iron technology and the State clearing jungles and enslaving the 'jungle men'. The Europeans failed or declined to admit that the killing of the mythical *Taraka*,[17] the non-Aryan forest leader, that had impressed Jones as an object of study, was not good for 'nature'. The point illustrates the general European view of indigenous forest use which was looked down upon.

FOREST ENCLOSED, NATURE CHAINED[18]

From the very ancient days Indian people lived with the forests and their interaction with forests did not do any harm to the environment. As Hardiman talks of the Bhils, '(they) had a strong affinity with these woods and hills—their home as well as place of refuge—and any destruction which they carried out was on so small a scale as to make very little difference to the environment as a whole'.[19] It was the colonialist British that for the first time rejected the Asiatic notion of mutual survival of both trees and men and their inter-productive existence. They disturbed this natural equilibrium first by encouraging cultivation through forest clearance for maximization of land revenue and then by introducing organized forestry for commercial timber production, viz., the sal (*shorea robusta*) and deodar (*cedrus deodara*) which were in great demand for making railway sleepers.

The first objective of the British in settling the Jungle Mahals in 1767 was to compensate for losses in the plains due to revenue remissions necessitated by floods and droughts.[20] It was also hoped that additional benefit would come through expansion of commercial agriculture. This is revealed in the observation of the assistant magistrate of Midnapore, who states that the land when cleared could profitably be turned to the production of sugar, cotton, mulberry, indigo, hemp and flax.[21] Production of commercial timber was equally important to the British. Travel journals of the 1790s mention travellers, encounter with teak, sal and shishu forests which were widely recognized as commercially valuable.[22] William Hodges toured the Rajmahal Hills with Cleveland in 1782 and wrote, '...the appearance of this part of the country is very singular, having immense masses of stone piled on another; from the interstices of which very large timber trees grow out—in many of these rocks I found the teak, a timber remarkable for its hardness and size.'[23] The British organized forestry in India to fell the trees when they were large and mature enough to suit colonial purposes. As Ramachandra Guha puts it, 'At a deeper epistemic level, the language of scientific forestry was purposely used to justify the shift toward commercial working.'[24] Thus, colonial green commerce and the resultant deforestation, decreasing rainfall and water scarcity in soil created a vicious circle. Taking Milnes' formulation for granted, less supply of rain or soil water than the amount evaporating from the foliage hindered the normal growth of forests in British India.[25]

The 'Centre', of course, interpreted destruction of forests in its own way. It blamed the ignorant and desperate Indians and their subsistence rights in forests for the deforestation. And State control over forests was suggested as the way out. Colonial intrusion into the forests of Bengal started officially in 1864 when the first conservator of forests was appointed. The next year the first Indian Forest Act was passed creating artificial notions of 'core and buffer' and placing the forests under revenue department. Reservation of forests started in 1874 and within ten years most of the reserve forests were 'gazetted'.This was accompanied by Wildlife Preservation Act (1873) and the Elephant Preservation Act (1879). Forests were now completely ruled by the Centre, the Panoptic State, and were prohibited to the Indian forest dwellers, the peripheral 'they' of the country. The centre thought it necessary both for commercial purpose and for its increasing hold over the subaltern society which would be a very important part of its task of rural penetration and state making. As Skaria points out, essential forms of state making were 'increase in information about forest tribes, demilitarization of forest chiefs, sedentarisation of forest tribes and demarcation of reserved forests...'.[26] In this process of statemaking conflicts between the Centre and the periphery sometimes took the form of 'ecological warfare'.[27] In many cases the people spontaneously protested against denial of their hereditary rights by spoiling forest resources. The best example of this was the people's burning of forests in 1921 when the alien rulers introduced the policy of fire protection which deprived the people of their traditional rights of burning pastures and forests for promotion of the growth of grass. To the centre restriction of burning was a way for forest development; to the people, on the other hand, development had a different meaning. The process of development planned by the centre, in fact, pushed the periphery to the opposite direction. To quote G.B. Pant, restrictions to burning 'is a source of widespread hardship and the opinion of all classes of people seems to be unanimous on this point'.[28] Reaction of the peripheral people to this was natural and they began to burn the forests. Incendiary fires in Kumaun affected about 8,40,000 hectares of forest; in July 1921 alone about 11,3,400 hectares of reserved forest in Kumaun division were burnt.[29]

The Post-Colonial Scenario

In post-colonial India the 'Centre' has changed—the colonial 'we' has been nationalized as the new 'authority' and the colonial 'they' have been further peripherized, raising intra-societal strands of environment. 'We' considers the progress of Europe as the standard and respects the European concept of 'dignified existence'. The 'they' are disqualified as 'backward' in the perspective of European time scale. This 'they' includes not only the tribal poor but also the declassed civil community migrating from one province to the other or from the neighbouring states. Science, technology, development, emancipation and progress have become watchwords of the Indian 'we' just as the colonial 'we' had set eradication of barbarism as its goal at the cost of the ordinary 'they'. In essence, all the words are clubbed in technological development which 'demands ample space, geographical space, colonies', and 'interiorizes the concept of the colonies—colonizing its own hinterlands, mostly settled with subsistent and ecologically harmonious communities, and subordinating them to the requirements of the industrialization programme'.[30] It is the 'we' and 'our' bureaucrats who only know 'modern science' and has the sole right to decide how the nature will be processed.

Environmental Conflicts in Forests

Roots of environmental disputes could thus be traced in post-colonial India not only to those between eco-system and non-eco-system people but also, perhaps more, to differences of perception among social classes, the fight being politicized between the 'we-state' and the 'they-citizens'. It is, in fact, a struggle between the powerful 'Centre' and the powerless 'Periphery'.

In colonial 1872 the Lieutenant Governor of the North Western Provinces, on a tour of Dehra Dun District, received repeated complaints from 'the natives'on the 'severity of the forest rules, dwelling chiefly on the fact that no forest or wasteland was made over to them in absolute proprietory right and so they were afraid that in some future period government might resume the whole of it and leave them destitute'.[31] As one Hillman 'succinctly' put it, 'the forests have belonged to us from time immemorial, our ancestors planted them and have protected them; now that they have become of value, government steps in and robs us of them'.[32] The same trend was visible in the post-colonial *Chipko* Movement of North India as is evident from a statement of S.L. Bahuguna, its leader, that the movement originated from a clash between the state contractors and local inhabitants over rights of cutting trees and from the demands of the Gangotri Swaraj Sangha and Dasholi Gram Swaraj Sangha for more rights of people on forest resources.

On 27 March 1973, a group of peasants in a remote Himalayan village in the upper Gangetic valley prevented loggers from felling the hornbeam trees which were auctioned by the state forest department to a sports-goods company of Allahabad. The peasants of the adjoining village *Mandal* prevented felling by threatening to hug or stick to (*chipko*) the trees. The *Mandal* episode was the beginning of a series of similar protests throughout the 1970s, a dozen or more, which collectively constituted 'the *Chipko* Movement, recognized as one of the most famous environmental initiatives of our times'.[33]

'Centre-state' behaviour was more or less the same in the case of Marichjhanpi of the Sunderbans of West Bengal. In 1978 nearly one lakh refugees, mostly the lower caste Namasudras, left Dandakaranya rehabilitation zone of the Andhra-Orissa belt, and created a new settlement at Marichjhanpi, a thirty-nine mile long and eight mile wide uninhabited island in the Ganga-Brahmaputra Delta in the Sunderbans. They reportedly established fisheries, workshops, cottage industries, bakeries, a dispensary and a primary school. They took a desperate view of the situation, unprecedented of its kind, and brought all their human resources together to resettle themselves in the forest lands against enormous odds.[34]

The response of the state of West Bengal, the 'Centre' in this case, was first of fear and then of anger. They declared the refugee settlements illegal encroachment on forest lands reserved for biospheric balance and protection of endangered tigers. The chief minister of West Bengal stated in the State Assembly on 10 February 1979 that no further settlement anywhere in West Bengal would be allowed and all the refugees would be pushed back to Dandakaranya. Brutal police operation followed and took the form of siege of the island by police launches, indiscriminate firing on the helpless poor and forced sinking of boats carrying refugee women and children.[35]

The peripheral perception of the settlement in forest lands was just the opposite of what the State maintained. Not that the question of ecological degradation was completely ignored by the 'they' when their survival was at stake. But they believed in their capacity to entertain harmony with nature and generate symbiotic relationship with forests. They were confident that they could introduce in the island a new pattern of development by way of establishing fisheries and planting renewable trees as a part of reclamation, which could both develop the forest resources and preserve their community. The refugees denied that they had destroyed the forest trees. This was so because tall and dense forest trees were not at all available in the island which was full of only weeds and firewoods like *garan* and *hetal*. Raiharan Baroi, General Secretary, Udvastu Unnayan Samiti, wrote in an open letter on 5 March 1979, 'Marichjhanpi is actually isolated from the main reserve forest by conjunction of two big rivers, Jhila and Garral. All its three sides are open fields, void of forest resources and suitable for human settlement.'[36]

Already in an open letter dated 16 February 1979, the same refugee leader had written that 'there were no such trees at Marichjhanpi in 1978 as could be categorized as forest resources. The trees which the refugees uprooted were mainly Garan, Chhitegaon and Hetal, all of the height between three feet to six feet, that could be used only as firewood'.[37] The refugees proposed to plant forest trees on the banks of the rivers if they were allowed to settle there. They also pointed out that robbery of forest wood might be stopped if they could settle and which in turn could increase the pace of forestation in the surroundings.

The refugees' observation that the newly raised Marichjhanpi land was suitable for Garan, Geugoa, Konkoba, Sundari and Pasur trees was, in fact, more or less correct.[38] It was only on the banks of the rivers that some Garjan trees could be planted which the refugees agreed to do. Majority of the trees were of short height and had little role in monitoring temperature and ecological balance in any fruitful sense. Nor were they very important in preventing erosion of land. Obviously an island like Marichjhanpi was not liked by the Royal Bengal Tiger who always prefers a dense forest of huge tall trees. A report of the Forest Department itself stated that even if no human settlement was ever allowed at Marichjhanpi only two tigers could be maintained there.[39] So technically the objections of the Government of West Bengal, the 'powerful Centre', raised against the settlements of the 'powerless periphery' as destructive of environment were not at all convincing.

This will become more clear if it is compared with the case of Dandakaranya. There also refugee rehabilitation required deforestation—but that was welcomed by the state serving industrial urban interests. The area of Dandakaranya Project had been rich in mineral wealth but had been backward and isolated due to its inaccessibility and self-sufficient nature of tribal habitation. Manpower and labour of the refugees were utilized there to develop the area. Deforestation went on but the 'Centre's' men who advocated for standard biosphere at Marichjhanpi did not object to it. They did not resist large-scale deforestation in the Duars of north Bengal by the Nepali migrants, establishing Nepali labour *bustees,* as the Nepalis were favoured as skilled tea-estate labourers. At Marichjhanpi, on the contrary, preservation of forest was absolutely necessary even at the cost of thousands of human lives, because its development for mineral wealth was not required, nor refugee labour needed in the area where industrial growth was still a dream. However whatever few trees could be planted in the island could be useful to some outer industrial sectors. The Sunderban Unnayan Board published a pamphlet in 1976 in which the Deputy Conservator of Forests wrote, 'the growth of trees in these zones is quite slow due to the site factor and attack of insects and fungus to trees rules out the possibility of quality timber, consequently the endeavour should be to grow industries which can utilize the small-sized timber for, say, particle board or paper.'[40] So Marichjhanpi was sought to be protected not for any biospheric interests but for industrial ones and this illustrates how the Indian 'Centre' in the 1970s and 1980s rejected the critique that identified techno-industrial pattern of development as the root cause of environmental degradation.

THE WATER DISPUTE

Experience of the Indian periphery with water resources was more or less similar. In colonial India the Britishers helped drying up water reserves by settling *jalkar mahals* as a part of all inclusive revenue structure. The *mahals* evolved from its earlier position, i.e. having separate status as a category of *sayer* as distinguished from *mal* of the Mughal land revenue system.[41] Access of the eco-system people to the *mahals* was restricted[42] and mass participation in the maintenance of lakes, bills and ponds was lost.[43] An article in the *Mihir–O–Sudhakar*, a vernacular newspaper of Bengal (1907-08), described in detail how the Chalan Bill of Rajshahi District of East Bengal dried up after colonial intervention. The author argued that the Cornwallis Settlements deprived the *'Projas'* (tenants) of their traditional rights to dig ponds and so the British were responsible for this natural degradation.[44] In the colonial period whatever little canal irrigation the State undertook adversely affected lands because of its structural evils.[45] Embankments did not contain adequate cross drainage works, water got held up and surrounding areas got submerged and damaged.

After 1947, big dams which Nehru welcomed as 'the temples of modern India' were erected in the country mainly for irrigating upper lands producing cash crops and for hydroelectric power generation. Interests of the powerless were neglected and the dams were built up under a shadow of misdirected planning emerging out of political-economic interpretation of development by dominant authorities. It was thus natural that the projects were carried out at the cost of deforestation, killing of wild animals as was reported from Koyna, Panchet and Bhavanisagar. In the Srisailam Project of the Krishna River, habitation of lakhs of people vanished and conflicts between the 'Centre' and the 'periphery' were frequent in Koyelkaro, Bhopalpatnam and Inchampalli Dam areas. In the Tehri Dam the cost of deforestation was about Rs. 30,000 crores.[46] The picture was almost the same in the projects of Punjab, Haryana, Rajasthan and Uttar Pradesh. Reddy's research has highlighted the extent of degradation of forests in south India due to construction of dams. He has cited that the construction of Idukki Dam over Periyar River in Kerala hastened the degradation of vegetation and sharply reduced the forest cover. Reddy has estimated the loss of forest lands to river valley projects during the period 1951-76 at 0.49 million hectares which was roughly 10 per cent of the area irrigated by canals.[47]

The Narmada Bachao Andolan raised its head in the 1990s against such a background. The 'Centre's' view of the project was that the Sardar Sarovar Dam on the Narmada River would stand as an illustration of India's economic development. But it suppressed the fact that the dam would submerge historic temples, rich deciduous forests and at least 250 villages and would force about 70,000 people to become ecological refugees.

Quite reasonably the Narmada people in the 'periphery', in apprehension of their ecological persecution, strongly stood for the anti-dam slogan of Medha Patkar.

Environmentalism Revisited

The Chipko Movement and the Narmada Bachao Andolan are the best examples of people's environmentalism in the Indian periphery as against that of the Indian Centre. Unlike the Chiko Movement of Brazil, the Chipko combined the idea of protection for common resources along with endangered species and the Gandhian back-to-land thesis practised through non-violent technique of protest. The Narmada Bachao Andolan, on the other hand, in contrast to the 'Save the Stanislaus' Movement organized by Mark Dubois of California against the New Melones Dam, was aimed to save not only the river itself but also thousands of peasants who had hereditary rights to the villages there. The Indian 'they', therefore, fought not only for the nature but also for the society, for the social right to mutual interaction with nature. In the colonial period 'they' shared the stage with anti-colonial political struggle; in the post-colonial period 'they' resisted the 'Centre' to ensure democracy, human rights and equal rights over common natural resources.[48]

The Middle Path

The Indian middle class between 'we' and 'they' have accepted, however, the technocratic view of environment. Their environmentalism has three stages. The first stage takes a romantic mythical view of nature, laments for what it had and what it has lost. In the second stage, it desperately finds out a group or groups whom it can blame for the loss. In the final stage it identifies the drawbacks of ongoing developmental and technological projects. Some of them become nature-centric environmentalists and human-right-activists and others set up organizations, if possible with nationalist flavour, to suggest cure for the evils with more sophisticated technology and environmental planning. With this managerial approach, operating within the scientific-developmental paradigm of a modern state, it calls for a new attitude towards nature, demanding more parks, lakes and wildlife sanctuaries. It at the same time is victimized by the new culture of technology, popularized by the 'we', which makes it enjoy both the nature and its destroyer. Samuel Cohen, the inventor of the Neutron Bomb, when asked in an interview why he engaged himself in making catastrophic weapons; replied, 'I enjoy'. This reply may find favour among the Indian middle classes too.

Environmentalism of the 'they', the urban and rural poor, the *bustee*-dwellers and the industrial workers are just the opposite—'they' have an anti-thesis, a survival approach, no question of sophistication, no question of romantic love for nature.

The Tata Factory of Gopalpur was not opposed by the 'civil society' or the middle class people. It was resisted by the local poor who feared not merely the loss of nature, but also huge lands spreading over 25 villages. In Karnataka the peasants challenged government's decision of eucalyptus plantation to feed a polyfibre factory, because they understood from experience that such plantation could lead to topsoil erosion and decline in water level.[49]

In contrast, the people between 'we' and 'they', who are very much opposed to rural backwardness and urban *bustees*, are not so vocal against jungles of highrises, automobile aggression, flyovers and bypasses, big bazars and arcades, whereas they are untired of clamouring for nature within their complexes.

Realization

So conflicts were, they are and will be. Outward stability will be maintained in terms of domination and hegemony. Sometimes image-building compulsions may work, as was in the case of Silent Valley Hydroelectric Project in the state of Kerala. Indira Gandhi, the then Prime Minister of India, stalled the project not because of her realization that Indian rainforests would be inundated but because, as Gadgil and Guha have explained, she wanted 'to enhance her image among the international conservation community'.[50]

NOTES

1. For an excellent discussion on these ideas, see Ramachandra Guha, *Environmentalism—A Global History*, New Delhi, 2000, pp. 10-24.
2. Francis Moore has called it a social construction, but to me it is more an elitist intellectual one than social as whole. See Francis Moore, *Environment and Society*, New Delhi, 2003, p. 1.
3. For an analysis of social myth, see D. Silverman and B. Torode, *The Material World,* London, 1980, p. 260.
4. Richard H. Grove, *Green Imperialism,* Delhi, 1995, p. 483.
5. Quoted in Rila Mukherjee, 'Space Knowledge and Power', in Ranjan Chakrabarti (ed.), *Space and Power in History: Images, Ideologies, Myths and Moralities,* Kolkata, 2001, p. 29.
6. Norman Hampson, *The Enlightenment,* Harmondworth (U.K.) 1979, p. 81.
7. Tapan Kumar Chattopadhyay, *India and the Ecology Question,* Kolkata, 1999, p. 12.
8. Quoted by Vandana Shiva in a review article published in *Chinta,* Dhaka, 15 August 1993, p. 15.
9. J.M. Mackenzie, *The Empire of Nature*, Manchester, 1988, p. 168.
10. William Binart, 'Empire, Hunting and Ecological Change in Southern and Central Africa', *Past and Present*, August 1990, pp. 62-86; Ronald Inden: *Imagining India*, Oxford, 1990, p. 3.
11. Cited in Debal Dev, *Unnayan Purakatha* (Bengali Monograph on Development), Kolkata, 2005, p. 19.
12. Kapila Vatsyayan, 'Ecology and Indian Myth', in Geeti Sen (ed.), *Indigenous Vision—Peoples of India, Attitudes to Environment,* New Delhi, 1992, pp. 157-80.
13. For a summary of *Vrkshayurveda* debt is acknowledged to K. Vijayalakshmi and Shyam M. Sundark, *Vrkshayurveda—An Introduction to Indian Plant Science*, Madras, 1993.
14. Kalhana's *Rajtarangini* is translated and edited by W. Stein (1900), reprinted by Motilal Banarasidass, Delhi 1961. Also see the Surjya episode narrated in Bengali by Dinesh Chandra Sarkar, *Prachin Itihaser Kahini* (Stories of Ancient India), Kolkata, 1984, pp. 82-6.
15. See *Srikrishnavijaya* edited by K.N. Mitra, Kolkata, 1944.
16. For an idea of 'folk literature' that evolved in *Mangal Kavya-Panchali* tradition illustrating man-nature relations in the Sunderban area, see Sutapa Chatterjee, 'Literature and Folk Deities of the Sunderbans', in Rajat Kanta Ray (ed.), *Mind, Body and Society*, Kolkata, 1995, pp. 425-48.
17. *Ramayana*, retold by Rajsekhar Basu, *Balmiki Ramayan* (Bengali), Kolkata (Bengali calendar year 1396), pp. 23-6.

18. In this section the author's findings are based on his earlier article, 'Environment as an Issue of Political Economy in Colonial and Post-Colonial India: Some Case Studies', in Chittabrata Palit and Amit Bhattacharyya (eds.), *Science Technology, Medicine and Environment in India: Historical Perspectives*, Kolkata, 1998, pp. 228-59.
19. David Hardiman, 'Power in the Forest : the Dangs 1820-1940', in David Arnold and David Hardiman (eds.), *Subaltern Studies,* vol. VIII, Delhi, 1996, p. 105.
20. W.K. Firminger (ed.), *Bengal District Records: Midnapore,* vol. 1, 1763-64, Calcutta, 1926, no. 60, dated 17 March 1766; Verelst to Graham, quoted in K. Sivaramakrishnan, 'British Imperium and Forested Zones of Anomaly in Bengal 1767-1833', in *Indian Economic and Social History Review*, vol. 33, no. 3, 1996, p. 248.
21. Quoted in Sivaramakrishnan, op. cit., p. 225.
22. Ibid., p. 249.
23. Ibid.
24. Ramachandra Guha, *The Unquiet Woods: Ecological Change and Peasant Resistance in the Himalayas*, Delhi, 1991, p. 60; also see two articles by Michael Mann and E.P. Flint, in Richard H. Grove et al. (eds.), *Nature and the Orient*, Delhi, 1998, pp. 396-458.
25. J. Lores and Milne Margery, *Water and Life*, Bombay, 1969, p. 23.
26. Quoted in Sivaramkrishnan, op. cit., p. 246.
27. Ibid., p. 253.
28. G.B. Pant, *The Forest Problem in Kumaun,* Allahabad, 1922, p. 65.
29. Madhav Gadgil and Ramachandra Guha, *This Fissured Land,* Delhi, 1993, p. 166.
30. Claude Alvares, *Science Development and Violence: The Revolt Against Modernity*, New Delhi, 1992, p. 6.
31. A.S. Rawat, 'Deforestation and Forest Policy in the Lesser Himalayan Kumaun: Impact on Peasant Women and Tribal Populations', in *Mountain Research and Development*, vol. 15, no. 4, 1995, p. 313; this is also referred to in the present author's article, 'Environmentalism, Environmental Movement and the Indian Scenario', in *Vidyasagar University Journal of History,* New Series no. 1, Midnapore, 2001, pp. 46-7.
32. Ibid.
33. Particularly the women were aggrieved because the encroachment by contractors deprived them of their access to fuel, water and fodder. See Aparna Mohanto, 'The Indian State and Patriarchy', in T.V. Satyamurthy (ed.), *State and Nation in the Context of Social Change*, Delhi, 1994, p. 104.
34. Memorandum to the Members of Parliament from the Udvastu Unnayan Samity dated 22 March 1979, signed by Raiharan Baroi, General Secretary of the Samity, private collection.

35. Gyanesh Kudaisya, 'Divided Landscapes, Fragmented Identities: East Bengal Refugees and Their Rehabilitation in India 147-79', in D.A. Low and Howard Brasted (eds.), *Freedom Trauma Continuities: North India and Independence*, Delhi, 1998, pp. 122-3; for further details see Jagadish Chandra Mondal, *Marichjhanpi—Naishyabder Antarale* (Bengali), Kolkata, 2002, pp. 51-68.
36. Letter dated 5 March 1979, private collection of Niranjan Halder, the then reporter of the *Anandabazar Patrika*, Kolkata.
37. Letter from Raiharan Baroi dated 16 February 1979, published in Jagadish Chandra Mondal, op. cit., pp. 138-9.
38. Saibal Kumar Gupta, '*Marichjhanpi Ki Marichika* (Is Marichjhanpi Only a Mirage), *Marichjhanpi Bulletin*, Kolkata, May 1979.
39. Ibid.
40. Ibid.
41. Proceedings of the Committee of Revenue, Calcutta, 3 August 1789; 1 July 1791; 1 and 19 November 1816.
42. Proceedings of the Board of Revenue, Calcutta, 24 February 1841.
43. Ibid.
44. Cited in Sumit Sarkar, *Beyond Nationalist Frames: Relocating Postmodernism Hindutva History*, Delhi, 2002, p. 106.
45. Elizabeth Whitcombe, *Agrarian Condition in Northern India: the United Provinces Under British Rule 1860-1900*, Berkeley, 1972, pp. 29-31, 64-91.
46. Prasad Ray, '*Unnayan Banam Parivesh—Bharatiya Chalchitra* (Development Versus Environment, the Indian Scenario)', in Mohit Ray (ed.), *Prasanga Parivesh* (on Environment), Kolkata, 1991, p. 6.
47. Venkat D. Reddy, 'Deforestation : Its impact on Indian Environment', in A.K. Tripathi et al. (eds.), *Advances in Environmental Sciences*, New Delhi, 1993, p. 69.
48. The present author's article in *Vidyasagar University Journal of History*, op. cit., p. 49.
49. Tapan Kumar Chattopadhyay, op. cit., pp. 26-30.
50. Madhav Gadgil and Ramachandra Guha, *Ecology and Equity : The Use and Abuse of Nature in Contemporary India*, Delhi, 1995, p. 73.

3. Forest, Land Use and Water in Colonial South Asia: Issues from Agrarian and Environmental History

Arun Bandopadhyay

Academia in the last twenty years has seen a significant growth of interest in environmental history, simultaneously approached from global, regional and local perspectives in many writings. There has been a remarkable transformation in the scope and purview of teaching and research in certain disciplines like economic history in the wake of this phenomenal rise of environmental history. The present paper on certain environmental issues of colonial South Asia is based on two broad assumptions. The first is that there is considerable mutual dependence between economic, specifically agrarian history and environmental history in general, though their specific distinctions should in no way be overlooked. Secondly, the environmental issues of colonial South Asia are important not only as 'new frontiers of knowledge'; there is something in 'this history' that makes it abidingly significant in understanding today's environmental debate at large.

These two assumptions are a prelude to certain general propositions, which we must highlight in the beginning. Environment is a multi-faceted concern in which practitioners of several disciplines participate. It is an academic query, a social activity, and a consciousness, each of which has its history. Besides scientists from various disciplines, politicians, activists, social scientists and philosophers participate in today's environmental debate concerning the state of environment, the sustainability of different technologies and the question of ideologies and social systems related to environmental change and movement. Social scientists have particular ways of looking at all these, and they include people from the disciplines of sociology and anthropology, economics and history, and sociologically sensitive scientists. Secondly, history has a very important role to play in explaining the origin of modern environmentalism. It is not merely because of the significance of understanding the administrative and social history of environment or for its general importance in contemporary world. Indeed, the simultaneity of modern environmentalism and 'modern history' including the rise of capitalism is striking. However, there is a problem of synthesis of theory and history in the study of broader socio-ecological change. Environmental historians often do not know what to do with social theory, while the environmentally oriented social scientists are generally ignorant about how to translate their perspectives into historical research. History, properly synthesized, not only provides a perspective but also a direction in today's environmental debate.

The present paper has three parts. In the first part, I am concerned with the extant approaches to environmental history, which have so far been guided by two broader paradigms of human-nature relations. If one is the key construction of nature and culture through history,[1] the other is what has been broadly defined as political ecology.[2] Strangely enough, both these paradigms have been recently criticized, and significant additions and modifications have been proposed. The second part of the paper deals with some questions on the origin of modern environmentalism as well as on the specifically agro-ecological explanation of the rise of capitalism in early modern period, particularly after 1600. While the former has been advocated by Richard Grove's recent work *Green Imperialism*,[3] the latter has been made possible by a rereading of Immanuel Wallerstein's celebrated work *The Modern World System* Vol. I through the writing of Jason W. Moore.[4] The role played by European science, capitalism and the colonial knowledge system has been evaluated. The views of Grove and Wallerstein are critically placed here. In the final part, three related issues pertaining to forest, land use and water are identified from South Asian colonial history and explained from their agrarian, environmental contexts. The arguments relating to colonial watershed in South Asian ecological change have been specifically judged. The broad ideological, social and ecological implications of the change are also analysed. The paper ends with a concluding note to argue for a broader synthesis of agrarian and environmental history in the South Asian colonial context and suggestively builds a case for colonial environmental history as a significant tool for understanding the contemporary environment question at large.

I

We can begin with four basic approaches identified for environmental studies: (a) biocentric, (b) ecological, (c) economic, and (d) ethical.[5] The biocentric approach is rooted in an aesthetic or quasi-religious commitment to nature and is a vital argument for the nature preservationists. It stems from the feelings that led ancients to both fear and respect nature, which gave plants, animals and other objects of nature their individuality and their ability to act on behalf of or against humans in the maintenance of the order of the universe. As a generalized statement of value, the biocentric argument can be developed in many directions, including those relating to biodiversity. The ecological approach to Environmental Studies starts by placing value on something like a stable system, a certain mix of species of plants and animals with natural conditions like climate and soil structure remaining in or near a state of equilibrium, which in its turn influence human ecology, including even human culture.[6] The economic approach by making efficiency a virtue has a two-way effect on the history of nature. On the one hand, economic efficiency urges progressively greater resource exploitation from nature, thereby becoming destructive. On the other hand, by an extension of the efficiency principle, the approach expresses apprehensions about the alarming rate of natural resource depletion for future, thereby becoming protective of nature. Finally, the ethical approach to nature seeks to develop sorts of 'rights of nature', in its multifarious meanings and abstractions, though not necessarily against man.[7] In particular, the argument speaks for the preservation of exceptional features in nature, unique natural objects and individual species of plants and animals for their own sake.[8]

The ecologic approach is further developed by the establishment of a link between ecology and history through the identification of the dominant frames and language of analysis for environment. Four modes of resource uses are identified in the long course of human history.[9] Each mode includes aspects of technology, economy, social organization, ideology and a specific ecological impact on surroundings. The four modes of resource use are: (a) food gathering, (b) nomadic pastoralism, (c) settled agriculture, and (d) industry. They are not strict chronological categories, one replacing the other conclusively in a long time series. However, the overall ecological impact of the first three modes was not devastating for nature. By contrast, the industrial mode, combined with arguments of economic efficiency for exploiting nature in the destructive sense, and 'scientific' prescriptions for resource use for capitalistic purposes has proved to be major disturber of environment.

Given these basic approaches, the two analytical paradigms for environmental history may be taken up for discussion. Admittedly, there are certain advantages of the nature-culture paradigm in analytic terms. It can critically distinguish between Western and Indian attitudes towards nature over the ages, and can even interpret colonial watershed as a major departure from the paradigm. Moreover, nature is not taken as a non-changing given, as the physical landscape is constantly changing. Similarly, culture should not be taken as merely ethno-biological, as it is varying and changing. Indeed, A.W. Crosby's definition of culture is better suited in this paradigm as 'a system of storing and altering patterns of human behaviour not in the molecules of genetic code but in the cells of the brain'.[10]

However, K. Sivaramakrishnan has questioned this paradigm in his book *Modern Forests: Statemaking and Environmental Change in Colonial Eastern India*. He has made two criticisms: (a) nature-culture dualism is simplified and (b) preoccupation with colonial watershed is far-fetched. In short, instead of seeing environment in the context of nature and culture, he problematizes nature and culture as social constructs, thus relinquishing large-scale systems approach to human ecology and history in favour of a mosaic approach stressing the effects of local ecological factors, social conflicts, events and culture.[11] Sivaramakrishnan has called this 'statemaking'. Here the history of colonialism rapidly dissolves into histories of colonial statemaking, in terms of control over resources and people. However, this history sometimes met with notable success, sometimes abysmal failure.

The other major paradigm is political ecology that constantly focusses on issues of social equality and justice in the sphere of conflicts over natural resources. Amita Baviskar writes that its strength lies in the fact that it 'has examined social movements large and small that bring together diverse and distant groups, address trans-national audiences and use international and national regulatory and judicial institutions to defend threatened livelihoods against the incursions of state-led extractive development'.[12] However, Baviskar criticizes this paradigm on two grounds. First, political ecology tends to look at development through the binaries of civil society versus state, 'virtuous peasants' versus 'vicious states'. Secondly, it assumes that 'cultural identities are pre-formed, derived directly from an objective set of interests based on shared locations in terms of class, gender and ethnicity that challenge nationalism and/or capitalism'.[13] In other words, political ecology creates a vacuum when it comes to the use of natural resources for collective representation beyond the concern of their immediate material value. A cultural politics of natural resources fills the vacuum by relating the materiality of the resource to wider structures of meaning. It treats identities, interests and resources not as givens but as emergent products of the cultural practices. In this sense, 'it has a greater appreciation of the complex and contingent conditions under which people make history'.[14]

Despite this criticism, the most striking advantage of political ecology remains its concentration on the political economy of resources, particularly the complexity of local resources intersecting with global commercial economy. More important, resource issues and conflicts are discussed here not only in spatial terms but also in temporal terms, and in this, imperial history matters considerably. As expropriation of wealth from the south and enrichment of the north was often achieved through direct physical violence from the seventeenth to the nineteenth centuries, Simon Dalby points out, 'longer perspectives for thinking about resources and history have to be considered'.[15] The remarkable historical change in ecological power relations in early modern period has also been hinted in Wallerstein.

Finally, I come to the relevance of moral issues or thought as such within environmental history or environmental debate at large. Environmental ethics is believed to be a guiding inspiration for the environmental movement. Even within environmental history, ethical issues may be less apparent but not altogether absent. Donald Worster detects a dilemma here when he writes: 'Environmental history was . . . born out of a moral purpose, with strong political commitments behind it, but also became, as it matured, a scholarly enterprise that had neither any simple or any single, moral or political agenda to promote'.[16] However, the role and place of nature in human life continues to be its subject matter. It proceeds on three levels, as argued by Worster. While the first copes with understanding nature itself, as organized and functioning in past times, the second dwells in the socio-economic realm as it interacts with the environment. But the more tangible or human type of encounter is found at the third level that tackles with the purely mental or intellectual issues. Here perceptions, ethics, laws, myths and other structures of meaning become part of an individual's or group's dialogue with nature. Worster adds,

> people are constantly engaged in constructing maps of the world around them, in defining what a resource is, in determining what sorts of behaviour may be prohibited and generally in choosing the ends of their lives. Though for the purpose of clarification, we may try to distinguish between these three levels of environmental studies, in fact they constitute a *single dynamic enquiry* in which nature, social and economic organization, thought and design are treated as one whole (emphases added).[17]

II

One striking fact about the origin of modern environmentalism and the rise of early capitalism is that they were concomitant: both began to take shape from the sixteenth century onwards. We make a brief study of the views of Wallerstein and Grove respectively on the agro-ecological roots of the early rise of Western capitalism and the European colonial origin of modern conservationism.

We begin with Wallerstein. There is a general consensus among analysts that however useful *The Modern World System* Vol. I may be for matters of large-scale economic history, it is silent on the environment. It is exclusively focussed 'on the ways of organizing relations among humans', dropping 'the ecological dimension that was part of the Braudelian framework'. Jason Moore has challenged this view in a seminal article published in 2003. He points to the volume's strong eco-historical content, and its importance for conceptualizing a world environmental history that highlights capitalism's historical-geographical specificity. Thus an eco-historical reading and critique of the volume forms the basis for the historical-geographical sketch of European expansion and environmental transformation that followed. Four elements of historical geography got special attention from Wallerstein: equalization, expansion, divergence and agro-ecological transformation. The process of equalization across space was made possible through the production of a new geographical scale where 'Europe's leading strata brought together formerly isolated or only loosely articulated areas into a single division of labour'.[18] It was an equalization of commodity production through socio-ecological relations encompassed by the new capitalist world economy. Secondly, geographical expansion was essential to the resolution of feudal crisis, finally leading to capitalist development. It was reinforced by the consolidation and expansion of the scale of territorial states and their empires that had suffered during feudal crisis but gained renewed vigour through overseas expansion. Thirdly, through the process of divergence, a new globalizing relation between the core and periphery took shape. As Wallerstein himself noted, 'The trend in the core was towards variety and specialization, while the trend in the periphery was toward monoculture'.[19] Finally, the agro-ecological transformation made the rise of capitalism possible as part and parcel of a radical reshaping of world ecology, whose most dramatic features were found in Wallerstein's analogy in the new American and eastern European peripheries.

Thus, Jason Moore argues that Wallerstein should be taken seriously for environmental history because of his proposition that nature and society are mutually relational. 'For Wallerstein, as for Marx, the degradation of the soil and the degradation of the labourer are dialectically bound.'[20] The second important argument of Wallerstein from the environmental perspective is that the trend toward monoculture was most evident in the periphery. Indeed, plantation-driven monocultures were the most dramatic, and quite possibly the most important, way that peripheral landscapes were produced in the emergent capitalist world economy. Thirdly, Wallerstein's breakthrough was to show how these local-scale transformations on the one hand were determined by world-scale structures and forces and on the other were constitutive of the very same world-historical patterns. Thus, for Wallerstein, the mutual determination of ecology and society was ultimately mediated by human labour power, which itself was at once a force of nature and a force of society. However, the most glaring limitation of Wallerstein's ecological perspective is his preoccupation with the agrarian geographical conception of capitalism. As a result, the 'metabolic rift' between the country and the city—so central to Marx and Engles in their ecological critique of capitalism and developed in myriad directions in recent ecological literature—remains a secondary concern to Wallerstein. The rural-urban dialectic in environmental history is not fully comprehensible in his analogy.

We now review Richard Grove's of thesis on the origin of modern environmentalism from a South Asian perspective. Though global environmentalism has been largely made a theme of the last quarter of the twentieth century, its modern origin has been generally traced to the nineteenth and the twentieth centuries.[21] Thanks to the works of Richard Grove, first *Green Imperialism* and then *Ecology, Climate and Empire: The Indian Legacy in Global Environmental History*, modern environmentalism now can be traced as far back as AD 1500. Grove's move is a major departure as he makes a 300-year backward journey for the origin of modern environmentalism, linking it with the historical experience of South Asia. The Grove thesis highlights two important issues that perturb today's environmentalists—global and local issues, both of which had something to do in the formulation and criticism of the thesis.

Richard Grove's unique departure is his attempt to link modern environmental thought with the mental and colonial expansion of Europe during AD 1500-1860. Colonial expansion thus becomes a double-edged sword for him. First, it created an imbalance in the vast part of the world in economic and ecologic terms. Second, initial 'modern' thought was made possible by the specific contribution of European science, which was variously attached to colonial expansion. Earlier (1995) the contribution was identified in two main areas: (a) the protection of tropical forests in colonies and (b) the construction of various botanical gardens. Now (1998) a further area called (c) the study of climate changes has been added, with special reference to the writings of Fernandez Oviedo on the connection amongst rainfall, vegetation and the hydrological cycle. Thus colonial science is given an exclusive position within imperialism, a position developing out of actual colonial experience and growing conscience of European science.

The search for environmental ideas has a long history. Grove emphasizes the importance of the oceanic island 'Eden' as a vehicle of the new conception of nature. During this period (between fifteenth and nineteenth centuries), Grove identifies two major influences which are broadly 'cultural'. First, conservationist practices could not be distinguished from the complex web of economic, religious and cultural arrangements.[22] Second, the search for 'Eden' was a phenomenon whose roots lay in a complex mixture of European, Arabic and Indian philosophical traditions.[23] Indeed, India and the Ganges Valley in particular found a prominent place in some medieval European texts as the location of some earthy paradise. The search for 'Eden' thus does not fit with Edward Said's construction of Orientalism based on power relations.

Then came the Portuguese and Dutch construction of tropical nature that was further mixed up by the indigenous knowledge of southwest India. Two cases can be cited. First is the case of the Portuguese physician called Garcia da Orta who published a book in 1563. The book contained description of plants in the East and India, from which medicines sold in Europe were extracted. This text was hostile to European and Arabic knowledge and gave more importance to accurate local knowledge.[24] The other is the famous twelve-volume Dutch botanical encyclopaedia called *Hortus Indicus Malabaricus*

(1678-93), compiled by Van Reede. Van Reede rejected methodologies propounded by Father Mathew, a European botanist, and depended more on the knowledge of the local Malayali physician Itti Achuden of the Ezhava community. Grove makes two major conclusions from this. First, van Reede was eager to acquire highest quality of indigenous knowledge. Second, he was elevating Ezhava knowledge.[25]

From about the middle of the eighteenth century to about the middle of the nineteenth century, we do get a form of state environmentalism. This period is also called the period of global environmentalism. Two things happened during this period: (a) institutional diffusion through wide development of professional science and (b) diffusion of climatic and medical environmentalism amongst intellectuals and governments. Three persons were important: J.R. Foster, Robert Kyd and Alexander von Humboldt. For naturalist Foster and his son, the voyages of Captain James provided the context of professional enquiry: 'the growing strength and direction of German Romantic science, *Naturphilosophie* and Orientalism both encouraged the search for empirical knowledge of natural and social variations'.[26] For Robert Kyd, the founder of the Calcutta Botanical Garden, the theories of the French agronomies and the physiocrats were most important. Kyd was even guided by the experience of the 1770 famine in Bengal. However, for Grove, Kyd was compelled to stress the commercial advantage that might accrue to the East India Company and deliberately underplay the merits of the project of famine prevention.[27] For Alexander Humboldt, during 1800-37, there was the Orientalist preoccupation with Indian conceptions of the relationship between man and nature, particularly through the writings of Forster, Goethe and Herder. Humboldt made two points. First, he had an interest in analysing deforestation. Second, highlighted the impact of Europeans on tropical environment and indigenous societies.

Finally, we get a period of gradual emergence of State conservationism during the years 1760-1857. Grove agrees that, on balance, indigenous knowledge and afforestation methods significantly contributed to the Company's environmental policy, though finally these get a less important position in his analogy.

During this period, deforestation was linked with the state of agriculture, health and climate.[28] Roxburg, for example, increased his interest in planting trees to provide famine food and to increase the incidence of rainfall.[29] Nathaniel Wallich criticized the deforestation of bamboo jungles in Bengal, which he said caused a local epidemic in 1815-16.[30] Sleeman initiated tree planting in northern India to promote forest protection for reasons which were neither strategic nor marked by timber deficiencies.[31]

The Grove's thesis brings the colonial framework from the periphery to the central focus in explaining the origin of modern environmentalism. For him, modern environmentalism is the child of European science and colonial experience as well as knowledge. Three major criticisms are in order here. First, Grove is restrained about the ecological imperialism of Europe, particularly its far-reaching impact on the natural, economic and cultural life of the colonies. His position is different from that of Crosby's. While Grove focuses on the relationship between deforestation and desiccationism, Crosby vehemently attacks European ecological imperialism and its impact on the various parts of the world including South Asia. Secondly, Grove does not distinguish pre-colonial deforestation from that of the colonial ones, notwithstanding his emphasis on ecological imbalances during 1500-1860. It seems that he attaches more importance to environmental awareness than to environmental degradation during this period, though the former is a natural corollary of the latter. Finally, Grove has talked about the combination of two knowledge systems in the birth of modern environmentalism, but throughout his work he has maintained a structural pre-eminence of the Western knowledge system. The cultural issue is not resolved by this account; it is only heightened. The origin of modern environmentalism thus remains mixed up with the onset of European colonial science, which itself was a cultural development. In the final analysis, Grove approached the global and local issues that make up modern environment in South Asia in the broadest sense of the term more from the global than from the local point of view. Herein lies a dilemma that is at once historical and environmental.

III

In the final section, I shall make a brief review of three crucial issues pertaining to forest, land use and water in colonial South Asia from the agrarian and environmental perspectives. However, the review should not be taken as a narrative of developments in these three broad areas over the last two hundred years. My intention is limited: to identify broader frameworks for analysing these issues; to highlight the dependence and distinction of agrarian and environmental perspectives in their historical formulations; and to highlight the importance of colonial experiments in understanding environmental history at large. As forest and land use are intricately linked, the changes associated with them in the colonial era would be taken together as the main subject of debate. Use of water would be briefly studied with reference to its implications for agrarian and environmental contexts in colonial South Asia.

It would be good to begin with a brief indication of the enormity of ecological changes in colonial South Asia with reference to any particular region. We take the instance of the highlands of Sri Lanka in the nineteenth century, as described in James Webb's work entitled *Ecological Pioneers*,[32] which is a text in the Master's Course on Political Ecology conducted by the Department of Cultural Anthropology and Ethnology, University of Uppsala. The crude story is the dramatic deforestation of the rainforests within the span of a century, leading to the collapse of the isolation of the Sri Lankan highlands. But the more important argument of the book is that new economic and ecological forces generated from far beyond the Indian Ocean came to bear on the highlands during the period. Several features of these new forces have been identified. First, the abolition of slavery within the British Empire led coffee and sugar planters to search for new opportunities, igniting their interest in the dramatic exploitation of the Kandian Highlands, as they are called in Sri Lanka. Secondly, the British planters through the model of 'scientific' plantation accomplished the most extensive conversion of rainforest agriculture into tropical plantation agriculture 'to be seen anywhere in the British Empire in the nineteenth century'.[33] Finally, this conversion virtually made way for monocrop plantations in the highlands by stages, first coffee, then cinchona, and finally tea, brought respectively from the Ethiopian Highlands, the Andes Mountains and the foothills of the Himalaya.

These specific changes are more intelligible in the context of a few broader frameworks of analysis and hereafter we shall dwell on them as applicable to the environmental history of colonial South Asia at large. The foremost among them is the vexed question of the relation between forests and settled cultivation. In much of South Asian history, these two categories were far from sharply demarcated spaces, their interdependence being a marked feature of peasant enterprise. A considerable part of new cultivation in colonial South Asia was often made out of forests. Moreover, forests—especially those near peasant village—were as much a part of the means of subsistence as settled cultivation. In Tamil Nadu in the early nineteenth century, 'waste has been treated as a part and parcel of local culture, often connected with changing agro-eco-system of the locality.'[34] Forest dwellers formed a composite group, including four main communities: settled peasants living close to forests and using forest resources, occasionally land; tribal groups practising settled cultivation and also using forest resources; pastoral and nomadic communities; and shifting cultivators. The modes of subsistence of these communities did change from time to time leading to movements from one mode to another. Hence the absence of any fixed boundaries between forest and settled cultivation in the strict sense of the term should be taken as the first general framework of our analysis.

However, the closed relation between forest and settled cultivation does not rule out major disturbance in the form of large-scale deforestation. Indeed, the argument that British colonial rule marks a crucial watershed in the ecological history of South Asia is based on such an assumption.[35] Historically speaking, this colonial watershed in world environmental history cannot be denied. The beginning of modern environmentalism and its subsequent formulations, we have seen, were inextricably connected with imperial design, ecological change and indigenous responses. However, there is a general argument that the continuity and break in the environmental history of South Asia have to be comprehended by going beyond the standard chronological framework, with reference to the dominant modes of resource use.[36] This argument is too vague and amorphous to deal with man's complex relationship with nature in South Asia in the last three hundred years. Indeed, colonialism has a very special place in historically interpreting nature and culture in South Asia as found, modified, regenerated, conserved and propagated at the various layers of authority and the intermediaries during the period. Indigenous knowledge of both nature and culture is equally relevant.

Two major formulations have been made out of this broad framework of colonial watershed. The first is that in the pre-colonial period there existed a cultural tradition of prudence at the level of community, called 'conservation from below', and that it was disturbed in various ways in the colonial era. The second is the level of use and control over forest resources at the level of the State. As regards the first, it has been argued that a collectively recognized set of restraints in using forest resources as imposed by the village communities or specialized caste groups was neither universal nor fully effective. They generally ignore the mechanism of rural power relations. It has also been doubted to what extent the tradition of prudence was based on conscious designs towards preserving the ecosystem. Moreover, non-arable environment even in the pre-colonial era was stated as 'far from being a paradise of so-called common property'.[37] However, despite these criticisms, the general consensus is that the scale of depletion of forest resources in the pre-colonial era was not big enough to disrupt the old ecological order, and its cause was not unrelated to the particular nature of the use of forests by the village community and the State. Even David Hardiman, who spoke so eloquently against the essentialist and 'distorted' presentation of the nature consciousness in the pre-colonial past, has to admit this about the Bhils, the erstwhile ruling community in the tribal region of Gujarat. He writes that the Bhils in the pre-colonial era 'had a strong affinity with these woods and hills—their home as well as place of refuge—and any destruction which they carried out was on so small a scale as to make very little difference to the environment as a whole'.[38] He describes a very different situation regarding the damage to environment in the same area in the colonial period between 1820 and 1940.

As regards the use of forest by the pre-colonial State, the general argument is that it did neither alter the existing pattern of resources nor disturb the continued existence of certain rights of forest dwellers. This argument has been revised recently. Even in the Mughal period, the State encouraged reclamation of forests lying away from settled villages for bigger income. Reclamation was also done in the wider context and requirement of the agrarian economy. Military and political needs had a dual role vis-à-vis forests: they led sometimes to their preservation to create obstruction for enemy movements, sometimes their destruction as part of the desired military security. The relatively easy access of forest-users to forest resources like land, grazing space and forest products continued but this was not because of any recognized principle of statecraft. Indeed, the access was not always free and universal. The more important reason for this relative freedom was that the State did not find it inconsistent with its needs, or its capacity and means to detect such access. But two qualifications against these revisionist positions remain. First, usual expansion of cultivation through reclamation in pre-colonial era was least harmful to ecology, as damage to it arose mainly out of needs unconnected with agriculture. Secondly, the massive deforestation occurred only in the colonial era as 'the colonial state arrogated to itself the right to regulate the ecological and social landscape of the country'.[39] The new motivations of the colonial state associated with the ideological question at large form another distinct, broad framework of analysing South Asian environmental history at this point.

The broader motivations of the colonial state and their implications vis-à-vis forest control and land use pattern may be approached from three standpoints: (a) the ideological question, (b) the framework of colonial policy, and (c) the implications of the activities of various private agencies in the forest. The role of ideology is a complex question. It was of course not autonomous of the changing imperial needs. A qualitative change occurred in Europe's economy in the wake of the Industrial Revolution and the contemporary economic teachings did reflect on them. The initial influence of the teachings was felt by the colonial state in its policy of first marking the forests as a backward 'primitive' economy and barbaric, then insisting on the replacement of shifting cultivation and pastoral-nomadic economy with settled peasant agriculture, and finally calling the tribal forest-dwellers as lazy cultivators with ecologically destructive farming methods. However, economic teachings did not lead to any virtual reorganization of Indian agriculture (except the investment in irrigation), and land revenue continued to be the mainstay of State's income. B.B. Chaudhuri thinks that the ideological influences on the colonial state's forest policy should not be overstressed as there was indication of continuity of 'an old norm of statecraft'.[40] He, however, himself admits that the needs of the colonial government significantly differed from those of the earlier governments, and that these had their decisive influence on policy.[41] Indeed, it may be argued that the ideological question should not be separated at all from the material requirements of the State in this case, as they were intricately connected.

The evolution of the colonial state's forest policy also requires scrutiny. Admittedly, it was not based on a fixed set of assumptions and changed over time. Indeed, ever since the creation of Imperial Forest Department in India in 1864 and the promulgation of the Indian Forest Act of 1865, environmental debate began among officials. D. Brandis, the German botanist became the first inspector-general of forests. Three kinds of policies were noted at this stage: (a) annexationist, (b) pragmatic, and (c) populist. The annexationist policy had claimed full right of the government over forests, and Baden Powell, agricultural secretary of the Government of India, was its greatest supporter. The pragmatic policy suggested that people had certain real, age-old rights over certain kinds of forests. The Madras Government went a step forward, claiming communal rights over certain kinds of forests. The populist approach developed over time, particularly in the course of nationalist agitations over forests during the colonial period. The debate finally ended in favour of the opinion of the Central Government, i.e. in the model of Indian Forest Act, 1878. Thus, three kinds of forests were created: (a) the 'reserved forests' (total State control), (b) the 'protected forests' (rights recorded but not settled) and (c) the so-called 'village forests' (the option not exercised for the most parts of the subcontinent).

The revisionist argument tries to distinguish between the short-term and long-term effects of the colonial state's intervention in the forests. Three major shifts are identified. First, as the government needed increased income from land revenue, it regarded control over forests, an ideal site of new cultivation, as an important source of it. Second, the government made increasing use of a particular forest resource, timber, first for shipbuilding in India and England and then for sleepers required for the fast growing railways in India from the second half of the nineteenth century. Thirdly, a decisive shift came with the 'preservation' of forests, in which 'scientific forestry' became an important element of policy.

It is important to note that the policy of commercial logging was most methodically and effectively carried out government scheme in colonial India. By 1878, railways used more than two million sleepers, all made of timber. Forests were thus denuded of most valuable and sturdy timber – deodar, sal and teak. Shifting cultivators did cut and burn trees, but the damage was temporary as they could afford to wait till the completion of the regeneration process. The revisionists insist on the absence of a far-sighted policy of prudent use of resources, but they fail to explain the implications of the keenness of the forest-users to maintain their subsistence. In the final analysis, the causes of major deforestation in colonial South Asia lay largely outside tribal society, its origins could be traced 'in the pressure to generate an economic surplus from the forest that began, or hugely intensified, during British rule'.[42]

As regards 'State Conservationism', there is no denying the fact that organized forestry in colonial India partly developed in response to the revenue and strategic needs of the empire. However, as discussed in Section II, an increasing number of botanists, medical men and desiccationists spoke of forests' connection with climate and environment. Depletion of tree cover would reduce rainfall, gradually damage topsoil and cause soil erosion, finally leading to drought and reduction of productivity. For many of them, 'fear of climate change' was a reality.

However, two qualifications are to be made. First, the government did not consistently follow its conservationist plans, less to mention 'scientific forestry'. Secondly, the government's policy of forest conservation did not prevent it from leasing huge forest tracts in different parts of South Asia to European tea and coffee planters. Ecological concerns did not at all appeal to it at the time of distribution of wastelands for this purpose. In short, commercial motives of the colonial state became increasingly decisive over the years, but these did not altogether rule out the prospects of 'scientific forestry' at certain stages of colonial environmental history.

Besides the colonial state, the presence of outsiders—individuals and other private agencies—in forests raises interesting analytical questions. One revisionist argument considers the role of the outsiders as largely autonomous of the State's needs and control. However, it is admitted that the initial presence of outsiders in forest tracts was mostly connected with needs of the colonial state. Private groups gained control over forests through short-term leases from government or from zamindars for the procurement of timber, opium and liquor as well as for the collection of grazing and forest taxes. Though government policy itself had much to do with the arrival of outsiders, the growth of a market system considerably determined the nature of the outsiders' roles. Indeed, 'reservation' and 'protection' of forests made sense only in the context of a market system, which enabled the government to send out its products to the market. But this market system was inextricably linked with the colonial state's vision and requirement. The latter even failed to prevent the consolidation of the outsiders in the traditional world of forest-dwellers, because it shared the 'dominant vision of land, leading to a misrepresentation of 'other landscapes'. In addition, labour demands by the Forest Department as well as by other private agencies over the forest dwellers increasingly tended to become arbitrary and coercive over the years. For example, the forest lease of the Midnapore Zamindari Company in West Bengal specifically enabled it to get cheap labour from the forest dwellers for various purposes.

The social and ecological implications of deforestation and changing land use in colonial South Asia form another framework of our analysis. M. Mann has talked about 'ecological destabilization' caused by large-scale deforestation in the Ganga-Jamuna *Doab* in northern India in the first half of the nineteenth century.[43] 'The destruction of economically unprofitable and therefore unvalued woodland areas in the Doab caused a warming of the regions within a few decades.' The quality of the soil suffered as a result, the amount of available water decreased and soil fertility declined. All these created severe scarcity conditions, leading to the catastrophic famine of 1837-8. Moreover, the spread of cash crop economy led peasants to ignore the old ecological norms. The increasing imbalance between cash and food crops had its effect on productivity, soil fertility, deforestation and climatic degradation.

'Social ecology' was reflected in the changes affecting the modes of subsistence of the forest dwellers. With the tightening of the State's forest control measures from the 1880s, the tribal groups suffered in two ways: (a) shrinking scope for new cultivation and (b) increasing restrictions on pasture. Restricted access to forest resources—timber and other products—was a bigger threat to their subsistence. The delicate integration of activities relating to agriculture and animal husbandry in the pastoral economy of the western Himalayas was broken through a series of measures initiated by the colonial government. The practice of taxation on animals grazed, systematically enforced from the second decade of the twentieth century, was a big disincentive for the pastoralists. The more numerous group of 'shifting cultivators' suffered as the 'conservationist' agenda severely disrupted their economic organization and threatened its survival. There was a strong cultural element behind their preference for shifting cultivation, particularly in the case of the Baigas, which was largely ignored by the colonial government. However, sometimes there were economic factors for their resort to shifting cultivation, as evident in the case of the Gonds: once settled cultivators, they were gradually driven by other 'colonists' (Marathas, for example) to move into forest tracts and take to shifting cultivation in the course of the eighteenth century. The colonial government's response came in three phases. Initially, they straightway banned the system. Then they insisted on the increasing replacement of shifting cultivation by settled plough cultivation. Thirdly, in the wake of increasing resistance, the government wanted to confine the shifting cultivators to some fixed places only. However, the legal position of their holdings remained undefined in the context of British ideas on private property. The net result was that they increasingly sank to the position of sharecroppers over time. Only in rare cases, as B.G. Karlsson's study of the Rabhas of North Bengal has shown, were they used in 'reserved' forests to grow food crops along with the planting of trees in the name of *taungya* (literally meaning hill-field) cultivation.[44]

We end this section with a short note on the agrarian and ecological context of the use of water in colonial South Asia. Our entry point is supply of water through irrigation, admittedly the most innovative domain of public works of colonial government since the 1840s. However, the irrigation question was closely linked with the quality of land (including wasteland) and environment. Indeed, the early colonial investment in irrigation was mostly guided by profit motivations from agriculture by bringing superior quality of land under its purview, and not general principles of development.[45] In her celebrated work published more than 30 years ago, Elizabeth Whitecombe showed that the vast irrigation investment made by the East India Company and the Raj in the Indus and the Ganges basins in the nineteenth century did not cause rapid economic development and only brought ecological disaster to many localities, through widespread salinization and reh deposition.[46] In a more recent article, whitecombe has covered the later period also, arguing that the environmental costs of waterlogging, salinity and malaria as emanating from the projects were never satisfactorily entered in irrigation accounts.[47] The construction of high canals caused obstruction to surface drainage, leading to waterlogging. People suffered from fever, principally malaria in these areas. The Malaria Survey of India of the early twentieth century provided the root-cause: 'the critical climatic factor in transmission was not rainfall as such in association with maximal annual temperatures, nor pooling, nor soil saturation, but atmospheric humidity'.[48] Whitecombe shows that malarial incidence was highest where atmospheric humidity was highest: 'in submontane tracts and in the waterlogged areas of the plains'.[49] Her main conclusion is that British India's irrigation projects succeeded in those areas where the natural order permitted. 'It failed where nature so dictated.'[50]

If there were ecological implications of the supply of water through irrigation, there were also social and economic implications of the use of this newly constituted economic good. It has been argued by David Gilmartin that the British irrigation engineers in the Indus Basin in the late nineteenth and early twentieth centuries linked nature, productivity and colonialism in such a way as to accommodate two competing notions of the indigenous community.[51] The binary distinction between proprietary land and 'wasteland' under the structure of Punjab's newly engineered irrigation systems is an indication. 'Whatever the state's role in bringing large new areas under irrigation, and in increasing aggregate agricultural production, its inability to use engineering science to break through the power of the local village communities and extend a technical system of irrigation control into the villages has sometimes (been) seen as a failure of development.'[52] But it is really not the case. It is rather 'one of the consequences of modern development generally that these two forms of community, defined here through an analysis of the term "waste"... have simultaneously shaped modern history'.[53]

IV

Two brief conclusions: first, the study does not purport to undermine the independent lines of enquiry followed in agrarian and environmental history, but highlights their mutual dependence in more than one sense. We are aware of the rift between these two important branches of history of colonial South Asia ever since the middle of the 1980s, but the rift is on the whole unwelcome. 'If the old agrarian history neglected the forests and pastures, environmental history now has banished the peasant fields from the realm of historical concern.'[54] It even narrows down the scope and canvas of much of environmental history in the process. We have seen that forest, land use and water were highly interconnected issues of environmental history of colonial South Asia. They can best be understood in their social and ecological contexts; not in their isolation from agrarian history, but in the complex process of their mutual dependence.[55] The second conclusion is even broader. There is much in the environmental history of colonial South Asia that is of cardinal importance in handling today's environmental debate. The ecologic content of the emergence of modern world system has been noted. The strange mixture of global and local issues is a fact of reality in modern environment. The conflict and convergence of these issues in today's world are much debated. Colonial environmental history, supported by capitalist enterprise of the early modern period, not only highlights the historical origin of the debate but also charts its future course to a large extent. Many of the significant questions concerning globalization and environment are rooted in colonial history. Perhaps some viable answers can also be hinted at from this kind of study of environmental history.

NOTES

1. Four scholars, namely Madhav Gadgil, Ramachandra Guha, Vasant Saberwal and Mahesh Rangarajan, have been specifically identified as early advocates of political ecology in South Asia. See Amita Baviskar, 'For a Cultural Politics of Natural Resources' in *Economic and Political Weekly* (hereafter *EPW*), vol. XXXVIII, no. 48 (29 November-5 December 2003), p. 5055.
2. See Richard Grove, *Green Imperialism, Colonial Expansion, Tropical Island Edens and the Origins of Environmentalism 1600-1800*, Delhi, 1995.
3. Immanuel Wallerstein, *The Modern World System I: Capitalist Agriculture and the Origins of European World Economy in the Sixteenth Century*, New York, 1974. The case for a rereading of Wallerstein's text has been vociferously suggested by Jason W. Moore, 'The Modern World System as Environmental History? Ecology and the Rise of capitalism' in *Theory and Society,* vol. 33, 2003, pp. 307-77.
4. These are some important approaches chosen from the huge environmental literature. See Joseph M. Petulla, *American Environmentalism: Values, Tactics, Priorities*, Texas and London, n.d., chapter 6, pp. 97-117. See also D.E. Worster, *Nature's Economy: The Roots of Ecology*, New York, 1979. For a critique from the point of view of 'progress', see William Tucker, *Progress and Privilege: America in the Age of Environmentalism*, New York, 1972.

5. Though this ecologic model is not fully static and rigid, its usefulness as a tool of historical analysis is being increasingly appreciated. However, the concept of a long-lasting 'climax eco-system' or a 'climax community' as developed by Frederick Climents or Donald Worster has been doubted by many who argue that ecology must not be 'subverse' to progress. See William Tucker, op. cit., p. 163.
6. Writers like H.J. McCloskey, however, have argued that 'The findings of ecology do not necessitate a basic revolution in ethics but simply a more informed, more accurate thinking out of our moral obligations and moral rights.' See H.J. McCloskey, *Ecological Ethics and Politics*, Totowa, 1983, p. 29.
7. See Charles Frankel, 'The Rights of Nature' in Lawrence H. Tribe, Corinne S. Schelling and John Voss (eds.), *When Values Conflict, Essays on Environmental Analysis, Discourses and Decisions*, Cambridge, Mass., 1976, pp. 106-9.
8. For a detailed discussion of the theory of ecological history, both generally as well as in the Indian context, see Madhav Gadgil and Ramachandra Guha, *This Fissured Land: An Ecological History of India*, Delhi, 1992. For a detailed critique of the view, see Arun Bandopadhyay, CHJ, op. cit.
9. See Alfred W. Crosby, *Ecological Imperialism: The Biological Expansion of Europe*, Cambridge, 1989 and Canto 1993, p. 14. A second view of culture is given by P. Corbet as 'a set of beliefs about the conduct of life and the organization of society; a set of beliefs about men's nature and the world in which he lives' in his *Ideologies,* London, 1965. A third view sees culture, developed in the process of evolution, as a non-biological form of satisfying the human needs and the preservation of common interests. For example, Napoleon Wolanski observes: 'It is a paradox that culture sustains . . . the "animal" nature of the humans, as it protects the organism against the necessity of the biological changes. Culture thus counteracts the evolution of human organisms towards the forms progressively more distant from the animals.' See Napoleon Wolanski, 'Modernization as a Form of Cultural Adaptation to Environment' in Kapila Vatsyayan *Prakriti: The Integral Vision*, volume 5, *Man in Nature* Baidyanath Saraswati (ed.), New Delhi, 1995, p. 247.
10. See K. Sivaramakrishnan, *Modern Forests: Statemaking and Environmental Change in Colonial Eastern India*, New Delhi, 1999, p. 14.
11. See Amita Baviskar, 'For a Cultural Politics of Natural Resources', op. cit., p. 5052.
12. Ibid.
13. Ibid., pp. 5052-3.
14. See Simon Dalby, 'Environmental Insecurities: Geopolitics, Resources

and Conflict' *EPW*, vol. XXXVIII, no. 48, 29 November-5 December 2003, p. 5077.

15. See Donald Worster (ed.), *The Ends of the Earth: Perspectives on Modern Environmental History*, Cambridge, 1988, p. 290.
16. Donald Worster, op. cit., p. 293.
17. See Jason W. Moore, op. cit., p. 311.
18. Wallerstein, op. cit., p. 102.
19. Jason Moore, op.cit., p. 357.
20. See Ramachandra Guha, *Environmentalism: A Global History*, New Delhi, 2000.
21. Grove, *Green Imperialism*, op. cit., p. 16.
22. Ibid., p. 19.
23. Ibid., p. 81.
24. Ibid., p. 85.
25. Ibid., p. 314.
26. Ibid., p. 335.
27. Ibid., p. 382.
28. Ibid., p. 404.
29. Ibid., p. 411.
30. Ibid., p. 416.
31. James L.A. Webb, *Tropical Pioneers: Human Agency and Ecological Change in the Highlands of Sri Lanka, 1800-1900*, New Delhi, 2002.
32. Ibid., p. 2.
33. See Arun Bandopadhyay, 'Environment and Identity in the Indian Historical Context: An Initial Vision' in Bharati Ray and David Taylor (eds.), *Politics and Identity in South Asia*, Kolkata, 2001, pp. 144-7.
34. See Gadgil and Guha, op. cit., parts 2 and 3.
35. Gadgil and Guha have explained this in their first ecological history of India described above.
36. Richard Grove, *Green Imperialism*, op. cit., p. 386.
37. See David Hardiman, 'Power in the Forest: The Dangs, 1820-1940' in David Arnold and Hardiman (eds.), *Subaltern Studies VII—Essays in honour of Ranajit Guha*, New Delhi, 1994, p. 105.
38. Nandini Sunder, *Subaltern and Sovereigns: An Anthropological History of Bastar 1854-1996,* New Delhi, 1997, pp. 105-6. Mahesh Rangarajan also takes an identical position on this issue, see his *Fencing the Forest: Conservation and Ecological Change in India's Central Provinces, 1860-1914*, New Delhi, 1996, pp. 15-16. Most scholars agree on this.
39. See section on Forest Control in B.B.Chaudhuri, *Peasant History of Late Pre-colonial and Colonial India: Eighteenth to Mid-twentieth Century*, New Delhi, forthcoming as a volume of the Project of Indian Science, Philosophy and Culture.
40. Ibid.
41. Felix Padel, 'Forest Knowledge: Tribal People, Their Environment and

the Structure of Power' in Richard Grove, Vinita Damodaran and Satpal Sangwan (eds.), *Nature and the Orient: The Environmental History of South and Southeast* Asia, New Delhi, 1998, p. 899.

42. M. Mann, *British Rule on Indian Soil: North India in the First Half of the Nineteenth Century*, Delhi, 1990.
43. See B.G. Karlsson, *Contested Belonging: An Indigenous People's Struggle for Forest and Identity in Sub-Himalayan Bengal*, Lund University, 1997, pp. 106-12.
44. See Arun Bandopadhyay, *The Agrarian Economy of Tamilnadu, 1820-1855*, Calcutta, 1992, pp. 41-78.
45. See Elizabeth Whitecombe, *Agrarian Conditions in Northern India: The United Provinces under British Rule, 1860-1900*, New Delhi, 1971.
46. See Elizabeth Whitecombe, 'The Environmental Costs of Irrigation in British India: Waterlogging, Salinity, Malaria', in David Arnold and Ramachandra Guha (eds.), *Nature, Culture, Imperialism: Essays on the Environmental History of South Asia*, New Delhi, 1995, pp. 237-59.
47. Ibid., p. 249.
48. Ibid., p. 250.
49. Ibid., p. 258.
50. David Gilmartin, 'Water and Waste: Nature, Productivity and Colonialism in the Indus Basin' in *EPW*, 29 November-5 December 2003, pp. 5057-65,
51. Ibid., p. 5063.
52. 'Process of development predicated on rational, market-driven behaviour have simultaneously generated visions of community rooted in the common drive to control nature for the purposes of production, and solidarities rooted in identification with nature's fundamentally non-productive values, whether embodied in the village commons or in the national patrimony.'
53. Ibid.
54. See Neeladri Bhattacharya's 'Introduction' to the special issue (on Forests, Fields and Pastures) of *Studies in History*, vol. XIV, no. 2, July-December 1998.
55. Neeladri Bhattacharya raises two questions: (1) Why did environmental history move its focus entirely away from agrarian history? (2) Why did the peasants not get due recognition from the environmental historians? Ibid. I add two more: (3) How can we explain the fate of the forest dwellers without reference to the land question in the colonial period? (4) How can we incorporate the ecologic implications of agrarian activities more fruitfully in environmental history?

4. Marginal People and Politics of Anti-Modern Development: Revisiting the Indian Environmental Movement

Archana Prasad

INTRODUCTION: THE INDIAN ENVIRONMENTAL MOVEMENT AND HISTORY

Contemporary India is in a crisis, facing three important challenges that affect the everyday life of its working people in general and the marginalized tribal and *dalit* communities in particular. The first challenge is that of neo-liberal globalization, which gathered momentum in the 1990s and has been effectively critiqued by radical environmental scholarship on the one hand and left-wing history and scholarship on the other hand. All varieties of the progressive movement believe that the current trend of neo-liberal globalization has increased inequality, hunger and disease amongst the people. The second is the challenge of *Hindutva* and right-wing cultural nationalism, which has been opposed in full strength by all progressive movements. Though many activists of the environmental movements have joined in struggles against these sectarian forces, there are also others like Chipko Movement's Sunderlal Bahuguna, who have resorted to using alliances with such forces to facilitate support for their position in their opposition to the dominant paradigm of development. The third challenge is that of the burgeoning ecological crisis with the rapid deterioration of land, water and forest resources. It is in this sphere that the Indian environmental movement has made major contribution. Proponents of the movement argue that sustainable development is not merely about global environmental politics of climate change and the Rio Declaration, but also the vital issues of how sustained and long-term interventions are to be made in the daily lives of the people. It is here that the notion of sustainable livelihood has been linked with institutions of governance by the Indian environmental movement. And by doing this they have managed to make ecological sustainability a key issue in the politics of development in India.

'The environmental movement' is an umbrella term used to describe a series of local struggles and conflicts that highlight issues of livelihood and ecological security in the development debate. The genesis of the environmental movement lay in the Chipko Movement (1973) in Garhwal (now in Uttaranchal). Between the early 1970s and 1980s, there were several struggles for forest and water rights that raised larger ecological concerns—restoration of community rights in forests, rehabilitation and displacement through large projects, and the unsustainability of large dams and the Green Revolution.[1] Such struggles hence questioned modern development and conservation ecology pursued by the State and its officials since colonial times. As the Indian environmental movement saw it, the post-colonial rulers had failed to from the colonial model of development, as they continued to push forward the modern capitalist agenda that was responsible for the penury of the masses in general and marginalized people in particular. They attributed the degradation of the environment to the development of large industries and there mode of resource use.

As an alternative, the Indian environmental movement advocates the ideology of 'environmentalism of the poor' within whose framework it has used tribal history and the reconstruction of 'traditional tribal livelihoods' as important instruments of advocacy against the paradigm of modern development. Because of this many scholars of tribal and environmental history have also been either actively or at least ideologically associated with many of the local tribal movements and struggles that form a part the Indian environmental movement. Thus there is a dialectical relationship between the rise of environmental movements and their documentation and justification through the writing of environmental history in the Indian subcontinent. Thus, a pioneer environmental historian of India wrote:

The environmentalism of the poor originates as a clash over productive resources, a third kind of class conflict, so to speak, but one with deep ecological implications. Red on the outside, but green on the inside. In Southern movements, issue of ecology are inter-linked with issues of human rights, ethnicity and distributive justice. These struggles of peasants, tribals are in one sense deeply conservative (in the best sense of the word) refusing to exchange a world that they know for an uncertain and insecure future. They are an attempt to defend the locality and the local community against the nation.[2]

This paper is an attempt to understand the assumptions behind this anti-modern politics and the historical writing that provides the basis for its ideological potency. In the process of doing this the paper provides a critique, that shows that the environmental movement's investigation of questions of tradition and communitarian practices, and indeed their critique of modern development itself, will be far more realistic if elements of political economy are integrated into their framework.

Colonialism and Modern Development: An Ecological Watershed?

The opposition between traditional and modern systems characterizes the work of the environmentalists of the poor. This dichotomy is especially revealed in their analysis of colonialism and imperialism. In most of these writings, the colonial period is considered an 'ecological watershed' or a time when the traditional coherence, stability and eco-friendly patterns of existence were destroyed by forces of industrialization and capitalism. This was done through the development of monopoly state capitalism over resources. This means that the colonial state declared its ownership over land, forest and natural resources, and this policy formed the basis of British rule in the early nineteenth century. It also served to establish a system of expropriation of resources in subsequent post-colonial regimes. The most significant part of the analysis is that activists fighting for tribal rights identify the use of resources for modern industry (or the industrial mode of resource use) as the main purpose of natural resource management in these two eras. This mode of resource use is said to have three features. The first is decline in food gathering and production for subsistence and the shift to a commercial economy. It was assumed that tribals were outside the money and market economy before this period. These two factors were considered the most important elements in the degeneration of tribal life. The second important characteristic of the industrial mode of resource use was the breakdown of cohesive local communities and the entire process of adjustment that had occurred in the pre-colonial era. This also meant that traditional cultural practices and systems of knowledge governing resource use were marginalized in favour of modern science and technology, which concentrated on ways of exploiting nature for big industries and the market. Lastly, there was the domination of trade and commerce in determining the status of the individual or group in the larger system of the market economy. This modern economy thus signified a basic displacement of community interests that were grounded in a stable and coherent system before colonial rule. Even though many contemporary scholars and activists have contradicted the notion of a stable pre-colonial economy and argued for a benign colonial state, their analysis has resulted in creating the same dichotomy between modern industrial societies and traditional non-industrial ones.[3]

But more than this the environmental movement and its scholars end up reconstructing the pre-colonial society in a manner that is a historical. For example *This Fissured Land*, one of the first comprehensive ecological histories of India, shows pre-colonial societies as well-adjusted caste institutions that regulated resource use where each community occupied a specific ecological niche in society. The books lay stress on prudence and project the modes of resource use in tribal societies as a part of the hunting-gathering economies that include shifting cultivation. Even though shifting cultivation is considered a part of the hunting-gathering mode of resource use, the links between hunting, gathering and cultivation practices are seldom alluded to in the model promoted by these authors. This is mainly because the economies are projected as stable and mutually exclusive closed systems that are based on prudent use of resources. They harm ecology in a minimal way because their resource use is centred on small populations, limited needs and socio-cultural practices that regulated resource use. Using early anthropology they describe nature worship, sacred groves, taboos and other practices as regulatory factors in resource use.[4] In this way ecological roles and niches were also representative of a particular socio-cultural identity that a community possessed.

This analysis has strains of the analysis of the anthropologists of the 1930s and 1940s who attempted to represent the tribal society in romantic times. Thus Verrier Elwin, one of the most influential figures in tribal policies from the 1920s to the 1960s wrote:

> The life of a true aboriginal is simple and happy, enriched by natural pleasures. For all their poverty, their days are spent in the beauty of the hills. A woman carrying a load to the hill top pauses a moment to see the scene below her. It is the 'sweet forest' the 'forest of joy and sandal' in which they live.[5]

The 'forest of joy' was Elwin's' dreamland—a place characterized by the devotion to the soil, the power to stage a magnificent and colourful tribal festival, the spirit of sharing and many others. To these he ascribed the term 'things of value'. For Elwin exclusion meant the restoration of tribal freedom and the preservation of tribal values. Elwin remarked that there was no use introducing conditions to which tribals could not adapt. Instead their natural tribal culture, especially dance, drama, art and religion had to be preserved.

The Indian Environmental movement used this analysis to show that the industrial mode of production was predatory and expanded at the expense of the non-industrial one. Thus all industrialized economies, whether socialist or capitalist were seen as having an equally devastating impact on the environment and its relationship with the tribals. Similarly, they saw no difference between colonial and post-colonial regimes as both seem to be using and furthering the interests of the industrial mode of resource use. Thus, we find that 'environmentalism of the poor' equates industrialization with colonization and the spread of capitalism and does not give imperialism the importance that it deserves. It is also for this reason that this analysis fails to recognize that the survival of some traditional forms of production and the underdevelopment of marginal regions are a result of colonization. Colonial processes impede the modern development of a colony because the colonial government does not work for the interests of the colony, but for itself. Thus, areas with feudal and semi-feudal social and economic relations in tribal areas are allowed to survive because they serve the interests of the global capitalist system and its system of unequal exchange.[6]

Any recognition of this factor would have led to a different reconstruction of tribal histories within the Indian context. Several studies, including my own, have shown that the tribal societies were firmly integrated with their local and regional political economies, contradicting the work of many environmental historians who have seen tribal economies as insulated from 'outside' influences. Thus in the case of the North-East we see that tribal people had links with the plains of Sylhet and East Pakistan. They exchanged forest produce for food, salt, and oil and thus supplemented the seasonal *jhum* economy. These links remained intact in a modified form till the partition of the country in 1947.[7] In comparison, the tribes of central India also had links with non-tribals, especially artisans and peasants to whom they sold seasonal forest products and in return bought food, oil and cloth from the pastoralists. The monopolistic control over forest resources and the process of land settlements in the late eighteenth and the nineteenth centuries led to a disruption of these linkages and laid the basis for the destruction of the production capacity of the tribes.[8] In both the cases the role of the colonial rule was not merely one of the alienation of rights of tribal people.[9] It was also the conversion of tribes from producers to landless labourers. This meant that the tribal people stopped being contributors to value addition and growth in the local economy but became providers of cheap labour and raw materials.[10]

But it is not as if the tribes themselves did not protest the restrictions on their movements. There are several instances of tribes like the Karens of British Burma and Baiga of central India fleeing from government forests once the reservation of forests took place. Accordingly the colonists were forced to alter the assumption that the controlled practice of shifting cultivation would allow them to pursue their own system of forest management. The decisions to grant concessions of shifting cultivators were taken to ensure regular supply of cheap labour to the forest department. The *taungya* system in British Burma and Assam, and the creation of forest villages and the *baiga chak* (a demarcated area for shifting cultivation) in central India were important mechanisms for integrating the tribes within a system of colonial and world capitalism.[11] This created isolated pockets of semi-feudal relations and the differential integration of different strata of the tribals into the wider regional political economy. In the process the tribes became ever more dependent on welfare measures of the State and others like missionaries and nationalist social workers for the fulfillment of their everyday needs. The 'colonial watershed' was thus not only ecological in character, but had a decidedly imperialist and capitalist stamp. It not only brought about the selective exclusion of people's rights from their surrounding natural resources, but also played an integrationist role by destroying the local and regional economic networks on which a relatively self-reliant but precarious tribal economy was based.[12]

Egalitarian Communities and Primordial Identities

In line with this thinking the inclusion of tribal households was part of a much more iniquitous system with more devastating implications than the pre-colonial system and changed the power relations within the community in a way that increased the gaps between the powerful and the not-so-powerful. The Indian environmental movement and its historians have been contending, that class differences within the local society and the community was one of the most important impacts of 'colonial intervention' that introduced the role of the modern State in natural resource management. The era of the modern State followed a golden age which espoused a certain type of cultural pluralism and diversity that helped in the conservation of resources. Community-based institutions were seen as egalitarian, democratic, and instruments of sustainable lifestyles: bodies that were outside the scope of the market economy and were self-sufficient villages where all people were treated equally. Community institutions also created social and cultural codes that ensured the preservation and conservation of biodiversity. In tribal life, this is exemplified by the existence of sacred groves that have been lauded as the best traditional examples of forest conservation. For example, in *This Fissured Land*, the authors argue that some hunting-gathering practices (which are considered as harmonious forms of natural resource use) still exist amongst the tribals of Mizoram and Manipur, and are evident in the prevalence of sacred groves and wood lots that promote prudent use of resources. It is for this reason that 'environmentalism of the poor' argues that the State should withdraw from the business of resource management and leave it to community institutions that have managed these resources for long.

The assumption that these practices existed from time immemorial and are an integral part of the cultural distinctiveness of a particular tribal community informs most of the tribal rights movements. These movements have been demanding the restoration of the tribal way of life and traditional systems of governance that are perceived to be eco-friendly and truly democratic in character. One of these was the Adivasi Sabha of Jharkhand that in the 1930s demanded a separate state of Jharkhand and the expulsion of outsiders. There were also several movements during the colonial times that demanded the restoration of their traditional rights on the natural resources of their own regions. The most prominent amongst these were the Bastar rebellion of 1910, the Munda and the Santhal rebellions of the nineteenth century, the Gundem Rampa Movement of Bengal, the Forest Satyagraha of the Central Provinces and several others.[13] Their relationship with mainstream nationalism was tenuous in character and often Congress nationalists decried them as traditional and non-nationalistic movements. But with the emergence of the subaltern studies project in the mid-1980s, historians of modern India recognized that the regional aspirations of specific communities signified the unequal relationship between the tribal and non-tribal communities. It is also during this time that the environmentalists started writing about movements such as Chipko and Narmada as defense of customary rights. The most prominent example of this is Ramachandra Guha's *Unquiet Woods*, which discusses the pre-

Chipko movements of the Garhwal region and in one sense also heralded the advent of environmental history in India. This was followed by a lot of work on forest rights by scholars like David Hardiman, Madhav Gadgil, and others who contextualized the movements in their descriptions of the clash of cultures of the indigenous and the modern worlds that has informed the identity politics of our times. Many of these movements form a part of the Indian environmental movement today.

The use of primordial identity in the politics of opposition is in line with these scholar's strident critique of the modern colonial and post-colonial state whose control of natural resources is seen as always having served the interests of industrial capital. This means that 'environmentalism of the poor' sees the modern State as an instrument of large-scale industrialization that has alienated people from their own natural resources. The system of state monopoly over natural resources prevalent in India is considered by activists as a shining example of both the capitalist and socialist models of development. According to the environmental activists, these developmental models have led to rising inequities, social unrest and instability in Indian society. They have used State control over resources to favour an elite that acts as a predator over the rest of society.[14] From the point of view of the environmental movement, there is a sharp opposition of interests between community institutions and the modern State where 'community' institutions are seen as serving the interests of the larger mass of the Indian population. By the same measure both capitalist and socialist regimes are considered undemocratic by tribal and environmental activists. According to them, the advent of socialism in China and Russia led to the establishment of totalitarian regimes, which wanted to impose the industrial mode of resource use on their societies. As in the case of capitalism, under socialism too, there was no true democracy as people were deprived of their natural resources. Further, the rhetoric of democracy was used to destroy the knowledge and practices of communities. Thus, the Indian environmental movement sees a similarity between capitalism and socialism because of the unstinted support of the two systems to large-scale industrialization and modern science and technology.

While the opposition of the environmental movement and its historians is understandable, this analysis is most ahistorical when it comes to the defense of the traditional system of governance, the first causalities of which were women and the youth who had no decision making power or property rights in many parts of central India. This inequality was reflected in the ways different sections of the community and tribal groups were integrated into the regional and local networks of production and exchange. In my own study of the Baiga community I have shown that communitarian codes also reflect the lack of access of women to ownership of property and technology.[15] For example, the wife or the daughter was not entitled to any land, and if they touched the axe (i.e. the primary technology of cultivation) the axe was considered impure or unholy. This meant that women only had an opportunity to increase their economic power through collection of forest produce and labour. But here too, the situation was not too encouraging. Both women and men undertook gathering activities. Women gathered roots, fruit, leaves, and *mahua* and sal seeds. Root and fruit gathering were important sources of food in periods when *bewar* crop was ripening. Men also gathered roots in times of drought and famine. According to Russell and Hiralal, a Baiga could collect a full basket of roots in a single day.[16] Mahua and sal seeds were collected by women and used as food or for brewing *tadi* (country liquor). Apart from this, the collection of leaves was useful for household purposes and bamboo was collected to make baskets and mats that were sold in the markets. This brought them in contact with people who did not live in the forests but depended in one way or another on them. The nature of the contact was, however, quite gendered in at least some respects. Men sold more lucrative produce like honey, lac sticks, silk cocoons, and tans to the craftsmen. In contrast the women sold flowers, leaves and seeds of trees like the sal as well as fuel wood to peasants. These were presumably less lucrative than the produce sold by men.

The self-image of Baiga men as patriarchs of the world was reinforced vis-à-vis the rest of the local people through oral tradition. For example, Russell and Hiralal record a an old Baiga myth which states,

> They [the Baiga and the Gond] had two sons one of whom remained a Baiga, while the other became a Gond and a tiller of the soil. The sons married their own two sisters . . . and while the elder couple are the ancestors of the Baigas, from the younger are descended the Gonds and all the remainder of the human race. In another version of the story the first Baiga cut down two thousand old sal trees in one day, and God told him to sprinkle a few grains of kutki on the ashes, and then retire and sleep for some months, when on his return he would be able to harvest a rich harvest for their children.[17]

According to this myth the Baigas are the ancestors of all the other races. Their practice of *bewar* was considered a boon because it gave them this superior status. Due to this the Baiga men looked down upon their women, the Gonds and other forest people as socially inferior. The Baiga patriarch reinforced his position vis-à-vis the women in their relationship with the peasants. Even as the Baigas considered cultivation by the plough a sin, and most peasant castes as socially inferior, the structure of the regional political economy ensured that peasants were wealthier and had more social influence than the Baigas. Apart from excluding women from the decision making process, the self-image of Baiga men as protectors of Mother Earth had little effect on their social and economic position within the wider economy. They continued to eke out their existence from the precarious combination of swiddening and gathering.[18] But by refusing to work as wage labourers, the men forced the women to do the bulk of the work and perform the tasks of transplantation and harvesting, especially during times of scarcity when *bewar* crops had failed. Men only hired their labour out for one specific task: the uprooting of rice seedlings before transplantation. This meant that women were forced to go outside the house and labour in the houses and fields of upper-caste and non-tribal people where they were often abused sexually and otherwise. Like many other identities of Jharkhand's Adivasi Sabha or the Santhal rebellions which reflected a harmonious relationship with nature, the primordial identity of the Baigas as kings of the forest and protectors of Mother Earth too, reflected the larger process of marginalization in the extension of imperial capitalism.

REDEFINING DEVELOPMENT: PROGRESSIVE TRIBAL MOVEMENTS OF THE LEFT

Though these identities were anti-imperialist in character they were backward looking because they looked to the past to construct the future. In this sense they were different from other progressive tribal movements of their time, movements which attempted to create a vision of an alternate and egalitarian modernity and whose antecedents were rooted in the mass base of marginal tribal farmers and the working class. These movements of leftist orientation were not anti-modern movements and therefore never a part of the Indian environmental movement as defined by environmental historians. Yet they were anti-capitalist and anti-imperialist movements which sought to build an egalitarian society with a democratic consciousness, and a modern society with non-capitalist relations of production. Early leftist writings reveal that the discourse of these local struggles was couched in terms of the need for liberation of tribals and other oppressed farmers from the class oppression of landlords and traders. These dominant classes were supported by the State apparatus, which wielded enormous repressive power that it had consolidated through the selective incorporation of pre-colonial forms of authority into the colonial structure. It is this process of integration and the resultant alliance between the feudal elites and the capitalists of the Western world that formed the colonial ruling class within India. The Left of the late colonial period attempted to build a united front of tribals, peasants, working classes, and middle-class youth against this dominant coalition.

Three major areas can be identified in the early work of the Left in the sphere of tribal rights. The first was in Tripura where the Ganamukti Parishad was formed in the 1940s to fight against the Tripura rulers' oppression of landless people, most of whom were tribals. Here the issues of land and forest rights were raised and land struggles carried out by the organization, often resulting in violent State repression. The other two prominent examples of leftist defiance are the Telengana struggle in Andhra and the Varli struggle in Dahanu, Maharashtra. As in Tripura, these early struggles led by the communists concentrated on fighting against State oppression and demanding rights that would form the basis of an alteration in class relations. Primary amongst these were demands for ownership rights over land in areas where tribals had been alienated, providing fair wages for landless labourers, fair prices for produce, and ending the system of forced labour.[19] The fact that the Left did not eulogize tradition is evident since it made a sharp critique of feudal oppression during these struggles, many of which were against the zamindars in the late colonial period and the semi-feudal systems of the early post-colonial period. As P. Sundarayya writes, the aim of the Kisan Sabhas in the 1940s was to organize peasants, agricultural workers and youths for their legitimate demand to overthrow the oppressive regime of the Nizam and Deshmukh. It tried to do this through a programme of cultural and political action that expressed the basic class demands of its members.

Another important struggle of the period was that of the Varlis of Dahanu under the leadership of Godavari Parulekar. Here again the Kisan Sabha fought not only for the rights of those working on the private properties of landlords but also for the rights of forest labour. In Tripura too, the Ganamukti Parishad redistributed the Raja's estate to landless peasants. In Dahanu too, the struggle of 1946 concentrated on minimizing the power and influence of the landlords and the timber merchants of the area. The main demands consisted of getting higher wages for cutting grass and timber in the Dahanu Taluk. Given this tradition of activism, the Left did not see its agitation a means only to meet the needs of the tribal people, but as struggles against an entire system that would result in a better future for all oppressed people. In this sense the tribal rights struggles were an integral part of a larger movement to democratize the larger economy, society and polity and free them of exploitative influences.

The Left appeared to aim at a new ideology-based identity that attempted to evolve a model of development where tribals identified with the demands of other peasant and working classes. In the process the Left made a critique of both tradition and capitalist development in a way that sought to ensure that the benefits of modern development would reach the working classes in both urban and rural areas. They believed this was only possible if the tribal consciousness was transformed from one that was communitarian in character to one that was democratic and civic in nature.[20] Thus, the early tribal movements of the Left were aimed at not only securing the legitimate rights of the toiling masses but also at their politicization and an effort to articulate a different view of modernity, or a model of people-centred development. Along with this most Left movements of the time also followed the path of instilling new values into the tribals and landless peasants through some constructive works like running night schools, dispensaries and opening credit cooperatives and common granaries. Most of these measures were aimed at freeing the oppressed people from the tight hold of the landlords and imparting them values that would help to expand the movement in these areas.

But the Leftist critique was ecologically insensitive—it did not introduce the elements of sustainability, or address the problems arising from the ecological crisis till the last decade of the twentieth century. The critique of the Indian environmental movement can add to this effort by introducing an element of ecological sustainability into the Leftist discourse. While critiquing tradition, the Left must attempt to look at local knowledge traditions in a more analytical and compassionate manner so that it can identify and upgrade viable local practices in order to empower the local tribal economy. On the other side, the environmental movement needs to give up its rabid opposition to State intervention and romanticization of tradition in order to ensure that a viable and realistic alternative can be found.

Community Control and Globalization: The Crisis of Environmental Movements

In the seminar 'Rethinking Environment' in the Delhi School of Economics and Sociology (2001) the popular and eminent scholar Ramachandra Guha pronounced that popular environmentalism or environmentalism of the poor was on the decline in India. At the same meeting many young scholars following his footsteps were dismayed at the fragmentation of an umbrella ideology that had united them since the late 1970s. The material basis for this ideology, they claimed, lay in the anti-dam movements of the early 1980s, peoples' movements for the rights on forest, land

and water resources, and above all the Gandhian tradition of constructive work. They noted that even though the environmental movements had achieved some success in the creation of tribal states, the events of the last decade had shown that the inability of the movement to provide a viable economic and ecological alternative was slowly leading to its demise.

This crisis was in fact characteristic of the other progressive movements, but the environmental movement suffered more because of the innate weaknesses in its ideology. The post-colonial project of building a strong nation-state was combined with the special measures to protect the marginalized sections of the society. In the debates that preceded this policy, the Indian nationalists argued for a policy of integration of all marginal people and areas. In 1952 Nehru wrote:

> We must remember that this experience of hundreds of millions of Indian people was not shared by the tribal folk . . . we must approach the tribal people with affection and friendliness and come to them as a liberating force. We must let them feel that we have come to give something and not take something from them. That is the kind of psychological integration that India needs.[21]

The Nehruvian view was essentially that the economic life of the tribals had to be upgraded and modernized even as their culture needed protection. Contemplating on some of the measures for intervention Nehru once again wrote in 1954 that,

> Normally speaking, these *tribal economies have not come within the scope of a market economy* which is governed by the rule of the survival of the fittest. It is therefore necessary, as our Constitution has laid down, that we should *prevent the incursion of the market economy in these people's areas.* We have to prevent the rich people from acquiring land and dispossessing the tribal people. *We do not want to upset the tribal economy.*[22]

Through statements such as these Nehru elaborated upon his plans for tribal development. His thinking was, however, not historically accurate as it assumed that tribal people were untouched by market economies. Like all his contemporaries, particularly Verrier Elwin, Nehru also felt that the main problems of the tribal economies stemmed from the marginalization of their traditional rights. He emphasized that these rights should be restored and implied that self-reliant development of the tribal economy could only take place if they were protected from exploitation. Thus the protection of the tribals was not only justified but also necessary for social and economic betterment through the process of indirect intervention. Autonomous tribal councils were created in the North-East and tribal majority areas in central India were considered special zones. In keeping with Nehruvian ideals, a separate Tribal Welfare Department was set up and all tribal areas were divided into special Tribal Multi-purpose Blocks for promoting welfare measures like education, public health and income generation activities. However, these programmes were seen in isolation from the larger aims of land use and forest conservation in the post-colonial period and did not show how tribal development could be compatible with the larger aims of nationalist development.

Thus the entire foundation of the Indian environmental movement was based on its opposition of monopoly State control over natural resources. It objected to Nehru's 'temples of modern development', the dams and large public-sector projects, as they led to the displacement of tribal people. It also argued for a more decentralized model of development where the State would only have a regulatory role to play in the control of natural resource use patterns. But by the 1990s the situation had changed considerably. The advent of neo-liberal globalization saw 'community control', 'withdrawal of the State' and 'decentralized management' of natural resources become the buzz words of externally aided forestry sector reform programmes. Donor agencies themselves argued that the control of natural resources should be handed over to village-level community institutions, and one such transitional programme was the Central Government's Joint Forest Management Programme. Fifteen states had begun to issue guidelines and implement the programme in their areas by the year 1995. Forest protection committees were to be formed under this programme and the State was to share benefits of forest management with these local villagers. The forest guard was the secretary of the committee which performed the policing functions that the Forest department had earlier been performing. In one sense, the widespread propagation of Joint Forest Management by the forest department was also the admission of the fact that their centralized system of management had not worked for forty years after Independence.

However, the euphoria that was raised died once the programme was a few years old. The design of the programme in fact promoted its demise in areas where the conditions for its introduction were not ripe. The structure of the forest department and laws governing the sector remained largely the same; only the attitude of individual foresters underwent a change. The most radical change was noted in the case of West Bengal, where the administration was under the influence of the Left Front Government, and where the programme had been started as an unconventional system of forest conservation. This change is noted by almost all field studies of the West Bengal programme, i.e. that a major reason for the change was the prevailing socio-economic climate of the state, where there was a political commitment to make the bureaucracy more accountable to the people. Beat officers and local officials were forced to go and negotiate with local people and institutions rather than dictate to them. In other cases the situation was different from this, as forest officers tended to impose predetermined conditions on the communities rather than formalize an already existing informal system.[23]

Thus, groups mediating between the forest department and the local people felt that the programme was one where there was decentralization of policing, and centralization of decision-making especially in aspects like choice of species, how the funds are to be spent, and benefit sharing. In all states, including West Bengal, the government cornered a majority of the benefits of Joint Forest Management, thus short changing the Forest Protection Committee. The system became socially and politically unviable in areas where there were no social movements to protect the Forest Protection Committee, and bargain for a fair deal for them. This was especially true in cases where the programme was introduced as a way of meeting the establishment costs of the forest department through externally aided projects. Many studies have shown that the amount spent on infrastructure and establishments was a significant part of the project. For example, Samata, an organization based in Visakhapatnam, noted that the amount of money passed down to the people for the regeneration of forests has been disproportionate to the rest of the expenditure. This reveals a lack of seriousness in the implementation of Joint Forest Management.[24]

The advent of these projects at the threshold of economic reforms is itself indicative of the fact that state governments had started looking for alternative methods to sustain their departments. This has led to their dependence on funds from externally funded projects that are also acting like catalysts in the opening up of the forest sector. This analysis has also been true of externally aided projects in other states like Madhya Pradesh, which have received the largest amount of aid for the forest sector. In this situation the introduction of Joint Forest Management and other such programmes has actually led to the disempowerment of groups that had spontaneously tried to protect and regenerate forests. Several organizations like the Ekta Parishad, Kisan Adivasi Sangathan and Adivasi Mukti Morcha have been making this point in central India. In a report of the Joint Mission on the Madhya Pradesh Forestry Project, some representatives of movements opposing the process of globalization stressed that there was an urgent need to review and rethink the project.[25]

But far from doing this the state governments started implementing the second stage of the project, designated as the Community Forestry Project under whose guise the World Bank has started to restructure and privatize common resources. In many states like Andhra Pradesh, Madhya Pradesh, Maharashtra, and now Orissa, Chhattisgarh, and Jharkhand, the forest departments are increasingly restructuring themselves and facilitating the privatization of forests. The most telling example of this is in Andhra, where the government issued guidelines for making the industry a third partner in the Joint Forest Management process. Similarly, the World Bank sought to restructure the forestry sector through the Madhya Pradesh Forestry Project, where it outlined a role for the private sector in forest management. It said that forest-based industries would play a more proactive role in securing raw materials by providing credit, buy-back guarantees, materials, and technological support. They would also set up small industries that would provide inputs for farm forestry programmes and quality planting materials. Thus, private industry would sponsor nurseries, seed banks, and plantations.[26] However, since small and marginal farmers, landless peasants and tribals cannot raise the capital to either create the assets for processing or providing industrial inputs, this policy would mostly help rich peasants, traders and private industries. In contrast to the benefits ensued for the private sector, the role of the State is envisioned as one that is regulatory and supportive rather than one that is involved in production. One of the main conditionalities of the project is that restrictions on felling of trees on private lands would be removed. Thus, it would appear that forest conservation is more concerned with ensuring industrial supply rather than assisting biodiversity conservation for ecological security even though the Bank's stated goal has been to help the state governments implement the National Forest Policy, 1988.

It would thus appear that the vocabulary of the Indian environmental movement has been incorporated into the strategy of global capitalism within the country. It is therefore not surprising that the ideologues of the movement find it unable to respond to the current crisis. It is here that the rewriting of tribal histories can play a major role in resurrecting and reinventing the environment movement and its historical basis. The aim of such history should be to provide an alternative understanding of tribal development and lay down the basis of forming a united front of all movements working with the tribal people so that a broad-based offensive can be launched against the impending challenges. The special interests of the tribals should be identified as they are the most marginalized people, and their integration should be negotiated in a way so that they also get legitimate access and control over land, forest and water resources. The second major task before the progressive movements and their historians is to define the role and nature of the nation state in a new world order. There is no doubt that State will have to play a greater, but a different role, to achieve the goals of building a strong, self-reliant and democratic tribal society. Though the State enjoys monopoly control over many natural resources its role is decreasing through the large influx of money by private capital and donor agencies into different sectors of tribal areas. For this, new institutional and technological options must be evaluated by taking the experience of different movements and local knowledge into account. The challenge of delineating and visualizing a positive relationship between the State and the people is an important one if neo-liberal globalization is to be challenged effectively. The dilemmas of environmental historians and their movements can only be resolved if they effectively meet this challenge and provide a credible vision of an egalitarian society where the problem of unequal exchange is addressed in a substantive manner.

NOTES

1. For a brief history of the Indian environmental movement, see Ramachandra Guha and Juan Martinez Alier, *Varieties of Environmentalism: Essays North and South*, Delhi, 1998, pp. 4-6.
2. Ramachandra Guha and Juan Martinez Alier, *Varieties of Environmentalism*, p. 18.
3. For this, see B.D. Sharma's *Tribal Affairs in India* (Sahyog Pustak Kutir Trust, New Delhi 2001), where he argues that the colonial state was a benign state from the tribal point of view and it allowed tribals to maintain their customary use patterns (chapter on the schedules). In fact even Richard Grove's analysis in *Green Imperialism* implied that development of capitalism in the West led the colonists to look for virgin environments in the east and then conserve them. This notion about the benevolence of the colonial state and officials as well as their ecological romanticism is misplaced and ignores the real nature of colonialism. Nevertheless even from this angle the association of the colonial state is more with modern capitalist development rather than exploitative imperialism. The dichotomy between the traditional and the modern is maintained.
4. Gadgil and Guha, *This Fissured Land*, pp. 17-26.
5. Ibid., p. 20.
6. For this point, see Archana Prasad, 'The Baiga: Local Economy and Survival in Central Provinces' in *Studies in History 1998* and Sumit Guha, *Environment and Ethnicity in India. 1200-1900,* Cambridge, 1999.
7. J.B. Bhattacharjee (eds.), *Studies in the Economic History of North East India*, New Delhi, 1994.
8. Archana Prasad, 'The Baiga: Local Economy and Tribal Survival in Central India', in *Studies in History*, July-December, vol. 2, New Delhi.
9. For this point see Ramachandra Guha, *The Unquiet Woods: Ecological Change and Peasant Resistance in the Himalayas*, New Delhi, 1989 and Mahesh Rangarajan, *Fencing the Forests: Conservation and Ecological Change in India's Central Provinces*, New Delhi, 1996.

10. For a greater elaboration of this point see Archana Prasad, *Against Ecological Romanticism: Verrier Elwin and the Making of an Anti-Modern Tribal Identity*, New Delhi, chapter 2, 2003.
11. See for instance the work of Bela Malik, Sumit Guha and Archana Prasad's work on Assam, Khandesh and central India respectively.
12. For this point see 'Verrier Elwin Papers Number 165, Notes on the Khonds' (hereafter Khond Notes), Nehru Memorial Museum and Library (hereafter NMML), 89. The dynamic nature of the swiddening cycles whose stability was based on the structural links between cultivation, gathering and hunting practices is revealed in the analysis of the Khonds of Orissa and Baigas of central India who were primarily considered shifting cultivators by anthropologists and historians. The seasonal cycle was as follows: In Chait women went to clearings to pick castor and cut stalks that were already ripened. While women did the gathering, men cut large trees and prepared the fields. In Baisakh, the firing of the forest took place, and the women gathered unburned wood to burn. Men continued to hunt, but only in nearby forests. The seeds were sown in Jeth, and hunting continued. From Asadh to Bhadon, men worked in the fields. In Kuar, the first beans were ripened and in Kartik, small millets or *kutki* became ripe. In Aghan every crop was ready and in Pus winnowing took place. Pus was also the time for dances and marriages. In Magh, shifts were made to new fields and hunting-gathering was the main source of survival. This was the agricultural cycle of the first year. In the second year there was more time for hunting because fewer crops had to be sown and harvested, but since there was enough food, the people lived on the *bewars*. It was only in the third year that the diet had to be supplemented with the forest products and game from hunting.
13. For work on tribal resistance movements, see A.R. Desai (eds.), *Peasant Struggles in India*, Delhi, 1979. Also see David Hardiman, *Coming of the Devi: Adivasi Assertion in Western India*, Delhi, 1987; David Baker, 'A Serious Time: Forest Satyagraha in Central India', *Indian Economic and Social History Review*, 1984; and Kumar Suresh Singh, *Birsa Munda and His Movement*, Delhi, 1983.
14. Madhav Gadgil and Ramachandra Guha, *Ecology and Equity: The Use and Abuse of Nature in Contemporary India*, Delhi, 1995, p. 34.
15. Archana Prasad, 'More Marginal than the Marginalised', in Shakti Kak and Biswamoy Pati (eds.), Exploring Gender Equations, Nehru Memorial Museum and Library, New Delhi, 2005.
16. R.V. Russell and Hiralal, *Tribes and Castes of Central Provinces*, vol. 2, Nagpur, 1910, p. 91.
17. Russell and Hiralal, *Tribes and Castes of the Central Provinces*, p. 79.
18. Ibid., p. 91. Also see settlement reports of various districts for evidence

of the employment of lower class Gond and Baiga labour by richer peasants of the same or other upper caste communities.

19. For instance see S.V. Parulekar, *Revolt of Varlis*, New Delhi, 1947. And P. Sundarayya, *Telengana Peoples Struggle and Its Lessons*, Calculate (CPI(M)) 1972, pp. 188-9.
20. It is thus not surprising that S.V. Parulekar records that the 'struggle [in Dahanu] not only made him [the Varli] conscious of his rights in the economic domain, but it also made him understand and value of civic and political rights'.
21. Jawaharlal Nehru, 'Tribal Folk', opening speech in the 'Scheduled Tribes and Scheduled Areas' conference in 1952.
22. Jawaharlal Nehru, 'Approach to the Tribes' in *Jawaharlal Nehru's Speeches 1953-57*, New Delhi, 1964, pp. 458-61. See p. 460.
23. See 'Introduction' in Mark Poffenberger and Betsy Mcgean (eds.), *Village Voices, Forest Choices: Joint Forest Management in India*, Delhi, 1996.
24. *Joint Forest Management: A Critique Based on People's Perceptions*, published by Samata, Hyderabad, and CRY Net, Visakahpatnam, 2001, p. iv.
25. *Report of the Joint Mission of the Madhya Pradesh Forestry Project* (Bhopal: Circulated by Ekta Parishad, 1999), p. 12. Instead of using the systems of local governance that prevail within the ambit of formal government structures these agencies are attempting to control the natural resources of the country by creating parallel systems of control. The Village Resource Development Institution is one such institution that is creating social unrest and conflict in remote tribal areas.
26. This is one of the main objectives of the impending Rs. 520 crore Community Forestry Project in Andhra Pradesh which has been opposed jointly by all tribal organizations in Andhra of which the Girijan Sangham (the CPI(M) tribal front) is one.

SECTION II
Communities on the Margin

5. Tribes in Indian History

Vinita Damodaran

Some current revisionism in environmental history and ecological anthropology has been focused on dismantling such long-established terms as 'tribe', 'forest', 'indigenous' as well as related words which have been used extensively by historians and anthropologists. A spate of studies in the South Asian context have been written recently with a view to unpackaging these categories and contextualizing them within colonial narratives of representation.[1] Those that come in particularly for criticism are the ideas of the ecological noble savage, pristine forests, isolated tribal peoples, and the belief in wild food abundance. It is not my purpose here to rehearse these arguments beyond noting that there are problems in denigrating these so called 'myths' without thought to the cultural, historical and ecological realities which underlie them. The revisionist argument that earlier ethnographers and colonial administrators had mistakenly thought that 'tribes' were static entities leads many of the revisionist critics to conclude (often despite very clear linguistic evidence) that distinct tribes never existed, and that the claims of indigenous people for autonomy must have no theoretical legitimacy or historical validity.

A closer look at the records reveals that we may be too hasty in dismissing colonial narratives in this summary fashion. Earlier generations of ethnographers did actually very often understand the complexities of ethnic identity and cultural dynamics. In similar ways colonial discourse did not just conjure up an imaginary landscape, but analysed real landscape differences. In fact, it can be said that the material and the imaginary landscapes constituted one another in complex ways. Colonial administrators did participate in and engage with the land and the people and were forced to contend with indigenous knowledge and ideas of place. The narratives of these travellers, surveyors and officials of the Company Raj were not merely a 'representation of place' that could be used to root colonial claims to possession, but a far more ambiguous relationship with the place and its native inhabitants. Such a post-modern reading of colonial narratives of a place and its people tends to establish an easy coincidence between aesthetic appreciation of the landscape, geographical science and colonial appropriation. That maps were a fundamental tool of colonial conquest cannot be denied but that the trope of conquest was wholly accepted by natural historians, scientists, artists and other imperial agents is more difficult to establish. To see all colonial images as constitutive of the colonial identity of India and as part of the regime of colonial control does not allow for individual agency to emerge and tends as Dane Kennedy notes to 'essentialise the west as an undifferentiated, omnipotent entity . . . imposing its totalising discourse on the rest of the world without check or interruption.., a discursive practice no less distorting than the west's tendency to essentialise the orient'.[2] The ambiguities, contradictions and often acute observations of colonial officials go unrecognized in such a reading. It is against this background that colonial representations of customary rights and constructions of indigeneity need to be seen.

In one of her articles, Nancy Lee Peluso criticized colonial constructions of customary rights as having little basis in reality and leading, in the Indonesian context, to the 'racialisation' of the landscape with 'ethnic access' to resource use.[3] This is a problematic position, for the history of debates on customary rights in the Indian context reveals clear colonial preoccupations with the detail of local rights and their practice, especially in the context of forest lands. Given the nature of the State and the dominance of the property interest, these rights proved difficult to recover and to legislate in favour of, because they belonged only to practise and to oral tradition. Despite this, genuine attempts were frequently made in the latter half of the nineteenth century to document local rights and land-use customs and to protect some customary practices. In the context of the discourse of indigeneity, these attempts are of enormous importance, although they are rarely given adequate attention. The recent extraordinary attempts of the Jharkhand government to award indigenous land claims not on the basis of oral evidence but specifically on the basis of colonial documentation dating back to the 1920s demonstrates the vital importance of understanding the colonial interpretation of customary rights.

One worrying example of the revisionist approach I have referred appears in Sumit Guha's book *Environment and Ethnicity in India*. This work examines the peoples of the Vindhydri, Sahyadri, Satpura and Satmala of western India over the past few centuries. In analysing the forest polities of the early modern period and the complex political economy of the region, Guha theoretically engages with the terms, 'indigenous' and 'tribe', in the process arguing that an uncritical adoption of these categories is not supported by historical records. This exercise is a problematic one, for while he is aware of the political implications of these terms (noting that the use of these very categories determines the entitlements of people, for example, displaced in recent times by dam projects), Guha condemns their usage as being historically inaccurate. But while Guha's revisionism has achieved prominence, he is by no means alone or indeed a pioneer in his revisionism. Indeed, Indian nationalists have traditionally been suspicious of such claims to an authentic 'indigenous' status and their critique of tribal or ethic claims for identity and autonomy have in recent times been coopted by right-wing proponents of the nation state based on the notion of a unified national culture and a singular national history. Despite these often sinister developments, Guha has persevered in his dismissal of the historical validity of 'tribal' identities. Indeed, he appears to sympathize with the position of the unashamedly assimilationist sociologist G.S. Ghurye, who held the position that *adivasis* were part of mainstream Hindu culture and needed to be totally assimilated. If, in the process they were further marginalized, so be it. Or so the argument would appear to run, astonishingly.

Recent work on ethnicity in other contexts has moved beyond these mere assumptions of the historical invalidity of such categories, and has effectively argued that ethnicity and ethnic ideologies are historically contingent creations. Some of what Guha says may be true in some cases. For example, it is true that the Chakmas of the Chittagong Hill tracts were by no means the first people to enter those regions; in fact they were only one of a succession of immigrant cultures following the Arkanese and Tripurans into the area. But today Chakma identity is firmly linked to the hill tracts where they have sought to develop an 'indigenous' model of state, society and culture.[4] Elsewhere in India, as Hardiman argues, the term *adivasi* relates to a particular historical development: that of subjugation during the nineteenth century of a wide variety of communities which, before colonial rule, had remained free, or relatively free, from the control of outsiders. The experience generated a spirit of resistance which incorporated a consciousness of the '*adivasi*' against the 'outsider'. As Hardiman notes, the term was used by political activists in the area of Chotanagpur in eastern India in the 1930s with the aim of forging a new sense of identity among different 'tribal' peoples, a tactic that enjoyed considerable success.

James Bodley has observed that 'the revisionists assault on the "noble savage" and the wilderness idea comes at the historical moment when the global culture's unsustainable cultural imperative of perpetual capital accumulation is reducing the earth's stocks of water, soil, forests, and fisheries to dangerously low levels and disrupting ecosystems and natural cycles on an unprecedented scale'. Similarly, as notions of indigeneity and customary rights come in for revisionist attack, the marginalization and proletarianization of many forest-based communities and the demise of their traditional livelihoods gains pace all over the world.[5]

What was the process that led to the marginalization of many local forest communities? This paper looks at the evidence from Chotanagpur in an attempt to answer the above question and in doing so to examine the validity of such essential concepts as 'forests', 'wild foods', 'common rights' and 'indigenous' peoples. While it may appear to refer to Chotanagpur as a monolithic whole, it attempts to look at interregional variations in colonial policy, indigenous responses and its effect on resource use and the environment.

FORESTS, DEFORESTATION AND FOREST RESERVES

The forested landscape of Chotanagpur provided the material background to colonial and nationalist debates on notions of indigeneity. A 'tribal' way of life was seen to be one intimately linked with the forested environment. That the landscape may have been imagined in various ways within the colonial discourse as wild, remote, pristine and so on has been the subject of much research in recent times. Agarwal and Sivaramkrishnan have argued that the separation of the woodlands from the surrounding agrarian environment allowed colonial foresters to 'construct a forest landscape removing it from the world of agrarian relations'.[6] This seems in line with the revisionist argument that there is a marked tendency in colonial reports to overdraw the relationship between the forest and local communities. To construct the forest as a 'naturalised' environment alone ignoring local practices and to consistently misread the landscape do not stand up to critical scrutiny.[7] As I have argued, in understanding what constituted the forested landscape the explorers and colonial administrators were forced to contend with indigenous knowledge and ideas of place. That these knowledges were accumulated as a result of careful observation and study often relying on indigenous ideas is not in doubt.

Also frequently missing in these revisionist accounts is the fact of the importance of the forest economy to many local communities of the region in the nineteenth century. The question of wild food abundance is one that has been debated on extensively in the literature elsewhere, though not so much for South Asia. The hypothesis that foraging humans could never have lived in tropical forests completely on wild foods is widely debated.[8] Those that appeared to do so relied heavily on cultivated foods. However, the extent of foraging foods in the diet is an indicator of the importance of forests to the local economy. In the case of Chotanagpur one can argue from the evidence in colonial reports and through the writings of authors as Valentine Ball that foraging was an important part of the diet of communities such as the Hos of Singhbhum in the late nineteenth and well into the twentieth centuries. In an anthropological study conducted in two villages in the Saranda forest division in the 1970s, Michael Yorke noted that the economy of the forest-based Hos was heavily dependent on collecting. The one household in Dubil village that was capable of growing all its cereal requirements, collected many other carbohydrate foods such as tubers from the forest, and also marketed large quantities of forest produce such as rope grass, bachom or *sawai* grass and broom grass.[9] The revisionist point that the relationship between the people and the forest has been overdrawn thus does not hold true, at least for the Chotanagpur case.[10] Neither can the relentless tale of deforestation in the nineteenth century be told any differently. At least, for eastern India, the standard narrative holds good.

That the dominant trend in the colonial period in Chotanagpur was one of deforestation is not surprising given the fact that the landscape that evolved under colonial rule clearly expressed British attempts to dominate the forest, mineral and water sources in the interest of production and profit. One can argue that it was redefined in these terms through the 'masculine' discourse of scientific forestry.[11] In the process it threatened the small and relatively autonomous economies of the 'tribal' communities,[12] with catastrophic effects on the subsistence ethic of all groups, but particularly of women.[13]

The forests were, in the early part of the nineteenth century, primarily regarded as a resource and as one source noted that the Hazaribagh and Ranchi plateau now contain comparatively little forest. One report concluded that the average net decrease in the area under jungle in fourteen villages was 11 per cent within a period of 25 years, in this case due to reclamation.[14] The major cause of the destruction of jungles in most districts was the sale or the lease of the forest to contractors for supply of railway sleepers. Large areas of forest were destroyed to supply the timber necessary for the railways. The forests of Singhbhum were subject to heavy fellings, and it was reported in 1898 that the 'selection fellings for the supply of broad gauge sleepers from trees over 6½ feet girth amounted to over 20,921 trees at the average of 10.4 sleepers per tree'. These fellings were reported to have greatly impoverished the forests.[15] Singbhum was the district with the largest proportion of forest in the 1880s and with over 80 per cent of its population still 'tribal'. This was now threatened. An attempt was made in the 1880s to acquire all private forests with a view to exploiting timber in even remote areas. The private forests in Dumka subdivision were thus acquired as were those of Parasnath and Gobindpur which were seen as particularly valuable for they lay between the railway and the Grand Trunk Road.[16] A recent study of land-use changes in Chotanagpur has concluded that most of the shift in land use took place prior to 1890.[17] Table 5.1 will further illustrate this point.

TABLE 5.1: FOREST AND WOODLAND CHANGES IN CHOTANAGPUR 1870-90

(in hectares)

Chotanagpur Plateau	*1870*	*1890*
Dhanbad	10,382	9,794
Hazaribagh	31,6,408	3,06,495
Palamau	5,55,413	5,30,025
Ranchi	3,44,317	3,38,749
Santhal Parganas	3,08,138	1,77,577
Singhbhum	2,74,258	2,44,826
Total	18,08,916	16,07,466

Source: J.F. Richard et al., 'Changing Land Use in Bihar, Punjab and Haryana 1850-1970', *Modern Asian Studies*, 19, 3, pp. 699-732.

It was in this context, and given a growing sense of injustice, that the landscape of Chotanagpur became a symbolic terrain for definitions of Chotanagpuri identity. Identities were transformed in the context of this rapid ecological and cultural change.[18] It must be noted here that the term landscape is a complex concept. As Cosgrove argues, the term can be seen as a 'socio-historical construct', a way of seeing projected onto the land which has its own techniques and which articulates a particular way of experiencing a relationship with nature. It can be argued in a similar fashion, that the landscape of Chotanagpur has been reclaimed and reconstituted in defining Chotanagpuri identity.[19] Sahlins has noted in the context of Hawaii that 'the landscape and its legends inscribe a criticism of the existing regime. In the current jargon, the landscape is text. Places and names evoke an alternate society older, truer and more directly related to the people'. In this way were the landscapes of Chotanagpur organized by stories and legends of conquest and through memories of better times. The revisionist point that the forest connection of tribal communities has been overdrawn needs therefore to be reexamined.

In the context of Amazonia, Peter Gow shows how the Bayo Urubanka River was lived as a human landscape by local native peoples through a multiplicity of engagements with the forest and the river, with each other in acts of generosity, in narration and in encounter with the dead and with spirits.[20] In a similar fashion were the landscapes of Chotanagpur lived as a human landscape in the past. The original forests were spread out over thousands of square miles, especially in the districts of Hazaribagh, Singhbhum, Palamau and Ranchi, all of which had large forest areas. Local rulers had preserved the forest for military reasons and as Walter Hamilton noted in 1820, in several parts of Chotanagpur the woods had been forested with great care by the rajas as a protection against invasion from without. The trees were mainly either moist deciduous or dry deciduous and the whole division had a rich growth of *sat (Shorea robusta)*.

In the valleys, especially in sheltered situations, the principal companions of the *sal* were the *asan, (Terminalia tomentosa), gambhar, kend* and *simal.* The *mahua* tree *(Bassia latijolia)* was common throughout Chotanagpur and was very important to the local economy. In the villages better fruit bearing trees grew like *the jamun (Eugenia jambolina), karanj (Ponamia glabra), tetar (tamarindus indica), bad (Aegle marmegos),* jack fruit (*Autocarpus integrifolia*), and *pipal (Ficus benglensis).* There were many other forest shrubs and trees which yielded fruit and which afforded valuable food supplements in years of scarcity. Slacke, in his report on the settlement operations in Chotanagpur estate in 1882, enumerated twenty-one species of seeds and the fruits of forty-five uncultivated trees which were used as food in addition to thirty-four trees the leaves of which were used as vegetables, and eighteen species of edible roots, Slacke also gives the names of ninety-seven forest products used as medicines, twenty-eight used as oil and gums, seventeen used as dyes and thirty-three creepers or barks of trees used as rope fibre. The length of these lists gives us some indication of the economic value of the jungles to the local inhabitants. Valentine Ball noted in the 1860s that several of the communities were heavily dependent on jungle products. For example, the Keriahs of the Jolhari Hills, who were not settled agriculturists, relied on the jungle for a supply of fruits, leaves and roots. This they supplemented with rice procured from the lowland agricultural communities by trading jungle products such as honey, lac, *sal* seeds and leaves, and *tusser* cocoons.[21]

Settlement reports note that most of the communities, even the settled agricultural ones, and particularly the women of these communities had a highly sophisticated technical knowledge of their jungles. The Hos of Singhbhum, for example, had names for all the common plants and those of economic importance to them and, like the forest Mundas, were well versed in the edible properties of plants. The Birhors, in the extreme east of Singhbhum, were a wandering community who lived by snaring monkeys and by collecting the fibre of the *Bauhinia vahlii* creeper.[22] The forest environment, and a knowledge of it, were thus of critical importance to the local people, particularly in dietary terms. This importance in terms of food was paralleled by an equal significance in terms of belief; and the two were not truly separable. Chotanagpur folk taxonomy was completely embedded in and mediated by the local cultural order.

Munda understandings of the landscape and its productivity seem to encompass conceptual links between women and forests. Every Munda village, for example, had its own particular spirits whose duty it was to look after the crops. These spirits were known as *bongas*, which was the generic name referring to spirits and the power and force of mountains, hills, forests, trees, rivers, houses and villages. One such spirit, known as Desawali, played a large part in Munda festivals which were connected with the cultivation of land. The home of this presiding deity was the *sarna* or sacred grove, a little path of jungle, that when all else was cleared for cultivation, was left as a refuge for the gods where they might live apart. At all seasons of the year offerings were made in the *sarna,* for on the favour of the Desawali depended the success and failure of the crops. The Hos too incorporated the forest in various ways. The two-fold division of the landscape into tame *(hatu)* and wild *(buru)* represented the ongoing attempt of the communities to pacify and live with the forest *(buru)*, and its spirits *Burubongako.*[23] As Yorke notes, religious boundaries ensured important notions of community. All the springs, hills and large forest trees left standing in the village after clearing still harboured spirits against which the protection of the village spirit was necessary. All animals and plants were divided into those that were domesticated and hence of the village and those that were wild and belonged to the forest.[24]

The propitiating of the female spirits of the grove was done mainly by men with women being excluded. The propitiation began by sacrificing a fowl before a rough image of mud or stone. At night the villagers returned home with sal blossoms and marched to the beating of drums and the blowing of horns, with much dancing along the way. The following morning the women bedecked themselves with sal blossoms, carried baskets filled with the same blossoms which they placed over the door of every house for luck. The festivals of the sacred grove were very important for the settled agricultural communities of Chotanagpur and emphasized the importance of the forest and its flowering seasons in the ritual life of the communities. The forest was central to human life and the forest and the village together made up a spiritual and moral entity. It was to be protected and preserved and the people must respect it. Clearly a symbiotic relationship prevailed between the people and the landscape in Chotanagpur.[25] Such symbiosis is not always found in forest communities. In a 1980 study of the Mende of Sierra Leone, the forest was found to be regarded as opposing mankind and as an obstacle to human progress; the Mende believing that the bush contained innumerable dangers including evil spirits and that it constantly threatens farms.[26] The Chotanagpuris, on the other hand, tended to experience the forest and village as ontologically part of each other, one being the life force for the other's continuing existence. An interesting study among the Nayakas of south India by Nurit Bird David argues for a similar cosmic economy of sharing.[27] The Nayakas converse, dance, sing and even share cigarettes with the spirits of the forest, which they invoke with shamanistic experience.

What can be forcibly argued here is that Chotanagpuri understandings of the landscape, their stories of nature, and their lived history were to differ radically from the perceptions of nature and the land of colonial scientists and policy makers and later of a modernizing nationalist elite. To say this is not to romanticize indigenous peoples and their relationship with nature. In his reply to Obeysekere, Sahlins has noted that the post-modern attack on the notion of a bounded and coherent culture has occurred at the very moment when groups such as the Maoris, Tibetans, Australian aborigines around the world 'all speak of their culture using that word or some other equivalent, as a value worthy of respect, commitment and defence'. He argues that no good history can be written without regard for 'ideas, actions and ontologies that are not and never were our own'.[28] To the Chotanagpuris therefore the landscape was an important context for their ritual and customary traditions. The destruction of forests that was to occur as a result of colonial intervention in the nineteenth century was to later change this relationship between the people and their environment. However, the memory of the landscape was to live on and it became a repository of Chotanagpur's nostalgic past to be revived in complex oppositional contexts.[29]

It can be argued that the despoliation of the forested landscape and the transformation of the people's relationship with their environment in Chotanagpur in the nineteenth century was a powerful memory that was revived in periods of cultural resistance. In the latter half of the twentieth century this resulted in specific cultural images of the landscape being evoked through ritual festivals of the sacred grove and emerging as a factor in protest. Images of the landscape have long played a role in cultural resistance in other regions. For example, as Daniels notes, the 'ethnic nationalism fuelling the dissolution of the Soviet Union was codified by pictorial images of independent homelands.[30] Resistance may have been fanned by memory of better times in a less despoiled setting. These memories were present in the 'landscape of their current servitude'. In the context of Chotanagpur, the 'remembered landscape' was to fuel a long cycle of protest.[31]

THE POLITICS OF MARGINALITY AND THE CONSTRUCTION OF INDIGENEITY

All through the nineteenth century the local communities of Chotanagpur had sought to protest against growing cultural and physical incursions into their lives. Beginning with the unrest in Tamar in 1816 and the Munda rebellion in 1832, disaffection continued through the mutiny of 1857 and the last decades of the nineteenth century saw unrest in the almost every district of Chotanagpur. W.J. Allen, who made an extensive tour of Singhbhum in 1861 noted 'that the love of freedom was the general characteristic of the wild and hilly country of the savage Kols and Santhals'.[32] The Birsa Munda uprising in the 1890s was the culmination of this period of rebellion.

British forest reservation laws had long proved irksome to the Mundas and in the context of the degradation of their forest environment, exploitation by Hindu moneylenders and a modernizing colonial state, they rose in protest. Perhaps it was through the mapping of the notion of the *diku* or outsider in these resistance movements that a new sense of community was renegotiated and a radical consciousness began to emerge. The resistance movements of the latter half of the nineteenth century were critical to this growing consciousness.

By the twentieth century there was thus an established tradition of protest in the region. In 1915 British reports began to mention the Tana Bhagat disturbances among the Oraons in Ranchi District. Their movement, which had strong religious overtones, aimed to redress local grievances against zamindars and traders. The Oraons were apparently enjoined by divine command to 'give up superstitious practices and animal sacrifices', to 'stop eating meat and drinking liquor', to 'cease ploughing their fields', and to withdraw their field labour from non-*adivasi* landowners.[33] 'One of the movement's leaders, Sibu Oraon, had been reported as distributing leaflets to the effect that zamindari raj had come to an end, that it was no longer necessary to pay rent or *chaukidari* tax, that the Marwaris were selling cloth very dear and should be turned out and their cloths burnt, and that the bones of Muhammadans should be broken because they killed cows. The movement had a large following and was said to resemble Birsa Munda's uprising of 1895'.[34] By the 1920s, the Tana Bhagat movement had acquired 'disturbing' links with the Congress movement in the rest of Bihar. Gandhi's non-co-operation struggle resulted in renewed agitation in Chotanagpur and the protesters intensified their demands for low rents, restoration of rights to the jungle and abolition of forced labour.[35] The restriction of access to forests and fresh-water fisheries resulted in a wave of protest among the Oraons, Mundas and Santhals in the 1920s and 1930s in Midnapur, Bankura and Singhbhum and the rest of Chotanagpur. Many of these were fuelled by memories of better times, by stories of their fathers' times when all jungles were free and all *bandhs* open to the general public.[36]

When they lost their lands and forest to *dikus* (outsiders), the local community refused to recognize the loss as legitimate. William Archer, a colonial official at the time, records the ceremonial taking possession of villages by Tana Bhagats, the planting of the Tana Bhagat flag in the village and the reallocation of land among followers. He recorded that to the question, 'Where are your title deeds?', the Bhagats replied, 'The answer is my spade, my axe, my ploughshare are my title deeds. . . . Ploughing is the writing of the golden pen on golden land' To the argument, 'Your lands have been auctioned for arrears of rent and purchased by another,' the reply was 'When a man buys a mat he rolls it up and takes it away. Similarly unless the purchaser has rolled up my land and taken it away how can he be said to have purchased it?'[37] This is similar to the native readings of the landscape in Amazonia. As Peter Gow notes, the native people of the region were implicated in the landscape through moving around in the landscape and leaving traces on it. It was a lived space and no piece of paper in a far off government office which determined who owned what could transform the people's own complex relationship with the land.[38]

The Tana Bhagat movement is interesting because the Oraon followers adopted vegetarianism and an austere lifestyle and incorporated other Gandhian symbols in an attempt to strengthen their hands against the landlords. It can be argued that the movement's appropriation of the symbols of the national movement helped to promote a feeling of solidarity with a wider struggle against an oppressor State. Gandhi was also understood in terms of the people's own religious consciousness. The Chotanagpuri world was filled with divine and semi-divine beings and Gandhi was considered a divine force of this type with powers to mediate between the local communities and nature.[39] While some of the prescriptions of the movement, mainly the move to vegetarianism, can be characterized as an internalization of a caste ideology, the striving for a higher status is not an unambiguous one. Even while there was an acceptance of some of the principles of Hindu religion the attack on Hindu landlords and local oppressors was clear and striking. From hindsight it is clear that the people of Chotanagpur were beginning to produce their own brand of culture and modernity.

Modernity and its Discontents

The second decade of the twentieth century saw the development of a modern political idiom which sought to arrest the marginalization of the local communities. The concept of *adivasi* begins to come into use. It is interesting to examine the changing notions of this term over this period. In the beginning a pan-*adivasi* identity was also asserted under the Chotanagpur Unnati Samaj, which was started in 1915. The leaders of this organization were mainly Christian converts, English-educated students belonging to the Munda and Oraon tribes and they embodied an interdenominational unity of the missions for political purposes.[40] At times however the Samaj tended towards sectarian behaviour against non-'tribal' autochthons.

Rising *adivasi* consciousness was given an impetus by the activities of Christian missionaries and by colonial writings which categorized people into essentialized tribal identities with fixed boundaries.[41] Hoffman's *Encyclopaedia Mundarica* and other early missionary writings on the tribes of Chotanagpur helped in part to construct their identities as distinct from the plains' Hindus and helped to distinguish between different tribal groups, the Hos, Oraons and Birhors for example.[42] The romanticization of tribes also continued to be part of the stereotype, and it was claimed that the government was responsible for the decay of an authentic 'tribal' culture where 'in ancient times they had no kings and were kept together by their conferences. The fields they cleared were their own and their whole land belonged to them.'

The link between tribes and territory was one that had been established in the nineteenth century through the many tribal rebellions over land and the special administrative status accorded to Chotanagpur.[43] This claim to territory was reformulated in the period after the Second World War once the discourse of indigenous rights began to be politically articulated by raising the issue of a separate state. In 1937, the Unnati Samaj was reorganized as the Adivasi Mahasabha and it, for the first time, raised the question of a separate Jharkhand state. We see here also for the first time the usage of the term '*adivasi*' in a political context. The immediate cause for the formation of the Mahasabha was the experience of the first elections held in 1937 under the Government of India Act of 1935. The Congress swept the polls and there was a growing realization among the educated tribals that unless they organized themselves, the Congress would hold sway in Chotanagpur as elsewhere. It was felt that the Congress had little in it to offer the indigenous inhabitants of Chotanagpur and was a party of the *dikus*. This provided the impetus for some Christian and non-Christian tribals to join forces under the Adivasi Mahasabha. The Mahasabha continued its efforts to forge a pan-tribal identity and also opened up its membership to non-*adivasis* of that region, although it must be remembered that the strict distinction between tribals and non-tribals in the popular mind crystallized only years after the announcement of the Scheduled Tribes List in 1936. In its manifesto in 1937, the Sabha emphasized unity among the different 'tribal' groups above all. This emphasis on unity was in keeping with a growing understanding that only a broad movement would strengthen the hands of the Sabha vis-à-vis the State. Its expressed objectives were to be the improvement of the economic and political status of *adivasis* in Chotanagpur.[44] The party was opposed to the Congress in this period and was seen as loyalist by the British. It therefore remained outside the mainstream of nationalist polities.[45]

The attitude of the *adivasi* leadership to the Congress in this period was in part because the Congress was seen as a party of the *dikus* which had little respect for 'tribal' tradition and culture. In the 1940s the party gained new support for its movement from the Muslim League, which hoped to establish a corridor through Chotanagpur to link India with East Pakistan. The nature of the relationship between the Congress and the Adivasi Mahasabha can be gauged by the violence which erupted during the elections in 1946. Fights broke out between the Adivasi Mahasabha and the Congress at various polling stations in the region. In Kunti District five *adivasis* were killed and several injured in the violence, generating widespread condemnation. A renewed period of mistrust and hostility between the Congress and the Adivasi Mahasabha followed.

Events in the preceding period had resulted in ethnic arguments based on the notion of a separate tribal identity losing its force in favour of regionalism, as the Jharkhand Party began to embrace the discourse of western modernity. In 1950 the Adivasi Mahasabha was wound up to form the Jharkhand Party, which gradually changed its policy vis-à-vis the Congress. The party had to broaden its base and attempted to enlist more non-Scheduled-Tribe members. By the 1950s it was clear that ethnicity alone could not be the basis of a political dialogue in Chotanagpur. The census of 1951 showed that the tribals had become a minority in Chotanagpur. The party was therefore thrown open, at least in principle (as embodied in its constitution), to all Chotanagpuris. A significant transition from ethnicity to regionalism emerged as the formative factor in the movement. This is not to say that ethnic arguments lost their force but only that the Jharkhand Party saw it as politically tactful to air more regionally based arguments. Notions of ethnicity had to be reconstituted in different historical moments. The history of cultural contact with the plains' peoples, migration both to and from Chotanagpur and growing inequality were challenging notions of a pure *adivasi* identity. Many of the more recent migrants into Chotanagpur were in fact poor low-caste plains Hindus. It was felt that the new Jharkhand parties had to contend with this change by abandoning the old political language.[46]

The foremost ideologue of the Jharkhand Party in the 1950s was a western-educated Munda, Jaipal Singh. He had been active in the Adivasi Mahasabha and epitomized the new breed of leadership, which was Western educated, Christian and had an urban outlook. A charismatic leader, he had a large following.[47] Under his leadership, the concept of Jharkhand was enlarged to include all the regions that once formed the Chotanagpur administrative division. The party had decided that it would use constitutional means to achieve its goal. That the policy worked is clear, for the popularity of the party in the 1950s rapidly increased. It swept the polls in 1952 and 1957, emerging as the major political organization in the Chotanagpur/Santhal Parganas area. The 1957 elections then saw it extend its influence into Orissa, where it captured five seats.[48] It displayed remarkable unity, and thousands of people turned up at party meetings to show support. However, despite this show of strength, the States Reorganisation Commission in the mid-1950s turned down the plea for a separate Jharkhand state.[49]

By the late 1950s, the party entered a period of decline. At the leadership level, there was a growing split between the Christian and non-Christian *adivasis* on account of the former controlling high party positions. There was also a growing realization among the people that the party had failed to deliver the goods. It did not have any concrete agrarian programme and the leadership was drawn from the high strata of tribal society, that is, mainly from Mundas and *Mankis* (village headmen) in many parts and from among the Manjhi and educated Christians in the Munda and Oraon areas. As agrarian conditions continued to deteriorate new measures were needed to remedy widespread impoverishment but the party organization was too weak, and it had no radical programme. Eventually, the search for funds led it into dealing with the hated *diku* class of exploiters. In 1962, the party accepted as member an ex-zamindar of Chotanagpur and appointed a secretary from the moneylending community.[50] By 1962 the Congress, with its programme of *garibi hatao*, actually seemed to be more in tune with mass demands to end poverty.

Support for the Congress correspondingly increased with the decline of the Jharkhand Party. In the 1962 elections, the Jharkhand Party was reduced to 20 seats in the Bihar Assembly and it appeared that it could no longer maintain itself as a viable political organization. The merger of the Jharkhand Party with the Congress was thus a natural corollary to these events. Jaipal Singh accepted a portfolio in the Bihar Cabinet and many of his supporters never forgot this betrayal.[51] The merger signalled the end of the Jharkhand Party as a party of the people and effectively outlawed the radical stream.

A period of dissent followed, with grassroots activists struggling to build a political base. A radicalization of politics was inevitable given the increased exploitation of the Chotanagpuri communities under the Congress regime. Indeed, Congress policy towards tribal areas in the post-Independence period had totally alienated the *adivasis*. After 1947, the 'isolationist' thinking of the colonial rulers was heavily criticized by the nationalist state wedded, as its imperial precursors had been, to the ideology of development.[52] The report of the Scheduled Tribes Commissioner, known as the Dhebar Report on the Indian State's policy towards tribals, argued that the British policy of isolating them had resulted in their exploitation.[53] Professor Ghurye, a long-time critic of British rule, voiced this change in thinking when he stated that 'the policy of protecting the so called aborigines through the constitutional expedient of excluded areas or partially excluded areas evoked a protest from politically conscious Indians and was resented by many of them'.[54] In a conscious attempt to move away from the British policy towards the tribes, the new policy was unashamedly assimilationist, its professed aim being to draw the tribes into the mainstream of Indian political culture. The consequences of such a policy were predictably disastrous and created more tension in the region.[55]

The government of Bihar pushed ahead with a massive exploitation of the forest and mineral wealth of the region while maintaining in its official 'tribal' policies that the 'tribals' should be allowed to develop according to their own genius. After the 1950s, thousands of acres of *adivasi* land were lost to new industries. The cities of Ranchi, Dhanbad and Jamshedpur continued to grow rapidly through an ever-increasing in-migration of *non-adivasi dikus*. By 1961, there were already half a million migrants in Dhanbad and Singhbhum. There was also an extensive loss of land through sales by *adivasis* to *non-adivasis* not only for business purposes but for erecting residential buildings. The result was an increasing 'de-tribalization', with communities such as the Bauris becoming descheduled on account of their development as coal miners. The 1971 census disclosed an alarming state of affairs. The percentage of the 'Scheduled Tribes' in the population of the districts of tribal Bihar had fallen sharply in the decade from 1961: in Ranchi from 61.61 to 58.08, in Singhbhum from 47.31 to 46.12 and in the Santhal Parganas from 38.24 to 36.22. This was not only due to the slow growth rate of the *adivasi* population, which was in fact among the lowest in India, but the influx of people from other parts of Bihar.[56] In this period, struggles to halt these dramatic changes developed under a new leadership and resulted in the creation of political organizations like the Birsa Seva Dal and the Jharkhand Mukti Morcha (JMM). The new political extremism was reflected most clearly in the formation, in 1973, of the JMM, whose object was to form a separate Jharkhand state, end the exploitation of 'tribals' by 'non-tribals', and secure preferential treatment for 'sons of the soil' in the matter of employment. Under the aegis of this organization *adivasi* consciousness acquired a new political orientation. It led large-scale movements of protest in the 1960s and 1970s to regain tribal lands. In 1968, a movement in the Santhal Parganas resulted in, among other developments, the Santhals forcibly harvesting standing crops on lands illegally occupied by moneylenders. The period 1967-74 also saw many struggles under the aegis of the JMM to recover alienated lands from moneylenders and rich peasants in Chotanagpur, amounting to a renewed assertion of strength of a people long exploited.[57]

A history of this period of obvious exploitation can help us understand the nature of the counter-discourse of the local people in Chotanagpur. Faced with economic and political marginalization, the *adivasi* leadership in Bihar under the Jharkhand Party first sought to assert its political views by emphasizing a broad convergence of interests with other *non-*

adivasi groups. In a region where the *adivasi/non-adivasi* distinction had been blurred through decades of migration and where the poorer parts of the Hindu migrant population were as badly off as their *adivasi* brethren, it would have been politically inept to emphasize only an *adivasi* identity. However, the constitutional policy followed by the Jharkhand Party through its embracing the language of modernity and the lack of a radical programme in the countryside soon resulted in its decline and its ultimate merger with the Congress in 1963.[58] That this happened with disastrous consequences for the *adivasi* people's struggle in the 1960s is evident from the attempts made in the later 1960s and 1970s to evolve new independent political organizations to meet popular demands and, specifically the emergence of the JMM as a radical organization developing out of the agrarian struggles of the 1960s. This organization was to attempt a successful cultural revival in the 1970s and 1980s and to revive the image of the Jharkhand people as the inheritors of their ancestral lands and forests. A new and interesting period in the struggle by what was increasingly beginning to be seen as the 'indigenous people' of Jharkhand against an oppressive state had begun.[59] It was in this context and given a growing sense of *adivasi* consciousness that the landscape of Chotanagpur became a symbolic terrain for definitions of Chotanagpuri identity.

JAL, JANGAL, JAMEEN: THE DISCOURSE OF THE INDIGENOUS FOREST

The JMM gave particular emphasis to a cultural revival of *adivasi* rituals related to the land and signalled the revival of the sarhul puja. This 'festival of the sacred grove', traditionally confined to the villages, now became a grand political event in urban centres, and was accompanied by large processions, drum beating and dancing, with large crowds lining the streets.[60] In the context of a despoiled landscape, the ritual harked back to the days of an idyllic environmental past. It can be seen as a selective use of memory, where the memory of a pristine environmental past is linked to the solution of contemporary political and economic problems. Given the ecological degradation in Chotanagpur today and the poor state of its village sacred groves, often left with only one remaining tree, this ritual has taken on enormous symbolic significance. It evokes a particular image of the landscape—'older, truer and more directly related to the people'—and was used to revive memories of better times and to criticize the inequities of the current regime. It symbolized a flamboyant assertion of 'tribal' identity and strength and can be compared to the Ramanavami or Moharrum processions[61] in demonstrating militancy.[62] The *puja* thus became a highly visible, elaborate and ritualized culture of public celebration involving both the performers and the crowds in a collective act articulating the special relationship of the Chotanagpuri peoples with nature and asserting their rights as true custodians of their lands and forests.[63] It is possible to argue, in this context, as Paul Gilroy does when he describes the performance of black expressive cultures, that these performances were an attempt to transform the relationship 'between the performers and the crowd in dialogic rituals so that spectators acquired the active role of participants in collective processes which are sometimes cathartic and which may symbolize or even create a community'.[64]

This reinvention of 'tribal' traditions happened, as James Clifford notes, in a complex oppositional context where indigenous populations were threatened by forces of progress and modernity. In-migration had changed the character of Chotanagpur society and by the late nineteenth century it was a society that could not really be categorized as predominantly *adivasi*. In their collection of essays Hobsbawm and Ranger have pointed to ways in which nationalist mythologies were historically contingent creations as was ethnic and tribal identity.[65] An understanding of ethnic symbols and myths is thus invaluable for our study. Elements of *adivasi* self-government were also revived or re-invented. The *biasi* (assembly) in the Santhal Parganas today functions as a court without fees and deals out simple justice. Traditions of collective farming, and preservation of jungles, pastures and common land began to be asserted more forcefully, while common grain pools were encouraged. The attitude of the JMM towards non-*adivasis*, however, was still ambivalent. While the concept of *diku* is central to the notions of *adivasi* identity and solidarity, the Jharkhand parties began to realize that they could not sustain an appeal based on ethnicity alone.[66] Many of the low-caste migrants who arrived in the region in the nineteenth century felt that they had as much a right to be in Chotanagpur as the *adivasis*. Any political programme for Jharkhand therefore had to include these groups and the Jharkhand parties today are, therfore, only partly constituted by ethnic meanings and groupings.

The attitude towards *dikus* in this period is important to our understanding of how the *adivasis* conceptualize themselves and others. Moreover, the concept of *diku* itself is important, for it amounts to a form of boundary-maintenance. By mapping the named category of *diku* we can, perhaps, uncover the vocabulary of group differences in the region. What groups call themselves and what they call others is related, of course, to a language of esteem and insult. Names, as Manning Nash has noted, condense the relevant cultural information into handy social and psychological packages for easy self- and other-identification.[67] The notion of *diku* has not been a stagnant one in Jharkhand. In the nineteenth and early twentieth centuries, as we have seen, there were already clear notions of difference between *dikus* and tribal groups. The *diku* was clearly seen as a recent immigrant and as an outsider and exploiter who seized tribal lands. A little later, while the *diku* was still seen as the outsider who occupies all the government jobs, the boundary differences between *dikus* and non-*dikus* began to blur. An *adivasi* identity was emphasized but these boundary mechanisms were breached with ease. Instead, a more regional identity was taking over based on secondary cultural markers, that is, on a shared history of exploitation, a territorial boundary and a shared culture of the *adivasi* groups. The latter is important because, although there was a growing understanding that the future of non-tribals was assured in the envisaged state of Jharkhand, the parties continued to lay importance on 'tribal' culture. The appeal to voters was made on grounds of a common economic and cultural predicament. Ethnicity continued to have force in Jharkhand to the extent that it was a politically powerful argument against the way in which state and national political arenas were structured in favour of the dominant outsider groups.[68] Thus, although the parties emphasized a regional identity, ethnic arguments continued to be aired at the popular level.[69] The flag of the

Jharkhand Party was green in colour, deliberately to emphasize the common cultural and ecological heritage of all Jharkhandi *adivasis,* while the election symbol was a *sismandi* (a kind of fowl sacrificed to a *bonga*). The JMM flag had the traditional weapons of the bow and arrow as symbols of tribal resurgence.[70] *Diku* culture, it was argued, shows little respect for any of these symbols. But there is little doubt that a homogenous '*adivasi* identity' can no longer be asserted given the history of the region and the impact of the long history of low-caste Hindu migration though ethnicity continued to rear its head in different guises.[71]

The Jharkhand parties also attempted in this period to attack the relatively careless attitude of the Bihar state government with regard to environmental issues in Chotanagpur. One of the most widespread movements in the area in recent times has been motivated against attempts by the Forest Development Corporation to replace sal by *sagwan* (teak), since the latter is more valuable as wood in the market. This has grave consequences for the lifestyle of the local people. As we have seen, sal products have been useful to them in various ways. In 1978, resistance to the planting of teak was sparked off when the forest department undertook to plant teak in 2,000 hectares of sal forest. A strong popular belief developed that nothing grew under teak, particularly not the grass and tubers on which the local wildlife and people subsisted. It was also alleged that since elephants did not eat teak leaves, they would be forced to seek food in areas where crops grew, thus increasing their depredations. The agitators also argued that fruit-bearing trees were being cut down to establish teak nurseries, thus depriving the tribals of a source of food.[72]

A detailed analysis of the forest *andolan* in Singhbhum District has been provided by Father Matthew Areeparampil, a Jesuit priest worked among the Hos for many years and was actively involved in defending them in the court cases against them.[73] It can perhaps even be argued that Jesuit mission activity in this region fired local protest. Father Areeparampil noted that 'the immediate cause for this sudden outburst were certain actions of the government which the tribals felt were detrimental to their interests. In 1973 the government nationalized the *kendu* leaves trade. In 1976 it took over the sal leaves trade and in 1978 all the

Minor Non-Forest Produce (MNFP) was taken over by the government. In 1975 the Forest Development Corporation was formed and a 1.92 lakh hectares were leased out to the corporations for purposes of clear felling and planting high yielding varieties like teak. The first major incident of uprising against these actions took place at Simdega on 4 August 1978 when the police fired at a crowd of *adivasis*, killing one person. As the *andolan* progressed the forest issue came to acquire greater prominence. Forest officials were assaulted on a large scale and as part of the direct action programme in support of the movement for a separate state 2,000 *adivasis* from the forest areas of Chakradharpur, Sonua, Goilkera and Bandgaon with their bow and arrows took part in this demonstration.

Areeparampil notes that the *jungle katai andolan* was started at the same time where trees were felled in forest areas for the purpose of making fields. The initial phase of the movement included sixty-seven villages in the Karaikela area. The movement also attempted to reclaim lands which had *sasandiri* (burial stones) of their ancestors as evidence that these lands once belonged to them. The resistance to teak plantation specifically targeted teak nurseries and at Searing several huts, a pump set and all the teak saplings were destroyed. In October 1978 eleven teak nurseries were destroyed in the Sonua and Goilkera areas, causing considerable loss to the Corporation. The *Singhbhum Ekta* newspaper described the reasons for the movement in the following manner; 'the planting of teak after cutting the natural forests is against the interests of the *adivasis*. *Adivasi* life depends very much on the produce of the forest like *mahua, kusum, karanj*, etc. . . . in many areas.'[74] The Bihar administration reacted by intensifying repression. Section 144 of the Criminal Procedure Code was imposed throughout the forest areas on 2 November 1978. On 3 November the Sub-divisional Officer Sadar and his party severely beat up several *adivasis* including women at the Goilkera market. Further shooting followed in Serengda and Goilkera killing five *adivasis*. On the 5 November the leaders of the Jharkhand Party, N.E. Horo, Haricharan Sinku and Sohanlal Aneja were arrested. However, the *andolan* was to come more firmly in the grip of the JMM as the Jharkhand Party gradually distanced itself from it. As the political leadership wavered the *Jungle andolan* spread to other areas and continued to gain momentum until it climaxed in the Gua firings. Here a peaceful demonstration of *adivasis* was fired on by the Bihar Military Police. Fifty-nine rounds were fired and three *adivasis* killed outright. What followed was indescribable. When the injured *adivasis* were brought into hospital 'they were surrounded within the hospital, assaulted and shot dead. To quote the official version, nine rounds were shot killing, nine *adivasis* within the hospital'. As the hospital staff cowered the 'dead bodies remained there until darkness and the blood until the next day'.

The police in southwest Singbhum District had moved at the behest of local politicians, mine owners and timber contractors to arrest 4,100 tribals and non-tribals for unlawfully cutting trees. The *morcha* was driven underground, only to emerge again in new guises and locations.[75] In the context of a state-declared scarcity and with famine stalking the land, the resistance of the Singhbhum *adivasis* was laudable and there is little doubt that the movement for a separate Jharkhand state was renewed and intensified during this period.

In recent years many ethnic movements have legitimized their claims by reference to a global environmentalism.[76] This involves arguing that the local people are the best stewards of the landscape and have the best claims to control it. The discourse of the rights of indigenous peoples to their forest was thus an important part of the struggle of Jharkhand parties. In the late 1960s and 1970s, the Birsa Seva Dal, Bihar Prant Hul Jharkhand Party and the JMM were each set up to contest what they saw as the tyranny of developmentalism both within and outside the parliamentary area. These organizations participated in elections, while their activists were also involved in the forcible cropping of *diku* lands, in sabotaging local transport lines and in organizing new forest *satyagrahas*.[77] There was also a renewed attempt to preserve the sacred groves of the *adivasis* and a growing protest against dam building as at Koel Karo. The effort to prevent the flooding of tribal lands and groves under this project has generated widespread support. The main outcry seems to be directed against the destruction of the sacred groves where the gods are said to reside.[78] Over the years they have been successful in stalling the project, indicating the power of collective resistance.

By the mid 1980s a full fledged movement was under way to claim the lands and the forests expropriated by outsiders and the state as their own. The attack on forest lands held in the reserved forest areas that was inaugurated in Singhbhum soon spread to other areas in neighbouring Ranchi where, under the auspices of the Jharkhand parties, large areas in the protected forest zones came to be legitimate targets for struggle.[79] As the forest department fought back, attacks on forest guards and the burning of forest department rest houses in the Saranda forest area became a regular feature of the protest. The slogans of *Jal, Jangal* and *Jameen* (water, forest and land) and the movement for securing 'indigenous' rights had come to acquire new significance. In Singhbhum alone 4,000 acres of forest were illegally cut. Areeparampil has provided an analysis of both the strong and weak points of the *jungle katao andolan.*

He argues, I believe rightly, that this was an important new phase in the history of the movement, a time when it became truly popular with a wide participation of all groups including women. However, it was plagued with problems, not the least being the ambiguous support of the traditional Jharkhand leaders to the movement. There was also little support for the movement from the plains *adivasis* or the non-*adivasis*. Furthermore, the large-scale looting of forests mainly benefited contractors, timber merchants and corrupt politicians. In Porahat, a raid unearthed timber worth Rs. 10 lakhs in several saw mills and timber godowns in the 1980s.[80] It is interesting to note in this context that a trend towards ecological vandalism had been noted by settlement officers in Ranchi in the latter half of the nineteenth century, fearing forest settlements and the imminent seizure of forest lands by the State. We can note a similar process here, but one that had markedly intensified given the inroads of the forest department in corrupt cahoots with timber contractors and middlemen in the post-Independence period. This extreme reaction of local communities to these excesses by the State and timber contractors was thus to be expected. Often their reactions further denuded the forest cover.

One effect of the movement was a marked deterioration in the lifestyles of local villagers in the Porahat and Chaibasa areas of Singhbhum—the region of my case study. A widespread denudation of the hills resulted in many protected forest areas here. In local memory, hills that had been as recently forested as ten years previously were stripped bare of their foliage. Local communities bartered their forest resources in the provincial towns and in 1997, for example, columns of bicycle poachers could be seen weaving their way down from the hills laden with wood.[81] In Pumea village in central Singhbhum, women complained of the extensive distances they had to walk to collect fuel. Interestingly, a reaction to this phase of the struggle is currently taking place in Singhbhum district. A local conservation movement invoking perceived age-old conservation values of local people has developed in several villages, actively encouraged by local Jesuits. Here the hardship of villages like Pumea, affected by uncontrolled local forest-cutting, has forced villages such as Basakuti, Thakurugutu and Gutuhatu, to name only a few, to voluntarily take up the conservation of their local forests and limit access in order to preserve their fuel and other wood resources for the future.

The phase of environmental vandalism that occurred in Jharkhand in the 1980s and 1990s leads one to a reassessment of 'indigenous' forest rights. It also leads one to question whether local people should have the right to freely pursue traditional practices or to develop their lands, especially when the exercise of these rights has implications in conflict with environmental values. This is an issue that is currently being debated globally.[82] The debate has been particularly controversial where threats to the survival of endangered species has been involved. It has been noted in the context of the American Indians that the traditional subsistence conservationist practices of indigenous peoples have not really led to a sound modern environmentalism.[83] Furthermore the granting of land rights to indigenous people in the American Indian context has repeatedly led to their not returning to traditional subsistence practices, but instead to their seeking to develop their lands economically without any respect for the environment.

In the case of Chotanagpur, whilst one cannot deny that

traditional indigenous practice incorporated valuable environmentalist lessons as we have seen, the terrible toll on the land associated with State intervention and capitalist interests in the colonial and post-colonial periods has resulted in these communities demanding the return of their forests, not necessarily to develop them sustainably as in the past but in order to harvest them, often uneconomically, in order that they may not loose out to commercial interests. Very often they have been abetted in the process by commercial interests. Meanwhile contractors, timber merchants and corrupt politicians have used the cloak of the popular movement of the *jungle katao andolan* to loot forests.

In an interesting article Roy Perrett has argued that the conflicts between indigenous rights and environmental interests can be seen as conflicts between local and global justice. He argues that it is unlikely that (given the history of injustice) local people are going to give way when the exercise of their land rights happens to conflict with environmentalist values. Using the discourse of rights and Amartya Sen's capability approach[84] he goes on to submit a theoretical model of freedom, rights, justice and equality where frill moral weight is given to the notion of indigenous rights but allows for an overriding of these rights in order to respect some more basic right, such as the right to be well nourished and disease free. In the case of Chotanagpur, the value of these debates lies in the framing of policy where local communities have a stake in protecting their environmental resources. Examples of what may happen when trees rather than local people become the objects of conservation have been provided in many accounts.[85] New policy departures need to be evolved that will prove effective in extending the life span of the world's remaining forests, and in countering the formidable interests in exploiting them for short-term gain. Co-management of resources and joint forest management have been seen as the way forward. Only individual case studies will show the extent of participation or the ways in which definitions of 'community' have in fact strengthened certain hierarchies in society.[86] The local conservation movement underway in some villages in Singhbhum is an example of community forest management operating without the approval of the forest department. The major fear of the local people engaged in managing their local forest by hiring their own forest guards is that their stake in the forests will be lost in a changed political climate.[87]

The cultural struggle for indigenous rights being waged in many parts of contemporary India must be seen as essentially a movement directed towards transforming the balance of power in the region. In Gramscian terms it may be seen as a struggle for hegemony in the cultural and political arena. In rejecting terms such as *jangali* that forms part of a discourse that aids compliance towards forms of economic and political domination, by forcefully claiming indigenous status and rejecting the notions of backwardness and inferiority in comparison with the plains Hindus, *adivasi* leaders in the twentieth century attempted to secure political advantage in the colonial and post-colonial period. In the process, claims about the inherent originality or purity of *adivasi* culture were made, while the history of acculturation with the dominant Hindu culture were pushed aside. It is in this moment of struggle against dominant values and the narratives of the State, as Homi Bhabha notes, that the 'meanings and symbols of culture are appropriated, translated, rehistoricized and read anew'.[88] It seems very likely that ethnicity will increasingly dominate Indian politics. As the discourse of the nation state in India becomes increasingly undemocratic, ethnic politics seeks to express itself more forcefully. Moreover, while regarding ethnicity as a process there is little doubt that with the creation of the new states of Jharkhand, Uttarakhand and so on, ethnic arguments in India have already come into their own but, they continue to tread a complicated path.[89] The extraordinary attempts of the Jharkhand government to award indigenous land claims on the basis of colonial documentation dating back to the 1920s must be seen in this context. More surprising is the limited success achieved by the BJP to coopt the *adivasis*. This has included a determined effort on the part of the Hindutva brigade to Hinduize tribals, in the process dropping the word *adivasi* from the lexicon and substituting it with *vanvasi* or forest dweller. This can be seen as a move to deny 'indigenous' status to the tribals because it runs contrary to the Hindutva notion that the Aryans are the original indigenous people. The attempt to ban cow slaughter and conversion to Christianity is part of the determined effort to 'return tribals to the Hindu fold'. The right-wing agenda to coopt these groups indicates the ways in which the term 'indigenous' continues to be a highly contested one.

The recognition of the invented nature of many traditions and the notion of the constructed nature of culture and ethnicity allows us to approach these complex developments meaningfully through a historial lens. What emerges then is the links between culture and power—culture as a form of power and domination, especially when it masks itself as a 'national' culture. Culture as a medium in which power is both constituted and resisted and one is thinking here of political separatist movements in a global context which use the notion of a separate ethnic identity to challenge the notion of a homogenous national culture. Instances of dramatic resistance to cultural hegemony and power of a particular class or group or western capitalism show also that culture need not be always be on the side of power. Examples of indigenous people's movements, such as the Jharkhand movement demonstrate this.

In conclusion, one might state that given the history of the Jharkhand movement, claims to an 'authentic indigeneity' cannot be so easily dismissed by revisionist writers. Dirks, Eley and Ortner have usefully argued the political significance of these categories for surbordinate and marginalized groups seeking to contest the power of hegemonic formations whether constituted within academic disciplines, institutional fields or at the level of whole societies. They note, 'if otherness is a category that must always be suspected, nevertheless it may facilitate our attempts to listen to the voices of anthropologist informants and colonized subalterns'. The fact that the term *adivasi* with its connotation of autochthonous power has found most favour with these communities is of great significance. It can be seen as a way of creating alternative power structures and of being outside the narratives of the Indian nation state.[90] As Skaria puts it 'being *adivasi* or indigenous is about the shared experience of the loss of the forests, the alienation of land, repeated displacements since Independence in the name of development, and much more.'[91]

The recent debate over the damming of the Narmada has highlighted the question of indigenous rights. Approximately 37,000 hectares of land and 1,52,000 people are scheduled to be directly affected by displacement due to the reservoir. Secondary displacement will add many more to these numbers, raising the total to one million.[92] While it is true that the hill *adivasis* are only one-third of the number ultimately affected, their plight has been highlighted by reference to global environmentalism. In this, the activists of the Narmada Bachao Andolan have been helped by the contemporary political prominence of the issue of indigenous rights and the international shift in the attitudes towards indigenous people since the Second World War. A reassessment of the post-1865 period, in particular, will need to take into account the local traditions and transforming historical developments that have led gradually to the emergence of the identity of the *adivasi*. In the absence of such an analysis, the argument made by writers such as Sumit Guha that invocations of indigeneity can only have explosive consequences, simply ignores wholesale the real and extant politics of such identity formations in India.[93] The embracing of the identity of indigenous or *adivasi* must be seen in political terms. Given the effects of economic exploitation, political disenfranchisement, social manipulation and ideological domination on the cultural formation of minority subjects and discourses, a redefinition of the subject position of tribes and an exploration of its strengths and weaknesses, and of the affirmations and negations of the term *adivasi* itself was inevitable. In this context, it becomes useful to see contemporary *adivasi* culture and the assertion of indigenous rights in many parts of India today as a form of continuing political struggle, albeit one deeply connected with a critical global environmental predicament.[94]

NOTES

1. See Sumit Guha, *Environment and Ethnicity in India, 1200-1901*, Cambridge, 1999; Amita Baviskar, 'Tribal Politics and Discourses of Environmentalism' in *Contributions to Indian Sociology*, 31, 2, 1997; S. Sinha, S. Gururani and B. Greenberg, 'The Neo-traditionalist Discourse in Indian Environmentalism' *Journal of Peasant Studies*, vol. 24 (3), pp. 65-99, 1997.
2. Dane Kennedy, Imperial History and Post-colonial Theory' *Journal of Imperial and Commonwealth History*, 24, 1996, p. 3.
3. Nancy Lee Peluso, 'Fruit Trees and Family Trees in an Anthropogenic

Forest: Ethics of Access, Property Zones and Environmental Change in Indonesia', *Comparative Studies in Society and History,* 38 (3), pp. 510-48, 1996, and 'Genealogies of the Political Forest and Customary Rights in Indonesia, Malaysia and Thailand', *Journal of Asian Studies,* 60, 3, 2001, pp. 761-812.

4. William Van Schendel, 'Invention of Jummas: State Formation and Ethnicity in Eastern Bangladesh' in R.H. Barnes, Andrew Grey and Benedict Kingsbury (eds.), *Indigenous Peoples of Asia,* Michigan, 1995.
5. James Bodley, 'Comment in Headland, Revisionism in Ecological Anthropology' in *Current Anthropology*, vol. 38 (4), pp. 611-13, 1997.
6. A. Agarwal, K. Shivaramakrishnan, *Social Nature, Resources, Representation and Rule in India,* Delhi, 2001, p. 2.
7. R. Grove, 'Indigenous Knowledge and the Significance of South West India for Portuguese and Dutch Constructions of Tropical Nature' in R. Grove, V. Damodaran and S. Sangwan (eds.), *Nature and the Orient: The Environmental History of South and South East Asia,* Delhi, 1998, pp. 187-236.
8. See T.N. Headland and R.C. Bailey, *Human Foragers in Tropical Rainforests*, cited in Headland, 'Revisionism in Ecological Anthropology' in *Current anthropology,* vol. 18, no. 4, August-October 1997, p. 608.
9. M.P. Yorke, 'Decisions and Analysis; Political Structure and Discourse among the Ho Tribals of India', Ph.D. thesis, SOAS, 1976, p. 50-1.
10. Another trend in recent revisionist Indian forest history has been to rather uncritically accept the Leach-Fairhead thesis, where it is argued in the context of Guinea that the Kissidougou landscape is one that is currently filling up with rather than being emptied of forests and that the notion of linear change with regard to deforestation and agricultural intensification is unhelpful. In their story social groups in Guinea carefully planted trees in a hitherto denuded landscape. While it is useful to retain a critical perspective, and to be wary of either romanticizing or indicting indigenous peoples and their attitudes to the environment, it is much harder to dismiss the very real evidence of ecological changes and deforestation that took place in India all through the colonial period. One is not making the case here for a pristine environmental past. Clearly the people's engagement with the forest in multiple ways saw the creation of a human landscape, one that was ever changing with past forests giving way to settlements, shifting agricultural practice and the altering of boundaries between villages and forest. Nature was not 'out there' but was a lived relationship for local communities. However, only a much more detailed environmental history of the locality will allow us to piece together these rich and complex stories.
11. The discourse of scientific forestry was no more accepting of indigenous ideas of conservation than the earlier ethics of exploitation had been.

It has be seen as a mechanistic science where nature, the human body and animals could be described, repaired and controlled, as could the parts of a machine, by a separate human mind acting to rational laws. The domination of women and nature was inherent in the market economy's use of both as resources. Subsistence production, oriented towards the reproduction of daily life, was disrupted by this new development discourse. This had a particularly negative impact on women's subsistence which was specifically linked to the forest.

12. For an interesting study on the redefinition of the landscape in America under the plantation economy, see M.A. Stewart, 'Rice, Water and Power: Landscapes of Domination and Resistance in the Low Country, 1790-1880', in *Environmental History Review,* Fall 1991.
13. See V. Damodaran, 'Gender, Forests and Famine' *Indian Journal of Gender Studies,* 9:2 (2002).
14. J.A. Reid, *Final Report on the Survey and Settlement Operations in Ranchi, 1902-1910*, Calcutta, 1912, p. 129.
15. *Annual Progress Report of the Forest Administration in Bengal, 1898,* Calcutta, 1898.
16. *Forest Administration Report for Bengal 1882-83,* Calcutta, 1883, p. 223.
17. The expansion of arable land increased after the mid-nineteenth century and 80-95 per cent of the optimal geographical limit to cultivation was reached between 1900-10. In Palamau District alone approximately 1,00,000 hectare. of forest were cleared for the specific purpose of cotton production between 1860-1910. As can be seen from the table woodlands in Chotanagpur declined by 2,01,450 hectares in the period 1870-90 or approximately by over 11 per cent. This was a large decrease with dramatic changes in lifestyle for the people affected.
18. As Steve Daniels notes (and this is certainly true both of ethnic and national identities), 'identities are often defined by legends and landscapes, by stories of golden ages, enduring traditions, heroic deeds and dramatic destinies located in ancient or promised homelands with hallowed sites and scenery. The symbolic activation of time and space often drawing on religious sentiment gives shape to the imagined community of the nation.' See Stephen Daniels, *Fields of Vision, Landscape Imagery and Identity in England and US,* Cambridge, 1993, p. 5.
19. For more recent writings on history, landscape and identity see David Lowenthal, 'British National Identity and the English Landscape', *Rural History,* 2, 1991.
20. Peter Gow, 'Land, People, Paper' in E. Hirsch and M. O'Hanlon, *Anthropology of the Landscape,* Oxford, 1995. See also similar studies elsewhere: Tim Thomas, P. Sheppard and R. Walter, 'Landscape Violence and Social Bodies: Ritualised Architecture in a Solomon Island Society',

Journal of the Royal Anthropological Institute, vol. 7, no. 3, 2001, p. 570.

21. Valentine Ball, *Tribal and Peasant Life in Nineteenth Century India,* Calcutta, 1880 and H.H. Haines, *The Forest Flora of Chotanagpur,* Calcutta, 1910.
22. See S.C. Roy's fascinating empirical study of the Birhors. See *The Birhors,* Ranchi, 1925.
23. M Yorke, op. cit., p. 53.
24. Ibid.
25. It could be argued as R. Freeman has done for Malabar, south India, that perceptions of the forest differ according to one's class position. In Malabar he argues that for the elites of settled agricultural regimes 'the forest becomes a symbolic repository for the demonic, antinomian, anti-social because of the presence of all those lower castes and tribals with whom the higher castes were dependently but ambivalently tied'. See R. Freeman, *Forests and Folk. Perceptions of Nature in Swidden Regimes of highland Malabar,* Pondicherry Occasional Papers, 1994, p. 27.
26. See M. Leach, op. cit., See also similar views, Roy Ellen, 'Rhetoric, Practice and Incentive in Nuanlu', in Kay Milton (ed.), *Environmentalism: The View From Anthropology,* London, 1993, p. 140.
27. See Nurit Bird David, 'The Original Affluent Society', *Current Anthropology,* vol. 33, no. 1, 1992, pp. 25-34.
28. See Marshall Sahlins, *How a Native Thinks about Captain Cook for Example,* Chicago, 1995.
29. Simon Schama has noted that 'Landscapes are culture before they are nature; constructs of the imagination projected onto wood, water and rock.... once a certain idea of the landscape, a myth, a vision establishes itself in an actual place, it has a peculiar way of muddling categories, of making metaphors more real than their referents; of becoming in fact part of the scenery'. Simon Schama, *Landscape and Memory,* London, 1995, p. 12.
30. Daniels, op. cit., p. 12.
31. See Marshall Sahlins, *Anahulu, the Anthropology of History in the Kingdom of Hawaii,* Chicago, 1992, for the idea of the remembered landscape.
32. 'Home public, No. 150-152 dt. 26 September 1861 (National Archives, Delhi) quoted in Purshottam Kumar, *Mutinies and Rebellions in Chotanagpur,* Patna, 1991, p. 87.
33. S.C. Roy, *Oraon Religion and Customs,* 1928, reprint Calcutta, 1972, p. 251.
34. Extract from the Confidential Diary of the S.P., Ranchi, 3 January 1919, Political Special Branch, India Office Collectionm, London, 1919.

35. Report of the Commissioner of Chotanagpur, 12 May 1921, Political Special Branch, India Office Collection, File 1921.
36. Mark Poffenburger, 'The Resurgence of Community Forest Management in the Jungle Mahals of West Bengal' in D. Arnold and R. Guha (eds.), *Nature, Culture and Imperialism,* Delhi, 1985, p. 348.
37. Archer collection, MSS Eur. 236/1 India Office Collection (London).
38. Peter Gow, 'Land, People and paper' in E. Hirsch and M. O'Flanlon, (eds.), *Anthropology of the Landscape,* Oxford, 1995.
39. In Gujarat, the Devi movement of the tribals developed similar links with the national movement, see David Hardiman, *The Coming of the Devi,* Delhi, 1987, pp. 168-76.
40. See K.S. Singh, Tribal Autonomy Movements in Chotanagpur' in K.S. Singh (ed.), *Tribal Movements in India,* vol. 2, New Delhi, 1982.
41. One can argue with some reservation recorded above, as the Comaroffs do in the context of the Tswana, that 'the long conversations with missionaries had set the terms of the encounter that sought to make Africans through their everyday dress, agriculture, architecture and so on-through formal education . . . the various ways in which culture shown by the churchmen took root in the social terrain of the Tswana to be reinvented or reified into ethnic tradition. . . . Some to be creatively transformed, some to be creatively redeployed to talk back to the whites parts of the evangelical message . . . giving rise to novel forms of consciousness and action.' See Comaroff, *Of Revelation and Revolution, Christianity, Colonialism and Consciousness in Southern Africa,* Chicago, 1991, p. 288.
42. See J. Hoffman, *Encyclopaedia Mundarica,* Calcutta, 1906 on customary rights, pp. 2390-401.
43. E. Dalton, *Descriptive Ethnology of Bengal*, Calcutta, 1872, p. 3.
44. See *Chotanagpur Unnati Samaj ki Varshik Mahasabha ka Report aur Chotanagpur Adivasi Sabha ka utpatti*, Ranchi, 1937, pp. 1-14.
45. Political Special Branch, 25 April 1946, File 116, India Office Collection (London).
46. Field Notes, 1997-98 in Ranchi and Singhbhum districts.
47. Interview with Cornelius Ekka, Ranchi, April 1992. Ekka remembers going to Jaipal Singh's meeting in 1945 where there was a crowd of nearly 50,000 people.
48. At an *adivasi* meeting in Pathkudua the slogans raised included '*Chotanagpur, Santhal Pargana ki Jai*', '*Adibasi ki jai*', '*Jharkhand le ke rahenge*'. That the integrity of the Chotanagpur Plateau was a major issue for Jaipal Singh and his associates came up in the debates leading up to the reorganization of the states. The 1948 Kharsawan firing, where the Orissa government attempted to gain control of the princely state of Kharsawan and many peaceful *adivasi* demonstrators

were killed brought home the fact that the spoils of the Chotanagpur Plateau were subject to division by the successor states in the newly independent India whose policies were no different from those of the colonial rulers.

49. The party fought in the 1952 Assembly Election, the first in free India, and won 32 seats out of 325, becoming a major opposition party in the legislature. It demonstrated an impressive show of strength before the State Reorganization Committee (SRC) when the latter visited the area in 1955. However, the SRC did not recommend separate statehood, the main reason being the lack of viability of the area as a linguistic unit. In the election in 1957 the party once again became the leading opposition party with 28 seats in the legislative assembly of Bihar.
50. See K.S. Singh, 'Tribal Autonomy Movements in Chotanagpur' in K.S. Singh (ed.), *Tribal Movements in India*, vol. 2, Delhi, 1982, p. 7.
51. Interview with Jharkhand party leader N.E. Horo, Ranchi, April 1992.
52. 'Verrier Elwin noted that at the time 'there was endless talk of tribal development', See Archana Prasad, Against Ecological Romanticism: Verier Elwin and the Making of an Anti-Modern Tribal Identity, New Delhi, 2003, p. 99.
53. For details of these views, see S. Corbridge, 'State, Tribe and Region: Policy and politics in India's Jharkhand 1900-1980', unpublished Ph. D. thesis, University of Cambridge, 1993.
54. 'G.S. Ghurye, *The Aborigines, So-called and Their Future*, Delhi, 1943, p. 293.
55. This was not just confined to Bihar. As Christopher von-Haimendorf has noted a massive invasion of tribal land by outsiders all over India occurred specifically after 1947. See Christopher von Furer Hainiendorf, *Tribes of India: Struggle for Survival,* Delhi, 1989, p. 39.
56. See Myron Weiner, *Sons of the Soil: Migration and Ethnic Conflict in India,* Princeton, 1978, p. 165.
57. For details see R.N. Maharaj and K.G. Iyer, 'Agrarian Movement in Dhanbad' in Nirmal Sen Gupta (ed.), *Fourth World Dynamics: Jharkhand,* Delhi, 1982, pp. 165-200.
58. The merger was declared illegal shortly afterwards and the Jharkhand Party was revived. It still, however, retained some of its constitutional tactics. In a memorandum sent to Indira Gandhi in 1973 the party demanded the rectification of the mistake committed by the State Reorganisation Committee in 1950 and noted 'We want peace with justice. We want the government and the parliament to consider this demand with justice and fairplay . . . we do not want a situation to develop which would breed bitterness, strife, violence . . . , our demand is one of the oldest in the country which involves people who have suffered thousands of years. It deserves immediate consideration on

merit'. See a memorandum by the Jharkhand Party submitted to the PM of India, 12 March 1973.

59. As Ram Dayal Munda notes 'A period of self search followed the direct action movement of 1978 and after its brutal repression by the government an all inclusive effort with better planning was launched. This included a series of seminars, symposia, workshops and orientation classes all over the Jharkhand region. At the same time Ranchi University opened the Department of Tribal and Regional Languages to promote teaching and research on the languages, literature and cultures of the Jharkhand region.'
60. I was told on a visit to Ranchi town in 1992 that the scale of the Sarhul Puja I had witnessed there was a new phenomenon and an 'invention of tradition', in Hobsbawm's terms. As James Clifford notes, 'throughout the world indigenous populations have had to reckon with the forces of "progress" and "national" unification. The results have been both destructive and inventive. Many traditions, languages, cosmologies and values are lost, some literally murdered but much has been invented and revived in complex oppositional contexts'. See James Clifford, *Predicament of Culture,* Harvard, 1988, p. 16.
61. The celebration of the Hindu religious festival of *Ramnavami* and the Muslim festival of *Muharram* were often used to assert the strength of these communities in urban areas and sometimes resulted in inter-communal rioting.
62. A reassertion of traditional cultural practices is an intrinsic element of the economy and political struggles of third-world peoples. For many minorities, culture is not a mere superstructure, all too often in an ironic twist of Sartrean phenomenology the physical survival of the minority depends on its cultural variable. As Arif Dirlik argues, cultural struggle is an essential counterpart to political and economic struggle. See Arif Dirlik, 'Culturalism as Hegemonic Ideology and Liberating Practice', *Cultural Critique,* vol. 6 (1987), pp. 13-50.
63. Some scholars studying 'festive culture' have interpreted rituals as manifestations of an evolving folk culture creating meaning and helping people to cope with an alien world, as instruments for the promotion of group solidarity and as public assertions of group power and demands. See Kathleen Neils Conzen, 'Ethnicity as Festive Culture: Nineteenth Century German America on Parade' in Werner Sollors (ed.), *The Invention of Ethnicity,* New York, 1989, p. 46.
64. Paul Gilroy, *They aint No Black in the Union Jack,* London, 1987, p. 214.
65. E.J. Hobsbawm and T. Ranger, *The Invention of Tradition,* Cambridge, 1992, and Leroy Vail (ed.), *The Creation of Tribalism in Southern Africa,* London, 1989.

66. Whereas in 1872, 51.38 per cent of Chotanagpuris were classified by the British as aboriginals and semi-aboriginals, by 1971 only 30.14 per cent of the region's population belonged to Scheduled Tribes in Bihar. See H. Beverly, Report on the 1872 Census of Bengal, Calcutta, 1872, p. 154.
67. Manning Nash, *The Cauldron of Ethnicity in the Modern World* Chicago, 1989, p. 9.
68. Recent scholarship in the field argues convincingly that ethnicity, i.e. belonging and being perceived by others as belonging to an ethnic group is an invention. Ethnic groups are part of the historical process and though they may pretend to be eternal and essential they are usually of recent origin and eminently pliable and unstable. They thus constantly change and redefine themselves. See Werner Sollors (ed.), *The Invention of Ethnicity*, New York, 1989.
69. As Nash notes, 'Ethnicity is a resource in political, economic and cultural struggle. When economic ends are sought (opportunity, wealth and income redistribution or claims to ownership of a national patrimony), the ethnic group may approximate a political class and exhibit a form of class struggle powered by an ethnic ideology, not a false consciousness but often a true appreciation of the existing state of economic affairs,' Nash, *The Cauldron of Ethnicity*, op. cit., p. 127.
70. P.C. Flembram 'Return to the Sacred Grove' in K.S. Singh (ed.), *Tribal Movements in India*, op. cit., p. 89.
71. Homi Bhabha has emphasized the 'Hybrid moment of political change where ideas and forms are rearticulated; where there is a negotiation between gender and class, where each formation encounters the displaced.' He argues that the agents of political change are discontinuous, divided subjects caught in conflicting interests and identities. See H. Bhabha, *Location of Culture,* London, 1994.
72. Ibid., p. 20.
73. See Writ Petition No. 371-5 of 1983 in the matter of Matthew Areeparambil and Others Versus State of Bihar and Others (personal copy), Father Matthew Arreparambil's died recently. His death is a serious loss to scholars of India.
74. 'Gua Massacre of Tribal's', *Economic and Political Weekly,* XV, 38, 1980, p. 1123.
75. See A.K. Roy, 'Sal Means Jharkhand, Saguwan Means Bihar', *Sunday* (weekly), Calcutta, 8 April 1979, pp. 46-7.
76. For an interesting discussion of this in India, see Pramod Panjuli, 'Beyond Capitalised Nature; Ecological Ethnicity as an Area of Conflict in the Regime of Globalisation', in *Ecumene, 5,* (2) 1998, pp. 186-217.
77. See K.S. Singh, *Tribal Autonomy Movements in Chotanagpur*, pp. 14-21.
78. The efforts of the BJP-led NDA government to recommence work on the project was met with stubborn resistance, resulting in the death of ten

adivasis in police firings. A PUCL bulletin signed by Thomas Kochery, M.G. Sanjay and Medha Patkar notes that this recommencing of the project is 'indicative of the fact that in these heydays of globalisation and liberalisation, the government and power elites of the tribal states of Jharkhand and Chattisgarh are preparing for mortgaging the forests and rights of tribals for the sake of national and multi-national capital.' See http://www.pucl.org

79. Matthew Areeparampil, 'Forest *Andolan* in Singhbhum' in S. Narayan (ed.), *Jharkhand Movement: Origin and Evolution,* New Delhi, 1992, pp. 143-86.
80. Ibid.
81. Field notes 1997-98 in Ranchi and Singhbhum districts.
82. Roy W. Perrett, 'Indigenous Rights and Environmental Justice' in *Environmental Ethics,* vol. 20, no. 4, 1998, pp. 377-91.
83. Ibid.
84. Sen's capability approach rests on the notion of developing people's basic capabilities to achieve functionings they have reason to value. These functionings can vary from elementary ones (like being well nourished and disease free) to rather complex achievements like having self-respect and being able to take part in the life of the community. See Amartya Sen, *Inequality reexamined,* cited in Roy Perrett, 'Indigenous Rights and Environmental Justice', pp. 386-9.
85. See Sato's account of the Karen people living in 'ambiguous lands' in buffer zones between areas designated for forest conservation and farming in 'People in Between: Conversion and Conservation in Forest Lands in Thailand'. See also Cohen's depiction of the upland Akha populations of the Laos People's Democratic Republic who have been shifted to settlements on lower slopes and incorporated into lowland commercial Tai agriculture as an important, opium-addicted wage labour force in 'Resettlement, Opium and Labour Dependence: Akha-Tai Relations in Northern Laos', These articles are in *Development and Change,* vol. 31, no. 1, January 2000, pp. 179-200.
86. Nandini Sundar, 'Unpacking the Joint in Joint-Forestry Management' in *Development and Change,* vol. 31, no. 1, January 2000, pp. 255-79.
87. That this is not an ill-judged fear can be seen from the examples that Gadgil and Guha cite in Uttara Kaimada which had its own systems of forest management. This involved keeping watchmen and regulating the harvest. These village councils were given formal recognition in 1926 and continued until the 1960s when they were disbanded by the Karnataka forest department. The timber rights were then passed on to a local timber contractor. See Gadgil and Guha, *This Fissured Land: An Ecological History of India,* Delhi, 1992, p. 41.
88. H. Bhabha, *Location of Culture,* London, 1994, p. 37.
89. This is not to argue that the politics of the new state will be radically different from the preceding state of Bihar. Corruption continues to

plague the new state and the NDA alliance of the BJP and the Samata Party is bogged down by controversies. The threat posed by the ultra-left MCC (Maoist Coordination Committee) in attacking small *zamindaris* has proved a major irritant to the new state in the period leading up to December 2001. The fact remains that the BJP and its allies are seen to soft pedal on the 'indigenous' issue. More recently to counter this allegation, the Marandi government has taken up the cudgels in favour of 'indigenes' by the 'domicile policy for clerical government jobs', causing outrage among the settled Biharis. The fact remains that the indigenous population in the current state of Jharkhand numbers less than 30 per cent. Any policy for ousting 'outsiders' or redistributing resources can only be painful and bloody. It remains to be seen how the state will fare in relation to its impoverished communities.

90. See writers like S. Guha, *Environment and Ethnicity,* op. cit.
91. A. Skaria, *Hybrid Histories, Forest Frontiers and the Wilderness in Western India,* Delhi, 1999, p. 281.
92. Baviskar, *In the Belly of the River,* Delhi, 1995, p. 200.
93. See S.Guha, op. cit.
94. Ibid.

6. Role of Women in the Joint Forest Management Programme: Case Study of Two Forest Villages of West Bengal*

Ritajyoti Bandyopadhyay

The term 'participation' has a wide connotation evoking simultaneously a sense of togetherness, common purpose and mutual understanding. Since the end of 'participation' is to ensure 'voice' and 'choice' by developing a humane management capacity to sustain the 'improvements', participatory research is fundamentally about the right to speak. Due to the development of the notion of sustainable development which maintains a delicate balance between the human need to improve lifestyle and well-being on the one hand, and preserving natural resources and ecosystems for the sustenance of the future generations on the other, the concept of community participation in managing natural resources gains importance in the contemporary policy discourses.

By taking community forest management in India, popularly known as Joint Forest Management (JFM), as a specific case of participatory development, the paper seeks to revisit the process of democratization through community involvement and its

* The present paper is a part of the researcher's project work funded by SYLFF (Sasakawa Young Leaders' Fellowship Fund, Nippon Foundation, Tokyo), J.U. The author expresses his indebtedness to the Foundation for offering him a generous grant for carrying out the research and field trips for writing this research article. I am also thankful to Prof. Ranjan Chakrabarti for his comments on an earlier draft of the essay. Prof. Anuradha Chanda supervised my work during the fellowship period. Prof. Joyashree Roy, Prof. Swapan Chakraborty, Dr. Abhijit Roy, Prof. Gautam Basu, Debarati Bagchi and Abhishek Basu, have made insightful comments and suggestions to develop this paper.

much problematized 'gender' dimension. Identifying a slippage between 'involving women' and 'addressing gender', it ventures to make participatory development in general, and JFM in particular, more 'gender' sensitive. In addition, the paper interrogates some of the 'essentialist' implications of existing theoretical paradigms in the light of field findings in two forest villages in West Bengal and calls for conceptualizing 'multilayered gender relations' in the contour of everyday livelihood experience of human beings.

The paper is divided into six sections. Section I presents the theoretical framework of the study. Section II deals with reviews of studies concerning formal provisions of women's participation in JFM along with some research studies in this context. Section III would briefly describe the West Bengal state perspective. Section IV describes the way in which the field survey was done, while section V submits the field findings. The last section gives some suggestions to policy makers.

THEORETICAL FRAMEWORK

The role of women in mainstream development practices began to receive attention since the UN Decade for Women (1975-85). To be precise, policy approaches have assumed two specific forms—the 'Women in Development' (WID) and 'Gender and Development' (GAD) approaches. The latter succeeds the former in an evolutionary path. WID rubric conceptualizes women as resources who must be tapped and accordingly mobilized to attain project efficiency. Thus, as Tinker puts it in the context of forest management, 'women's productive roles' rather than 'their needs' justifies their inclusion in official management practices.[1] Providing the justification for sexual division of labour, WID asserts that since women are more exposed to nature, they have 'special knowledge' and 'innate connection' with the environment.[2] The WID position bears close resemblance to the Eco-feminist position since both these approaches assume women's 'essentially' 'closer' relationship to the environment.

In contrast, GAD, which began to dominate development literature in the 1980s, focuses on 'gender' (women in relation to men) rather than on women alone by challenging the idea that women have any essential connectedness with nature.[3] Going beyond a mere incorporation of women into existing paradigms of development, GAD proponents try to transform existing 'gender' relations (including the division of labour) in order to achieve 'gender' parity and empowerment for women. While WID has traditionally focused on such interventions as credit for women or access to employment or visibility in public meetings, GAD concentrates on unpacking the households and suggesting what measures can improve women's control over resources and their bargaining capability. Thus, GAD considers both 'gender' and caste/class in explaining women's development problems.[4]

The notions of 'capabilities' and 'entitlement', the two pillars of GAD rubric, propelled development to embrace 'human agency' and 'freedom', beyond its economic connotation. Dreze and Sen's now famous 'capability perspective' involves concentration on freedom to achieve in general and capabilities to function in particular (especially when assessing freedoms to pursue well-being). It has a precise agenda for women in terms of rendering education, health care, and constructing both intimate and public spaces that would benefit them as socially useful and influential beings and enjoy 'real freedoms' rather than merely fulfill larger social goals.[5]

Since GAD rubric has been able to expose some of the serious shortcomings of WID, and also promotes the need to problematize 'gender relations' at all levels of development business[6] the task in this paper is to essay its own foray to tease out some serious 'essentialisms' in the GAD perspective. Firstly, as Cornwall mentions, despite the pervasive use of the term 'gender', operational frameworks equate women with 'gender' and treat men as threat in women's empowerment.[7] Secondly, it is often felt that 'gender aware' development practice fails to be effectively engaged in comprehending the complexities of 'gender relations' within communities.[8] It thus tends to see 'gender relations' in terms of a potential or actual heterosexual relationship and overlooks multilayered existence of 'gender relations' which equally includes the dynamics of other kinds of man-woman relations (e.g. between elderly sister and her younger brother in the household which is an important relation for intra-household resource allocation) and the relations between women themselves at the interjection of generation, class and caste. Thirdly, the pervasive use of the term 'agency' in the context of women's[9] issues is theoretically problematic, for, in contemporary critical theory, it hinges on the question of whether individuals can freely and autonomously initiate action or whether the things they do are in some sense determined by the way in which their identities have been formed. Even those who take agency for granted in order to assert the importance of political action suggest the difficulty for the subjects to escape the effect of those forces that 'construct' them.

Therefore, so far as the 'women's agency' is concerned, it is important to understand the nature of the hegemonic project of patriarchal socialization in which the 'agency' of both men and women are exposed. Also it may be suggested that while women's education, access to property and participation in public deliberations can empower them with new aspirations, they are potentially unequipped to bargaining with patriarchy. A collective bargaining with patriarchal expressions is the most important step in the realization of women's 'voice', 'agency' and 'choice'. Fourthly, the very approach of GAD has a profound universalist tinge which often obscures regional socio-economic and cultural specificities, existence of histories of participation management and conservation and fails to nuance varied expressions of patriarchy. If JFM is to succeed, it will have to accommodate regional 'difference'.

The next section will show how JFM-specific literature oscillates from WID to GAD with a nominal epistemological value addition.

Past Studies

The watershed National Forest Policy in 1988 recognized the importance of involving women in forest management.[10] The implication of it was, however, restricted to the creation of berth for women in Forest Protection Committees (FPCs). Again, the 1 June 1990 circular providing JFM guidelines to the state governments forgot to specify any action plan to involve women and referred only to beneficiaries (MOEF, 1990).[11] This omission indicates the initial dilemma of 'governmental' action to the question of women's involvement in mainstream project work. The recent 2000 guidelines is said to have set rules for promoting 'gender' equity in an attempt to rectify its earlier passivity. But a close reading of the orders will tell the reader how the official standpoint fails to acknowledge the fact that unequal 'gender relations' cut across the broader issues of inequality due to class, caste and ethnicity divisions. Without enlarging the capabilities of women in terms of education and so on, it only suggests a 33 per cent representation from women in the General Body (GB) and the Executive Committees (EC) of the FPCs. No state legislation addresses 'gendered' social norms ('gender' division of labour, space of congregation, the female behavioral norm, etc.), 'gendered' perceptions which undermine women's capability and strength, and 'gendered' employment system (it has been observed that employees of the forest department in all the states are mostly 'men'), which often help sustain women's 'invisibility'.[12] The study of Britt-Kapoor in central Himalaya has shown how women are 'effectively conscripted' to forest committees in order to fulfill the requirements of JFM resolutions.[13] In the entire process, then, women's 'voice' and 'choice' are thoroughly marginalized inspite of their visibility in decision-making bodies.

As Menon mentions, individual state resolutions and project policies functioning in the context of micro-policy framework fail to imaginatively apply JFM to different regional contexts and most of them 'lack clarity' regarding the role of women.[14]

Half of fourteen state resolutions analysed by Hobley stipulate that one adult representative per household may be a member of the GB of the local forest management institutions.[15] Although some resolutions add the qualification that this may be either a man or a woman, in practice it is usually a man. Sarin's review of 'gender' equity in JFM notes that 'JFM is effectively equating' people's participation because of its assumption that as 'heads of the households' men adequately represent the interests of all household members.[16]

In four of the resolutions analysed, there are provisions for joint membership of both husband and wife (as in West Bengal) or for one man and one woman representative per household; and only in two states are all adults in a household considered to be GB members.[17]

Sarin notes of the first two variations that 'although a substantial improvement of the one representative per household formula, these provisions still exclude a large number of both women and men' such as younger nuclear families within extended or joint family units.[18] Apart from that, most of the state resolutions are silent about the right of widows and deserted women. Although in many cases sharing has not yet occurred, the implications of these provisions for women's membership are likely to mean that women are unable to exert significant control over a share that is seen as a household entitlement.

Correa's field survey in Uttara Kannada[19] reports how in every level of Joint Forest Programme Management (JFPM), women's participation was virtually non-existent owing to (a) their duty to cook meals of official staff, (b) non-incorporation of their views (if they were present in the meetings) in the recorded minutes, (c) lack of knowledge about the objectives of JFPM. The third observation supports Kameswari's analysis that women remain 'passive receivers' of information while 'men' act as 'active senders'.[20]

For Agarwal[21] JFM experimentations have effectively failed to ensure both women's participation in management and 'gender' equity in benefit sharing. Their membership in committees rather than citizenship determines usufructs sharing principles. Since the state does not involve women in law making, they are often used by the community in law breaking. Many cases exist, as she points out, where women have been banned from entering the protected areas where they formerly collected firewood.

In the context of JFM, Agarwal draws attention to some constraints to women's participation and then goes on to give a plausible solution. The flaws identified by her include organizational constraints relating to women's time use, gendered attitudes of the male forest staff, social constraints ranging from seclusion to the norms about women's capability and roles, lack of experience in public speaking and lack of recognized authority.[22]

Agarwal seeks to resolve the problem in two ways: first, by chalking out strategies to ensure women's confidence and awareness of their rights; second, by increasing their number in the representative bodies. A larger representation of women can, as she believes, enable some women at least to raise their voices and be heard.

As is evident from this account, inspite of having a commendable analytical capability, Agarwal is silent in addressing the difficulty to trace out women's 'agency' from their representation in public bodies. Phillips and Goetz have pointed out the complexities involved in the question whether women can necessarily represent women's 'gender interests'.[23] As Phillips makes clear, caution may need to be exercised in moving beyond particular concerns that are clearly shared to identify female representation with enhancing the position of women in general.

Thus, a simple increase in the number of women involved serves only the instrumental goals and remains inequipped in itself to address some of the issues of power at stake.

West Bengal Scenario

The West Bengal State Government was among the foremost Indian states to distribute surplus agricultural land to the landless people. It has been estimated that one in three landless families received land in this way.[24] Yet, the number of landless in the state is around 30 per cent who work as wage earners for landholders, generally at a lower rate than the labour rate fixed by the state. According to Bardhan and Mukherjee's sample analysis in 89 villages, for a majority of villages, there was a tendency for the land reform effort to decline as the Left Front gained increased control of the local government.[25] For them, the reason behind this was the fact that the left share was driven principally by sharing in voters' loyalty based on events at the district or state level, combined with historical pattern of incumbency within the village. In particular, they do not seem to have been influenced either by the existing land distribution or past land reforms carried out in the village. The existing political order, then, helps sustaining the existing inequalities and categorization in rural Bengal. The field findings of the paper suggest that right over landed property, in many cases, determine the success or failure of JFM in West Bengal.

The performance of literacy programme in the state is also dismal. According to Pratichi Education Report, Santiniketan, the rate of literacy (among those Children who are seven years old) as per the 2001 census is 69.22 per cent (eighteenth position in all-India ranking).[26] Health care is poor and therefore it inflicts negative impact on individual's productivity.

One of the reasons for unsatisfactory land distribution, health and education, as for the States, *Economic and Political Weekly*, Pal et al. note, can be traced to a rather poor public delivery service practiced in the state.[27]

STATE FOREST AND INSTITUTIONAL EVOLUTION OF JFM IN WEST BENGAL

The total forest area in the state is 8,349 sq km. of this 4,905.82 sq km. of area falls under JFM. The major forest areas are located in North Bengal low hills and plains (38.80 per cent), in South-west Bengal (36.35 per cent) and in Sundarbans (23.59 per cent). Presently the estate has 3,431 FPCs under JFM[28] (MOEF 1999).

Despite its early success in Arabari in the early 1970s, the JFM ventures in the state gathered momentum in 1989 (dated 12 July 1989) when government orders were issued to formalize the FPC, wherein the duties and responsibilities of FPC members, usufructury and other benefits to which they would be entitled were laid down. But the amended state resolution on JFM does not make explicit mention of women—the membership is either joint or male/female. The state resolution states that the number of members under 'elected representative' of the beneficiaries will not exceed six in the ECs. Beyond this, the resolution is silent on women's role and their involvement in JFM. However, when JFM started, the field-level foresters realized the importance of women's involvement in JFM. The State Forest Report 2000 shows that in West Bengal, 75.20 per cent of Non-Timber Forest Produce (NTFP) is gathered by women. Since NTFP gathering and its marketing constitutes the economic backbone of the system, and women are the principal users and gatherers of it, the involvement of women in JFM becomes a field-level reality in West Bengal. In the early 1990s the automatic joint membership to the GB of FPC was recognized. But the system remained unimplemented for many areas. Thus, in the FPC record book of

Midnapore (West) forest division, only 2 per cent women membership was recorded in no less than 72 FPCs. The State Forest Report 2000 shows that women's involvement in JFM is insignificant (5.7 per cent against male participation of 94.30 per cent).

By understanding the fact that women are being deprived of their rights, the West Bengal Forest Department (WBFD) has made an effort to establish a unique management system of women FPCs in West Bengal. To this end, seventeen All-Women FPCs have been established, primarily in three forest divisions in Bankura district. In these cases, the members of FPCs and ECs are all women. And the women folk are supposed to take all the decisions in these FPCs.

To substantiate the paper's theoretical premise, some of the seventeen All-Women FPCs were chosen. It was done intentionally because in all the 17 FPCs the 'critical mass' of women[29] has been attained—a veritable step which, for some GAD proponents, at least, can ensure women's own 'voice', 'agency' and 'choice' in public deliberations. The paper seeks to understand the 'correlation' between women's participation and their 'agency'—whether participation can really promote their own worldviews.

STUDY AREA: METHODOLOGY

This section is divided under different subtitles. I have, so far, conducted field survey in six All-Women FPCs. For this paper, I have chosen two among the six, since they have the potential to represent the others. The Surveyed FPCs are (1) Brindabanpur (Reg. no. B Kn/292, Forest/Range: Joypur, Forest Division: Bishnupur P.S.C.) and (2) Tribanka (West) (Reg. no. : N.A., Forest Range: Bishnupur and formerly Joypur, Forest Division: Bishnupur P.S.C.).

(A) NATURAL RESOURCE ENDOWMENT

The Joypur Forest is characterized as tropical, dry, deciduous forest.

(B) CHARACTER OF POPULATION AND THEIR LIVELIHOOD PRACTICES BEFORE JFM

The fringe area of Joypur and Bishnupur range is thickly populated by Scheduled Caste people who are mostly landless. Before the implementation of JFM, their livelihood was to fell trees and to sell them in the non-forest villages and mainly the markets. Chiefly the women folk used to do this. They were often forcefully employed by the men folk to clear the forest for subsistence. The male members were completely dependent on them, as there was no employment for them.

(C) SOCIO-ECONOMIC CLASSIFICATIONS AND PUBLIC INSTITUTIONS

Brindabanpur: Brindabanpur is a homogeneous village with 56 Scheduled Caste households (HHs) containing 290 inhabitants. Till date 53 HHs have been enrolled as FPC HH. They are all landless. It has been observed that the maximum number (35 out of 56) of HHs are dependent on wage labour; seventies HHs are engaged in government/non-government services; while rest four HHs are engaged in some sort of business. The village does not have any primary school or health centre. Recently, a Sishu Siksha Kendra (SSK) has been opened in Brindabanpur, which caters to the needs of mothers and children of the locality. Still the village lacks a motorable road and electricity. Literacy level is low; only two male members, Madan and Bikash Lohar can read and write in vernacular. The women interviewed can only sign their names.

Tribanka: It is a slightly developed village with a predominant Scheduled Caste population (Scheduled Caste 101 + General 18 = Total 119). Since all the HHs have membership in the FPC, it is heterogeneous group. So far as the land holding distribution is concerned, two HHs have large holdings, and three HHs have medium holdings. The considerable presence of small farmers (forty-four to be exact) makes the life of Tribanka economically vibrant. There are at least seventy families who can be designated as marginal farmers. Five HHs have been identified in the course of fieldwork that do not have any land. Six HHs earn their livelihood by wage earning. The remaining HHs are involved in the service sector or in business. The village does have a primary school (though with negligible infrastructure) but lacks a health centre and good communication with Basudebpur. Five male members have education upto secondary level, while women have no education. Some of them can only sign their names.

(D) REASONS BEHIND SUCH CHOICE

Brindabanpur and Tribanka have been chosen owing to three specific considerations:

(1) Both of them are All-Women FPCs in which the 'critical mass of women's representation has been attained.
(2) Brindabanpur is a homogeneous FPC while Tribanka is a heterogeneous one. This distinction is important in our analysis since we wanted to see caste-class interface within the contested domains of 'gender' and 'gender relations'.
(3) As has been shown in sub-section (C), Brindabanpur is a representative village in the state lacking basic public amenities and material entitlements, while Tribanka is a little more developed.

(E) QUESTIONNAIRE CONSTRUCTION

At first a pilot questionnaire was administered among the women of two tribal FPCs, Niljhora and Zillakhana in Modgoda range, Bankura (South) forest division. Based on their responses, the questionnaire was reviewed and revised, and the final format prepared. It encompasses issues related to demographic background, economic roles, household resource control, autonomy, education, nutrition, health, family planning, organizational participation, leadership, experiences of discrimination within and outside home, involvement in microplanning, NTFP gathering and processing and the responder's overall assessment of JFM.

(F) METHODOLOGY

The method of experimental study consisted of the following steps:

(1) Listening of the expected nature of outputs (as explained

in section E) based on the objectives of the experiment and preparation of survey forms.

(2) Preliminary reconnaissance of the selected villages.

(3) Interview of the household and recording of data in forms.

(4) Interpretation of data to produce the outputs decided upon at the outset and preparation of the paper.

FINDINGS

By interviewing the local people and the former Range Officer Swapan Banerjee (JFM was implemented in Joypur Range during his tenure), we came to know that in both the villages some committees were initially formed by the male villagers, but they failed to protect the forest cover. They forced the FD to dissolve their own committees and form new ones by incorporating women since (as they argued) women were traditional users of forest. A separate group interview with the male members of both the villages revealed that they were less inclined to protect the forest since they, at that time, did not understand the economic magnitude of JFM. They failed to envisage the benefits that they could accrue from JFM in future. As a result, they quietly 'left the place for women'. But, as we proceed, we will see that after JFM attained a certain degree of prosperity, the men folk came back in the programme with much interest. But initially it was the time to bring the women into the forefront of forest management as 'managers'. It was not easy for Swapan Banerjee to 'persuade' women to take 'public responsibilities'. It was decided that they would go for patrolling on rotation basis but would be accompanied by two forest guards. In course of time they became confident enough to go for independent patrolling. They were also 'generously' given economic incentives.

Thus, during 1991, the women members of Brindabanpur FPC were given a Kisan Nursery to raise seedlings and they earned Rs. 3,000 on its sale. They opened a bank account in favour of FPC. Different trainings were given to them for time to time. They started the protection in a group on roaster basis and successfully detected the cases of poaching. In 1988, one pond was excavated and pisciculture was started. A community hall, a ringwell and paddy thrasher were given to them as JFM support activities. By selling the rice gathered as 'musthy sanchaya' (daily collection of a fistful rice from each family), they women earned money which they deposited in a common account.

The women FPC members of the village also benefitted from the micro-credit system. The women saved a portion of their wage earnings from JFM activities in a bank account and loaned it to members when they were in urgent need of it.

The same developments in a larger magnitude took place in Tribanka. Better functioning of the FPC unit resulted in substantial increase in additional income of the members. For instance, the share of usufructs, collection and sale of NTFP, pisiculture and above all expansion of irrigated agriculture raised an additional income of Rs. 36.21 lakhs during the period six-year (1994-9). During the pre-FPC years, the average earnings in six years had not gone above Rs. 29.80 lakhs. Provision of irrigation water, better land reform, proper training in farming and other trade, and better input in agriculture besides proper protection of forest contributed to the additional income. The FPC purchased two ponds from community funds and again earned a lot. Regular and additional income significantly transformed the lives of villagers.

A standard success story of the two FPCs will describe the changed status of women in the villages. It will argue that JFM returned the dignity of women head loaders. Before the introduction of JFM, the women collectors were considered to be offenders and often treated disrespectfully. It will aptly quote a local woman, say, Shila Lohar in Brindabanpur who remained in police custody in the early 1980s. In the words of Parul Lohar, 'Before the introduction of JFM, we used to destroy the forests, now we protect them. Many of us had the experiences of eating burnt bread in police custody. Now we love our forests, because we have nurtured them. The foresters are our relatives'. 'The success of the 'success story' lies in highlighting this collaboration between the department and communities. As an index of women's empowerment, the story will highlight the aspirations of women—village women asking for practical help with things like handicrafts, food processing and poultry raising. FD and other NGOs thought these projects should be supported—this, after all, was what women wanted.

At this juncture of the success story, I can now posit the first disagreement. It is feared that supporting traditional gender roles without adequately addressing basic inequalities in terms of educational facilities, health care and property rights might reinforce, women's inequality and formalize their exclusion from the main project. And, as the fieldwork suggests, in both the instances this happened.

In Brindabanpur, the subsistence of its inhabitants is heavily dependent on forestry. They have no land or any other substantial source of income. As a result, JFM fails to improve their livelihood. In other words, since Brindabanpur is deprived of getting primary preconditions of development (health care, education, land), the next stage, i.e. JFM is bound to fail. Although women were given many facilities and initially they gained a 'voice', they failed to sustain it owing to their incapability to handle newly generated resources. Madan Lohar and Bikash Lohar who had knowledge of the 3 'Rs', soon captured authority. The male forest staff also implicitly supported it since it was easier for them to communicate with the community via persons like Madan and Bikash.

In Tribanka, JFM as a policy was materially more successful since the village had other resources too, by virtue of successful land reforms. But so far as the question of 'gender' is concerned, its experience was not very different from that of Brindabanpur. Due to illiteracy, here also, women failed to sustain the 'voice' they had initially gained. They simply did not know how to manage everything (including huge budgets).

The proponents of WID will still be satisfied with the Tribanka experience, since it has a good success rate. By concentrating on 'success', they would argue that it was possible as women were 'successfully involved' in the work. The GAD proponents will identify the 'retrogression' and suggest policies calling for expansion of 'capabilities' and 'entitlements' of people in terms of property right, education and health.

Conclusion

As argued in Section II, a simple expansion of basic public amenities is not enough to bargain with patriarchy. In order to listen to 'voice', 'agency' and 'choice' of women who are constantly exposed to patriarchal socialization, it is essential to initiate 'gender-sensitive' change in every sphere of life. In the public sphere the process should start from reviewing highly 'gendered' primers'. It is proposed that a simultaneous effort should be made to make lists more 'gender' sensitive. Also, infrastructural facilities should be extended to the deprived regions.

Secondly, grassroots movements (such as the works of Udvash among the children of Dhakuria Slum in Kolkata, India) should be encouraged by the state and efforts should be made to forge a link between these movements and intellectual feminism.

The next propositions are project specific:

1. The state government should pay attention to public delivery system. As the fieldwork reveals, some of the basic public amenities are scarce in the surveyed villages. JFM cannot add colour to the lives of the 'beneficiaries' unless the region attains a certain level of development.
2. The state should chalk out a strong action plan to combat the elephant menace. In Tribanka, every year, crops worth lakhs of rupees are lost.
3. The forest people should be treated as citizens and not as mere 'beneficiaries'. They are entitled to all civic amenities. A history of criminalization in the region in the post-JFM era will compel us to accept the fact that still they are treated as mere objects of public policy experimentation.
4. FD should adopt different attitudes to implement JFM in different regions. JFM in West Bengal was modelled on the Arabari line. It is important to note that in north Bengal or in Sundarbans, due to regional diversity the same model cannot be applied. Statistics shows that JFM attained more success in southwest Bengal than in Sunderbans or north Bengal. The reason is the Arabari model was applicable only to the kind of forests that exists in southwest Bengal.
5. In order to make JFM more successful, the policy makers should take lessons from the regional histories of forest conservation, management and expressions of patriarchy.

6. A proactive intervention from feminist corners is important to make JFM more equitable.
7. As has been argued earlier, over-emphasis on traditional gender roles would leave unaddressed, or reinforce women's inequality and formalize their exclusion from the main project. As the case of Brindabanpur suggests, such activities are often unlikely to lead to genuine empowerment and development of women. Instead they should be incorporated into explicit project aims.

Notes

1. I. Tinker, 'Women and Community Forestry in Nepal: Expectations and Realities', *Society and Natural Resources*, 7(4), pp. 367-81.
2. M. Leach and C. Green, 'Gender and Environmental History: Moving Beyond the Narratives of Past', *Contemporary Women-Environment Policy Debates*, Sussex, 1995, p. 2.
3. S. Joekes et al., Gender Environment and Change, *Development and Change*, 25 (1), 1994, pp. 135-65 and A. Sen, 'Gender and Cooperative Conflicts', World Institute for Development, Economics Research Working Paper 18, 1987, pp. 17, 30.
4. G. Sen and C. Grown, *Development, Crisis and Alternative Visions: Third World Women's Perspectives*, New York, 1987.
5. J. Dreze and A. Sen (eds.), '*The Political Economy of Hunger*, vol. 3', Oxford, 1991, pp. 10-11.
6. C. Jackson and R. Pearson, *Feminist Vision of Development: Gender Analysis and Policy*, London, 1998.
7. A. Cornwall, 'Making a Difference? Gender and Participatory Development', http://www.ids.ac.uk, 2005.
8. A. Cornwall, 'Gender Participation and Politics of Difference' in I. Guijit, and M. Kaulshah (eds.), '*The Myth of Community*', London, 1998, pp. 46-57.
9. E. Said, *Orientalism*, London: Routledge and Kegan Paul, 1978.
10. Ministry of Environment and Forest (eds.), 'National Forest Policy Resolution 1988', New Delhi, 1988.
11. GOWB, State Forest Report , Kolkata, 2000.
12. D. Arora, 'From State Regulation to People's Participation: Case of Joint Forest Management in India', *Economic and Political Weekly*, 29(12), 1994, pp. 691-8.
13. C. Britt-Kapoor, 'A Tale of Two Communities: Villager Perceptions on Local Institutions, Forest Management and Resource Use in Two Central Himalayan Indian Villages', Overseas Development Institution

Rural Development Forestry Network Paper 17, London, 1994.
14. A. Menon, 'Constructing The "Local": Decentralizing Forest Management', *Economic and Political Weekly*, 30 (34), 1995, pp. 2110-1.
15. M. Hobley, 'Participatory Forestry: The Process of Change in India and Nepal'. ODI Rural Development Forestry Study Guide 3, 1996, pp. 168-9.
16. M. Sarin, 'Joint Forest Management in India: Achievements and Unaddressed Challenges', *UNASYL*, 180, 46, 1995, pp. 30-6.
17. M. Hobley, 'Participatory Forestry', ODI Guide 3, 1996, pp. 168-9.
18. M. Sarin, 'Joint Forest Management in India', UNASYL, 1995, p. 50.
19. M. Correa, 'The Need for Emancipatory Research: Experience from JFPM in Uttara Kannada', in R. Jeffery and N. Sundar (eds.), 'A *New Moral Economy for Indian Forests?*', New Delhi: Sage, 1999, pp. 216-34.
20. V.L.V. Kameswari, 'Gendered Communication and Access to Social Space: Issues in Forest Management', *Economic and Political Weekly* 37 (8), 2001, pp. 797-800.
21. B. Agarwal, 'Re-Sounding the Alert-Gender, Resources and Community Action', *World Development*, 25 (9), 1997, pp. 1373-80.
22. Ibid.
23. A. Phillips, *Endangering Democracy*, Cambridge: Polity Press, 1991; A.M. Goetz, 'Introduction' in A.M. Goetz (ed.), *Getting Institutions Right for Women in Development*, London, 1997, pp. 1-28.
24. P. Bardhan and D. Mukherjee, 'Poverty Alleviation Efforts of Panchayat in West Bengal', *Economic and Political Weekly*, 28(8), 2004, pp. 965-7.
25. Ibid.
26. K. Rana, A. Rafique and A. Sengupta. The Pratichi Education Report, Santiniketan, 2002.
27. S. Paul, S. Balakrishnan, G.K. Kumar, S. Sita and M. Vivekananda, 'State of Indian Public Service', *Economic and Political Weekly*, vol. XXXIX, no. 9, 2004.
28. Ministry of Environment and Forest, State Forest Report, Kolkata, 1999.
29. B. Agrawal, 'Re-Sounding the Alert Gender', *World Development*, 25 (9), 1997.

SECTION III

Colonialism, Post-colonialism, the State and the Management of Nature

7. Managing the Environment: Disease, Sanitation and the Army in British-India, 1859-1913

Kaushik Roy

One of the principal pillars of the British-Indian State was the military. In addition to the white troops of the British Army, the Raj possessed Indian military manpower organized in the Sepoy Army. Utilization of Indian manpower was necessary because brown soldiers were cheaper and more efficient than the white soldiers in the subcontinent's climate and terrain. From Plassey till World War II, more soldiers fell victim to disease rather than to the enemy bullets. It took time and money for the State to train a recruit into a soldier. But sickness depressed the morale of the troops. So, the Raj in general and the army in particular attempted to manage the environment in order to protect the vulnerable military manpower from the ravages of disease.

Till 1857, the East India Company maintained its private white troops as well as units of the British Army. After the 1857 Mutiny, the Company's private white army was abolished. The rank and file of the Sepoy Army were Indians but the army was officered by the British. The units of the Sepoy Army and the British units were stationed in the three presidencies and were named after them respectively as Bombay, Madras and Bengal armies. From 1840 onwards, the British Government in India (hereafter GoI) maintained the Punjab Frontier Force for guarding the North West Frontier. In addition, the GoI also controlled different princely armies officered by the British but paid for by the 'protected princes'. The various armies together constituted the army in India and its strength fluctuated with time.

Institutional care for the sick soldiers became common in the European armed forces during the nineteenth century.[1]

For European doctors in the nineteenth century, writes Philip D. Curtin, tropical medicine and military medicine were nearly synonymous.[2] The British assumption was that disease originated either in hereditary traits or due to ingestion of various poisons that generally disseminated themselves as miasma arising from decaying organic matter and unclean human bodies. Sumit Guha writes that the ignorance of the exact aetiology of infectious diseases led the medical authorities to wage a campaign of environmental sanitation. Sanitation involved the removal of filth and refuse, purification of water and provision of ample ventilation in all dwelling places.[3] David Arnold argues that the bodies of Indians were the platform for colonial contestation and Western medicine was the instrument for colonizing the body.[4]

This paper argues that Western military medical practice was concerned with manpower economy. In this article the term environment is defined to include physical geography as well as the inhabitants who the British believed were influenced by the former factor. This article analyses the nature of disease that afflicted the imperial troops and the army's response to improve sanitation and hygiene of the soldiery with special reference to climate and terrain. The army's programme to counter the harmful effects of environment is tackled both from micro and macro perspectives. The British concern regarding army's health, hygiene and climate became systematic from mid-nineteenth century. In terms of scope, intensity and lethality, World War I marked a complete break with the 'little wars' of the nineteenth century. The first part of the essay introduces the period before 1857 Mutiny. The second part points to military medical reforms involving moral and environmental strands in the post-Mutiny era directed to the imperial garrisons scattered across the subcontinent. And the last section focuses on the army's campaign against disease when its units were engaged in 'small wars' till the onset of the Great War in 1914.

Encountering India's Environment: Manpower Losses and the Military's Response

Even in pre-British India, the militaries were ravaged by disease. Cholera spread from lower Bengal.[5] In 1757 cholera broke out in

Ahmad Shah Abdali's Afghan army when it was encamped at Madhavan, 13 miles downstream of Vrindavan. The season was hot and the river was almost dry. It was choked with half-burnt and dead bodies. In three weeks, the sun set them rotting. Every day about 150 soldiers died.[6] Records of cholera in India go back to the sixteenth century. In sixteenth-century Goa, the most common diseases were cholera, malaria, dysentery and syphilis. Syphilis was introduced from America to Europe in the 1490s and then to India by the Portuguese. It was known among the Indians as *firangi roga*. Between 1604 and 1634, about 500 Portuguese soldiers died annually from syphilis and other venereal diseases.[7]

The principal assumption of the British medical authorities was that high and fluctuating temperatures, high humidity, and exposure to intense sunlight weakened the constitutions of the Europeans who were not designed for warm climates. Notions of humoralism, which assumes that various disease reside in the fluids of the body, also influenced the British doctors. The early nineteenth century texts explain in humoral terms, the blood throwing off fiery and acrid elements in the form of fever and ulcers. By mid-nineteenth century, the medical texts argued that excessive heat disrupted normal circulation and reduced metabolism of the stomach and liver. To an extent, military medical knowledge was influenced by the Hippocratic texts which stressed careful observation and description of local meteorological, dietetic, and geographical features and their correlation with health, habits, race and character of a region's inhabitants.[8]

Between 1788 and 1795, in the European manned Bengal Artillery, annual wastage was about 13 per cent.[9] With the passage of time, the manpower losses due to disease somewhat declined. In the period 1840-6, mortality due to sickness in Meerut and Dum Dum amounted roughly to 5 per cent of the total strength. This was probably due to immunization resulting from exposure to India's climate. Two-thirds of the sickness and death at Dum Dum occurred among the recruits after landings. The table (7.1) illustrates the point further. This was because the recruits were not acclamatized. Again the veterans learnt to avoid the sun. And most of the death among the recruits was due to sunstroke. At Dum Dum liquor was cheap and easily available. This also caused death in the long run.[10]

TABLE 7.1: AVERAGE RATES OF SICKNESS AND DEATH IN THE BENGAL ARTILLERY STATIONED AT MEERUT AND DUM DUM BETWEEN 1840-6

Year	*Meerut*			*Dum Dum*		
	Monthly average strength of the artillery	*Annual number of deaths*	*Average sick in hospital on the 1st of each month*	*Monthly average strength of the artillery*	*Annual number of deaths*	*Average sick in hospital on the 1st of each month*
1840	312	16	25	747	31	58
1841	300	13	23	719	33	48
1842	212	14	14	606	27	36
1843	380	15	23	622	32	23
1844	328	11	20	639	26	15
1845	440	24	22	314	22	16
1846	178	9	15	404	25	22
Total	2,150	102	142	4,051	196	218

Source: 'The Bengal Artillery', Article V, *Calcutta Review*, vol. 9, 1848, p. 503.

Initially, the British depended on indigenous medical knowledge for fighting the diseases that afflicted Indian soldiers. In the last decade of the eighteenth century, for the Indian regiments, the Madras Army recruited Indian doctors, each of whom was paid Rs. 25 per month.[11] Each sepoy company was provided with two *bhisties* (water carriers) and two tents. Further for carrying the tents, two bullocks were kept in each company. While the *bhisties* provided fresh drinking water to the soldiers, the tents protected the troops from rain and sun.[12] However, with the passage of time, the role of Western medicine in the regiments increased. During the 1830s, there were three surgeon doctors for each regiment of white soldiers.[13]

Some regions like Burma and Sind proved to be especially harmful for the troops. On 1 April 1851, the 28th Bombay Infantry Regiment was ordered to Sind to relieve the 2nd Baluch Infantry Regiment. The Bombay Infantry Regiment had men recruited from Kathiwad, Poona, Deccan and a few from north

India. By November 1852, out of 754 soldiers of the Bombay Infantry, 482 suffered from Sind fever. By 7 December 1852, only 316 men were fit for duty. The regiment for purposes of garrisoning was divided into right and left wings. In the right wing, 30 men were sick and 5 died after they were sent to Karachi for medical treatment. On 10 February 1853, from the left wing 85 sick personnel were left behind at Karachi and Hyderabad in Sind.[14] During the Second Burma War in 1852, the British paid attention to diet and sanitation. But still mortality was high due to fever, dysentery and cholera.[15]

In 1857, the Company had 3,11,000 Indian troops in the subcontinent.[16] In the summer of 1857, about 1,20,000 Indian soldiers of the Company rebelled and captured Delhi. A rag-tag force of the Company, which included white as well as loyal Indian soldiers besieged Delhi. In August 1857, when the monsoon broke, 2,000 out of the 9,000 Company troops in front of Delhi suffered mainly from cholera.[17] The strength of the Company's force before Delhi rose slowly. On 11 September 1857, the Company's heavy batteries opened fire and the rebels also launched a counter-attack.[18] From Table 7.2 it is evident

TABLE 7.2: CASUALTIES IN THE DELHI FIELD FORCE BOTH FROM SICKNESS AND REBEL ACTIONS ON 11 SEPTEMBER 1857

Branch of the Army	*Total Strength of that Branch*	*Number of Sick Soldiers*	*Number of Soldiers Killed*	*Number of Soldiers Wounded*	*Total Number of Soldiers Killed and Wounded*
Engineers	936	214	40	67	107
Artillery	1,607	257	70	267	337
Cavalry	2,040	618	45	98	143
Infantry	8,357	1,985	828	2,224	3,052
Total	12,940	3,074	983	2,656	3,639

Note: Soldiers here also included officers.
Source: G.W. Forrest, *A History of the Indian Mutiny Reviewed and Illustrated from the Original Documents*, vol. 1, 1904, reprint, Delhi: H.K. Publications, 1992, pp. 152-3.

that among the engineers, casualties resulting from sickness was double than the casualties due to enemy's action. In the cavalry branch, casualties due to sickness was roughly about five times higher than casualties resulting from rebel actions. Overall about 40 per cent of the troops were down with sickness. The pacification campaign against the rebels involved gruelling marches over sun-baked plains. And many European troops suffered from heat strokes.[19]

During the siege of the Lucknow Residency, due to overcrowding and insanitary conditions, the loyal Indian troops and the European soldiers cooped up within the narrow confines of the Residency suffered from malaria, cholera and dysentery. When in November 1857, Colin Campbell marched from Kanpur into Lucknow, he issued a training memorandum on clothing, diet and exercise.[20] The dominant opinion was that intemperance in diet and sexual relations caused debility in the tropics.[21] Mark Harrison notes that hygienic rituals constituted a part of the new discipline that started emerging in the European armed forces during the eighteenth and early nineteenth centuries.[22] This trend became stronger in the second half of the nineteenth century.

Disease was a problem for the British Army even outside the subcontinent. In the second half of the eighteenth century, yellow fever wiped out about 40 per cent of the British military strength in the Caribbean. Between 1793 and 1796, the British lost 80,000 men in the Caribbean with over half of these to yellow fever.[23] The Crimean War lasted from 1854 to 1856. Out of the 4,05,000 men sent by Britain and France to Crimea, 25,600 were killed in battle but 38,800 died of disease.[24] Florence Nightingale, already famous for her service in the army hospitals, and Sidney Herbert, the reforming War Minister, forced the government in Britain to create the Army Sanitary Commission. On the basis of its report, the army started the programme of cleaning the barracks of filth and dirt.[25] This was because the dominant medical opinion linked disease with filth. The European medical men in India also equated epidemics with overcrowding and sanitary ignorance.[26] Curtin asserts that the heavy losses in India during the first half of the nineteenth century led to medical reforms. And the success of the reforms made imperialism cheaper in terms of manpower losses.[27] The next section turns the spotlight on military-medical reforms in post-1857 India.

Environmental Sanitation in the Post-Mutiny Era

After 1859, the colonial state in India took a more aggressive posture for checking and if possible in eliminating disease. The policy was not only to introduce welfare measures for the soldiers but also to gather knowledge about the climate and terrain of India. Environmental sanitation held sway even in the armies outside India. As late as the 1890s, military medical authorities of the American Army believed that if proper sanitary regulations were observed along with prompt isolation of the infected troops, then the subsequent outbreak of diseases could be controlled.[28] Roger Cooter and Steve Sturdy rightly assert that from late nineteenth century onwards, military medicine resulted in greater regimentation and regulation of military manpower.[29] This section shows that the GoI took active steps to shape the environment and introduced several welfare measures[30] plus hygienic discipline for training the soldiers to adapt to India's environment in a far more effective manner. All these developments brought the issue of public health to the forefront.

William Farr (the Compiler of Abstracts at the Registrar-General's Office in London in 1839) believed that all physical phenomena were law abiding and capable of being predicted. During the 1860s and the 1870s, Dr. James Lumsdaine Bryden was the Statistical Officer in the GoI's Sanitary Department. Like Farr, he believed that all physical phenomena were governed by natural laws. And the nature of these laws could be measured and manipulated for the benefit of humanity. His task was to gather as much data as possible relating to diseases and physical surroundings. From these data, he attempted to deduce the laws governing various diseases. Thus he attempted to impose order on the 'alien and hostile environment' of India.[31] The British authorities collected data for statistical analysis of the rate and types of sickness of the troops deployed at various regions at different times of the year. A basic understanding of the incidence of various diseases, the army hoped, would enable it to counter the ravages of nature far more effectively. To an extent, the military department in India increasingly adopted statistical methods, a process that is evident from the files.

Cholera was regarded as the principal killer of the troops in the Bombay and Madras Presidencies. Dr. J. Forsyth, Principal

Inspector General of the Medical Department, on 13 February 1862 informed H.W. Norman, the Secretary to the GoI's Military Department, that despite the advice of medical practitioners of Britain, dilute sulphuric acid was useless to check and cure cholera and diarrhoea.[32] But Norman persisted with the medical advice from the metropole. In August 1862, he informed the Adjutant General that Dr. McCormac had advised the GoI's Military Department to go on using dilute sulphuric acid for checking cholera.[33] The British military authorities in India deduced that inadequate physical hygiene and unsatisfactory state of water supply, especially of drinking water in the stations were the principal factors for this disease.[34] Table 7.3 below will throw further light on the sickness and mortality patterns in the army. In 1869, when Lord Napier was Commander-in-Chief of Bombay, he ordered that in case European troops were affected

TABLE 7.3: SICKNESS, MORTALITY AND INVALIDING IN THE MADRAS ARMY BETWEEN 1 APRIL AND 31 DECEMBER 1860

Troops	*Average Strength*	*Number of Admissions into Hospital*	*Deaths due to Cholera*	*Percentage of Death by Cholera to Strength*	*Percentage of Numbers Invalided to Strength*	*Percentage of Death from All Diseases to Strength*
Europeans of British Army	10,701	11,614	12	0.10	4.60	1.10
Europeans of the Sepoy Army	3,181	5,643	21	0.66	1.20	2.60
Indians of the Sepoy Army	35,401	355	107	0.30	1.70	1.40

Source: From Lieutenant-Colonel R. Hamilton, Deputy Secretary to Govt. of Madras, Madras Military Department, to the Secretary to the GoI, Military Department, Fort St. George, 4 July 1862, Progs. no. 271, Military Department Proceedings, August 1862, National Archives of India, New Delhi.

by cholera then enquiry should be made regarding the conditions of their latrines and rations.[35] In 1871, Rs. 3,250 was spent by the Madras Army for repairing and deepening the tanks to ensure supply of proper drinking water to the soldiers.[36]

From the above table, we can deduce that either the Indian soldiers were not admitted into the hospitals or they had little faith in European medical practice. Nevertheless, mortality due to disease was insignificant when the troops were stationed within the Madras Presidency. However, the scenario appears a bit different if we take a micro view of the situation. Particular regiments suffered severely from cholera. The 3rd Cavalry Regiment of the Hyderabad Contingent theoretically belonged to the Nizam but for administrative and operational purposes was under the Madras Army. In December 1863, this regiment had 135 cases of cholera. And out of them 69 cases were fatal.[37] An Indian regiment required public followers for logistical purposes (i.e. servants, *dhobis*, foragers). Table 7.4 shows that both among the soldiers and public followers of the 3rd Brahmin Infantry Regiment of the Bengal Army, about 70 per cent of those who contracted cholera died within 48 hours. Tables 7.5, 7.6 and 7.7 show that British environmental sanitation was not particularly successful against cholera.

TABLE 7.4: RATE OF CHOLERA IN THE 3RD BRAHMIN INFANTRY REGIMENT BETWEEN 18 FEBRUARY AND 3 MARCH 1876.

Date	*Sepoys Afflicted*	*Dead*	*Followers Afflicted*	*Dead*
February 18			1	
19	2	1	3	2
20	1	1		1
21	1	1	2	
22				1
23	1			
24				
25			2	
26	1			2
27	4	1	2	
28		3		
29	1	1	1	1

March 1	2		3	2
2	3			1
3			1	2
4	1	1		
5		1	1	
6	1	2	1	
7				
8		1		
Total	18	13	17	12

Source: Digest of Services of the 3rd Brahmin Infantry Regiment, 1861-1914, Return of Cholera cases and details of the Regiment between 18 February and 8 March 1876, Military Department, National Archives of India, New Delhi.

Guha says that the army attempted to construct little islands of purity in the miasmatic landscape of India for protecting the health of the soldiers.[38] The general assumption was that the Indian population was a reservoir of dirt and disease.[39] Even in the first half of the nineteenth century, the idea was gaining ground that the European troops ought to be isolated from possible physical contagion of the surrounding Indian population.[40] The Raj bought land for constructing lines for both the white and brown soldiers in an attempt to separate them from the 'diseased' civil society. Though the programme of constructing barracks for the soldiers was costly, still the army pursued this policy in order to conserve the lives of the troops. To give an example, for housing the Indian irregular cavalry, in 1860, the government bought land in Digha near the sea coast at Bengal. For accommodating the soldiers comfortably and to ensure proper supply of drinking water, trees were planted; houses and wells were constructed. The total expenditure came to about Rs. 71,715.[41] Gradually, the accommodation facilities of the soldiers improved. In 1884, General (later Field Marshal) Frederick Roberts informed Lord Napier that in the new lines constructed at Trichinopoly by the soldiers themselves, each Indian officer had his own house and the bachelors had their separate quarters. Further, each regiment had a gymnasium which was built from the regimental funds. Under the British instructors, the recruits and line boys were trained in the gymnasiums.[42]

Malaria was due to breeding of mosquitoes in stale water. In January 1870, the Commander-in-Chief ordered improvement of the drainage facilities in the cantonment of Nagode where both Indian cavalry and infantry regiments were stationed.[43] In an attempt to improve the personal hygiene of the soldiers, from 1872, each personnel of the 28th Bombay Infantry Regiment was issued new clothes annually.[44] Still, the problem was not fully solved. The 28th Bombay Infantry Regiment suffered heavily from malaria. Between June and October 1901, about 200 men and many British officers were hospitalized due to malaria.[45]

The theory about adaptability of physical constitutions in different climatic zones was influenced by Hippocratic notions of environmental influence. The belief was that climate exerted a powerful influence on human character and physical characteristics. The British assumption was that Europeans were incapable of becoming fully acclimatized to the subcontinent. Europeans thrived best in climates that most resembled the cold climate of Britain. Hence, relatively healthy localities had to be identified for the white troops.[46] So, in 1893, the Commander-in-Chief of India General Geo S. White suggested that if the political scenario permits, then the British troops should be quartered away from Peshawar where they fall ill in large numbers and shifted to the hills.[47] The general was backed up by Surgeon General A.T. Sloggett, Director of Indian Medical Service who in 1912, told the Nicholson Committee set up to reform the army in India, that it was necessary to move to the hills for the benefit of health. In the plains, Sloggett claimed, malaria, sand fly, fever and anaemia destroyed the health of the European soldiers.[48] Sloggett continued that as a result of sending the European soldiers to the hills, the death rate between 1907-11 had fallen from 8.18 to 4.80 per 1,000. And the number of cases invalided to England had decreased from 1,766 to 487.[49]

Besides proper accommodation, the army assumed that good food would improve health of the troops and hence their immunity to disease. In 1866, Robert Napier claimed that most cases of mortality among the European troops were due to bad meat supply. The mutton provided by the contractors was considered not of good quality. So, the army set up the Alligaum Sheep Farm. The commissariat was unwilling to take up the task of raising and feeding cattle under clean conditions and then slaughtering them for the troops. Napier was for buying cattle from the Rann of Kutch, Sind, Ahmedabad and Poona with the help of the political officers. There were good sheep available at Sholapur. He also encouraged grazing. Napier also wanted the commissariat to supply bread. This was because the Indian contractors' kneading rooms were dirty. Amidst dust and flies, the nearly naked and prespering workmen half buried themselves in the dough which produced the daily bread of the Europeans. Napier urged the Poona Bakery to take up this task.[50]

The army also intervened in ensuring a 'proper' food habit among the soldiers. Messes for the recruits were established in each regiment. Roberts reported that the messes were becoming popular and even the bachelor sepoys were joining them. Messes played an important part in building regimental ethos. Due to the presence of the messes, the soldiers did not have to cook their own food, which reduced the logistical burden of the army. Since the soldiers did not have to waste lot of time in cooking, more time could be devoted for training.[51] Thus, messing not only improved the health of the soldiers but also aided military training and the generation of regimental spirit, which was an important glue that held together the men in the battlefields. At times, the ration of the Indian soldiers caused problems. The 28th Bombay Infantry Regiment was a class company regiment. In 1900 it had two Sikh companies, two Pathan companies, two companies of Deccani Marathas and two Rajputana Muslim companies.[52] In June 1903, the 28th Bombay Infantry Regiment was stationed at Quetta. And seven Sikh soldiers of this regiment died. Of them six died due to food poisoning and one died due to sunstroke.[53] When in 1906, the 28th Bombay Infantry Regiment was stationed at Kohat it had 732 personnel. Within one year due to lack of good food in harsh climate 25 soldiers died.[54]

Occasionally health requirements of the troops forced expansion of the colonial state's reach over its subject populace. In 1861, of the 91,000 British soldiers stationed at Britain, there were 32,000 hospital admissions due to venereal disease.[55] For the British troops deployed in India, syphilis was a major problem.[56] In 1866, Robert Napier noted that many soldiers' health was permanently destroyed by venereal diseases.[57] In order to reduce the impact of these diseases on the European troops, Napier asserted that the soldiers should be encouraged to marry and the clergy should concentrate on the troops in the hospitals and in the prison cells. More facilities, he argued, ought to be provided to the clergymen to interact with the soldiers for religious conversation, prayers and lectures.[58] Nevertheless, the British soldiers continued to visit brothels. Most of the British privates were long-term volunteers drawn from the dregs of the society by a mixture of bribery and coercion.[59] On 18 June 1868, Robert Napier asserted: 'I would suggest for the consideration of the government, whether more general supervision over the health of the Indian population is not practicable.'[60] In 1881, the Contagious Diseases Act in India, which allowed medical inspection of prostitutes in the lock hospitals was suspended. This Act was repealed in 1888.[61] In January 1890, one Indian Medical Service officer claimed that in peacetime, at the micro-level, one half of a British regiment became ineffective due to venereal diseases.[62] On 2 December 1893, White wrote to His Royal Highness that at the Rawalpindi hospital, out of 360 British patients, 199 were suffering from venereal diseases. This was because, claimed the general, the safeguards, i.e. the lock hospitals, were removed due to the resolution of the House of Commons. White warned that due to this factor, in future, the incidence of venereal diseases would increase. Since soldiers could not be punished for visiting brothels, White like Napier argued, that the only way out of the impasse was moral improvement of the troops.[63] White, in a letter dated 4 September 1894, informed the Duke of Cambridge that venereal diseases were increasing among the British troops stationed in India. About 46 per cent of the British soldiers in India were infected with them.[64] In contrast, during the first half of the nineteenth century, 30 per cent of the European troops in India were hospitalized due to sexually transmitted diseases like syphilis, gonorrhoea and penile ulcers.[65] Between 1907-11, the admission rate per thousand of strength of European troops stationed in India was 53.10.[66]

The other problem for the British soldiers was spirits. Drink, rightly asserts John Keegan, strengthened the soldiers' steadfastness. Many British soldiers took spirits before and during battle.[67] According to Brigadier-General Owen, the inspecting officer of the Madras Army (1874-5), the British officers, '. . . drink more than is good for them'.[68] So spirits were prohibited in the bazars and discontinued in the canteens.[69] Still, the British soldiers continued to drink heavily. In 1893, White calculated that admission to hospitals amongst the non-abstainers was 10.50 per cent while among the abstainers it was only 5.50 per cent.[70] In 1894, White claimed that half of the diseases of the British Army were due to excessive intake of alcohol. However, due to the moralizing activities of the army, there was some improvement. In 1894, White claimed that about one-third of the British soldiers in India had become teetotallers due to the activities of the Army Temperance Association. As a result, the health of the troops was improving slowly.[71]

In the last decade of the nineteenth century, each Indian cavalry regiment had one British medical officer.[72] An Indian infantry regiment of 600 sepoys had one surgeon, two assistant surgeons and one Indian doctor. Let us have a macro and micro view about the state of health of the Indian soldiers when the army implemented its sanitary programme. On 8 March 1864, in the 3rd Brahmin Infantry Regiment, only one person (the British Captain) was sick.[73] On 17 April 1866, this regiment had 48 sick Indian soldiers.[74] On 5 March 1868, this regiment registered 62 sick Indian soldiers.[75] On 22 February 1869, in the same regiment, 1 British Major and 52 sepoys were down with sickness.[76] On 5 April 1870, the 3rd Brahmin had 95 sick soldiers. The British responded by increasing the number of Indian doctors to three.[77] In the years 1874-5, in the Madras Army the average death rate was 6.80 per 1,000.[78] The percentage of sick among the European troops due to fever in the Madras Army was 7 per cent. In contrast, the Indian troops were quite healthy; only 2 per cent among them were in the hospital.[79]

We cannot totally negate the private and public sanitation programmes initiated by the army. Overall, in the Sepoy Army, as evident from Table 7.7, and in the Hyderabad Contingent (see Table 7.5), mortality and the rate of sickness somewhat declined. However, Table 7.6 shows that instead of improvement in the health of the Bengal Army's Indian soldiers, mortality increased. This was because while for most of the time the Hyderabad Contingent was stationed within Madras Presidency, bulk of the

TABLE 7.5: SICKNESS AND MORTALITY IN THE HYDERABAD CONTINGENT BETWEEN 1881 AND 1890

Ratio per 1,000

Year	*Strength*	*Admission into hospital*	*Constantly sick*	*Deaths from cholera*	*Deaths from all causes*	*Mortality including absent deaths*
1881	7,068	673	24	0.57	7.78	8.52
1882	7,061	630	21	0.29	3.12	4.47
1883	6,983	572	20	2.15	7.59	9.31
1884	7,014	574	19	0.29	4.56	5.30
1885	6,969	522	17	1.00	5.88	7.57
1886	6,370	483	16		5.34	6.06
1887	5,018	614	20	1.39	9.16	12.66
1888*	6,242	734	27	0.96	6.73	10.94**
1889	6,933	555	19	1.30	8.65	9.48
1890	7,071	553	17		4.81	6.71

Notes: * Excluding men on active service in Burma for the first three months of the year.

** Including deaths in Burma in the first three months of the year.

Source: *Annual Report of the Sanitary Commissioner with Government of India 1890*, Calcutta: Office of the Supdt. of Govt. Printing, 1892, p. 75, Central Secretariat Library, New Delhi.

TABLE 7.6: SICKNESS AND MORTALITY IN THE INDIAN SOLDIERS OF THE BENGAL ARMY BETWEEN 1867 AND 1890

Ratio per 1,000

Year	*Average strength*	*Admission into hospitals*	*Constantly sick*	*Deaths from cholera*	*Deaths from all causes*	*Mortality*
1867-76	30,508	1,360	42	2.12	13.84	17.25
1881*	36,896	1,495	51	0.92	19.76	27.73#
1882	40,256	1,250	41	0.72	13.34	16.49
1883	40,932	985	32	0.56	10.55	13.98
1884	40,580	1,193	35	0.71	10.97	12.56
1885**	40,753	1,076	34	0.29	10.11	14.18
1886***	40,547	1,065	34	1.87	14.45	22.29
1887***	54,547	1,195	36	1.52	12.47	18.94

1888****	63,312	1,066	33	1.83	13.6	16.93+
1889@	65,360	1,116	37	0.38	12.96	11.30
1890@	64,080	1,306	42	3.28	19.16	21.82

*Notes:** Excluding troops in Afghanistan.
** Excluding men on active service in Burma and Egypt.
*** Excluding men on active service in Burma.
**** Excluding men on active service in Burma for the first three months and in Hazara for October and November.
@ Including the Punjab Frontier Force.
# These ratios are calculated on the basis of total regimental strength including the units in Afghanistan.
+ Including deaths in Upper Burma in the first three months of the year.

Source: *Annual Report of the Sanitary Commissioner with the Government of India 1890*, Calcutta: Office of the Supdt. of Govt. Printing, India, 1892, p. 72, Central Secretariat Library, New Delhi.

TABLE 7.7: SICKNESS AND MORTALITY IN THE SEPOY ARMY: 1877-90

Ratio per 1,000

Year	*Average strength*	*Admission into hospitals*	*Constantly sick*	*Deaths from cholera*	*Deaths from all causes*	*Mortality*
1877-81	118,669	1,422	48	1.94	24.90	27.4
1881	114,612	1,305	46	0.97	19.24	22.62
1882	114,894	1,129	37	1.02	12.24	14.76
1883	114,830	923	31	1.15	11.76	14.31
1884	114,827	1,042	33	0.71	10.50	12.22
1885*	115,486	978	32	1.61	13.67	16.09
1886*	106,010	973	31	1.27	13.27	19.46
1887*	105,254	1,045	33	1.31	11.68	18.17
1888**	124,822	995	33	2.14	12.84	16.14***
1889	128,642	1,003	35	0.68	12.94	16.19
1890	127,746	1,137	39	1.83	15.91	18.64

*Notes:** Excluding men on active service in Burma.
** Including Upper Burma for the last nine months of the year.
*** Including deaths in the Upper Burma in the first three months of the year.

Source: *Annual Report of the Sanitary Commissioner with the Government of India 1890*, Calcutta: Office of the Supdt. of Govt. Printing India, 1892, p. 71, Central Secretariat Library, New Delhi.

Bengal units and especially the Punjab Frontier Force were engaged in the North West Frontier and in Afghanistan between 1878 and 1880. The ineffectiveness of environmental sanitation is clear when the army was deployed in the 'vicious' north-east and north-west India and west of river Indus. The next section turns the spotlight on the military's attempt to protect the soldiers in those regions.

NUTRITION, DISEASE AND MORTALITY IN CAMPAIGNS

Harrison claims that as regards military medicine the British Army's experience of campaigning in the colonies gave it an edge in the Second World War vis-à-vis the Axis armies in the North African desert.[80] So, the Raj's medical paraphernalia during the colonial campaigns ought to be examined. When the regiments were marching and counter-marching towards the battle zones, lack of good water, sanitation facilities and properly cooked food became serious problems. As a result, the soldiers suffered. In the period under review, the Raj's army fought a war with Afghanistan, another with Burma and was engaged in numerous counter-insurgency campaigns against the tribes who inhabited the north-west and north-east India. This section portrays the nature and incidence of diseases that afflicted the soldiers while campaigning. It also focuses on the imperial policies for checking the 'ravages' of nature.

In 1860, when the Ludhiana Regiment was transported by ship to China, wood and coal was provided to them for cooking.[81] When the Indian soldiers were transported on ships for overseas service, care was taken to lodge them comfortably. To prevent overcrowding, for each Indian soldier without baggage, at least 7.50 square feet of space was allotted. In February 1860, Captain C.D. Campbell of the Indian Navy commanding HM's steamer *Feroze* refused to take 360 Indian soldiers with baggage because then each Indian troop would be able to occupy only 5.5 square feet of space.[82]

The 3rd Brahmin Infantry Regiment had three Brahmin companies, two Rajput companies and two Hindustani Muslim companies with a total strength of 800. In 1869, when the 3rd Brahmin Infantry Regiment was operating against the Bazotli tribe around Kohat, there was an outbreak of cholera. In September 1869, out of the 36 cases admitted, there were 20 deaths.[83] On 18 March 1873, as the regiment was moving out of north-east India for Dinapore, 35 cholera cases were admitted and out of them 25 died.[84] During the Manipur expedition of 1891, among the Gurkha regiments, more personnel died due to cholera and malaria rather than due to enemy actions.[85] On 31 March 1891, while proceeding towards Manipur, the 3rd Brahmin Regiment suffered heavily from cholera.[86] When the 3rd Brahmin was at Cachar in March 1895, cholera broke out. As the unit moved through the Hooghly River in country boats, further death due to cholera occurred as the soldiers drank water from the river.[87] On 13 September 1899, while the 3rd Brahmin Regiment was ordered from Allahabad to Manipur, cholera broke out. So, between 12 October and 13 December 1899, this regiment was quarantined at Shillong. This unit finally reached Manipur on 26 January 1900.[88] When the Regiment participated in the Lushai expedition, in order to ensure that the soldiers got food regularly, bullock convoys were used for moving supplies.[89]

The Second Afghan War lasted from 1878 to 1880. On 10 December 1878, General Frederick Roberts warned the GoI about the adverse environmental conditions that would be faced by the troops in Afghanistan. He argued that the government should be more liberal with the commissariat and medical establishments. More *gomastahs* and victualling sergeants along with apothecaries, Indian doctors, dressers and sweepers ought to be provided for the troops moving into Afghanistan. In addition, the Indian soldiers should be provided with boots and warm clothing.[90] The troops suffered especially from cholera which broke out during May 1879.[91]

The dominant assumption was that good food would make the soldiers healthy and resistant to various diseases. During campaigns, the army did not provide rations to the Indian soldiers. They had to buy articles of food from the market and cook their own food with firewood. The Madrassi sepoys consumed rice, mutton, *ghee*, pepper, salt.[92]And the Sikh soldiers consumed *chappatis* made of wheat and *dhal* (pulses).[93] But, in arid Afghanistan, the bazars failed to supply the troops with these items in adequate quantities. On 5 July 1879, Major-

General P.S. Lumsden, the Adjutant General in India told the GoI:

> The Native Army of the present day in a great measure consists of men of northern races of greater physique than the sepoy of the old army previous to 1857; that animal food whenever procurable, forms a portion of their diet, and that the men eagerly secure such diet; that the climate of the north stimulates the appetite and requires men exposed to it to be better clothed and fed than in more tropical climes, and that to maintain soldiers in work on a campaign demands a ration rather fuller than that found sufficient for warmer regions.[94]

To an extent, cold climate requires more heat, hence more calorific food. The military administration in India accepted that the Indian troops operating in Afghanistan in addition to meat, required cereals and vegetables. And these items were not easily available in Afghanistan. In fact, Lumsden argued that the troops should be provided with rations free of cost.[95]

In October 1879, the troops fell victim to malarious fever and a large percentage showed scorbutic symptoms.[96] Some regiments entering Afghanistan failed to protect the soldiers from the ravages of climate and provide them with adequate facilities for cooking hot food. On 2 February 1880, when the 28th Bombay Infantry Regiment was in Afghanistan, the bullocks bringing carts filled with baggage failed to come. At about 7 a.m. a dust storm rose and due to the unavailability of baggage, tents could not be pitched. In the night, due to its effect, two soldiers died. So, the army sent orders that every regiment while campaigning in Afghanistan must be accompanied by tents.[97] This defect was rectified in the later campaigns in the North West Frontier. In 1897, during the Malakand Expedition, every 12 soldiers were provided with a tent.[98] On 15 February 1880, Roberts demanded that the troops should be supplied with cooking pots.[99] On 7 November 1880, each company was allowed cooking pots weighing 160 pounds. Each soldier was allowed one pair of socks, one pair of boots, one pair of pyjama, one khaki coat, one cloth coat and one great coat. In addition to the tunics, each soldier was provided with a warm trouser.[100] The Punjab Frontier Force organized a Sick Train which comprised camels for conveying the sick to Multan via Dera Ghazi Khan.[101] The Eden Commission which was set up to improve the army's operational capabilities submitted its report to the GoI in 1879. It recommended that the clothing department should make hospital clothing and it should be stored in the commissariat depots. From these depots, the clothing for hospitals should be distributed to various hospitals as per requirements.[102]

Let us concentrate on a particular field unit named Vitakri Field Force that operated in Afghanistan and was composed of Indian regiments. From Tables 7.9 and 7.10, it is clear that malaria was the principal problem. Like the other troops serving in Afghanistan, the Vitakri Field Force also suffered from scurvy. This was because the army failed to procure fresh vegetables and water for the personnel.[103] Since Scurvy is caused by Vitamin C deficiency, lime juice was supplied to the scurvy patients.[104] Table 7.9 tells us that 194 soldiers were in hospitals, which comprised about 18.3 per cent of the total strength of the Vitakri Field Force. The number of camp followers sick on 31 August 1879 was 85.[105] From Tables 7.8 to 7.12, it is evident that service in Afghanistan proved unhealthy for both the Tamil and Telugu soldiers of the Madras Army as well as for the Punjabi soldiers of the Bengal Army. Nevertheless, the British generals took a racist view. In 1886, Roberts noted that the troops recruited from Bombay Presidency and Deccan were ruined by the climate when stationed in Baluchistan, Quetta and Pishin.[106] However, on 12 November 1897, Secretary of State for India George Hamilton

TABLE 7.8: AVERAGE DAILY SICK OF VARIOUS UNITS COMPRISING THE VITAKRI FIELD FORCE IN AUGUST 1879

Unit	*Average Daily Sick Among the Combatants*	*Average Daily Sick Among the Camp Followers*
15th Bengal Cavalry	64.7	32.8
Mountain Battery	16.2	1
21st Madras Infantry	36.9	18.5
30th Madras Infantry	48.7	19.7
Sappers & Miners	4	

Source: Report on the Health of the Troops Forming the Vitakri Field Force, August. 1879, Progs. No. 7152, Military Department Proceedings, February 1880, National Archives of India, New Delhi.

TABLE 7.9: NUMBER OF SICK SOLDIERS OF THE VITAKRI FIELD FORCE IN HOSPITAL ON 31 AUGUST 1879

Disease	*15th Bengal Cavalry Regiment*	*Number 2 Bombay Mountain Battery*	*21st Madras Infantry Regiment*	*30th Madras Infantry Regiment*	*9th Sapper Company*	*Number of Soldiers Suffering from Various Diseases*
Malarial Fever	38	7	18	44		107
Diarrhoea and Dysentery	4		1	1	6	
Scorbutic Affections	11	7	2	10	4	34
Rheumatic	2	1	7			10
Others	9	5	17	6		37
Total	64	20	45	61	10	188

Source: Report on the Health of the Troops Forming the Vitakri Field Force, Progs. No. 7152, Military Department Proceedings, February 1880, National Archives of India, New Delhi.

wrote to the Viceroy Lord Elgin that the performance of the white troops in the North West Frontier due to terrain and climate was worse than the Indian soldiers.[107]

The army's welfare measures and environmental sanitation somewhat improved the health of the troops during the Third Burma War. General Prendergast invaded Burma in November 1886 with 10,000 troops (three British infantry regiments and nine Indian infantry regiments). Of the Indian troops, seven were Madras Army's regiments and two were from the Bengal Army. Diarrhoea, fever and malaria afflicted the troops. Hospital provisions were provided for 10 per cent of the troops and 2 per cent of the followers. This was divided into field and general hospitals in equal proportion. There were six field hospitals of which two were for the British, three for the Indians and one for the followers. Medical officers, medical subordinates and hospital attendants of the Army Hospital Native Corps staffed these

TABLE 7.10: ADMISSION IN HOSPITAL DUE TO DISEASE IN THE VITAKRI FIELD FORCE DURING AUGUST 1879

Disease	*15th Bengal Cavalry (345)*	*21st Madras Infantry (395)*	*30th Madras Infantry (225)*	*Mountain Battery (82)*	*Number of Sick Soldiers Down with Various Diseases*
Malarial Fever	78	68	98	12	256
Diarrhoea and Dysentery	6	2	4		12
Scorbutic Affections	9	2	8	10	29
Rheumatic		4			4
Others	15	2	12	7	36
Total	108	78	122	29	337

Source: Report on the Health of the Troops Forming the Vitakri Field Force August 1879, Progs. No. 7152, MDP, February 1880, National Archives of India, New Delhi.

hospitals. The British Field Hospital used quinine and supplied bedding and blankets to the patients. The sick British soldiers got a diet which included wine, brandy, tinned milk, beef and arrowroot. The British soldiers found their beef and bread ration adequate but very often the bread was indigestible. The Sikh, Gurkha, and the Pathan soldiers were given rations of rice, *dhal* and *atta*. The Madrassi soldiers liked rice but the Punjabi soldiers were accustomed to meat. Initially, the commissariat refused to import sheep and goats from India on account of high expenses. In accordance with the British medical opinion, due to a rice diet, the Madrassi soldiers were not fit for continuous exertions. And the *dhal* resulted in colic and diarrhoea. After due representation by the medical authorities, the commissariat agreed to import goats from India and meat was issued biweekly to the troops. The coolie corps in Burma was supplied from Madras, but most of them suffered from syphilis and ulcers.[108] For those Indian soldiers suffering from scurvy, each patient got one ounce of lime juice and one ounce of sugar daily.[109]

TABLE 7.11: SCURVY IN THE VITAKRI FIELD FORCE ON 22 SEPTEMBER 1879

Unit	*Soldiers*	*Camp Followers*
15th Bengal Cavalry	13	
Mountain Battery	14	5
21st Madras Infantry Regiment	25	1
30th Madras Infantry Regiment	23	12
Total	75	18

Note: Of those suffering from scurvy, one patient belonging to the 15th Bengal Cavalry died. In addition, one camp follower died from heart disease and another from pneumonia.

Source: From Lieutenant-Colonel G.A. Prendergast, commanding 15th Bengal Cavalry, and commanding at Vitakri, to the Quarter Master General in India, HQ, Camp Vitakri, 22 September 1879, Progs. No. 7152, Military Department Proceedings, February 1880, National Archives of India, New Delhi.

TABLE 7.12: SICKNESS IN THE VITAKRI FIELD FORCE ON 20 OCTOBER 1879

Unit	*Number of Sick Personnel Combatants*	*Bearers*	*Followers*	*Total Number of Sick Combatants*	*Remarks*
21st Madras Infantry Regiment	145	70	9	224	Of them 32 required carriage.
30th Madras Infantry Regiment	90	20	5	115	Of them 33 required carriage.
Mountain Battery	11			11	On sick certificate for six months.
Total	246	90	14	350	

Source: From Colonel T.C. George, Commanding at Vitakri, to the Deputy Assistant Quarter Master General, Lahore Division, 20 October 1879, Progs. No. 7152, Military Department Proceedings, February 1880, National Archives of India, New Delhi.

When the British flotilla advanced towards Mandalay, cholera broke out. At Mandalay, the ships were cleaned and fumigated. All possible sanitary measures were implemented still the disease continued till December. The theory of miasmas held sway over the medical authorities. One British medical officer, a surgeon-major, in 1890 wrote: 'We were aware that cholera was endemic on the river at all seasons. That the peculiar moist state of the atmosphere, and the crowding of the ships may have been inductive means for inviting it, is highly probable.'[110] A cholera hospital was established around the river Irrawaddy but still the disease spread to the region around river Chindwin. The British medical doctors assumed that the subsoil around the bed of Chindwin was affected. The 43rd Gurkha Regiment lost 50 per cent of its strength to cholera as it moved along Irrawaddy. The doctors claimed that this was because the Gurkhas had consumed large quantity of melons and cucumbers. Besides cholera, the troops also suffered from dysentery. During the wet season, many wounds turned septic. Beriberi also spread among the troops stationed at Bhamo and Katha. In general, concluded the medical authorities, the diseases were due to bad climate, bad hygiene, insufficient food, impure water and excessive exposure to sun and rain.[111] However, the emphasis on sanitation was not totally misplaced. During World War II, unlike the Axis troops, dysentery and diarrhoea among the British soldiers were prevented due to good personal hygiene and sanitation.[112]

The fatal effect from disease in the Third Burma War was a far cry from the ravages caused during the First Burma War. During the First Burma War (1824-6), six out of seven men deployed became casualties due to sickness.[113] In that war, the average number of admissions to hospitals each year amounted to 3,540 per 1,000 strength. Among the British troops who participated in this war, 1,215 men died due to disease whereas only 60 died in action and 36 from wounds.[114] By contrast, between 1 November 1886 and 6 August 1887, the 3rd Hyderabad Contingent Cavalry in Burma had 497 men. It received a reinforcement of 20 men. Only 2 died due to disease; another 12 suffering from sickness were invalided to India.[115] Table 7.13 gives a macro view of the effect of cholera on the troops in Burma. The situation was not much better for the militaries campaigning outside South Asia.

TABLE 7.13: TROOPS AFFECTED BY CHOLERA IN BURMA BETWEEN 1 NOVEMBER 1886 TO 18 JANUARY 1887

Date	*British Troops Attacked by disease*	*Died*	*Indian Soldiers Attacked by disease*	*Died*	*Followers Attacked by disease*	*Died*	*Total Sick*	*Died*
1 Nov.-30 Nov. 1886	5	4	37	16	13	6	55	26
1 Dec.-31 Dec. 1886	25	19	74	31	83	56	182	106
1 Jan.-18 Jan. 1887	5	5	2	1	12	8	19	14
Total	35	28	113	48	108	70	256	146

Note: Total of deaths to attacked by disease: Europeans 80 per cent, Indian soldiers 42.4 per cent, Followers 57 per cent.

Source: 'Mackinnon on the Burma Campaign', *Indian Medical Gazette*, vol. 25 (January 1891), p. 28, All India Medical Service (AIMS) Library, New Delhi.

The American Army's Cuban campaign lasted from June to July 1898. While 3,700 died due to typhoid, malaria and yellow fever, only 300 were killed in combat.[116] During the Boer War (1899-1902), enteric fever (typhoid and paratyphoid) did more damage to the British troops than the Boers.[117] In the Boer War, the British Army lost 13,000 men from disease.[118]

In the last decade of the nineteenth century, within the medical discourse, the shift was from focus on body humours and environmental miasmas to microbes and germs. From 1898 onwards, the germ theory of disease advocated that disease in the tropical regions was not specifically linked to climate and could be overcome by medical science.[119] The germ theory asserted that microscopic organisms cause specific and infectious diseases. Partly, this theory was somewhat influenced by the development of bacteriology under Pasteur and others.[120] Almroth Wright, professor of pathology at the Army Medical College, Netley from 1892 to 1902 was an advocate of vaccine therapy and in the face of continual opposition, pushed for anti-typhoid inoculations. Measures like vaccines were aimed towards individual soldiers rather than wholesale reform of the environment. Social behaviour and environmental factors that were crucial in the army's sanitary programme became less important. The aim was to promote personal health through technical means. Instead of temperature, rainfall and topography of the military stations, properties of the blood serum of the soldiers became more vital.[121] Rather than sanitary science or hygiene, the laboratory became more important for understanding the outbreak of disease. In the first decade of twentieth century, within the discourse of public health in Britain, the focus shifted from the environment to the individual.[122]

Vaccination against smallpox was made compulsory for the new Indian recruits in the 1860s. And from the 1890s, there were attempts to inoculate the sepoys against typhoid and plague, but these measures were not strictly enforced. Inoculation against typhoid was considered as polluting by the high-caste Hindus as the bacilli from which the vaccine was prepared was usually of unknown origin.[123] Arnold writes that the Indian soldiers tried to resist vaccination indirectly. When they were ill, they turned to the indigenous practitioners of medicine in the bazars of the towns and followed their own folk and religious remedies. Nevertheless, the trend was towards increasing medicalization of the military personnel in the first decade of the twentieth century.[124]

The early twentieth century also witnessed marked improvements in the field sanitation of the Raj's army due to the increasing introduction of technology. There was improvement in the construction of latrines.[125] The sappers and miners constructed abulation trenches. The British regiments disposed of solid excreta in incinerators. Night urinals were made of tins which were placed on stands and lighted by red lamps.[126] All refuse was burnt in incinerators and they were cleaned in the morning to prevent choking. Then the ashes were disposed in a specially marked trench.[127] In 1912, Sloggett asserted before the Nicholson Committee that if mosquito nets were provided to the soldiers then the incidence of malaria could be checked and this in turn would reduce the wastage of manpower due to invaliding.[128]

Conclusion

India unlike the Caribbean Islands did not prove to be a graveyard for the white soldiers. The environmental sanitation programme of the British in India was tinged with racist assumptions. In general, the Indians were regarded as carriers of disease. It is wrong to assume that only the 'non-martial' Madrassis fell victim to disease. Even the 'sturdier martial races' from Punjab and Nepal fell victim to disease while campaigning in the harsh climate of north-west and north-east frontiers. In the post-1857 era, the army and the State became more interventionist in order to ensure proper food and accommodation facilities for the troops. The military medical authorities were not able to realize the causality behind disease but emphasis on clothing and food to an extent improved the health of the soldiers. Malaria and cholera were certainly not eradicated. But one must note that the militaries outside India were no more effective in combating disease. Gradually, a shift occurred away from environmental policing due to the emergence of the germ theory. Towards the end of the nineteenth century, one witnesses increasing use of technology for combating disease and the focus was on managing the germs rather than the tropics' 'exotic environment'.

NOTES

1. Mark Harrison, 'Medicine and the Management of Modern Warfare: An Introduction', in Idem, Roger Cooter and Steve Sturdy (eds.), *Medicine and Modern Warfare*, Amsterdam-Atlanta, GA: Rodopi, 1999, p. 4.
2. Philip D. Curtin, 'Disease and Imperialism', in David Arnold (ed.), *Warm Climates and Western Medicine: The Emergence of Tropical Medicine, 1500*-1900, Amsterdam-Atlanta, GA: Rodopi, 1996, p. 99.
3. Sumit Guha, 'Nutrition, Sanitation, Hygiene, and the Likelihood of Death: The British Army in India *c.* 1870-1920', *Population Studies*, vol. 47, 1993, pp. 389-90.
4. David Arnold, *Colonizing the Body: State Medicine and Epidemic Disease in Nineteenth Century India*, Delhi, 1993, pp. 2-10.
5. Mark Harrison, 'A Question of Locality: The Identity of Cholera in British India, 1860-1890', in David Arnold (ed.), *Warm Climates and Western Medicine*, p. 133.
6. Jadunath Sarkar, *Fall of the Mughal Empire: 1754-71*, vol. 2, 1934, reprint, New Delhi, 1991, p. 73.
7. M.N. Pearson, 'First Contacts between Indian and European Medical Systems: Goa in the Sixteenth Century', in Arnold (ed.), *Warm Climates and Western Medicine*, pp. 23-4.

8. Michael A. Osborne, 'Resurrecting Hippocrates: Hygienic Sciences and the French Scientific Expeditions to Egypt, Morea and Algeria', in Arnold (ed.), *Warm Climates and Western Medicine*, p. 81; Michael Worboys, 'Germs, Malaria and the Invention of Mansonian Tropical Medicine: From "Diseases in the Tropics" to "Tropical Diseases"', in Arnold (ed.), *Warm Climates and Western Medicine*, p. 183.
9. Brigadier R.C. Butalia, *The Evolution of the Artillery in India: From the Battle of Plassey (1757) to the Revolt of 1857*, New Delhi, 1998, p. 178.
10. 'The Bengal Artillery', Article V, *Calcutta Review*, vol. 9, 1848, p. 504.
11. Lieutenant-Colonel W.J. Wilson, *History of the Madras Army*, vol. 2, Madras, 1882, p. 182.
12. Ibid., vol. 1, Madras, 1882, pp. 114, 226.
13. Arnold, *Colonizing the Body*, p. 92.
14. Lieutenant Adjutant Carter, Record Book of 28th Bombay Infantry Regiment: 1846-1913, vol. 46, Military Miscellaneous, Military Department (hereafter MD), National Archives of India (henceforth NAI), New Delhi. This volume is not paginated and the information is organized under various dates. 1846; 1 April 1851; 9 Nov. 1852; 7 Dec. 1852; 10 Feb. 1853.
15. A. Ghosh (ed.), *History of the Armed Forces Medical Services India*, New Delhi, 1988, p. 63.
16. Major D.H. Cole and Major E.C. Priestley, *An Outline of British Military History: 1600-1937*, London, 1937, p. 199.
17. Ghosh (ed.), *Armed Forces Medical Services*, p. 64.
18. G.W. Forrest, *A History of the Indian Mutiny Reviewed and Illustrated from Original Documents*, vol. 1, 1904, reprint, Delhi, 1992, p. 131.
19. Ghosh (ed.), *Armed Forces Medical Services*, p. 66.
20. Ibid., p. 65.
21. Mark Harrison, *Public Health in British India: Anglo-Indian Preventive Medicine, 1859-1914*, New Delhi, 1994, pp. 56-7.
22. Harrison, 'Medicine and the Management of Modern Warfare', in Idem, Cooter and Sturdy (eds.), *Medicine and Modern Warfare*, p. 3.
23. Kenneth F. Kiple and Kriemhild Conee Ornelas, 'Race, War and Tropical Medicine in the Eighteenth Century Caribbean', in Arnold (ed.), *Warm Climates and Western Medicine*, pp. 68, 70.
24. Field Marshal Viscount Montgomery of Alamein, *A History of Warfare*, London, 1968, p. 426.
25. Richard L. Blanco, 'The Attempted Control of Venereal Disease in the Army of Mid-Victorian England', *Journal of the Society for Army Historical Research*, vol. 45, 1967, p. 234.
26. Mark Harrison, *Climates and Constitutions: Health, Race, Environment and British Imperialism in India, 1600-1850* (New Delhi, 1999), pp. 43, 153.

27. Curtin, 'Disease and Imperialism', in Arnold (ed.), *Warm Climates and Western Medicine*, p. 106.
28. J.T.H. Connor, '"Before the World in Concealed Disgrace": Physicians, Professionalization and the 1898 Cuban Campaign of the Spanish American War', in Cooter, Harrison and Sturdy (eds.), *Medicine and Modern Warfare*, p. 34.
29. Roger Cooter and Steve Sturdy, 'Of War, Medicine and Modernity: Introduction', in Cooter, Mark Harrison and Sturdy (eds.), *War, Medicine and Modernity*, Phoenix Mill, Thrupp, Stroud, 1998, p. 17.
30. Some welfare measures related to the construction of better barracks and hospitals for the sepoys and *sowars* is studied in Kaushik Roy's, 'Logistics and the Construction of Loyalty: The Welfare Mechanism in the Indian Army, 1859-1913', in P.S. Gupta and Anirudh Deshpande (eds.), *The British Raj and its Indian Armed Forces: 1857-1939*, New Delhi, 2002, pp. 99-116.
31. Harrison, 'A Question of Locality', in Arnold (ed.), *Warm Climates and Western Medicine*, p. 136.
32. From Dr. J Forsyth, Medical Department, Principal Inspector General, to Lieutenant-Colonel H.W. Norman, Secretary to the GoI, MD, Fort William, 13 February 1862, Progs. no. 329, Military Department Proceedings (henceforth MDP), August 1862, NAI.
33. From Lieutenant-Colonel H.W. Norman, Secretary to the GoI, MD, to the Officialing Adjutant General of the Army, Fort William, 13 August 1862, Progs. no. 331, MDP, August 1862.
34. *Report of the Sanitary Commission for Bombay 1864*, Bombay, Byculla, 1865, p. 211, National Library (henceforth NL), Kolkata.
35. 'Cholera', Memo by Napier, Poona, 16 May 1869, Notes and Minutes by Napier of Magdala Commander-in-Chief, Bombay, 1866-9, MSS. EUR.F.114, I©, Oriental and India Office Collection (hereafter OIOC), British Library, London.
36. Records of Chief Commands 1865-76, Appendix B, Expenditure, Madras Army, 1871, Notes and Minutes by Napier.
37. Digest of Services of the 3rd Cavalry Regiment of the Hyderabad Contingent, December 1868, MD, NAI.
    This document is unpaginated and the information is organized under various year.
38. Guha, 'Nutrition, Sanitation, Hygiene and the Likelihood of Death', p. 390.
39. Harrison, *Climates and Constitutions*, p. 22.
40. Douglas M. Peers, 'Imperial Vice: Sex, Drink and the Health of British Troops in North Indian Cantonments, 1800-58', in David Killingray and David Omissi (eds.), *Guardians of Empire: The Armed Forces of the Colonial Powers c. 1700-1964*, Manchester, 1999, p. 31.
41. From E.H. Lushington, Officialing Secretary to the Govt. of Bengal,

to the Officialing Secretary to the GoI, MD, Camp Bankipore, Progs. no. 91, 21 February 1860, MDP.

42. Roberts to Lord Napier, Bangalore, 10 October 1884, in Brian Robson (ed.), *Roberts in India: The Military Papers of Field Marshal Lord Roberts, 1876-93*, Stroud, Gloucestershire: Alan Sutton for the Army Records Society, 1993, p. 311.
43. General Orders by the Commander-in-Chief, Calcutta, no. 149, 2 March 1870, NAI.
44. 28th Bombay Infantry Regiment, April 1872-3.
45. Ibid., June-October 1901.
46. Harrison, *Public Health in British India*, pp. 38, 44.
47. Letter from Geo S. White to HRH, 2 December 1893, no. 57cc, George White Collection, MSS.EUR.108/18, OIOC.
48. *Proceedings of the Army in India Committee 1912*, vol. 3, Simla, 1913, Minutes of Evidence, Sloggett Examined, p. 800, NAI.
49. *Proceedings of the Army in India Committee 1912*, vol. 3, Sloggett Examined, p. 801.
50. 'Meat Supply for Troops', Minute by Napier, Poona, 22 October 1866 Notes and Minutes by Napier.
51. Roberts to Napier, 10 October 1884, in Robson (ed.), *Roberts in India*, p. 311.
52. 28th Bombay Infantry Regiment, 1900.
53. Ibid., June 1903.
54. Ibid., 16 March 1907.
55. Blanco, 'The Attempted Control of Venereal Disease in the Army', p. 237.
56. *Report of the Sanitary Commission for Bombay 1864*, p. 212.
57. 'Prevention of Venereal Disease', Minute by Lieutenant-General R. Napier, 27 August 1866, Notes and Minutes by Napier of Magdala Commander-in-Chief Bombay, 1866-9.
58. 'Prevention of Venereal Disease', Minute by R. Napier, 29 May 1866, Notes and Minutes by Napier.
59. Brian Bond, *The Victorian Army and the Staff College: 1854-1914*, London, 1972, p. 8.
60. 'Visitations of Cholera as Connected with the General Health and Sanitary Conditions of the Indian Population', Minute by Napier, 18 June 1868, Notes and Minutes by Napier.
61. Harrison, *Public Health in British India*, p. 75.
62. 'Mackinnon on the Burma Campaign', *Indian Medical Gazette* (henceforth *IMG*), vol. 25, January 1890, p. 27, AIMS Library, New Delhi.
63. Letter from White to HRH, 2 December 1893, 57cc, White Collection.
64. Letter to the Duke of Cambridge, Simla, 4 September 1894, Letter no. 90, LB 13, White Collection.

65. Peers, 'Imperial Vice', in Killingray and Omissi (eds.), *Guardians of Empire*, p. 34.
66. *Proceedings of the Army in India Committee, 1912*, vol. 3, Sloggett Examined, p. 805.
67. John Keegan, *The Face of Battle: A Study of Agincourt, Waterloo and the Somme*, 1976, reprint, Harmondsworth, Middlesex, 1978, p. 183.
68. Records of Chief Commands 1865-76, Inspection Reports of the Madras Army 1874-5, Notes and Minutes by Napier.
69. *Report of the Sanitary Commission for Bombay 1864*, p. 212.
70. Letter to the Duke of Cambridge, 1 August 1893, no. 34cc, LB 13, Book no. 3, White Collection.
71. Letter to Cambridge, Simla, 17 July 1894, Letter no. 82, White Collection.
72. Major R.G. Burton, *History of the Hyderabad Contingent*, Calcutta, 1905, p. 309.
73. Digest of Services of the 3rd Brahmin Infantry Regiment, 1861-1914, MD, State of the Regiment on 8 March 1864, NAI. This document at times is unpaginated and the information is organized under various headings and years.
74. 3rd Brahmin Infantry Regiment, State on 17 April 1866.
75. Ibid., 5 March 1868.
76. Ibid., 22 February 1869.
77. Ibid., 5 April 1870.
78. Records of Chief Commands, 1865-76, Inspection Reports of the Madras Army for 1874-5, Notes and Minutes by Napier.
79. General Frederick Roberts, *Correspondence with England while Commander-in-Chief in Madras: 1881-85*, Simla: Govt. Central Printing Office, 1890, To the Duke of Cambridge, no. XLIX, 21 July 1883, p. 96, L/MIL/17/5/1615, Part 3, OIOC.
80. Mark Harrison, *Medicine & Victory: British Military Medicine in the Second World War*, Oxford, 2004, p. 283.
81. From Colonel W.B. Thomson, Commissary General, to the Officialing Secretary to the GoI, MD, Fort William, Progs. no. 318, 24 February 1860, MDP.
82. From R.B. Chapman, Under Secretary to the GoI, Home Dept., Progs. no. 86, 29 February 1860, NAI.
83. 3rd Brahmin Infantry Regiment, p. 26.
84. Ibid., p. 27.
85. E.D. Smith, *Valour: A History of the Gurkhas*, 1997, reprint, New York: The Overlook Press, 1998, pp. 38-9.
86. 3rd Brahmin Infantry Regiment, 1887, March 1888, 31 March 1891.
87. Ibid., Para 90-1.
88. Ibid., p. 23.
89. 3rd Brahmin Regiment, p. 21.

90. Roberts to Colley, Private, Camp Alikehl, 10 December 1878, in Robson (ed.), *Roberts in India*, p. 37.
91. Lieutenant F.G. Cardew, *A Sketch of the Services of the Bengal Native Army to the Year* 1895, 1903, reprint, New Delhi, 1971, p. 347.
92. Wilson, *Madras Army*, vol. 1, p. 114.
93. Diary of E.H.E. Collen, Royal Artillery Officer in North West Frontier Expedition, 1897-8, p. 28, NAI.
94. From Major-General P.S. Lumsden, Adjutant General in India, to Colonel H.K. Burne, Secretary to GoI, MD, HQ, Simla, 5 July 1879, Progs. no. 7213, MDP, February 1880.
95. Lumsden to Burne, 5 July 1879, Progs. no. 7213, MDP, February 1880.
96. From Surgeon H.G. Archdall, 30th Madras Infantry Regiment, Senior Medical Officer, Camp Vitakri, to Officer Commanding Camp Vitakri, File no. 124, 18 October 1879, MDP, February 1880.
97. 28th Bombay Infantry Regiment, 1880.
98. 'Accommodation, Scheme for Continued Maintenance of Communications with Chitral by the Dir Chitral Route', by Major-General A.R. Badcock, Proceedings of the Govt. of India, MD, Malakand, 1897-8, NAI.
99. General Order by Roberts, Kabul, 15 February 1880, in Robson (ed.), *Roberts in India*, p. 162.
100. 28th Bombay Infantry Regiment, 7 November 1880.
101. *Appendices to the Report of the Special Commission Appointed by the Governor General to Enquire into the Organization and Expenditure of the Army in India*, vol. 4, Calcutta: Govt. Central Press, 1880, Appendix XLV, p. 1653, NL, Kolkata.
102. *Report of the Special Commission Appointed by the Governor General in Council to Enquire into the Organization and Expenditure of the Army in India*, Simla: Govt. Central Branch Press, 1879, p. 130, NAI.
103. From Colonel T.C. George, Commandant, 30th Infantry Regiment, to the Deputy Assistant Adjutant General, Lahore Division, Camp Vitakri, 19 October 1879, Progs. no. 410, MDP, February 1880.
104. From Lieutenant-Colonel G.A. Prendergast, commanding 15th Bengal Cavalry, and commanding at Vitakri, to the Quarter Master General (hereafter QMG) in India, Progs. no. 7152, MDP, February 1880.
105. Prendergast to the QMG, 3 September 1879, Progs. no. 7152, MDP, February 1880.
106. Note on the necessity for increasing the efficiency of the Native Army, Simla, 25 September 1886, in Robson (ed.), *Roberts in India*, p. 352.
107. George Hamilton to Elgin, Confidential, no. 153, 12 November 1897, Accession no 1573, Reel no. 2, Hamilton Papers, Microfilm, NAI.
108. Medical Arrangements for the Burma Expeditionary Force, From Surgeon-General, HM's Force, Bengal, to Secretary to the GoI, MD,

Simla, Progs. no. 46, 21 October 1885, Proceedings of the GoI, MD, Burma, 1885-6, NAI; 'Mackinnon on the Burma Campaign', pp. 24-6.

109. Medical Arrangement, Progs. no. 46, Para 27, Proceedings, Burma.
110. 'Mackinnon on the Burma Campaign', p. 26.
111. Ibid., p. 27.
112. Harrison, *Medicine and Victory*, p. 278.
113. Cole and Priestley, *British Military History*, p. 173.
114. Ghosh (ed.), *Armed Forces Medical Services*, p. 62.
115. 3rd Cavalry Regiment of the Hyderabad Contingent, Report by Colonel Commandant, 1887.
116. Connor, '"Before the World in Concealed Disgrace"', in Cooter, Harrison and Sturdy (eds.), *Medicine and Modern Warfare*, pp. 30-1.
117. Cole and Priestley, *British Military History*, p. 282.
118. Claire Herrick, '"The Conquest of the Silent Foe": British and American Military Medical Reform Rhetoric and the Russo-Japanese War', in Cooter, Harrison and Sturdy (eds.), *Medicine and Modern Warfare*, Endnote 63, pp. 121-2.
119. David Arnold, 'Introduction: Tropical Medicine before Manson', in Idem (ed.), *Warm Climates and Western Medicine*, pp. 1, 4.
120. Worboys, 'Germs, Malaria and the Invention of Mansonian Tropical Medicine', in Arnold (ed.), *Warm Climates and Western Medicine*, p. 181.
121. Michael Worboys, 'Almroth Wright at Netley: Modern Medicine and the Military in Britain, 1892-1902', in Cooter, Harrison and Sturdy (eds.), *Medicine and Modern Warfare*, pp. 77-8.
122. Mark Harrison, 'Sex and the Citizen Soldier: Health, Morals and Discipline in the British Army During the Second World War', in Idem, Cooter and Sturdy (eds.), *Medicine and Modern Warfare*, p. 227.
123. Mark Harrison, 'Disease, Discipline and Dissent: The Indian Army in France and England, 1914-15', in Idem, Cooter and Sturdy (eds.), *Medicine and Modern Warfare*, p. 187.
124. Arnold, *Colonizing the Body*, pp. 95-6.
125. Sanitary Report Maneuvers Mandalay Brigade 1911, p. 1, GP 62375(591)3927, Annexe Building, NL.
126. Sanitary Report Mandalay Brigade 1911, p. 2.
127. Ibid., p. 3.
128. *Proceedings of the Army in India Committee, 1912*, vol. 3, Sloggett Examined, p. 819.

8. Plague and Prophylactics: Ecological Construction of an Epidemic in Colonial Eastern India

Arabinda Samanta

This paper seeks to engage in two things. First, it intends to explore how the plague epidemic in colonial eastern India during the closing years of the nineteenth and the opening decade of the twentieth centuries was constructed in official perceptions as a disease of dirt and filth, and as such led to an ecological construction of the disease. Second, it identifies the contested terrains that arguably informed the perception of the colonial masters about ecological disruption, and led to a protracted showdown with the native contenders.

Epidemic diseases are more often than not functions of environmental decay and ecological disruption. The plague in eastern India, particularly in the capital city of Calcutta, was a vexing dilemma for the government. The insanitary and unhygienic conditions of the towns and villages in eastern India were held responsible for the outbreak of the epidemic plague. To improve the situation by reducing rodent population, roofs were removed, floors dug up, and houses flooded with disinfectant. The rats simply moved away and spread the infection with renewed vengeance. By pumping the sewers with disinfectants, rats were again driven into houses and carried with them fleas that infected the inhabitants. It proved a vicious circle exit from which was well nigh impossible.

The British in India realized that the country would never be safe enough so long as the native population and its towns and countries were left uncleansed to act as a reservoir of dirt and disease. But despite an overarching perception of threat of disease, sanitation and sewers, town planning and public health never seemed to figure prominently in the project of colonial imperatives. The colonial state was not willing to incur the cost involved. Nor was it keen to bear the political risks of sanitizing India. For such a project would require the British to meddle deeply and dangerously in the habits and customs of the natives.[1]

If the problem of public health was thus conceived in terms which could not possibly allow its resolution, the view expressed in the officialdom was that if the natives preferred to live amidst filth, it was their fate designed by their own tradition. It was from this official perception that the colonial state formulated its strategy to combat the plague. Instead of negotiating the epidemic medically, they sought to develop a prophylactic mechanism, which amounted to an ecological construction of the disease. The present paper seeks to identify the multiple sites which tended to underpin the divide between plague and prophylactic, and environment and disease.

The Great Pandemics of Plague

The first definitely established pandemic of plague occurred in the sixth century AD and was known as the Plague of Justinian. The disease broke out in Egypt and spread 'to the ends of the inhabitable world'. The number of victims of this pandemic, which lasted over 50 years, is sometimes estimated as high as 100 million, and the historian Gibbon in his masterly summary considers this staggering figure within the bounds of possibility.

The second pandemic of plague, the Black Death, began in the neighbourhood of Constantinople and spread westward through Europe in the early months of 1348. It is clearly described by Guy de Chauliac, body physician to Pope Clement VI, and was the subject of nearly 300 'plague tracts', popular treatises which were intended to teach people how to cope with the appalling menace. These tracts represent the first large-scale effort ever made to educate the public in health matters.[2] The social dislocation, which resulted from the Black Death, was in some ways even more serious than the immediate mortality. A.L. Maycock has said that 'the year 1348 marks the nearest approach to a definite break in the continuity of history which has ever occurred'.

After the initial catastrophe of 1348 plague continued to rage in Europe for more than three centuries. The last major outbreak of the pandemic occurred as 'the great plague' of London in 1665, immortalized by Daniel De Foe. In the week of 19-26 September the statistical report of the city showed 8,297 deaths from all causes, of which 7,165 deaths were due to plague.[3] At the end of the seventeenth century the disease died out in Europe; the reason for this decline remains a puzzle for epidemiologists. Many theories have been advanced such as decrease in trade with heavily infected Eastern countries, control of the rats by better sanitation, and replacement of the house rat by the sewer rat, which has less intensive contact with human beings; but none of these hypotheses are wholly convincing. It is suggested by some authorities that cyclical changes may occur in the virulence or in some other characteristics of the germ itself.

Plague did certainly persist in Asia, and in the late nineteenth century broke out in the third great pandemic of this disease. Its increase began to be noted in South China about 1870 and at Canton and Hong Kong in 1894, and shortly reached most of the larger seaports of the world. Plague appeared at Bombay in 1896. By 1904, there were more than a million deaths from the disease in India; by the end of 1936, 40 years of plague in India had killed more than 12 million people.

The Rat, the Flea, and Man

Any contagious and fatal epidemic disease was originally called a plague (from *plaga*, a stroke). But this term is now applied to that particular kind of plague which is characterized by the appearance of high fever with inflammation of lymphatic glands or bubo, and is therefore called the Bubonic Plague. In Sanskrit medical books it has been described as *Vidradhi* and *Visharpa*, and in *Yunani* as *Taoon*.[4]

By the end of the nineteenth century medical tracts emerging from Bombay sought to locate the aetiology of the disease in climate and social position. The climate and season, they argued, had 'special influence' upon the onset of plague.[5] A moderate amount of heat as a rule was found to be favourable to its occurrence, whereas a very high or low temperature was unfavourable to it. But, they argued, there had been exceptions; it had prevailed during the severest winter on the Volga and in Moscow, and in extreme heat, as in Smyrna.[6] As regards social position, it was argued that poverty had been found to be the chief predisposing cause of plague. The Great Plague of London of 1665, which was called the Poor's Plague, and of Baghdad and Mesopotamia in 1878 where it was called by Cabiadis as *miseriae morbus* are illustrations of this fact. But in Bombay, poverty had nothing whatever to do with the outbreak of the disease. There had been neither famine nor poverty; it broke out there among the well-to-do classes.[7]

A disease so fatal in its nature and against which human power was so futile was in ancient times naturally attributed to wrath of the gods. Supernatural, astrological and in some instances rationalistic causes were assigned to it. In the fourteenth century the College of Physicians of Paris ascribed it to the influence of constellations in India. But more natural explanations however followed. Putrefaction of dead animals was assigned as a cause in Egypt, as was the poisoning of water supply. Undue heat, rain, night sweats, and absence of the Etesian winds were thought to cause plague.

Leaving the ancient theories on the causation of the disease, we find that scientists in the late nineteenth century divided themselves into two classes: those who believed in the germ theory and attributed plague to a specific germ, holding that germs can never arise *de novo*; second, those who believed that atmospheric changes and certain telluric conditions or insanitary surroundings engender the seeds of pestilence which are carried through air, water or other media.[8] The arguments in favour of the first theory were however so strong that it was almost universally accepted that plague was due to a specific poison which grew and multiplied under favourable conditions, and that wherever it occurred it was caused by the implantation of those germs in a suitable soil. The soil best suited for the plague seed was one where insanitary conditions prevailed. Dirt and filth, bad ventilation, and overcrowding were supposed to be its manure.

The causative agent of plague, a bacterium, was discovered very early in the late pandemic, and the intimate relation among rat plague, the flea, and human plague was also elucidated. During the Hong Kong epidemic, the great Japanese bacteriologist S. Kitasato, who formerly worked with Koch in Germany, described a bacillus in plague-stricken patients, and showed by experiments that those bacilli if injected into lower animals produced in them symptoms of plague. A. Yersin simultaneously discovered the same germs in connection with plague. Kitasato and Yersin argued that these germs must be considered to be the specific poison which produced the symptoms of plague. The bacilli were found in the blood, in the buboes, and in all internal organs of the victims of plague.[9] Thus in 1894 in Hong Kong, Yersin and Kitasato described the plague bacillus. In 1897, M. Ogata isolated the organism from rat fleas. In 1898, P.L. Simond claimed the demonstration of flea transmission.[10]

By the closing years of the nineteenth century it was maintained that plague was a miasmatic or soil-bred disease, and that the germs found in earth, water or in some form of fermenting or decomposing material a suitable nidus for growth. In this sense it was like malaria, which was endemic in a particular suitable area, appearing and disappearing as climate or other conditions were favourable or unfavourable. The Chinese had a peculiar idea of the infection of plague. They thought it to rise from the soil, and believed that it first attacked small animals with breathing organs near the soil, such as rats, then animals with breathing organs a little higher, such as poultry, dogs, goats, cows, so on till it reached man whose breathing organs are higher from the soil than those of other animals.[11]

Rats are undoubtedly infected with plague before and during the disease's prevalence among human beings. Rats even play an important part in the spread of plague infection. In Kumaon this rat plague was recognized as a forerunner of the plague. *The Times of India* observed on 30 September 1896:

> It was known more than a month ago to all the people of Mandavi and to all municipal sweepers in the district that the rats were dying in thousands all over the districts. They were found dead and dying almost everywhere, and in places where dead rats were never found before.

It was ten years later however that the whole problem was analysed in a rigidly scientific fashion by a plague commission appointed by the Government of India. The commission in its report presented a survey of human plague cases in relation to the prevalence of the disease in rats in the same localities. This study showed a close and roughly quantitative relation between the epizootic among rats and the epidemic among human beings, the course of the former preceding that of the latter by one or two weeks.

Later sections of the report gave epidemiological evidence to show that direct transmission of plague from man to man is not an important factor, that insanitary conditions are significant only in so far as they favour breeding and harbouring of rats, and that the spread of plague from one locality to another is generally due to imported rat fleas on the bodies or in the luggage of persons who themselves are often in good health. It is probable that the infected rat plays a major role in place-to-place dissemination. In transport of the disease by sea, the rat is undoubtedly the chief agent. So far as the rat-flea-man links in the chain are concerned the commission laid a sound basis for knowledge in this field.[12]

History of Plague in Eastern India

The first known case of plague in Calcutta was discovered in April 1898, and at the end of that month the city was declared infected.[13] It continued to be so until October of the same year, when cases ceased to be reported, and the city was accordingly declared free from plague. During these six months, attacks and deaths reported were 230 and 192 respectively. The outbreak therefore cannot be said to have been an epidemic, as that word is commonly understood.

During the next four months the disease remained quiescent. A few isolated cases were reported which bacteriological examination showed to be plague. There were a considerable number of cases in which the cause of death was not sufficiently apparent, and it was considered advisable to disinfect the houses in which they had occurred. The mortality during the whole of this period was above the average, and in the opinion of the health officer the greater part of the excess was in fact due to plague.

It was not however till the end of February 1899 that the existence of plague was sufficiently demonstrated to warrant a declaration that Calcutta was again infected. This outbreak lasted until the end of June 1899, and during these four months 1,336 cases and 1,223 deaths from plague were reported.[14] It was however the decided opinion of the two medical officers who dealt with the disease during this period that the above figures by no means represented the actual mortality for which plague was responsible. What true plague mortality was can only be conjectured. There appears to have been extensive concealment of cases, and the estimates of the authority vary, the highest being slightly over 3,000. This was reached in March and April. From April onwards it fell rapidly, and in June the mortality rate was again normal. During the second half of 1899, 1,131 cases were reported as plague, and 898 as 'suspicious'.

In 1900 the disease assumed very different proportions, and became for the first time an epidemic. Between January and June, 7,897 cases and 7,373 deaths from plague were reported.[15] Of these deaths, 3,667 cases or nearly half of the total occurred in March, and 1,996 in April, after which the virulence of the epidemic abated rapidly. During this period cases were freely reported, and the Chairman of the Medical Board appointed by the Government showed by an interesting set of figures that information was obtained of practically all deaths due to plague.

The total mortality due to plague in Calcutta from its first outbreak in April 1898 down to 30 June 1900, a period of two years and three months, had been according to the official returns, 10,997. If in accordance with the opinion of the chairman and medical authorities, suspicious cases and excess mortality not otherwise accounted for were put down to plague, the total might be fixed at 13,000 in round numbers.

A striking feature of the plague in Calcutta was the continued prominence of Ward No. V, Jorabagan, and this was still more noticeable when the figures for 1907 which accounted for more than all the other periods together were examined. During that period no less than 1,555 cases occurred in Ward No. V, or more than the total of any other two wards together. Describing the southern portion of the ward, Dr. Simpson writes:

> Everyone I have taken over the area . . . is unanimous in condemning

it as unfit for human habitation and a source of danger to the town.... The narrow, ill-ventilated streets; the passages to which neither light nor fresh air have access; the filthy condition of both; the close proximity of the houses to one another, and their overcrowded state, combine to form conditions which render proper sanitation impossible. It is a standing menace to the rest of the city; and should plague once obtain a firm footing in this quarter, which is the worst I am acquainted with in any city I have seen, there is every likelihood of the disease becoming endemic.

By 1900 plague was rampant in Gaya, Mungher, Bhagalpur, Bukhtiarpur, Dinajpur, Chakberia. The authorities were thinking of the expedience of using force for evacuating and disinfecting the infected houses and villages.[16]

PROPHYLACTIC INTERVENTION REVISITED

Plague in India was primarily a disease of the long-tailed house rat, *rattus*. Other rodents were of comparatively little importance. They were less numerous, they tended to live in sewers or fields rather than in houses and some varieties did not harbour many plague fleas. In the vast majority of cases man was infected more or less accidentally by hungry infected rat-fleas, which had strayed from the carcasses of house rats, which had died of plague.[17] When there was epidemic plague among rats the severity of the human epidemic depended on the closeness of the association of rats and man. Human plague would cease to be a serious problem, it was believed, when man no longer provided food and shelter for rats in our houses. The real anti-plague measure, it was argued, was therefore 'rat-exclusion'.[18] This entailed a radical change in the habits and housing conditions of the people, which it was argued would come about eventually through education and social uplift.

It had been the practice to deal with plague outbreaks by certain time-honoured temporary measures, namely (i) evacuation, (ii) inoculation with anti-plague vaccine, and (iii) rat destruction by trapping and poison-baiting. These measures had undoubtedly controlled plague epidemics to a considerable extent.

When plague attacked Calcutta, Mungher and Patna in 1898 certain measures had been formulated and prescribed for general adoption throughout India by the British Government. These included carefully enforced death registration, house-to-house visitation, segregation of the sick and of contacts, the evacuation of infected localities, disinfection, and the enforcement of general sanitary precautions. The Government of Bengal too issued certain regulations to combat the epidemic by prophylactic intervention.[19]

Right of Entry and Examination: The owner and occupier of any house should permit the health officer to enter the premises and examine any person whom the health officer had reason to believe to be infected with bubonic plague. If the person be a female who according to the custom of the country did not appear in public the examination should be made through a female doctor, female hospital assistant or other female agency.[20]

Segregation: If on examination the health officer suspected any person was suffering from or infected with plague he might cause such person to be removed to a hospital, and might arrange for his detention, dieting and medical treatment therein. He might also cause the other occupants of the house in which such a person resided to be removed to a segregation camp and to be detained under observation for ten days. The relatives, friends, *hakims*, *baids*, priests of sick persons would be allowed free access to them during day time, subject only to such precautions as the health officer might consider necessary.[21]

Disposal of Dead: The friends of the deceased should be permitted to dispose of the corpse by cremation or burial in accordance with their religious practices, but they should obey the directions of the health officer or other sanitary or executive authorities as to the time, route, and method of removing the corpse to the burial or cremation place. The corpses of Europeans or Mohammedans who died of plague should be buried if possible at least six feet deep. The place of burial if not an authorized cemetery should be far from inhabitations and should so situate that there might be no risk of contaminating sources of water supply. In case where cremation was the custom the body should be completely burned at the usual burning ghat or other isolated locality in accordance with customs, the clothes brought in contact with the body being either burnt according to customs or disinfected.[22]

Inoculation: In 1900 the Government of Bengal had ordered the district officers to resort to Mr. Haffkine's system of anti-plague inoculation. In 1903 it modified the order and argued that inoculation should be *encouraged* wherever possible, and that in places which were threatened with a visitation of plague, no efforts should be spared to *explain* to the people the advantage of becoming inoculated before the disease was among them.[23] It was at the same time strictly enjoined that compulsion must on no account be resorted to, and that the choice whether or not they would be inoculated must entirely be left to the people. In Patna Division, in Mungher, and probably in other districts of the Bhagalpur Division, nothing must be done for the present, for, it was argued, in the present temper of the people, the mere mention of inoculation would probably create a panic and intensify the difficulty of obtaining early information of the occurrence of plague.

Prophylactic Measures in Practice

In eastern India the provisions regarding segregation and evacuation were modified by offering inoculation as an alternative, and by permitting isolation in private houses of the better classes. People were up in arms in June 1900 in connection with plague regulations regarding evacuation and disinfection. This was particularly so at Bukhtiarpur, Dinajpur and Chakberia in Patna District, at Chaitantola in Monghyr and elsewhere.[24] The Lt. Governor of Bengal therefore directed that local officers should abstain from employing force for the purpose of carrying out evacuation and disinfection. They should encourage people to adopt them in every way, by advice, by persuasion, and by supplying them with desired materials and labour. If any person or class of persons nevertheless refuses to comply, force should not be used to coerce them.[25]

In spite of this, however, the first appearance of plague was signaled by unprecedented panic and exodus from the towns of Calcutta, Mungher and Patna, and by several disturbances. Fortunately the outbreak in Calcutta was but a slight one, and it served the purpose of indicating how far the general policy prescribed till then was practicable in Calcutta. When plague reappeared in the succeeding year, the government's policy was stated in a resolution of which the following is an extract:

> In order that effective measures may be taken to prevent the spread of infection, it is of the first importance that every case, which occurs, shall be promptly brought to notice of the authorities. Foreign Governments would have just cause for complaint if the regulations in force were repugnant to the sense of the people affected as to drive them to withhold information and hide away their sick instead of bringing them forward for treatment.[26]

Compulsory removal to hospital and segregation were accordingly abolished. The policy, which had been followed from that time, was that of making every effort to obtain information of cases, and of inducing people to accept the measures which experience had indicated to be of most avail in preventing the spread of the disease. Of these the principal, in fact, practically the only one generally used in Calcutta had been disinfection. The measures were:

INFORMATION OF PLAGUE CASES

Such measures as house-to-house visitation and the offer of rewards for information of cases had never even been suggested in Calcutta; nor had penalties for not volunteering information been enforced, except in occasional instances. Volunteer agencies had in many instances done most valuable work, but the task of reporting cases was not one with which they had been able to cope, except to a limited extent.

From the beginning of June 1898 however a new feature of some significance appeared in the weekly returns. This was close approximation of the number of cases with the number of deaths. In the 20 weekly returns from 2 June to 13 October 1898 the numbers had been identical in nine returns, and in none of the remainder had the figures differed by more than four.[27] If the figures were correct, they would denote that virtually every case of plague terminated fatally. This is of course not the truth. Roughly speaking, the proportion of plague attacks which ended in death was 80 per cent. If it may be assumed that all deaths due to plague had been traced, these figures would indicate that during the period in question some 470 cases ending in recovery escaped discovery.

Meanwhile the total mortality from all cases had been in excess of the normal. The average number of deaths from all cases from 1 June to 13 October 1898 was 7,213, whereas the actuals had been 10,207, showing an excess of 2,994 or more than 40 per cent. When all due allowance had been made for the known prevalence of malarial fever and for deaths due directly to the floods of September, these figures are disquietening, and suggest that a certain number of deaths due to plague had escaped record. If there had been failure in the procedure of investigation, it is of significance; for the sheet anchor of the plague policy observed in Calcutta was disinfection of every room or apartment in which a case occurred, whether ending fatally or not. And if non-fatal cases were not discovered, the work of disinfection must be incomplete. This emphasizes the importance of the more widely extended process of disinfectioning.

DISINFECTION

Of the recognized preventives against plague, disinfection had been practically the only one on which reliance had been placed in Calcutta. The procedure throughout had been to disinfect every room in which either a case of ascertained plague or a case suspected to be plague had occurred. Thus, between January and June 1899, only 1,336 cases of ascertained plague were reported, but 4,750 premises were disinfected. And since February 1900, this policy had been extended to the disinfection of whole *bustees* or streets in any part of which a case of plague occurred. From 1 January to 8 September 1900, 42,314 rooms had been subjected to 'extra-infection'.[28]

In carrying out these measures, the Chairman of the Medical Board rightly observed that the influence of men of local standing was enormous. He quoted three instances, in which local opposition was readily overcome by invoking the aid of the landowners Raja Binoy Krishna Bahadur, Maharaja Sir Narendra Krishna, and Babu Sarat Chandra Mukherji respectively.

In many places human plague disappeared in the hot weather only to resurface in the following cold season. It was then realized that the temperature and humidity in the depths of rat burrows were such that plague infection might continue among rats and fleas over the hot weather. Further, experiments in Madras Presidency in the 1930s had shown that infected rat fleas remain capable of conveying plague infection after as long as 29 days' starvation in rat burrows.[29]

By the 1930s certain known methods of destroying fleas were found to be of little value. Thus disinfection of grain by exposure to the heat of the sun or in hot air chambers had been largely given up. The use of kerosene oil emulsion to spray plague-infected houses was of some value but it could not affect fleas hidden in burrows or crevices or under rubbish.

A note on 'trapping and baiting as anti-plague measures' by Dr. G.D. Chitre was circulated in 1919 and these methods were widely employed. Various fumigants such as sulphur dioxide and carbon bisulphide had been used from time to time. Hydro cyanic acid (HCN) gas was recognized as the fumigant of choice as far as the lethal effect on rats and fleas was concerned. By 1930s experiments had been carried out in the Cumbum Valley in Madras Presidency, and also in Bombay and Lahore under the auspices of the Indian Research Fund Association, the Travancore Durbar and the Bombay and Punjab governments with the hope that HCN fumigation of rat burrows might prove a more effective means of arresting plague and might even be successful in obliterating endemic plague.[30]

SERUM THERAPY

Serum therapy in 1897 was at an interesting stage of development, but as a practical method of treatment it was of uncertain value. Laboratory prophylactic experiments with anti-plague serum had been so successful that its use as a preventive or protective measure might perhaps ultimately allow modification of the segregation thought so necessary in dealing with Asiatic suspects.[31] Even a weak anti-toxic serum gave good results but as a curative agent in practical medicine, it had been a comparative failure in Bombay and in China, in spite of statements to the contrary. This failure was scarcely to be wondered at because the serum employed was admittedly of weak anti-toxic power. Moreover the practical difficulty of bringing the patients under treatment early enough to give him a fair chance of recovery had been against the success of serum therapy.[32]

INOCULATION

Inoculation of vaccine material was carried on by Haffkine in Bombay Presidency, but with what success it is difficult to say. Figures given of what occurred in the House of Correction, would show that its use was of benefit, but such figures are incomplete and much more information is required. James A. Lowson, Plague Commissioner, Bombay, argued in 1897 that this form of protection would never come up to that provided by an anti-toxic serum. The reason was that the pain and discomfort of inoculation was so great that unless the inoculation could be 'sprung' on a whole community at once, the results of inoculating a few were generally sufficient to cause the remainder to fight shy of any such vaccination. Laboratory work in connection with the vaccine, according to Lowson, had so far not given very successful results, and the results on man at least had not proved so striking as one could wish.[33]

At first sight, the figures of 1907, with their improvement over the previous year, indicate that this measure was at last to emerging from the shadow of popular disfavor under which it had languished so long. It was argued that an increase from 101 inoculations to 3,122 might very well be taken as an indication that some of the educated were beginning to realize the benefits of plague prophylaxis and its safety.[34] A few Europeans and educated Bengalis had had themselves and their children inoculated, but with these extremely rare exceptions the whole of the inoculations were done on people attracted by the reward of eight *annas*—beggars, drunkards, and victims of opium, hasheesh or cocaine, habit, the drugs of the streets. Moreover the same persons presented themselves for inoculation two or three times within the same month. Many of them probably did a round of the different districts and were inoculated several times.[35] It was impossible to verify this from the registers, as nearly all the names in them were false.

RAT KILLING

In 1907 as many as 1,22,090 rats were killed. The number seems large, but it is doubtout if it affected the rat population in the city, particularly when Kitisato reported that in Tokyo even after the pilling 40,00,000 rats in three years, the result had been disappointing. The number of rat killings was greater in northern Calcutta because this is where the chief grain centres were situated. Many of the grain men or *dalwallahs* found rat collecting sufficiently paying to take up as a regular calling.[36] In other parts of the city the rats were too scattered to make it worthwhile catching them, and the class of professional catchers did develop. In the European parts of the town where active measures were taken by private individuals, there was some diminution in the rat supply.

The result of rat trapping was more educative than practical. The reward for every live rat brought in was lessened from two *annas* to six *pice* from January 1907. The attention of people was directed to the importance of rat destruction, and it was anticipated that a time would come when each householder would rid his house of rats. In fact it was suggested in 1906 that the first step would be to insist that all grain godowns be rat-proof. It was argued that it should be possible to legislate for Calcutta in such a way as to cause little, if any, hardship; the law could be framed so as not to include the petty traders. As a matter of fact, some of the more recently erected *dal* godowns had as the result of Dr. Crake's (District Medical Officer) persuasion been built *pucca* and rat-proof.

Rat destruction had often been unpopular with the people for religious reasons, and had more often than not received little or no cooperation on the part of the public. Any reduction of the rat population by trapping could be only temporary because rats bred so rapidly that they soon replaced the casualties. A still more serious objection to rat destruction by trapping and baiting was that the infected fleas were not destroyed. It might be argued that to kill rats when plague was raging merely released plague-infected fleas and increased the chances of man being infected.

Pathology of Popular Response

The measures taken by the authorities were of course designed with the sole object of preventing the spread of plague among people and of protecting from its ravages. But the motives of the government were always misconstrued. At different times rumours were circulated that the government desired to poison the people. The object of its action was variously stated to be the reduction of the superabundant population, the spread of the disease in order to deter foreigners from invading India, the seizure of people's money and property, the propitiation of the plague demon, and the permanent consolidation of British rule in India.[37] Among other absurd rumours circulated was that the government wished to destroy caste and religious observances, with the ultimate design of forcing Christianity on the natives of India.

SEGREGATION SCARE

Dr. Mahendra Lal Sarkar argued in 1898 that if the hoopla about the plague had produced any result, it was produced one that must be regretted, and that was the scare.[38] There had been an exodus from Calcutta as a consequence of the panic caused by the report that everybody suffering from the disease would be taken to segregation camps for treatment.[39] Crowds of men and women were seen thronging the streets of Calcutta; the thoroughfares presented a scene that was shocking; and the railway stations were so overcrowded that many returned home as the carriages were not sufficient to carry them away.[40] The cart men, coolies, *mehters*, and *dhangars* had struck work and gone back to their village homes. Domestic servants and cooks were also leaving the town for fear of being inoculated or segregated, and it was becoming difficult to get washermen. The mercantile community was meeting with the greatest difficulty in removing their goods and working their godowns for want of sufficient coolies.[41] The landholders were suffering from loss of tenants who were leaving the city, and the general public from want of menial servants of all classes.

Even when the inoculation scare was gradually dying away, the segregation scare was increasing. The government under the rules of the Venice Convention was bound to observe them to prevent the spread of plague. The Venice Convention held that segregation was one of the best means that could be adopted to prevent the plague taking an epidemic form. But the question is whether the Convention meant that by segregation the patient was to be separated from other members of the family and placed in a separate apartment of the house, or that he was to be taken for treatment to a plague hospital. That the latter was not the intention of the Convention seems to be evident from the concession already made by government that the members of a plague-affected family might be lodged in a separate apartment of the house, subject to the approval of the authorities. People wondered then 'why remove patients of the poorer classes to the Manicktollah Hospital, if they dread to be taken there? Then why not allow them to be treated in their own houses'.[42]

People also argued that in order to disabuse the minds of the masses of the segregation scare, they should be treated, where possible, in separate apartments of their own houses by their own doctors, under the supervision of the health officer and his assistant. But in cases where accommodation for this purpose was not considered sufficient or where this could not be done for other reasons, the patients might be treated in the ward hospitals which the commissioners had opened in their respective wards under instructions from the authorities. This, the people argued, would be in consonance with the feelings, habits, and customs of the people, and in no way calculated to raise unnecessary alarm in their minds regarding the intentions of the government.[43] People were leaving the city in large numbers as they considered their hearths and homes as sacred, and did not like to be invaded by police officers.

The *Times* had also taken up the subject of segregation scare. 'The Indian Press', it argued,

> continues week after week protest against the stringency of oppressive measures, which could with difficulty be forced upon a European population, and which are so opposed to the most sacred traditions of Eastern life.... Europe understands this perfectly well in regard to Turkey. It realizes that to compel the Sultan to apply to his Oriental provinces the same that may with safety be applied in London or Berlin would shake the Ottoman Empire to its foundation.[44] As regards the measures adopted in Bengal the *Times* asked: 'How far is a Government justified in introducing measures at the instance of foreign advisers which can only be enforced at the cost of panic?'

CONCEALMENT

Some members of the Vigilance Committee suggested that they might be given the authority to enter the *zenana* (women's quarter) of Bengali homes to enable them to examine inmates thereof.[45] The issue generated acrimonious debate in the newspapers. People argued that those who knew how keen the religious feelings of Hindus and especially Mohammedans, who observed *purdanashin* (veiling), must agree that such powers should not be given to anybody. They further contended that there could be no fear of any case of plague being concealed by members of respectable families since they would know that by adopting such a course they would have much to lose, and nothing to gain. As in the case of respectable gentlemen, it was argued, so with regard to the masses.[46]

PLAGUE HOSPITALS

Alarm spread that a person suspected to be suffering from plague had been carried away to the isolation hospital at Manicktollah, and that it had no provision of separate wards for the treatment of Mohammedan and Hindu patients. To allay the fear, it was suggested that the *baithakkhanas* or ground-floor rooms of the outer block of Bengali homes be allowed to be used as segregation hospitals for the use of plague patients.[47]

AMBULANCE VAN

Ambulance van was another aspect, which was contested by the people. Rumour was afloat that people dreaded the ambulance van more than death itself. They believed that when a patient was put into it, his sufferings were great, and the disinfectants made the van more uncomfortable.[48] The people argued that the *palki* (palanquin) instead of the ambulance van should be introduced to carry patients to plague hospitals. If *Uriah* (people from Orissa) bearers could not be found to carry plague patients in *palkis*, *Romoni* or up-country bearers might be employed on the duty. *Palkis*, it was argued, which had no cloth covering inside, might be used as they could be easily disinfected.

When the epidemic was at its worst, the urban literati suggested that a day of general prayer be observed in all churches, chapels, *masjids*, Brahmo Samajis, Hindu temples, and other places of public worship for the sake of the poor Calcuttans who were threatened with an outbreak of plague.[49]

> Let us then make pujah to propitiate the Deity according to the customs of our various nationalities. Let the Hindu worship his idol, utter the mantras, which his Shastras have taught him, and make *homa* and observe other propitiatory rites. Let the Christian pray in his Church. Let the Brahmo pray in his Samaj. Let the Mahomedan utter his prayers in his Masjid. I have no doubt that the united prayers of His children would be heard and we would be freed from the plague by the Almighty Giver of all good and blessings.

In the previous years, it was argued, when an epidemic of cholera or small pox had appeared in the city, *sankirtan* (chorus singing) parties used to be formed in different parts of the town. These groups chanted hymns and went from door to door singing the name of Hari in loud chorus with a view to driving away the epidemic.[50] They found no reason why similar parties should not be formed when the fear of plague was driving them mad.[51]

STREET RIOTS

A series of riots and disturbances paralyzed Calcutta and other towns in eastern India. The troubleshooters took full opportunity of the situation and resorted to all sorts of violence.[52] Ambulance vans were burnt down, and at places some Europeans were beaten up and inoculating officers brutally attacked by frenzied rioters.[53]

CONCLUSION

Perusing through the contemporary literary tracts and vernacular periodicals emanating from colonial eastern India, it appears in retrospect that the incidence of plague was popularly viewed as a visitation of fate, and as such, to submit to it with patience, but without an effort to do what was humanly possible to mitigate the calamity. They were also distrustful of the methods which western science had championed as the most efficacious for the protection of public health and extirpation of the epidemic.

Added to this, both Hindus and Mohammedans viewed with greatest dislike any intrusion into their homes, and especially any possible interference with the privacy of their women. Among Hindus, again, the caste system and its elaborate rules prevented intimate association, and especially common together of the so-called superior and inferior castes. In the city of Bombay, the greatest opposition was experienced from the Sunni Mohammedans, especially the Konkani Sunnis. In eastern India, the riots, strikes and disturbances were the actions of the marginalized social groups, both Hindus and Muslims—the municipal coolies, scavengers, sweepers, carters, butchers, *durwans*, menial servants, railways coolies, mill workers, who were hit the hardest by the plague regulations.

Where the incidence of plague had been really severe, people had readily given information to the plague authorities and had sought their aid. They had also taken refuge from it in flight. But once the virulence of the epidemic had abated and the fear of death no longer shared them in their eyes, they became indifferent to the precautionary measures and unwilling to undergo the slightest inconvenience in order to guard against future calamity. It was this attitude which became an obstacle in dealing with plague in eastern India. Of this government cannot complain. It is human nature to case precaution should anxieties abate. That the original animosity and suspicion of the people had been so remarkably changed was due to the unsparing energy and unfailing tact of the officers to whom the administration of plague in Calcutta had been entrusted.

NOTES

1. C.E.A. Winslow, *Man and Epidemic*, Princeton, 1952, p. 198, also R. Chandavarkar, Plague Panic and Epidemic Politics in India in Terence Ranger et al. (eds.), Epidemics and Ideas, Cambridge, 1992, pp. 203-40.
2. C.E.A. Winslow, op. cit., p. 199.
3. Ibid., p. 199.
4 A. Mitra, *The Bubonic Plague*, Calcutta, 1897, p. 1.
5. 'Bubonic Plague in Bombay', a paper read by Dr. A.G. Viegas at the Meeting of the Grant College Medical Society on 24 November 1896, Bombay.

6. Dr. A.G. Viegas, op. cit., p. 23.
7. Ibid., p. 24.
8. A. Mitra, op. cit., p. 8.
9. Ibid., pp. 9-10.
10. C.E.A. Winslow, *Man and Epidemic*, p. 200.
11. A. Mitra, op. cit., p. 12.
12. C.E.A. Winslow, op. cit., pp. 200-01.
13. Report on the Epidemic of Plague in Calcutta during 1898 and 1899 and up to June 1900, by E.N. Baker, Secretary to the Government of Bengal (hereafter GoB). Home Department, Sanitary A, February 1901, National Archives of India (hereafter NAI), New Delhi.
14. E.N. Baker, op. cit., p. 7.
15. Ibid.
16. *The Bengal Plague Manual*, Calcutta, 1903, p. 30.
17. Major W.J. Webster, 'A Note on Hydro Cyanic Acid Gas Fumigation of Rat Borrows as an Anti-Plague Measure', *Health Bulletin*, no. 21, Central Research Institute, New Delhi, 1935, p. 1, Oriental and India Office Collection (OIOC), British Library, London, V/25/850/94.
18. Major W.J. Webster, op. cit., p. 1.
19. *A Compilation of Regulations Issued by the Government of India and Local Governments in Connection with Plague*, Calcutta, 1898, V/27/856/6A, OIOC, BL, London.
20. Ibid., p. 89.
21. Ibid., p. 90.
22. Ibid., p. 91.
23. *The Bengal Plague Manual, Being a Collection of the Extant Regulations and Executive Orders in Connection with Plague Issued by the Government of India and the Government of Bengal*, Calcutta, 1903, p. 68.
24. *The Bengal Plague Manual*, Calcutta, 1903, p. 30.
25. Ibid., p. 30.
26. E.N. Baker, op. cit., p. 8.
27. Ibid., pp. 9-10.
28. Ibid., p. 10.
29. Major W.J. Webster, op. cit., p. 2.
30. Major Webster, op. cit., p. 3.
31. James A. Lowson, *Report on the Epidemic of Plague from 22 February to 16 July 1897*, Bombay, 1897, p. 40, OIOC, BL, London, V/27/856/13.
32. James Lowson, op. cit., p. 40.
33. Ibid., p. 41.
34. T. Frederick Pearse, *Report on Plague in Calcutta for the Year Ending 30th June 1907,* edited by W.C. Hossack with Appendices by Hossack and Crake, Calcutta, 1907, NAI, New Delhi.
35. Frederick Pearse, op. cit., p. 3.

36. Ibid., p. 4.
37. *The Bengal Plague Manual,* Calcutta, 1903, p. 29.
38. *Calcutta Medical Journal*, May 1898.
39. *Swasthya*, Shravan (1305 BS), 1898.
40. *The Indian Mirror*, 5 May 1898.
41. Ibid., 11 May 1898.
42. Ibid., 10 June 1898.
43. Ibid., 11 June 1898.
44. Cited in by Gobin Chunder Dhur's, *The Plague*, Calcutta, 1898, p. 18.
45. *The Statesman*, 17 June 1898.
46. *The Indian Mirror*, 23 June 1898.
47. Ibid.
48. Ibid., 17 June 1898.
49. Ibid., 29 May 1898.
50. Ibid., 1 June 1898.
51. *Swasthya,* Chaitya, 1306 (BS), 1900.
52. *Swasthya*, Shravan, 1305 (BS), 1898.
53. *Amrita Bazar Patrika*, 4 May 1898.

9. Industrial Workers, their Environmental Crises and Empire: Perspectives on Colonial Bengal

Amal Das

Labour historians have enriched Indian labour history by their important contributions and in-depth analyses of workers' struggles, trade union movements and the influence of political and ideological actions on these struggles and working class organizations. However, historians of working class movements have done little work in the field of larger themes of culture, ideology, mentalities, gender, ecology or environment. Scholars dealing with social history, including those dealing with the social history of the working class are silent about environmental problems encountered by the workers. The present paper has taken up as its theme the nature and extent of environmental decay in urban industrial areas that affected the industrial workers during the colonial period. It also focuses on the attitude of the Empire towards these crises. My attempt is to bring to light the environmental conditions prevalent in one particular industry, namely the jute industry, which was eastern India's largest colonial enterprise.

In the second half of the nineteenth century, the jute textile industry witnessed rapid growth along with other industries such as railways, cotton textiles, tea, coal, iron and steel, metal and so on. With this growth of modern industries and the development of a modern transport system , an industrial labour force began to emerge in eastern India. Although the mills and factories, in the early stage, engaged local hands, the situation had changed by the turn of the century. The large jute mills, situated on both banks of the river Hooghly, employed a large number of up-country migrants from Bihar, the United Provinces, Orissa and

Madras who began to far outnumber local Bengalees.[1] The industrialization and urbanization and the consequent emergence of a new industrial labour-force gave rise to a variety of social, economic, physical and human environmental crises. The unplanned urbanization and industrialization brought in its wake the imbalance of natural atmosphere everywhere. The ecological and environmental decay arising out of such industrial changes had far-reaching and enduring impact on the labouring society. The changing infrastructure started to create problems more or less similar to those of the Industrial Revolution in England. The industrial changes in England resulted in the massing of population in industrial towns and 80 per cent of industrial population lived in towns of over 10,000 inhabitants. The concentration of people in towns and the development project of the administration, induced ecological and environmental decay. The growth of large towns towards the end of the eighteenth and early nineteenth centuries occurred at a time when building regulations were not in existence. In the factory towns thousands of dwellings were built up on the back-to-back principle. A dwelling touched an adjacent dwelling on three of its four sides. Ill-ventilated and dirty, these dwellings quickly became foul and verminous. The sanitary provisions were inadequate.[2]

The present paper is divided into four sections. Section one will discuss the nature and extent of ecological and environmental hazards of the industrial workers in Bengal. Section two will highlight the adverse effects of the filthy environment on the health of the workers that led to diseases and high mortality rate. Section three will critically examine the role of the Empire and the various pressure groups that were active in urban politics in handling the situation. Finally, the paper will draw certain observations and conclusions.

Ecological and Environmental Crises

The new development projects of the colonial government in Calcutta and around, the unplanned industrial expansion, the acute scarcity of space, the filthy condition of the workers' working and living places created new problems for the industrial workers in Bengal. The mills and factories where the workers had to work for hours together were built without any plan and slightest consideration of air, water, light and sanitation. These were ill-ventilated, dark, dirty and dingy and the atmosphere was suffocating. Usually the doors and windows of the factories were kept shut. The migrants in mills and factories, who came from a different social and cultural environment, found it difficult to adapt themselves to the new condition. They had to lead a life completely different from their village life. The illiterate villagers working in such unhealthy and unhygienic places knew nothing about the laws of health. To add to their misfortune, the smokes, foul gases, and chemicals emitted by the mills and factories in polluted both water and air. The jute mills situated on both banks of the river Hooghly threw their poisonous wastes into the river. The smokes and dust coming up from the chimneys were potential health hazards. The wells and ponds used by the urban industrial population became polluted due to industrial effluents. It is strange that none of the industries discharged wastes in municipal sewers. Even groundwater became polluted by industrial pollutants. The contaminated water caused enteric diseases. Typhoid fever, dysentery, cholera, gastrointestinal troubles and respiratory problems were common diseases among industrial workers.

Besides workplace, the areas where the industrial workers used to live were also unhealthy and without any sanitary provision. The influx of rural poor into urban industrial towns in search of jobs led to congestion. Owing to the rapid and extensive development of industries and the colonial development project, land for housing became scarce and expensive. To tide over the crisis and to accommodate the migrant rural population, slum settlements arose in urban industrial towns. These slums were built back to back without the slightest consideration of space. They became 'filthy, dirty, disease-ridden hovels' with no arrangement for light, windows, chimneys or fireplaces. The rooms were tiny, varying from 8′ × 6′ to 10′ × 8′, and devoid of any kind of sanitation or minimum amenities. Bathing and latrine facilities were non-existent. There was no arrangement for drainage, conservancy and water supply. The municipal taps on the roadsides were the only source of water supply. The municipal tanks were in a bad shape, full of weeds and mud. The slum dwellers bathed and washed their linen in the same tanks and drank the same polluted water. In the jute-growing districts, jute-steeping was also done in the same tank. There were open sewers gulching filth, swarms of flies and every sort of ecological horror. The latrines, if these existed in any *bustee* area, were too few and filthy so that men, women and children had to use street drains and open fields at a distance.[3]

B. Shiva Rao, a trade unionist observed: 'with a small room 8′ by 6′, I found nine people living, in the next, which was hardly bigger, were eleven people and two goats on the tiny mud-floored verandah.'[4] He stated with emphasis: 'Slums have grown up round mills and factories in most parts of India, but nothing can equal, for squalor and filth and stench, the *bustees* in Howrah and the suburbs north of Calcutta.'[5] The Royal Commission on Labour in India had no option but to confess frankly that this was the common scene of all the mills on both banks of the Hooghly.[6] The slums could only be reached through narrow winding lanes. The inadequate ventilation was cut off by the workers themselves by means of old kerosene tins and gunny bags for privacy. To reduce the burden of rent, the practice of sub-letting these huts was common and this made the slums extremely overcrowded.[7] The filthy and insanitary environment of the slums was such that investigating officers often became ill during their investigations. Scavenging in the slum areas was irregular and unsatisfactory and haphazard.

The workers frequently met with fatal accidents and faced fire hazards in their living places. As most of the huts were made of mud plaster with thatched roofs there was every chance of accidents from fire. To add to this, the workers often used a part of the room for cooking purposes as there was no separate kitchen. When the adult members of the family went out for work in the mills and factories, there was no one to attend to the children. As a result accidents often led to loss of life of children. For instance, a young boy and his seven-year old blind sister lived in a hut in a crowded *bustee* of Sibpur. The boy worked in a jute mill in Howrah. When he went out for work the blind sister was left alone. One day, on his return from work, the boy found his little sister burnt to death. Their 'thatched hut' had caught fire while she was asleep.[8]

Thus, unhealthy and insanitary environment of the slums, impure drinking water, stagnation of waste for want of drainage system, irregular cleaning of public and private privies and urinals, highly objectionable and unhealthy location of night soil depots and the abominable condition of the workers' workplace and living quarters made their life hell.

The environmental decay became worse when the railways was introduced in Bengal. Railway tracks were laid and as a result long embankments were made on the sides of the tracks which created newer problems. These environments obstructed the natural drainage system and water became stagnant, which made it a haven for mosquitoes. During rains, the slum dwellers were faced with acute drainage problem. But no steps were taken either by the urban municipal authorities or the mill employers to clear the obstruction to ensure effective drainage.

Impact of Environmental Decay on the Labouring Society

The workers with their meagre and uncertain wages lived and died in debt. Ill-fed they became weak and prone to diseases. The high cost of living and poverty below subsistence level affected the general health of the workers. A dietary and nutrition survey conducted among the working population in early 1940s revealed that in one jute mill of Howrah District, 42 per cent males suffered in anaemia. In another jute mill this disease was most common among the mill hands. Bad nourishment and malnutrition were the potential factors for this disease. The survey also found that the workers lacked the minimum requirement of protein, fat, calcium, phosphorus, iron and vitamins A, B and C.[9] As a result they suffered from sickness such as rickets, pernicious type of aneamia, ostcomalacia, pain in eyes and blindness.[10]

The ecological changes and filthy environment were responsible for the spread of diseases among the labouring poor. Countless numbers either perished or suffered from permanent disabilities. The stagnant water caused mosquitoes to breed which spread malaria. There was an interrelationship between ecological and cultural changes, particularly in the case of diseases such as malaria. Irrigation, irrigated fields, embankments, seasonal swamps and waterlogging increased the number of mosquitos causing malaria. A worker affected by malaria could easily infect hundreds of others. The slum areas or the coolie lines became the hotbed of infectious diseases. Impure drinking water or polluted tank water helped the spread of water-borne diseases like cholera, typhoid, stomach disorder, and diarrhoea. These diseases had killed thousands of labouring men and women.

The industrial workers were often victims of epidemic diseases. Plague, small-pox, malaria and influenza epidemics had a pernicious impact on the poor labourers. The plague epidemics in Bombay followed by the one in Calcutta in 1898 were so massive in scale by 1930 they had claimed more than 12 million lives,[11] a sizeable number of which were labouring poor. The malaria, small-pox and influenza epidemics in 1918-19 in Bengal also caused innumerable deaths in the urban and rural areas. Many migrant workers left their jobs and fled to their native towns. The desertion of labourers parlyzed industry and commerce. The plague in Calcutta in 1898 created panic among the workers.[12] *Amrita Bazar Patrika* observed: 'Trade, commerce and business of every description was dislocated.' In official perception, dirth and filth were responsible for the outbreak of epidemic diseases and there was an ecological construction of diseases by officials. The health hazards and diseases made workers' life insecure and uncertain.

This insecurity and hopelessness about the situation had a pernicious impact on the social life and habits of the workers. As they had little scope for recreation and amusement to get rid of the drudgery of day-to-day life, they took to drinking and gambling. The mill coolies were frequently addicted to alcohol and *ganja*, causing further demoralization the workers. Gambling and drinking in public area often led to law and order problem causing enormous trouble for the police and the common people.[13] The disproportional sex-ratio and the preponderance of males over females in the slums had its own effect. Sex vices were common among the mill coolies which corrupted both the human and social environment. Dr. Curjel , a civil surgeon who visited 76 mills in the year 1921-2 commented that up-country migrants from Bihar, and the United and Central Provinces brought women with them and these women worked in the mills. But they 'are not usually the wives of the men with whom they live'. She saw prostitutes living in the village of Fort Gloster in Howrah Dristrict.[14]

Role of the Empire and Urban Pressure Groups

What did the colonial state do to control the ecological and environmental decay that was causing diseases and deaths of hundreds and thousands of labouring poor? Did it take any positive step or did it simply evade the issue? These questions need to be seen in the perspective of development and improvement of public health and environment in Britain vis-à-vis in the colonies such as India.

The Industrial Revolution in Britain changed the population map to a remarkable extent. From the second half of the eighteenth century the growth of population was rapid. The next half century saw the population rise by 50 per cent, as the census of 1801 shows a population of nine million. This doubled by 1851 and doubled yet again by 1901. The influx of people from the countryside to the industrial towns caused environmental, social, economic and cultural problems. Industrial changes, population stress and space shortage brought about changes in the human environment making it a haven for infectious diseases. Extreme stress on ecology contaminated air, water and food, thus affecting the general health of the people. In the factory towns, thounsands of workers were faced with acute housing shortage and sanitary hazards. No adequate sanitary provision was made and it was not considered necessary to install an independent water supply for each house in London. No system of drainage was established and the existence of ill-constructed cesspools was not abolished in the city of London until 1850. It took many more years to introduce universal drainage system throughout London. House refuse was not collected and destroyed; it was deposited in gutters or on waste ground, giving rise to diseases and death. The water supplied was frequently polluted. Water taken from wells or streams in the proximity of cesspools or burial grounds became a source of death rather than of life.[15]

Environmental decay became a prime concern following the outbreak of cholera epidemic in England in 1847-8. Finding themselves in a critical situation, the leaders of the sanitary movement started a campaign for necessary action. Public opinion was aroused in favour of sanitary reforms. The persistent campaigners for better sanitation and public health laws in Britain were the Utilitarian Sir Edwin Chadwick and the Registrar-General Thomas Farr. The energetic endeavour of Chadwick saw the enactment of the Public Health Act of 1848 and the acceptance of the principle that the British Empire was responsible for the health and sanitary improvement of its people. Chadwick's brilliant Report on the Sanitary Condition of the Labouring Population of Great Britain', published in 1850, stressed on the link between poverty and sickness and sought remedies for the eradication of poverty and the social policies to be adopted by the government. British health policies developed from the mid-nineteenth century through parliamentary action. Besides Chadwick, the proponents of the new sanitary movement and parliamentary reforms were Benjamin Disraeli, Lord Shaftesbury, John Simon, Southwood Smith and Edward Bulwer-Lytton. In 1848 a Central Board of Health was established with power to set up a Local Board of Health 'in any city, town, borough, parish or place' which desired it or in which the death-rate was high. The duties of these local boards were to 'manage sewers and drains, wells and water supplies, gas works . . . and slaughter houses, and to regulate offensive trades, remove nuisances, control houses unfit for human habitation, and provide burial grounds, recreation areas and parks, and public bath houses.'[16] But the progress was slow, partly because of the volume of works and partly because of conflict between central and local authorities.

The Public Health Act of 1872 divided the country into sanitary districts, urban or rural, thus extending the organization begun under the Act of 1848. The Public Health Act of 1875 dealt with many aspects of sanitation for the control of physical environment. The sanitary authority was empowered to appoint a medical officer of health, a surveyor and a sanitary inspector. Power to deal with a wide range of matters relating to public health was conferred on the sanitary authority. The measures that the authority had undertaken included supply of water, improvement of drainage, sewerage, the making, paving, lighting and cleaning of streets, the removal of refuse, the supervision and control of markets and slaughter houses, and the isolation of infected patients. It was also empowered to provide public baths and wash houses. During the next few years the local sanitary inspectors were given the power to look into the welfare of the labouring population and inquire into the sanitary condition of workshops.[17] The Artisans' and Labourers' Dwelling Act of 1868 empowered the local authority to condemn property which was not fit for habitation. Power was given to demolish slum property if the owner failed to comply with necessary repairs. This was the first real attempt to deal with the problem of slums although success in this regard was limited due to objections raised by the property owners and the slackness on the part of the local authority. By early twentieth century, reforms in England began attacks on 'overcrowding' and labyrinthine 'honeycombed' tenements, a prelude to the campaign for 'eradicating the slums'.[18]

It is evident that by the end of the nineteenth and the early twentieth centuries, Britain had developed tremendously in the sphere of sanitary improvement and public health policies and the success was the outcome of the government's thoughts, planning and organization.

Imperial health policy and sanitary reforms were introduced and developed in Bengal in the late nineteenth and early twentieth centuries. The vanguard of the British political consolidation in India army, and the protection of the health of this army from tropical diseases and filthy environment was the headache of the colonial government. This anxiety figured prominently in the minds of British rulers when they found that a large number of British soldiers had died of cholera in the 1817 war against the Marathas. The same calamity happened in 1857; 6 per cent of the British soldiers lost their lives in warfare and the rest (percentage not known) died due to tropical diseases, mainly from fever, malaria, dysentery, small pox and cholera.[19] This catastrophe created fear and panic not only in the British army, but also among the ruling classes, their families and the European civilian population. The colonial government thus considered the protection of the health of its men its first and foremost duty in India. Another consideration was economic. The British rulers in India throughout the colonial period were most concerned with the uninterrupted economic prosperity of British India. So they wanted to keep the commercial and industrial zones free from tropical diseases as these would hamper production and profit. The losses incurred by European industrialists and businessmen was often heavy in diseased areas. The labourers in order to save themselves from diseases deserted the towns, which disturbed the normal running of mills and factories and hampered production. During such times, industries suffered from acute shortage of labourers and labour became expensive. Therefore, the mill employers and their powerful organizations cried out for immediate and appropriate actions in order to save the industry. The government, compelled by the Indian Jute Mills' Association (IJMA), the Bengal Chamber of Commerce, and Traders' Association rushed to avert the serious danger and took necessary actions to solve the sanitary and health questions of the workers.[20] This attitude of the government was evident from the reports of the inspectors of factories published annually which stated that the health question of the workers was normally a question of epidemics, and not one of diet, nutrition or standard of living. The report 'General Health of the Operatives' described the workers' health as 'good' unless an epidemic or endemic diseases broke out. The report read 'The general health of the operatives—men, women and children was good, and no epidemic and endemic diseases appeared amongst them.'[21] This attitude of the British rulers caused enormous sufferings for the labouring class. Even at the hour of crisis the medical aid the labourers received was meagre. No expensive or curative treatment was provided to them, no planned and organized sanitary reforms and public health schemes were undertaken to eradicate diseases and control environmental decay. The measures undertaken were piecemeal, need-based and inadequate. They did not produce any permanent effect. Labourers' sickness was never equated with their poverty and as a consequence, these labourers with usual hard work and without good, sufficient food or medicines not only became weaker but also fell easy prey to diseases.

It was only in the late 1920s and 30s when workers became more restive, militant and more conscious of and assertive about their demands, and their trade union organizers became more vocal in favour of their demands that the government and the mill employers took notice of their pitiable condition and implement some welfare schemes. The years following the General Jute Mill Strike of 1929 in Bengal witnessed the initiation of maternity benefit and a few other schemes. The IJMA decided to establish welfare units, baby clinics and creches in mills.[22] A few of the mills also set up schools in industrial areas.[23] The mill employers thought of building better coolie lines within the mill compound with some sanitary provisions.[24]

Undoubtedly, there was no hesitancy in introducing sanitary reforms and health measures in European populated areas in Calcutta and some selected urban pockets. Measures were undertaken to protect the residential areas of the Europeans by improving the drainage system, insuring purified water supply, improving sewerages, lighting and cleaning of streets, and removal of refuse. Attention was paid to protect European managers' bungalows and quarters which were susceptible to contagion due to the living of native servants in close proximity. Their quarters were segregated from the servants' dwellings. The coolie lines in mill boundaries were built at a safe distance from the managers' bungalows. This was because of the conflicting theories of hygiene between the incoming and the host cultures that required that 'Indian dwellings and servants' houses (should) be at a safe distance. . . . For hygienic reasons, especially in the malarious and unhealthy districts , close proximity is not desirable.'[25] Attention was paid to keep as the bazars free from of filthy. In selecting sites for bungalows, the concepts of sanitation, free air, light, and in some cases solar protection by maximizing the open area around the house and planting trees round the edges of the compound were given due importance. Most of the bungalows were laid out with beautiful gardens. The motive was to protect European lives that had to live and work with the natives. It was an attempt, according to David Arnold, calls 'to build a *Cordon Sanitare* around the white community'.[26]

The British rulers in India devoted attention to the development of a distinctive medical research in India and the establishment of a grid of Western-oriented hospitals, clinics and public health policies to ensure the protection of health of their countrymen. Medical authorities and sanitary engineers were entrusted with the responsibility of cleansing the filthy environments. The diseases peculiar to tropical countries were still ill understood and therefore the means of preventing them were unknown to the Western doctors. This failure to understand tropical diseases induced Western scientists to undertake serious and sincere researches. The result of such researches was unique. Robert Koch's discovery of the cholera bacillus, Ronald Ross's discovery of the mosquito-human cycle of the malarial parasite, W.M. Haffkine's discovery of anti-cholera and anti-plague serums, the original and decisive researches of W.B. Bannerman, William Glen Liston, Indian Plague Commission, A.C. Bacot and C.R. Martin, and L.F. Hirst's work on plague transmission and epidemiology were some of the major advances in Western researches.[27] By the late nineteenth century, the significant expansion of Western medical knowledge in India, growth of medical institutions, advances in researches, discoveries of insect vectors and microbes against tropical diseases, identification of modes of infection, familiarity of Western doctors with Indians' maladies and epidemic diseases all these gave confidence and encouragement for greater government intervention against tropical diseases with the hope that these could be easily won over by the scientific Western medical treatment. This growing understanding of etiology of diseases stood in the way of development of indigenous medical culture.

While the colonial government made concerted efforts to control environmental decay and eradicate tropical diseases in European populated areas, the reverse was the case with the areas inhabited by Indians. Sanitary improvement and public health was slow and irregular in coming to native towns, slums and rural areas. The industrial regions of Bengal—the jute mills on the Hooghly River, the tea gardens in the Dooars, the collieries in western Bengal, the engineering concerns in and around Calcutta were the hotbed of diseases because of the poisonous environment. The industrial workers were the hardest hit. Problems of drinking water, drainage, cleaning of slum areas, sewerages and all other environmental hazards remained unsolved. The workers received just the skeleton of the British sanitary reforms and public health policies. Due to inadequate medical facilities, want of charitable dispensaries and health clinics, and medicines, labourers in the slum areas died in large numbers. Their requests, prayers and memoranda for better sanitation and medical facilities in the early decades of the twentieth century were of no use. The colonial government and the mill employers either neglected or ignored their justified demands.

Although some of the large municipalities had health clinics and charitable dispensaries, these were ineffective and run by inexperienced doctors, subordinate compounders and dressers and as a sequel, wrong treatment often led to unfortunate incidents. The district and union boards were financially not solvent to take proper steps against diseases. Many of the district and rural dispensaries and health clinics were without any doctors and nurses. The attendance of the staff was irregular and admission and treatment of patients depended on the whims of the staff and not on the condition of the patients. Medicines, if supplied, were of poor quality and some even spurious. In fact, all the good hospitals were in Calcutta to serve the interest of the 'whites' and the Indian elite who could afford expensive treatment. The majority of the native population and the slum dwellers had to rely either on irregular government dispensaries or on the tricks of quacks.[28]

The urban municipalities, barring a few, were in a bad condition and unable to spend money for better sanitation and medical service. There was absence of any organized control activities by the government during epidemic or endemic diseases. No preventive measures were undertaken since these would cost much on the exchequer. The colonial state was reluctant to spend imperial funds to extent health schemes and sanitary reforms in the native-populated areas. Various health and sanitary improvement schemes formulated by officials ended with the proposing of new taxes, the maximum to be borne by the native population. Naturally the poor labouring coolies feared any such scheme that would rob them of their money. Many new taxes were imposed in the name of sanitation and health schemes but the amount collected was spent not for the welfare of the natives but for imperial purposes and colonial development projects. The district and local boards spent little on sanitation and health, expressing incapability due to shortage of funds.[29] Although the native newspapers expressed resentment against the insanitary and unhygienic conditions existing in the urban and rural areas these were of no avail. Thousands of villagers were depopulated due to epidemics and insanitary conditions.[30]

Even the mill dispensaries established in some mill municipalities ignored the health and nutrition deficiency disorders of their mill coolies. Medical investigation in mill areas received scant attention from the government and from the mill managers. An investigation into the condition of women workers in the jute mills in 1931-2 following the recommendations of the Royal Commission on Labour in India discovered several serious disorders among women which, however, found no mention into the records of the mill dispensaries. Even the mill doctors who accompanied the investigation team to the coolie lines were not familiar with these cases.[31] This clearly indicates how far the mill doctors and the mill managers were negligent about the health of the labourers.

To add to the misfortune of the slum-dwellers, the politics of the urban pressure groups often stood in the way of better sanitation and improvement of slums. The intrigues, tussles and tensions among various interested groups in the municipalities, and district and local boards affected the condition of the poor slum dwellers in urban areas. The powerful groups in the municipalities decided the resource allocation and the orientation of the development projects. The municipal schemes of slum improvement and the opening out of insanitary *bustees* were dependent on the understanding and compromise between the municipal authorities and the slum owners whose diverse interests had somehow be reconciled. The landlords after created obstacles to prevent the improvement of the slums, and often filed heavy law suits. As labour supply to the Bengal jute mills was abundant towards the close of the nineteenth and early twentieth centuries, the slum owners found it profitable not to effect any improvement in the slums but to profit by increasing rent and subletting, at the enormous physical, cultural and emotional cost of the migrant workers.[32] A triangular tussle often occurred among the municipalities, the mill authorities and the private landlords on issues such as land acquisitions, housing of the workers, water connections and the supply of drinking water, drainage system and so on. The mill authorities found it difficult to own lands for housing their workers. A practical difficulty arose in the case of mills which were built in the centre of towns where land was dear. The problem was that under the Bengal Municipal Act, land acquisition from private owners was extremely difficult for the mill employers.[33] G.M. Broughton highlighted this problem by stating that mill authorities faced difficulty in securing lands in the vicinity of the mills. Compulsory acquisition was not permissible under the existing Bengal Municipal Act and the owners often demanded exorbitant prices for their lands.[34]

Acrimonious debates between mill authorities and *bustee*-owning landlords often led to municipal politics that hampered slum improvement. Majority of the workers who lived in *bustees*, let out by petty landlords and zamindars were in depressed conditions, but the owners made their profits. The problem became acute by 1895 when there was an abundant supply of migrant labourers. The scarcity in accommodation reached a new height and it was difficult for mills outside Calcutta municipal limits to retain labour. These mills 'started around 1895 an agitation to incorporate the mill sites into the new "mill municipalities", thereby separating these areas from the existing municipal boundaries.' The jute mill owners were often able to use public money for the housing of workers through the 'mill municipalities', i.e. municipalities that were controlled by jute mill managers.[35]

Progress in the construction of drainage work, sanitary improvements and the supply of drinking water was frequently stopped by litigations and the obstacles created by the landowners. In draining the town, the municipalities were frequently involved in law-suits which had been filed by owners of private drains. The port commissioners and the railway authorities—two powerful organizations—frequently created problems in the drainage work by their independent projects.[36]

CONCLUSION

This paper shows that industrialization, population stress and colonial development projects in and around Calcutta caused environmental decay and diseases in the urban industrial areas of Bengal. The slums where the industrial population lived were the worst affected. The dirth and filth in all native towns and slums helped the spread of diseases. For many years the colonial government was apathetic to such environmental crises and diseases. It blamed the Indians for the filthy environment and diseases and left them at the mercy of indigenous medical culture and fate.

By the late nineteenth century, the British rulers in India, for several reasons, realized the urgent necessity of penetrating into the native towns and villages with superior Western sanitary reforms and public health policies. Discoveries of insect vectors of epidemic diseases and the familiarity of Western doctors with new medical developments encouraged and inspired the colonial government and its medical officers to intervene and fight against tropical diseases with greater confidence and better results. Thus, Western public health measures and medicine reached the shores of India in the garb of Rudyard Kipling's ideology of 'White Man's burden' and Western 'civilizing mission'. The distinctive public health policies and sanitary measures penetrated deeply in 'white'-populated Calcutta and some urban pockets. Although it reached the native towns and villages, progress was slow and irregular. Preventive measures were never encouraged in native towns and villages and there was no systematic pursuit for environmental solution. What the British sincerely and seriously did for their countrymen including the working class in Great Britain in the domain of environment and public health remained undone for the colonized. Beyond creating modern water supplies and some sanitary improvements in Calcutta and a few large municipalities, and providing the benefits of Western medical treatment to 'whites' through hospitals and clinics, the Indian masses, barring a few rich, remained outside the orbit of Western medical treatment, hospital facilities and better sanitation. The colonial government did not make any serious endeavour to transmit Western medical and environmental knowledge to the Indian population. In order to avoid conflict, they thought it prudent not to interfere with indigenous beliefs, customs and cultures. As a result their attempt to control environmental decay and diseases in colonies like India remained unimpressive, highly selective and imperfect throughout the colonial period. Despite an overarching perception of threat of disease, sanitation, town planning and public health never seemed to figure prominently in the colonial project. Government policies had little control over the ecology of disease in the subcontinent. Liberal environmentalists in the Indian Medical Service attributed the unimpressive results to narrow, ineffective assaults on diseases and agitated for broad 'social policies', subsidizing 'nutrition for poor children' through schools, training midwives in 'antiseptic births', slum clearance, systematic elimination of village compost heaps and other breeding grounds of disease.[37] Unfortunately, while in Britain the 'cult of cleanliness swept the middle classes' and was carried with 'religious fervour down to the masses' and 'the cult of soap and water' had replaced 'the cult of religion and pedigree' in the late nineteenth and the early twentieth centuries, the same did not occur in India under British rule. There was no administrative or upper class pressure for environmental improvement and health practices in India. No evangelical movement, no Utilitarian Chadwicks for sanitary movement and no leaders for reform of Indian health practices and hygiene emerged in India to champion the cause of the downtrodden. The lonely voices with no backing from social reformers or nationalist political leaders were the liberal environmentalists in the IMS, its directors and the inspector-general who agitated for resources for more and better sanitation, water supplies, hospitals and dispensaries, doctors and trained midwives, nutrition and housing.[38]

As Ira Klein comments, 'Flawed western theories, inability to weaken the social and environmental roots of much Indian illness, and failure to diffuse new ideas and health practices helped thwart attempts to contain death.'[39]

NOTES

1. B. Foley, Report on Labur in Bengal, Calcutta, 1906, para 29.
2. G.W. Southgate, *English Economic History*, London, 1960, pp. 123, 290-1.

3. B. Shiva Rao, *The Industrial Workers in India*, London, 1939, pp. 110-15; Jurgen Kuczynski, *The Rise of the Working Class*, London, 1967, pp. 222-3.
4. Rao, p. 114.
5. Ibid., pp. 113-14.
6. Report of the Royal Commission on Labour in India (henceforth RCLI), Calcutta, 1931.
7. 'Annual Report on the Working of the Indian Factories Act in Bengal', (henceforth ARWIFAB), Calcutta, 1908, General Department Miscellaneous Branch, Proceedings A, Nos. 53-4, July 1907, Government of Bengal, West Bengal State Archives, Calcutta.
8. *The Englishman* , 9 April 1896, p. 6.
9. Dr. B. Mookherjee, 'Nutrition and Diet Survey in Howrah, Calcutta, 1940', pp. 161-2; 'Report of the Health Survey and Development Committee' appointed by the Government of India in 1943, vol. 1, p. 11 in *Indian Labour Year Book*, Government of India, 1946, pp. 200-01.
10. Commerce Department, Commerce Branch, Proceedings A, nos. 2-6, July 1932.
11. 'Annual Report of the Public Health Commission with the Government of India 1929', Calcutta, 1932, p. 69. The plague epidemic was at its height between 1898 and 1908, during which time over six million deaths were recorded. See L.F. Hirst, *The Conquest of Plague: A Study of the Evolution of Epidemiology*, London, 1953, p. 299.
    Also see D. Arnold, 'Touching the Body: Perspectives on the Indian Plague, 1896-1900' in R. Guha (ed.), *Subaltern Studies V* Delhi, 1987; Amal Das, 'Plague and People in Calcutta 1898-1900', in A. Guha et al. (eds.), *Explorations in History, Essays in Honour of Prof. C. Palit*, Calcutta, 2003.
12. Das, pp. 117-37.
13. *The Englishman*, 13 October and 1 November 1899; *Howrah Hitaishi*, 18 August 1906 , Report on the Native Papers (Bengal) for the week ending the 25 August 1906, Judicial Department; Police Branch, Progs A, Nos. 6-11, January 1896.
14. Commerce Department, Commerce Branch, Progs B, No. 77, April 1923.
15. Southgate, p. 291.
16. Southgate, pp. 291-3; Ira Klein, 'Medicine and Culture in British India' in *Explorations in History*, pp. 83-5.
17. Southgate, pp. 291-3.
18. Anthony Wohl, *Endangered Lives*, Cambridge, Mass., pp. 292, 294, 299, 313 as cited in Klein , p. 84.
19. For details see Sandip Sinha, *Public Health Policy and the Indian Public-Bengal 1850-1920*, Calcutta, 1998.

20. J.N. Cook, 'Report on Plague in Calcutta' in *Report of the Epidemics of Plague in Calcutta during the Years 1898-99, 1899-1900 and upto 30 June, 1900*, Calcutta, 1900, pp. 10-14, *Amrita Bazar Patrika*, 3 May 1898, pp. 8-10.
21. ARWIFAB, General Miscellaneous Br., Progs A, Nos. 22-23, August 1893. It contains the annual report on the working of the Indian Factory Act in Bengal in 1892.
22. 'Report on the Administration of Bengal', Calcutta, 1930-1, pp. 79-80.
23. RCLI, vol. V, part I (Memorandum for the RCLI by J.M. Mitra, Registrar of Co-operative Societies, Bengal), see pp. 53-4 on 'Education in the Industrial Belt'.
24. RCLI , vol. V, part I, p. 282 and part II, p. 284.
25. A.D. King, *Colonial Urban Development: Culture, Social Power and Environment*, London, 1976, p. 131. For details see pp. 131-53.
26. D. Arnold, 'Smallpox and colonial medicine in 19th Century India' in Arnold (ed.), *Imperial Medicine and Indigenous Societies*, Delhi, 1989, p. 48.
27. Klein, p. 100.
28. Sinha, pp. 70-103.
29. Ibid., Amal Das, *Urban Politics in an Industrial Area, Aspects of Municipal and Labour Politics in Howrah, West Bengal 1850-1928.*
30. See the editorial in *Sanjibani*, a Bengali weekly, 11 February, 1989; '26th Annual Report of Sanitary Commission for Bengal', p. 45; Sri Sri Vishnupriya, *Ananda Bazar Patrika*, 6 August 1902.
31. Commerce Dept., Commerce Br., Progs. A, Nos. 2-6, July 1932.
32. Dipesh Chakraborty, 'Communal Riots and Labour: Bengal's Jute Mill Hands in the 1890s' in *Past & Present*, no. 91, 1981, p. 27.
33. Foley, appendix.
34. G.M. Broughton, *Labour in Indian Industries*, London, 1924, p. 138.
35. 'Report of the Committee for the Year Ended 31 December, 1904, Indian Jute Mills Association, Calcutta, 1905, p. IV; Chakraborty, pp. 26-28.
36. J. Bonnerjee, *Howrah Civic Companion*, vol. I, Published from Howrah municipality, 1955.
37. 'Report of the Commissioner of Public Health of India', 1930, pp. 158-61; *RCPH*, 1936, pp. 106-13, 125-7; *RCPH*, 1937, pp. 87, 178, 230-1, as cited in Klein, p. 101.
38. Klein, p. 102.
39. Ibid., p. 101.

10. Conflicting Claims: The Colonial State Forests and Forest Dwellers in the Jalpaiguri District, 1869-1947

Sahara Ahmed

A vignette of the imperial phase and its 'predatory nature' precipitating a negative impact on the Indian subcontinent is evident in some recent literature on ecological history. Colonial ecological history is more intelligible if we comprehend British notions of absolute property in marked contrast to the Indian idea of property as a hierarchy of user rights. Colonial intervention in the management of local forest resources, for example, came through a long process of discussion and debate at various levels among extremely heterogeneous constituents—working foresters, the state bureaucracy and, lately, the local people.[1] The significance of colonial scientific projects has been accepted as a major area of research amongst social scientists, environmentalists, anthropologists and other interested groups in the recent past. At an academic level, the history of forest management has been a history of graduation from simple utilitarian demands on the woods to an appreciation of the dynamics of the natural system.[2]

In this paper I try to explicate the historical determinants of imperial intervention and ecological change in the Jalpaiguri District, ensconced in the foothills of the Himalaya. Two broad areas of focus have emerged, namely changes in imperial attitude to the natural world and the responses and strategies of forest dwellers to new systems of resource extraction. The issues related to the conservation of forests and the processes of statemaking in

* I am grateful to Professors Arun Bandopadhyay and Ranjan Chakrabarti for their critical scrutiny of my various drafts and their valuable observations which have enriched my understanding of the subject. The shortcomings and mistakes, if any, are entirely my own.

colonial Jalpaiguri are inextricably connected.[3] These processes and strategies, incorporated without much variation into the post-independent state, were nuanced by diminishing forests and conflicts over natural resources.

The British annexation of the Duars in 1864-5 resulted in massive depletion of natural forests and their conversion into tea-plantations and reserved forests under the regime of scientific forestry. From 1770 to 1860 Jalpaiguri witnessed a new commercial possibilities for timber sales or cash crops, with no public agency yet in place to enforce any systematic timber management. Then gradually as the imperial bureaucracy spread its administrative tentacles, greater planning and use evolved, especially after the Indian Forest Service was established in 1865 and the formal constitution of the Jalpaiguri District in 1869. Three problems proved to be the beté-noire of the colonial government, viz., forest fires, graziers and forest dwellers. The government dealt separately with each problem according to its comprehension.

The flat level strip of land, averaging about 22 miles running along the foot of the Bhutan Hills was known as the Bhutanese Duars or the Western Duars. The East India Company was eager to initiate friendly relations with the Bhutanese government with the ulterior motive of inaugurating a trade route to Tibet through the Bhutanese kingdom. The Cooch Behar Raj held considerable sway over this tract in the seventeenth century but its influence waned in the eighteenth century. Taking advantage of this predicament the Bhutanese Raja invaded cooch-Behar. These depredations continued unabated until the cooch Behar Raja's repeated appeals for military aid to the East India Company provided the much desired ground for armed intervention. In attempting to interpret this official version as a mere excuse to annex the Duars, myriad possibilities are detected. The Duars area could be an interesting possibility for tea cultivation and being rich in forest resources could be a ready asset for timber extraction. The Anglo-Bhutanese War was triggered off by the futile efforts of a diplomatic mission to mitigate the Bhutanese depredations in 1864-5.[4] The Bhutanese forces gave way under the British onslaught and accepted the terms spelled out by the British Government. The Bhutanese Duars, like the Assamese

Duars became an integral part of British territory. A yearly tribute of Rs. 25,000 was stipulated to be exchanged for the Bengal Duars. The border demarcation between Bhutan Hills and the Duars was accomplished and the district of Jalpaiguri came into being in 1869.[5]

British Entry into the Duars and the Beginning of Forest Conservation

The Jalpaiguri Forest Division bears one of the best sal forests of India and within its small area of 40 Square miles has various forest tree species, other flora and fauna.[6] It comprises about 72 estates bordering the forests and a population directly or indirectly dependent on it, rendering every bit of forest produce saleable. In this division even an insignificant tree would fetch good revenue.[7] Francis Buchanan-Hamilton's report confirms that the jungles of Duars were not virgin forest at the time of British annexation. His report purveys well-organized timber operations in northern Bengal. He corroborates that the assimilation of labour gangs (indigenous population—Koch, Mech, Rabha) in organized timber operations was observed, trees were cut and floated on the Teesta River and later sold to timber merchants.[8] Although state control was extended over the forest in 1866, it remained in the words of the Forest Department open to 'indiscriminate felling' until 1874 when the first blocks of forest were properly reserved.[9] The reserved forests in Duars were administratively divided into two forest divisions, i.e. Jalpaiguri and Buxa, with the river Torsa separating the two. Despite the unbridled timber operations, according to the Forest Department, 'the best timber had been cut prior to the reservation, the Duar forests were still regarded as most valuable, in fact, the best sal forests in Bengal'.[10] On 1 April 1877, the following areas had been gazetted as reserves: the Apalchand forests, Tundu forests, Dainah forests, Moraghat forests, Dumchi forests, Dulgaon forests and Khairbari forests. The proprietor at a rental of Rs. 3,000 per annum farmed out the Baikunthpur Jungle Mahal Estate.

The building of the railway network is undeniably a landmark in the history of Indian forestry. The systematic management of forests of the Jalpaiguri and Buxa divisions commenced with the construction of small blocks of reserved forests to furnish a permanent supply of fuel and timber to the administrative centre of Jalpaiguri Division and the cantonment at Buxa.[11] Soon after the initiation of reservation, merchants were allowed to fell trees on payment of a fixed price per tree. The purchasers generally selected the best stems and worked only in accessible areas. Thus the forests were gradually depleted of the stock of best and selected stems in accessible areas. During 1870-1, the Government of Bengal laid down that no tree should be felled except by the direct agency of the Forest Department. This was perhaps the genesis of departmental operations.[12]

Conflicting Interests Over Forests

It is interesting to identify the competing interests within the colonial state itself. The state was not the homogenous actor as is often assumed or taken for granted.[13] This was particularly evident in relation to the conflict between the tea industry and the Forest Department. The focus was particularly on the difficulties of operating the tea gardens, which had to counter the triple-edged problem of fuel for factory engines, firewood for the labourers and above all, wood for tea boxes needed for the export of tea.

Wood suitable for tea boxes was available in Duars, but it was sold by the Forest Department at exorbitant prices, forcing the tea managers to import it from abroad. The officer in charge of the Survey Report was reprimanded by his superiors for his 'unsuitable and sometimes ignorant' ways of criticizing the work of other departments, i.e. the Forest Department.[14] Faced with the embarrassing fact that the tea-industry in dire need had turned to Japan and Sweden, the government in 1918-19 decided to grant concession to a private firm, Messrs Davenport & Co., for the extraction of timber within the Buxa Reserve, to be used for the local manufacture of tea boxes and also for timber and other wood products.[15]

Communities, Forests and the State

The State and its ensemble of institutions and sub-structures converged on the aspect of protecting forests from forest-dwellers, even if they diverged on the issues of commercial exploitation and environmental preservation. For a considerable period of time, communities living in the vicinity of forests persisted as peasants, resolutely cultivating shallow degraded forest soils. The social attachments to subsistence agriculture were so strong that the forest-dwellers found their self-image only through it.[16] Another important factor was the stratification noticed in forest dwelling communities. This is counter-indicative because the concept of a tribe came to be equated with a single rank.[17] In actuality, forest communities were stratified to some extent even in pre-colonial times. Henceforth, such communities were subject to further stratification on the basis of economic, social and political positions.

Forest dwelling communities can be analysed from the perspective of the articulation of modes of production.[18] Besides, forests being a tangible category also imply relationships. But the agency of control (i.e. a forest controlled by forest-dwellers and a forest owned by the government) would have different implications for the forest dweller.[19] Enmeshed in this maze, it would be interesting to explicate the relationship between forest-dwellers and forests as a tangible category and the changes perpetrated by the colonial state that necessitated the marginalization of these communities.

Confronting the Challenge of Colonial Forest Policy

Most colonial documents refer to the indigenous population of Duars as Mech, Kachari and sometimes Garos (Garrows), Totos and Rabhas. The Mech were nomadic husbandmen who wandered in the jungles, breaking up the virgin soil with their *daos* or billhooks, cultivating cotton and rice, and seldom remaining more than two years in the same place. Prior to British annexation they paid a capitation tax of Rs. 2 per annum per man to the Bhutanese government in return for which they were allowed to cultivate land. However, since they were accustomed to shifting cultivation they encountered severe dislocation due to the reservation of forests and extension of commercial agriculture.

It is a probable conjecture that the phenomenal timber demand of the railway network had triggered off the need for conservation. The establishment of the Indian Forest Service as per the Government Forest Act of 1865 heralded a more systematic and efficient planning. In course of time the colonial forest administrators expressed dissatisfaction with the Act's special provisions for village communities and their forest use practices. The Act clearly stated that the law should not abridge or affect any existing rights of individuals or communities to forest lands. This triggered of the famous debate between the first Inspector General of Forests, Brandis and other scientific foresters. Brandis's work in Burma convinced him of the vital importance of State control over forest ownership and management. The fusion of forestry with the State and its logical corollary, and the hostility to private enterprise were among the basic tenets of scientific conservation to which Brandis whole-heartedly subscribed.[20] Where Brandis was to depart radically from the consensus among 'scientific' foresters was in his enthusiasm for community ownership as a parallel but complementary system to state forestry. Experiences in Burma had made him conscious of the fact that valuable teak forests were controlled by militant tribes such as the Karens. He was aware of the potentially disruptive effects of a state forestry system that was too extensive and exclusionary.[21] Keenly cognizant of village forest rights and demands, Brandis had himself suggested a system of forest management based on a collaborative relationship between the State and the local communities. During his tenure in Burma, Brandis helped in developing a unique method of conciliation and village participation known as the *taungya* system.

In the Act of 1878 Baden Powell's (one of the chief architects of the official British forest policy in India) position prevailed and limited private property right only pertained to continuously cultivated land. This position was based on a highly selective and legalistic reading of Indian history, wherein it was argued, 'Oriental Sovereigns' had the right to dispose of forests and wastelands as they wished.[22] The Act, however, made some special provisions for certain 'channels' for the villagers. Communities were given three months to contest the reservations following the declaration of the State's intentions for reservation.

If the villagers failed to file a claim within this period, their rights were revoked. Unfortunately, this philanthropic gesture of the colonial government was futile since the illiterate villagers were ignorant of any survey and settlement programme or the intricacies of the legal procedures. The demarcation of all the reserves in the Jalpaiguri district was completed in 1876-8.[23] Large tracts of forests declared as 'wastelands' were opened up for tea cultivation and leased out to Europeans planters at very nominal rents. A substantial portion of the primeval forest disappeared and was replaced by tea gardens and sal plantations.[24] Railways and a network of roads were built to connect the Duar plantations with the outside world, and above all, the expanding industry brought about a demographic change.[25] The indigenous people were few in number, and they shunned the work in the tea gardens and sal plantations.[26] The planters instead recruited a major portion of the labour force from Chotanagpur in southern Bihar and the influx of groups like the Oraons, Mundas and Santhals proved to be a great boon to the tea industry.[27]

The population size of Jalpaiguri district altered phenomenally within a few decades. At the time of the 1921 census, the population of the district was 9,36,269 with a density of just 319 per square mile. As Table 10.1 indicates that peasant cultivators were attracted to the Western tract of the district and also to

TABLE 10.1: POPULATION GROWTH IN JALPAIGURI DISTRICT (1872-1931)

Census Year	*Jalpaiguri District*		*Western Duars*	
	Population	*Increase (%) over the previous year*	*Population*	*Increase (%) over the previous year*
1872	4,17,855	–	90,668	–
1881	5,80,570	26.97	1,82,687	101.49
1891	6,80,736	28.30	2,96,348	62.21
1901	7,87,380	15.66	4,10,606	38.55
1911	9,02,660	14.64	5,19,372	26.49
1921	9,36,269	3.72	5,58,971	7.62
1931	9,83,357	5.00	6,61,068	18.26

Source: Census reports of the relevant years.[28]

the neighbouring Rangpur district and the Cooch Behar State. Jalpaiguri district came to be composed of the greatest proportion of immigrant population just after Calcutta and Darjeeling.

The colonial records mention pastoralists and shifting cultivators resorting to passive resistance in the form of flight, by simply moving elsewhere, and by breach of rules of the Forest Department. For instance, they started forest fires and grazed cattle in the reserved forests, since forest fires and grazing were anathema to the scientific foresters who promulgated prohibitive regulation from the very outset.[29] Forest fires were endemic during most of the nineteenth century. Four cases of breache of rule were filed 1877-8 and in all these cases convictions were obtained. One was a case against two Bhuteas for setting fire to the forest and obstructing forest produce at the same time. A fine was imposed for the latter part of the offence, but the lighting of the fire could not be proved. Of the eight fires in the Buxa Reserve, six were extinguished, but two caused extensive damage due to the presence of high winds. Both fires were lighted inside the Reserve, one by cattle-owners and the other by a blacksmith who resided at Rajabhatkhawa and worked for the Forest Department.

Since grazing was anathema to the colonial foresters, the issue was subject to bitter polemics. 'Of many forest questions, on which discussion would tend to throw light, none appears of greater importance or more complicated in its general features than that of grazing.'[30] Treated in connection with its results on young forest growth, or with regard to the large population interested in obtaining good pasturage for their cattle, this subject ranked foremost with those relating to forest management, necessitating special consideration from both departmental and civil officers. The former were sometimes hesitant in reflecting that grazing was indispensable to the *gaoli* and his herds, or did much injury, or did not consider how dependent they were on the forests for their requirements. The latter persistently discredited the fact that cattle did much injury, or did not appreciate the real extent of damage caused by admitting them into a forest.[31] It would be a mind-boggling experience to deliberate on this issue, since it is till date a cause for consternation to the Forest Department.

Majority of persons acquainted with an iota of conservational perception adhered to the view that damage was caused by allowing cattle to graze forests that were being restored. It was not sufficient to simply prohibit felling or carting away of usufruct from a tract that was desired to facilitate a more wooded condition. Experience had proved that a timber crop could not be materially increased so long as large herds of cattle, goats and sheep were allowed to graze at will over the forest. All, or nearly all, seedlings were trampled or browsed down by animals, and much of the sapling growth was injured by cattle rubbing against it, or by the cowherds lopping its young branches for fodder, in those places where the grass had dried up or been thoroughly grazed down.[32]

A somewhat different version on grazing has been unfolded in another account. With reference to the proposal rendering all grazing illegal in the Duars with an aim to protect the sal forests, the cultivators were dislocated, removed to a distance, leaving the forests to be surrounded by a howling wilderness of grass, aggravating the fear of forest fires.[33] Instead, if the best forests were fenced by cultivation, and in turn if cultivation and grazing within the edges of the forest proved a check to fires, the district officer and forest officer would be able to share a lot of bonhomie and the class of woodmen would not be driven away from their old quarters, but would be handy in case of want of labour.[34]

The government decided that cattle grazing could not be totally discontinued. As milk was required for the regiment at Buxa, cattle grazing were to be confined to the burnt part of Panbari Block to curtail damage prospects. The British blamed the forest fires on ignorance; it was claimed that the local people were oblivious of the aims of the British forest policy. The conservator of forests wrote, 'Although our measures were only partially successful, still we have achieved more than would have been considered possible a few years ago. . . . When the people come to understand what our object is, and when they see they cannot set fire to the forest without becoming liable to severe punishment.'[35] This also became the common way of handling the indigenous cultivators. Not being permanent settlers, they had no right to claim the land, and the government could simply inform them to 'move outside' the area of forest declared as 'reserved'. In some cases villagers were offered small sums in compensation for their transfer. A Rabha man corroborated that all of a sudden a realization dawned on them much to their displeasure that the forests were limited and one day they would find themselves deprived of further living space.

Plantation and Regeneration

The plantations of north Bengal constitute an interesting chronicle. Baffled by the problems of natural regeneration, plantations of different species were raised in a planned manner. The conversion of high forests by means of planting was conceived as early as 1867. Immediately after the reservation of the forests in the year 1867 a group of foresters thought of converting the existing forests and sporadic trial of many species were made all over north Bengal.[36] In the Terai and the Duars, the earliest plantation (1867) was aimed at introducing teak and mahogany near Sukna. This, however, ended in a faux pas on account of the poor quality of the seeds and also due to drainage inherent in the site chosen for the trial.[37] Teak was further experimented upon Bamanpokhri (from 1868 onwards) but the series of plantations, despite the earlier promise, was not pushed beyond 1888. The area under teak plantation was not subject to any further enlargement. The planters thought that if teak failed to thrive in the subsequent years, it should be heared in conjunction with toon, sisoo and sal. However, plantations with an increasing emphasis on sal were created wherever the site was found suitable.

However, the success of sal stupefied the foresters in the beginning and as a consequence sal was popularized. Plantations with increasing emphasis on sal were created wherever the site was found suitable. Soon sal was to monopolize large tracts of forests in north Bengal. The preference for sal is perceptible considering its commercial value and hence its consequent depletion. It immensely enhanced the value of the forests wherefrom stock was being decimated of many valuable species. As a consequence the invasion of many useless evergreen species took place due to edaphic changes induced by rigid fire control

TABLE 10.2: POPULARIZATION OF SAL PLANTATIONS

Locality	*Name of the Species*	*Age*	*Total Stem Yield of Timber Volume per Cu.M*	*From High Forests when Clearfelled (in Cu.M per hectare) (Average)*
Lower Tundu	Sal	15	–	
		20	12.41	
		25	37.29	
		30	62.86	72.10
		35	87.02	
		40	111.87	
		45	136.04	
Apalchand	Sal	15	–	
		20	10.00	
		25	27.50	
		30	82.50	29.50
		35	120.00	
		40	155.00	
		45	195.00	
MoraghatRange	Sal	15	1.05	
		20	10.60	
		25	35.38	
		30	70.77	34.50
		35	114.65	
		40	159.22	
		45	205.25	
UpperTundu	Sal	15	–	
		20	16.50	
		25	48.90	
		30	78.80	58.70
		35	111.40	
		40	145.80	
		45	177.80	

Source: District Gazetteers and Settlement Records for the years 1867-77.

measures, and also due to selective exploitation of better trees.[38] Table 10.2 will provide ample evidence for the wide-scale popularization of sal plantations.

From Conflict to Compromise

The necessity for fire protection was one of the truths that the new forest science had established in the late nineteenth century. 'The exclusion of fires from reserved forests... became emblematic of what care and modern management could accomplish in the forest in India.'[39] The outcome, however, was quite unexpected. Fire prevention in the Duars had almost eradicated the young sal saplings. In other words, the tall grass and weeds provided a sort of protection to the young saplings, the destruction of which led to the eradication of the young plants. The remnants of such a failed venture are still evident in Damanpur area, where the entire plantation perished. It was also known that clearance of undergrowth made the young pure crop of sal susceptible to the disease Loranthus.[40] It is a strange paradox that the Herculean efforts to propagate sal plantations resulted in no gains. Nature perhaps has its own ways of striking back. Despite the initial hurdles, the Forest Department managed to control fires, but a new problem emerged: the sal forest stopped regenerating itself. The reduction of forest fires caused a tremendous spread of creepers. Worse, a thick layer of undergrowth replaced the savannah grass cover favourable to sal seedlings. Myriad unsuccessful methods were attempted until the situation became acute. G.S. Hart's (inspector general of forests) proposals were based on experiments in the Duars. The new method constituted initial clear felling of trees followed by field cultivation, or the so-called *taungya* cultivation, and artificial regeneration or direct sowing of the seeds of the particular trees wanted.[41] The term originates from the method of shifting cultivation that was practiced all over the Burmese highland. Edmund Leach, writing on the Kachins, said that the term '*taungya*' means '*hillfield*' and is a technique of cultivation resembling that, which in Assam is known as '*Jhum*'. There is, however, a technical difference between ordinary *jhum* or shifting cultivation, and the method Brandis learned from the Karen people from whom he borrowed the term *taungya*. Shifting cultivation implies desertion of land following some years of cultivation, whereas in *taungya* along with the cultivation of food crops particular species of trees are planted for harvest at a much later date.

Paradoxically, the new knowledge introduced to reformulate forest operations was antithetical to what the scientific foresters advocated. The question, however, was not limited to application of techniques, but rather to unanimous effort of foresters responding to an acute local crisis. The indigenous communities, who were earlier referred to in pejorative terms, became an invaluable asset to the Forest Department. Hart initially thought it an easy task to involve the forest communities—'indeed the people show a great keenness to take up this work'.[42] Suitable labour remained a limiting factor to the development or extensive usage of the *taungya* method for 'there are now so few villagers who habitually *jhum*'.

The establishment of forest villages was considered absolutely essential in order to ensure a permanent supply of labour. Shebbeare was assigned the task of restructuring of the system of forest villages in view of the prevailing circumstances. According to him, in 1894 the first labourers had been settled inside the reserved forests, but the early settlements for fire prevention were shortlived and by 1902 all of them were deserted. From 1904 it became a regular policy in the Jalpaiguri Division to establish forest villages.[43] *Taungya* system brought in new rules. In the 1930s independent shifting cultivators were transformed into settled forest villagers under the rule of the Forest Department. This paradigm shift was not imposed upon them, but with the loss of the jungle—which was reserved, converted into tea gardens, or made into agricultural land—there were not many options left. Consequently, the forest villages were in a state of flux. Households and often entire villages were deserted while others came into being.[44] The Forest Department, however, was not in apposition to force people to settle or remain in a forest village. Any form of coersion would lead to flight or desertion.

The crops obtained from the *taungya* plantations proved insufficient to maintain a household throughout the year. It was also a risky type of agriculture, both the villagers' own crops and the saplings often perished due to the depredations of wild pigs, elephants or other wild animals. The Forest Department, therefore, had provided the forest villagers with an additional land for permanent cultivation instead of shifting cultivation.

Forest being the forest-dwellers' *sine-qua-non* for living and the colonial government's source for resource generation, coping with scientific forestry proved to be an arduous task for both. To return to the question of legal status of the lands already possessed or cultivated by the tribes, the Forest Department considered these lands as leased or granted to the forest villagers in return for the services rendered. 'The lease is only temporary, and the land remains the property of the State.' This was the position expressed in the forest officials' general rhetoric, and in the land documents some of the forest villagers possess till date.[45] All government authorities have uncritically accepted this position. In his work on Rabha society, M.K. Raha pointed out that 'the land, the house, and other constructions are not their own, but actually belong to the Forest Department of the State Government. The forest authority only permits them to enjoy these temporarily in exchange of their labour rendered to this department on year to year contract.'[46]

The need of a permanent labour supply remained the crux of the *taungya* system throughout the British period. The people who put their shifting cultivation skills to use in the Forest Department's *taungya* plantations were none other than the indigenous people (Koch, Mech, Rabha, Toto, etc.). With the implementation of the *taungya* system, these shifting cultivators who had earlier become a left-over population with no place in the new colonial plan, suddenly became a crucial asset to the Forest Department. This heralded the era of compromise from conflict. The initial difficulties persisted as compromise was imposed from above. This structure, absorbed with minor variations during the post-colonial phase, was also confronted with similar difficulties. Independent India experimented with methods of social forestry: with *Vanmahotsav* of the 1950s paving the way for a more balanced cooperation in the 1970s and 1980s and the creation of Forest Protection Committees in the 1990s.

NOTES

1. Satpal Sangwan, 'Making of a Popular Debate: The Indian Forester and the Emerging Agenda of State Forestry in India, 1875-1904', *Indian Economic and Social History Review* (hereafter IESHR), vol. 36, no. 2, April-June 1999, p. 187.

2. Satpal Sangwan, op. cit., p. 187.
3. K. Sivaramakrishnan, *Modern Forests: State Making and Environmental Change in Colonial Eastern India*, Delhi, 1999, pp. 2-3.
4. D.H.E. Sunder, *Survey and Settlement of the Western Duars in the District of Jalpaiguri: 1889-95*, Calcutta, 1895, pp. 18-22.
5. D.H.E. Sunder, op. cit., pp. 18-22.
6. West Bengal District Gazetteers, Jalpaiguri, Calcutta, 1981, pp. 1-2.
7. Seventh Working Plan for the Reserved Forests of the Jalpaiguri Forests Division (Calcutta, 1975-6 to 1980-4) in Jalpaiguri Forest Office Library (hereafter, JFO), p. 1.
8. Proceedings of the Revenue Board, 16 November 1773, Nos. 2, Calcutta, 1774, p. 10. West Bengal State Archives (hereafter, WBSA), Kolkata.
9. Proceedings of the Revenue Board, 16 November, op. cit., pp. 10-15.
10. E.O. Shebbeare, Working Plan for the Reserved Forests in the Jalpaiguri Division of the Bengal Forest Circle, 1920, p. 8, JFO.
11. 'Brief History of the Forest Department in Bengal (with Assam from its Inception to 1870)', Revenue Proceedings, WBSA, Kolkata, 1870, pp. 20-4.
12. 'Progress Report of Forest Administration in Bengal 1871-1900' in E.P. Stebbing's '*The Forests of India*', vol. III, John Lane the Bodley Head Limited, London, Calcutta, 1902, pp. 225-30.
13. B.G. Karlsson, *Contested Belonging: An indigenous People's Struggle for Forest and Identity in Sub-Himalayan Bengal, Lund University*, Department of Sociology, 1997, pp. 90-91.
14. Resolution by C.E. Buckland, Secretary to the Government of Bengal, 8 July 1895, published together with Sunder's Settlement Report op. cit., p. 10.
15. The issue of tea boxes was discussed in various letters and documents during this time. The private firm that finally got the concessions started large-scale forest operations, clear-felling the forest around Rajabhatkhawa, where a light railway had been constructed to transport the timber. See G.S. Hart, 'Note on a Tour Inspection in the Goalpara (Assam), Buxa, Jalpaiguri, Kalimpong, Kurseong Forest Division, Bengal', April 1920, p. 12.
16. Akhileshwar Pathak, *Contested Domains—State, Peasants and Forests in Contemporary India*, Delhi, 1994, p. 15.
17. Akhileshwar Pathak, *Contested Domains*, op. cit., pp. 15-17.
18. Arun Bandopadhyay, 'Towards an Understanding of Environmental History', in *The Calcutta Historical Journal,* vol. 16, no. 2, Calcutta, 1994, p. 154.
19. Ramachandra Guha, *The Unquiet Woods*, Delhi, 1989, pp. 5-7.
20. B.G. Karlsson, op. cit., p. 99.
21. Progress Report of the Forest Administration of Bengal, 1877-78, Calcutta, 1878, p. 34.
22. R. Guha, 'Dietrich Brandis and Indian Forestry: A Vision Revisited

and Reaffirmed' in M. Poffenberger and Betsy McGean (eds.), *Village, Voices, Forest Choices,* Delhi, 1998, pp. 86-8.
23. Progress Report of the Forest Administration of Bengal, 1877–78, Calcutta, 1878, p. 34.
24. Ranajit Dasgupta, *Economy, Society and Politics in Bengal: Jalpaiguri 1869-1947*, Delhi, 1992, p. 9.
25. R.P. Tucker, *Himalayan Foothills of Assam*, London, 1988, p. 46.
26. R.P. Tucker, op. cit., pp. 32-3. Tucker argues that this system of recruiting labour mainly from Chotanagpur was already practiced in the tea gardens of Assam. A possible reason may be availability of cheap labour.
27. A. Mitra, *Census 1951: West Bengal District Handbook, Jalpaiguri*, Calcutta, 1954, p. 30.
28. Data collected from Census Reports for the relevant years.
29. See letter from Peterson to Ulick Browne, 29 August 1876 in Annual Progress Report Calcutta, 1877, p. 5.
30. 'On the Effects of Grazing in Sal Forests', WRF Notes and Queries, in *Indian Forester*, vol. 2, October 1877, Calcutta, 1877, pp. 203-6.
31. 'On the Effects of Grazing in Sal Forests', pp. 204-6.
32. J. McKee, 'On Grazing', in *Indian Forester*, vol. 2, Calcutta, October 1875, pp. 100-7.
33. 'On the Effects of Grazing in Sal Forests' pp. 203-4.
34. J. McKee, op. cit., *Indian Forester*, pp. 100-7.
35. Annual Progress Report on Forest Administration in the Bengal Presidency, Calcutta, 1924, p. 3.
36. R.C. Ghosh, 'Plantations of North Bengal—A Review' and A.B. Chowdhury, 'The Forests of Jalpaiguri District – A Study in Composition', op. cit., p. 113.
37. R.C. Ghosh, op. cit., p. 113.
38. Annual Progress Report for the Forest Administration in the Provinces of Bengal for 1909-10, Calcutta, 1911, p. 10.
39. R.C. Ghosh, op. cit., pp. 113-14.
40. Annual Progress Report for Bengal Presidency 1937-38, Calcutta, 1939, pp. 25-30.
41. See Dr. Schlich's (Conservator of Forests) letter to the Secretary, Govt. of Bengal Presidency, Financial Dept. 2, November 1876 in Progress Report of Bengal Presidency, Calcutta, 1877, p. 15.
42. See the 'Notification on Reserved Forest Tracts in the Western Dooars, Julpigurее District', by the Financial Dept., Govt. of Bengal, in Progress Report of Bengal, Calcutta, 1876, p. 13.
43. Annual Progress Report, Calcutta, 1877, p. 4.
44. *Progress Report of Forest Administration of Bengal, 1930-35*, Calcutta, 1936, pp. 15-20.
45. Working Plan for the Reserved Forests in the Jalpaiguri Division, 1920, Calcutta, 1922, pp. 23-4.
46. M.K. Raha, *The Rabhas of West Bengal*, Calcutta, Scheduled Castes and Tribes, Welfare Department, Govt. of West Bengal, 1967, p. 30.

11. Congress and Conservation: A Look at the NPC Reports*

Jagdish N. Sinha

Introduction

Apart from its political agenda, the Indian National Congress was interested in almost anything that had resulted from the colonial rule and intervention which could facilitate the party's fight for freedom. For, the nationalist leadership had perceived from the beginning that colonialism was all-pervasive; and so, any effort to end it could not be a piecemeal affair. This is why what literally started as a war against the foreign rule concluded as a cultural confrontation with unique tools of truth and non-violence under the leadership of Mahatma Gandhi. Of the many things that came in between, the finesse of the nationalist discourse on man and nature in terms of imperialism and nationalism is noteworthy. It is from this angle that this paper seeks to examine the concern of the Congress for conservation and environment, with reference particularly to the endeavours of its National Planning Committee (NPC) in the last decade of the colonial rule in India.

To begin with, the Congress focused on the economic problems and tried to promote technical education; later, scientific and technical services attracted its attention. The question of industrialization came on its agenda with the rise of *Swadeshism*

* I take this opportunity to express my gratitude to late D.P. Singh, Supreme Court Lawyer and Congress M.P., and P.N. Haksar, bureaucrat and diplomat, both closely associated with the Congress and its leader Indira Gandhi for initiating me into research. The materials for this paper were collected under an INSA (Delhi) project. The author expresses his sincere thanks to the Indian National Science Academy for its generous funding.

(urge to use things indigenous); and by the outbreak of World War I, its leaders like Madan Mohan Malaviya presented elaborate nationalist discourse on it. Mahatma Gandhi gave a new orientation to the Congress programme in which nature and environment assumed significance in relation to social progress and political freedom. However, the rising young leadership, within the Congress and outside it, interpreted Gandhi's ideas as an ambiguous ideology bereft of any direct relevance to the problems of the country. With their background of Western education and liking for Western way of life, they came forward with new ideas and new solutions based on Western science and technology. In order to realize their dream, the Congress constituted a National Planning Committee in October 1938, for drawing a 10-year plan for developing India as soon as she would be free. While making this plan, the NPC also took into account the questions of conservation, environment and ecology. The issue was taken up also by other organs and forums of the Congress, including its individual members and sympathisers. [1]

The Genesis

The genesis of the Congress' concern for conservation and environment may be traced to Gandhi's *Hind Swaraj* written in 1908. In this book, Gandhi presented his views not only against imperialism and material culture of the West but also on the holistic approach of the Indian culture, in which nature occupied a pivotal position.[2] The Mahatma raised the discourse to a higher level where human well-being and happiness on the one hand and nature on the other were seen in a mutually inextricable relation.[3] His philosophy of 'truth' and 'non-violence' was not confined to politics alone; it had deep implications for conservation in the widest possible sense. Initially and for many decades to come, however, Gandhi's exposition was read as an ambiguous and abstract philosophy—retrogressive in concept and impractical to follow. Obviously, this was sure to have no takers in the colonial corridors; for many in the Congress and outside it, it was of no use either. Even Jawaharlal Nehru, a favourite of Gandhi, did not subscribe to the Mahatma's views;[4] so was the case with M.N. Saha, the rising leader of the Indian scientific community.[5] Yet, the ideas of the Mahatma were never rejected outright. On the contrary, he had already found some like minded thinkers in personalities like Anand K. Coomarswamy[6] and Rabindranath Tagore,[7] among others. However, the Congress did not promote Gandhi's ideas until he came at the helm of affairs in the early 1920s.

From this time onwards, Gandhi's philosophy was begun to be translated through rural reconstruction, which once again brought the issues of nature and environment in the limelight. The programme envisaged promotion of small-scale cottage industries and emphasized sanitation and natural life, which was reflected in Gandhi's preference for naturopathy and indigenous medicine.[8] The problems of poverty and backwardness bothered many others too; but the issues on their agenda and the means of solutions differed from those of the Mahatma. For M. Visvesveraya, the noted engineer and technocrat, the panacea for India's problems lay in large-scale industrialization on the capitalist lines.[9] Noted scientist M.N. Saha, too, wanted large-scale industrialization but on the Soviet model. He pleaded for a wholesale transformation of the national life with the help of modern science and technology, with a meticulous management of the natural resources of the country.[10] In this way, both of them were addressing in some way the problems of natural resources and environment; yet their means and the ultimate goals were different from each other as well as from those of Gandhi. This predicament was bound to influence the Congress policy and the national concern on the subject at large in the years to come. By mid 1930s, the young leadership within the party came out with similar ideas for national reconstruction, which, once again, brought the question of management of the natural resources, hence of environment and ecology to the fore.[11]

NPC on Conservation

After the call for *Purna Swaraj* (complete self-rule) in 1930 and the colonial effort to placate the demand leading to the grant of Provincial Autonomy in 1935, things changed fast. With the elections in the provinces and formation of popular ministries there, the nationalist leadership felt emboldened to look ahead to the approaching independence. The Congress felt so enthused that it constituted in 1938 the National Planning Committee to plan for the development of a free India. The NPC was directed to prepare a 10-year plan for national reconstruction with the help of modern science and technology to be implemented by the national government after independence. The National Committee worked through 29 sub-committees dealing with the various aspects of the national life. It was chaired by Jawaharlal Nehru and hundreds of top Indian experts worked on its different sub-committees.[12]

While defining national plan in a Note for the Guidance of its Sub-Committees, the NPC stated that:

> The different sectors of the Plan have necessarily to be co-ordinated. The essence of planning is an advance on all fronts. There must be agricultural planning, the object being that the country should be at least self-sufficient as regards foodstuffs measured in terms of the food index given above, and as regards the quantity of raw material this should be raised by a pre-determined percentage. Soil conservation, afforestation, grass land management, flood control and river management, and improvement of inland navigation and transport, improvement of livestock and fodder supply, are items in the planned programme which have not yet been taken up systematically. Power development of coal and other kinds of fuel for industrial power also demand planning. More important is the planning of different kinds and types of industries, large, medium and cottage, which alone may effectively mitigate the present pressure of population on the soil. Within a decade the aim should be to produce a balanced economic structure in which half the population would depend on agriculture.[13]

Going by the above guideline of the NPC and its views expressed elsewhere, it is clear that though its main concern was planning and development and not conservation or environment, it was very much aware of the latter's crucial role in national reconstruction, and so, many of its sub-committees addressed the subject again and again. In fact, it appointed an exclusive sub-committee on soil conservation and afforestation[14] and many of its other sub-committees also took note of the subject, at times in greater detail, in their respective fields, such as, those dealing with River Training and Irrigation, Mining and Metallurgy, Health, Population, Power and Fuel, Crop Planning and

Production, and Transport and Communications.[15]

Initially, the concern for conservation arose in the context of exploitation of natural resources for development of the country. As expected, these committees began with queries and surveys in order to understand the condition in their respective fields so that they could suggest ways and means to solve the problems and contribute to development in the future. For this, detailed questionnaires were circulated widely. The data and information received revealed disturbing facts: lack of information, dangerous equation among various aspects of environment and society, lack of coordination among the various official agencies concerned, and indifference or faulty approach of the government in the matter. All these facts were discussed and analysed, and finally reports with recommendations were submitted to the parent body, the NPC, which, in turn, passed its own recommendations, generally agreeing with the views and recommendations of the sub-committees.[16]

SOIL AND LANDMASS USE

This subject was taken up in detail and directly by the Sub-Committee on Soil Conservation and Afforestation.[17] The terms of reference of the inquiry were: (1) protection against erosion, floods and other detrimental factors affecting the soil; (2) treating it with manure and fertilizers; (3) providing drainage and other facilities needed to guard against water-logging and weeds; (4) planting of new forests in areas denuded of them; (5) care of existing forest and sylviculture; (6) development of forest produce and establishment or development of industries founded upon them; (7) provision of transport facilities needed to develop forests; and (8) reclamation of land and such other things relevant to the subject.[18]

Thus, the Sub-Committee took a wider view of the subject. However, it was soon faced, as most of its sister committees, with the problem of the lack of information and data. It, therefore, also drew upon the knowledge of individual members of the committee and its collaborators but an attempt was made 'to avoid individual bias or predilection'.[19] Whatever information was thus culled in was full of distressing facts: there was no state machinery to deal with the subject properly; and the existing ones lacked in mutual coordination. But what was most disconcerting was the serious imbalance among the various contenders of land mass use. Its use by the population was faulty; the forest cover was not adequate, and whatever existed of it was mal-distributed. While looking into the problem, the sub-committee took into consideration several factors, such as volume and distribution of population, factors responsible for soil erosion, agricultural and cultural practices, impact of war, land relations and India's climate. In this connection, it remarked that 'The most apparent feature of the present maladjustment in relation to soil conservation is the small proportion of the total area devoted to village or minor forests, fodder crops, pastures, fruit trees and other trees, e.g. for fuel, timber etc.'[20] It also took note of the disastrous consequences in this regard of the cash crops and uncoordinated expansion of the railways, both of which were an outcome of the colonial rule in the country.[21]

Apart from suggesting various administrative measures and considerably enhanced initiative by the state, the Sub-Committee underlined the 'importance of coordination of policy, research, efforts and programmes of land use'. It put special emphasis on research and development (R&D) and propagation of new knowledge and skill. It underlined the necessity of village planning and wanted it to be accorded importance along with drainage, water supply, communications and such other matters in connection with future plans for rural reconstruction.[22]

After the final deliberation on the subject, the National Committee resolved: 'Soil and Forests constitute a national heritage. On their successful conservation, depend the present and the future of the nation. The State, must, therefore, step in and accept responsibility for their conservation.' It further wanted that the problems of conservation of soil and forests be treated as a whole after the closest investigation. For the control of the management and use of land, it proposed the establishment of a Land Development Board, both at the Centre and in the provinces and the states. The provincial and the state organizations were to look after the local aspects and the organization at the Centre would take up matters of interest to more than one province. This was expected to serve the purpose of coordinating all efforts for conservation of soils and forests and enable the problems to be visualized and grappled as a whole.[23] The Central Land Development Board was expected to deal with: soil conservation including soil surveys, soil maps, soil fertility and land reclamation; anti-erosion measures; afforestation, reafforestation and improvement of existing forests; and land utilization and coordination.[24]

Other connected subjects like irrigation and drainage, crop production, grasslands and pasture, industrial utilization of agricultural and forest produce, and marketing of produce from the land should be dealt with in consultation and cooperation with corresponding organizations.[25] The whole area in a province or state was to be divided into physigraphic units, each of which would have a research station. A central institute for the study of soil was proposed for the whole country.[26] The National Committee also resolved that adequate facilities should be provided for training in forestry and agriculture in the universities and technical institutes, especially with a view to making the results available to the public.[27]

While the 'State must accept the responsibility for soil conservation and take all necessary measures to overcome these limitations and work out plans for conservation', remarked J.N. Mukherjee, chairman of the Sub-Committee, 'Public cooperation must be obtained and it is therefore necessary to rouse public conscience and create soil and tree sense in our people and more especially in our politicians and administrators.'

FOREST AND WILD LIFE

Directing attention to the existing problems of land mass and its use, such as utterly inadequate forest cover, soil erosion and infertility of land, this Sub-Committee on Soil Conservation and Afforestation recommended several remedial measures, including afforestation, control over shifting agriculture and reclamation.[28] Giving very special importance to forest, the NPC resolved: 'Forest must be preserved as a national heritage, and Forestry should be judged by the long-term financial results rather than the immediate surplus.' Therefore, it suggested several remedial measures for improvement, including creating organizational bodies in the provinces and the states, control of grazing and fire, contour trenching and gully plugging. Finding the general condition of privately owned forests unsatisfactory, it recommended that they should be acquired by the State or strictly controlled by it in the public interest. Forests were to be developed and worked with a view to produce raw materials for various industries, including the cottage industries.[29]

The NPC showed a deep concern for the depletion of the wildlife and hence recommended a ban on organized large-scale hunting. For the protection and preservation of wildlife in the jungles, it suggested the creation of national parks and sanctuaries in various parts of the country. Finally, it highlighted the urgency of developing suitable means of transport and communications to enhance accessibility to the forests so that they could be developed and exploited properly.[30]

LIVESTOCK

The Sub-Committee on Soil Conservation and Afforestation was prompt to note the 'deplorable condition of livestock' in the country. It attributed it to 'insufficient production of fodder crops, bad conditions of grazing grounds, unmanageable numbers of cattle and the neglect of proper methods of breeding.'[31] It went into the details of these and other factors connected with the subject.

But it was the Sub-Committee on Animal Husbandry and Dairying that delved deep into the subject. It studied the problems and prospects of various types of animals used in economic activities, for transportation and for food.[32] To begin with, it took stock of all types of livestock available in the country at the time, and of the colonial measures, the initiative by the newly-formed Congress ministry in Bombay in the matter, and trends abroad. The Sub-Committee noted that India had the largest number of cattle in the world (more than 31 per cent of the world cattle population), but qualitatively it was 'perhaps the poorest'.[33] Therefore, it placed special emphasis on improving their food supply, health and breeding. It discussed in detail the problems of fodder and suggested increased emphasis on nutritional research.[34] Preventive measures to control diseases were emphasized, and the value of R&D at every level and of veterinary education was underlined.[35] With a view to maintaining harmony between the cattle population, their natural food supply and the volume of demands by the society, it was suggested to keep a control over their population through sterilization and slaughtering, which was to be supervised by veterinary experts.[36]

Veterinary science was a privileged sector under the British rule though essentially for military purposes.[37] The NPC report differed in that it pleaded for promoting the services for wider use. It placed special emphasis on veterinary education, making it an integral part of the national education system, and wanted to take the knowledge and skill generated by both of them to the village and the actual farmer.[38] Secondly, it acknowledged, unlike most of the British, India's great indigenous tradition in the field of animal husbandry and the good quality of the local breeds, which could be used beneficially with the help of modern knowledge. Its emphasis on reviving and conserving the indigenous pedigree animals is particularly significant from the view point of conservation.[39] It also studied smaller animals such as sheep, goat, and poultry that supplemented the economy of the poorer section of the Indian society, and made appropriate recommendations for their improvement.[40]

Apart from calling for creating a system for intelligence gathering on the subject, the NPC stressed the necessity of pedigree reproduction, conservation of the indigenous livestock (miltch, draught and others) and maintenance of its general health and utility. It showed concern, at the same time, for maintaining a balance between the cattle population, and the natural and social environment.[41] It also discussed the problems affecting sanitation on account of animal husbandry and dairying and suggested to locate their establishments away from towns and human habitations.[42] The subject was discussed also by other sub-committees like that on soil conservation and afforestation.

AQUATIC LIFE

The NPC also paid attention to the aquatic life in the country. A separate sub-committee examined the various aspects of fisheries as a prospective industry and made recommendations in this regard. What is, however, important from our point of view is the emphasis on R&D,[43] as the subject had been badly neglected during the colonial rule. This was so in spite of the fact that fishes and other aquatic animals were an important source of protein and other vital nutrients for a sizeable section of the poor throughout the country.[44] Moreover, India had a large number of rivers and varieties of other water bodies besides possessing one of the longest coastline thriving with marine life in the world that[45] no wonder, her ecological balance was crucially dependent on them.[46] Yet the fact that the colonial government neglected the subject amply speaks of the official indifference to the basic interests of the local people.

WATER RESOURCES

The Sub-committee on River Training and Irrigation was one of the first and most important bodies to deliberate on conservation and ecology directly.[47] One of its important members, M.N. Saha, had by now made the problems of flood and urgency of managing rivers an important issue in relation to the socio-economic development of the country.[48] This committee considered the rivers as an important natural asset of the country; and so it made detailed recommendations as to how to train them to control flooding and devastation, and harness their waters for irrigation, power generation and transportation. In this connection, it also examined the problems of soil erosion and landmass-population ratio.[49] After discussing the recommendations of the Sub-Committee, the National Committee made its recommendations.

It suggested for creating a Water Resources Board for obtaining a high degree of coordination and correlation of efforts for conservation and utilization of water resources in the country. It wanted to have a thorough study and evaluation of the water resources—both surface and underground—for which it asked for creating a Department of Hydrographic Survey and advised to have a section on hydrology attached to the Meteorological Department. It considered river water a major aspect of the subject that deserved meticulous and holistic approach. Instead of haphazard building of flood banks here and there, it advised scientific management of the natural river systems. It recommended careful training of rivers through reservoir system and other appropriate measures, and emphasized the importance of taking into consideration all factors affecting the society, economy and environment of the whole basin of the rivers. As such, besides flood control and irrigation, it pleaded for making use of river water also for transport and power generation. All this was to be achieved through development of integrated river valley projects on the model of Tennessee Valley Authority (TVA) of the USA.[50]

A separate Sub-Committee on Power and Fuel examined the question of power generation from alternative sources.[51] Both the Sub-Committee and the National Committee emphasized the necessity of developing and exploiting the vast resources of hydroelectricity in the country. For this, they recommended the constitution of a Hydro-Electric Survey of India, like the Royal Water Power Board of Sweden, or the Federal Hydro-Dynamical Survey of Canada, as a permanent body with the same status as the Trigonometrical and Geological Survey of India. It was to work in cooperation with the National Water Power Resources Commission, and the survey was to be undertaken according to the natural hydrological divisions of India (e.g., Ganga Basin, Indus Basin, Western Ghats and Deccan Plateau), in a comprehensive manner laid down by the World Power Conference.[52] It was in the field of water resources that the NPC recommendations were the first to be translated into practice. In the very first session of the Dominion of India Parliament, in November-December 1947, a bill was introduced to establish the Damodar Valley Authority, a Statutory Corporation, and the Damodar Valley Corporation (DVC) came into being in 1949. This was soon followed by other river valley projects like Kosi and Gandak projects in Bihar and others elsewhere.[53]

MINERALS

Concurring with the report of the Sub-Committee on Mining and Metallurgy, the National Committee accepted the vital importance of the mineral wealth of the country, and since it belonged to the community collectively, the Sub-Committee wanted it to be carried on as public enterprise.[54] It suggested: 'Restriction should be imposed on the export of ores of national importance, such as manganese, mica, limonite, etc. A definite policy should be laid down in respect of minerals of which India has a virtual monopoly, or of which she has supply in excess of her requirements.' It wanted that the Central Geological Survey Department to carry out a thorough survey of the mineral resources of the country, and for this purpose, it be extended and adequately strengthened with expert staff. Taking a serious view of the problem of waste in the mining process, it wanted it to be investigated by experts and stopped wherever possible.[55] It found the existing rules and regulations regarding mining and prospecting highly unsatisfactory and so desired them to be revised. Besides, it advised Indian nationals to be trained in sufficient numbers for all types of work, to replace the then employed foreign experts at the earliest possible.[56]

The Sub-Committee on Power and Fuel also examined the minerals connected with energy generation.[57] In its report, the NPC called for a definite National Power and Fuel Policy treating the power and fuel resources of the country 'as a national property, which should be fully conserved, scientifically developed and utilised'. In view of the limited reserves of coal, which could not be replenished, and its very wasteful mining, processing and supply, the NPC wanted to have a 'very strict State control' on the coal industry. Moreover, in order to conserve coal, it advised to encourage exploitation of alternative sources like hydro-electricity.[58]

Realizing the vital importance of minerals for the country, the sub-committee on minerals and metallurgy enquired in detail into their existing condition, and the laws governing them.[59] In view of the poor endowment of mineral resources of the country, it regretted that even the known or available mineral resources of the country had not been developed with the intensity they deserved, if the objective of national self-sufficiency in the matter of industries was to be attained. On the contrary, the matter had been made worse because of the negative colonial policy allowing uncontrolled, haphazard mining and inroads of foreign firms in the sector. The sub-committee therefore, warned against the growing oil imperialism and of the phenomenon later perceived as neo-colonialism.[60] Here again, the recommendations of the sub-committee were executed as soon as the national leadership assumed powers of governance. A Fuel Research Institute (FRI) was established at Dhanbad, which was followed by the nationalization of the mineral resources of the country.[61]

HUMAN RESOURCES

While the human resources drew attention of other subcommittees, too, it was directly dealt with by the sub-committees on population,[62] health[63] and education.[64] A separate Sub-Committee on Population examined the problems of the number and quality of population, its co-relation with the means of subsistence and the remedial measures against over-population. It discussed the question of redistribution of population both within the country and outside it, and several other factors affecting its quality and growth.[65] Some of its findings with regard to population growth were revealing and disturbing. While confirming the steady growth in the Indian population, it noted certain trends not only hostile to the progress and well-being of the nation but also tending to create liabilities in terms of increase in the enhanced demand for food, healthcare and education.[66]

The Committee highlighted the special characteristics of the population structure in India. In the country's 'population pyramid', it found heavier piling up at the base and shrinking in the middle and violent fluctuations relatively common at every level. Such a structure suggested an abundance of unproductive population (children), shortage of productive population (mature adults) and presence of an element of uncertainty due to fluctuations in the growth of various age groups, sex and regional distribution—a condition unfavourable for proper planning and growth.[67] These characteristics were not common for the population pyramid in the West. Showing concern for the declining ratio of the upper middle-aged group (40-45) from 100.4 in 1891 to 96.8 in 1931, the Committee did not fail to notice that everywhere in the world this group showed lowest mortality ant that the best leadership came from it. The decline in India in the proportion of this group, already one of the lowest in the world, did not augur well for social progress in the near future.[68]

The Committee, therefore, placed emphasis on quality of the population as it considered population an important factor in the developmental process. The question of number did not bother it much at that time, though it was not altogether indifferent to it. For improving and maintaining the quality of population—its health, and its mental and physical capacity—the committee accorded importance to two factors: first, adequate food supply and proper means of subsistence, and, second, health, both of which, in turn, involved several other factors including nutritional planning and eugenic innovations for better human reproduction.

The Committee pleaded for a planned food policy. This entailed extension of cultivation through reclamation of wasteland. It advocated a scientific policy with emphasis on production of more nutritive cereals, pulses and beans, and root vegetables and fruits.[69] In addition, it underlined the importance of enhanced production of animal protein and dairy products.[70] It felt that planned crop production in adjustment to the nutritional needs of the rural masses could be promoted only by setting up in each province a special Department of Applied Botany and Ecology, and suggested close cooperation between Nutrition Research Laboratories and agricultural and other departments connected with food supply. In order to support its views the committee pointed out that this was one of the major recommendations of the Inter-Governmental Conference of Far Eastern Countries on Rural Hygiene, and, further, that Indians could not grapple with the problems of food supply until they brought about a 'marriage between agriculture and public health'.[71]

The National Committee felt that the prevalent under-nutrition and malnutrition should be tackled by a systematic crop planning oriented particularly towards producing heavy-yielding energy-producing and protective foodstuffs. It recommended in this connection the establishment of a Central Nutrition Board with regional branches, for developing a nutritional policy in coordination with the Departments of Agriculture and Public Health. Concurring with the views of the Sub-Committee on population, the National Committee resolved that the existing food resources should be more effectively utilized and supplemented, particularly by vegetables or animal proteins, so as to give a more balanced diet, and an attempt should be made to improve the food habits and methods of food preparation, aiming at obtaining more nutrition from the foods consumed.[72] On most of these questions, the Committee's approach was scientific and dynamic, and clearly reflected an attitude marked by concern for public welfare which was grossly lacking in the colonial policy.

Since matters concerning health were dealt with by a separate sub-committee, the Sub-Committee on Population kept itself confined mainly to such matters as reproduction and birth control, malnutrition and impairment of functional capacity, and maladjustment of certain individuals or groups in the society. As regards human reproduction, the Sub-Committee studied in detail its various technical aspects including fertility patterns of different regions, race and social groups in the country. It stressed the need of eugenic innovations aimed at better selection for reproduction and elimination of mentally and physically handicapped and defectives. For the latter, it recommended sterilization of persons suffering from transmissible diseases of serious nature such as insanity and epilepsy, and legal restriction on the marriage of lepers.[73] This, indeed, was a revolutionary idea far ahead of its time.

However, the NPC was concerned not only with the section which was useful for the society but also with that which was not. Its initiative and understanding in the matter are significant in that NPC's was probably the first effort, at the all-India level, to look into the problems of the handicapped and disadvantaged with a very rational and humanitarian approach. Its treatment of the subject is based broadly on three levels: prevention and cure, pragmatism in dealing with the existing realities, and resort to eugenic measures.[74]

The Committee was concerned also with imbalance in the different sections of society and the consequent trend of 'mispopulation'.[75] So, to check this malady they suggested both birth control measures as well as eugenic measures referred to above.[76] The population that was bound to exist in any case, needed to be provided with suitable employment. The NPC, therefore, paid its attention to that also. Industrialization was a paramount issue before the national leadership by then, which the Committee considered a priority sector from the viewpoint of employment. It, therefore, pleaded for promoting agriculture as a full-time industry so that employment could be provided to the vast multitude of people engaged in it. Until the goal of full-scale employment was achieved, it suggested certain other measures like unemployment insurance and relief to industrially unemployed.[77]

In connection with managing the vast population of the country, the Sub-Committee Report initiated a discussion on a global approach to the problem and underlined the need for an officially coordinated and controlled redistribution of population within the country as well as outside it. In this connection, it pleaded for a rationally coordinated migration of population from one country to another in order to achieve a balance between the local resources and the population subsisting on it. It considered the anti-immigration policy of countries like the USA, Africa and Australia, based on nationality, race or colour, a menace to world peace, and called for international action in the matter.[78] Here again, the thinking of the NPC was far ahead of its time.

Referring to the articles of the Atlantic Charter providing for freedom of movement for everybody all over the world, the Sub-Committee emphasized that only a theoretical right of this sort 'will not suffice to solve the grave problem of extremely unequal distribution of population in the several countries of the world, as viewed particularly, in comparison with the available food supply' that led to intense international rivalries resulting ultimately in global wars.[79] It, therefore, concluded: 'Unless the conscience of the whole world is roused, and a world-wide movement is adopted to redistribute by concerted action the entire population of the Globe, with a view to adjust the man power to the material resources in every corner of the earth, the Population problem of countries like India and China would be all but impossible to solve.'[80]

A separate Sub-Committee on Health looked into the problems of health and sanitation in the country. It tried to cover virtually every conceivable aspect of the subject: the existing state of affairs, major shortcomings, and suggestions for improvement. To begin with, the Sub-Committee came out with startling facts—unreliable data in certain cases and total absence of data in others, disturbing statistics on health (high mortality rate, short average life span, rampant malnutrition and diseases prevalent on endemic level, and abysmal facilities of public health).[81]

Concurring with the Sub-Committee, the National Committee called for raising the dietary standards substantially and in the light of the recommendations of the League of Nations. It wanted the state to be responsible for the preservation and maintenance of health of the people. It underlined the necessity of research in public health, elaborate organizational infrastructure equipped with local experts and personnel, and self-sufficiency in the production of drugs.[82] The elaborate coverage of rural health in the report reflects the colonial neglect in the matter.[83]

After taking stock of the public health and the services concerned,[84] the Committee made detailed recommendations for creating appropriate infrastructure for management of public health and research, staffed by adequately trained Indians,[85] with special emphasis on rural health,[86] food and nutrition,[87] and health of the mother and child.[88] It also emphasized the necessity of self-sufficiency in drug manufacture indigenously,[89] and of creating a system for maintaining vital statistics, for which it provided elaborate guidelines.[90] Moreover, for all this, the National Committee joined its Sub-Committee to call upon the State to take initiative and share responsibilities in a big way. Problems of public health, sanitation and environment were taken up also by other sub-committees like those dealing with housing and industry.[91]

Meanwhile, the Government of India (GoI) appointed, in 1943, a high power committee under Joseph Bhore to examine and advise on the problems of health, subsequently known as the Bhore Committee. The fact that most of the NPC concerns about health, hygiene and sanitation were incorporated in the Bhore Committee report and elaborate suggestions made about them suggests that the NPC's concerns were taken note of by the official bodies.[92] Needless to say, the Bhore Committee recommendations were widely welcomed in the country and they, together with the recommendations of the NPC, served as a basis of the national health programme soon after Independence.[93]

The Sub-Committee on Education looked into its subject from the view point of all-round development of both the individual as a useful citizen and the society as a whole.[94] It studied the problems of education at all levels: primary, secondary and higher secondary. The Committee gave utmost importance to the elimination of illiteracy (90 per cent of population at the time) as the first step towards educational reconstruction.[95] Technical education was needed to solve the problem of unemployment, and higher education was expected to be oriented towards research addressing the immediate problems of the country. It may be recalled that the chairman of the Sub-committee was M.N. Saha who had started a crusade against recurring floods and a movement for training the rivers for integrated development. Conservation and development of the natural resources for national reconstruction was his life-long mission. Needless to say, wherever he worked, as on the Power and Fuel Sub-Committee, his understanding of the subject naturally permeated his views and recommendations.[96] From the view point of enriching the cultural qualities of human resources, the Committee's emphasis on introducing cultural subjects in technical courses, 'if necessary at the sacrifice of some amount of technical knowledge' merits special attention.[97]

TRANSPORT

Apart from their crucial role in the economic and social progress of the country, we have seen in the preceding pages that transport and communications were considered important also for conservation, development and judicious exploitation of the natural resources, for health and hygiene, housing, and for movement of population and the necessities of life like food and medicine. For this and other reasons, separate sub-committees dealt with transport and communications as major components of national reconstruction. In this connection the Sub-Committee on Transport Services made a detailed study of the existing transport facilities in the country. While it noted the gross neglect of the prime modes of movement in India, roads and waterways, it found the impressive growth of railways unbalanced in view of the local needs.[98] We may like to point out that by this time even the government was worried about the adverse environmental effects of the railways.[99]

But more important for our subject, the Sub-Committee also took stock of the draught animals of the country as a means of transportation. Looking at the statistical data of 1942, which counted horses at 16,30,708, mules at 65,470, donkeys at 14,67,593 and camels at 5,26,674 in 1937-8, the Sub-Committee highlighted the importance of these animals as means of transport, especially in inaccessible areas and for haulage of goods, which it estimated at not less than Rs. 1,000 crores per annum. However, it was intrigued at the absence of the elephant in the list, and expressed its concern at the depletion of this 'mighty monarch of the forest' through 'uncontrolled hunting' and 'indiscriminate entertainment for distinguished visitors by such devices as *Kheda*.'[100]

While discussing the future needs of transportation, the Sub-Committee pleaded, among others, for greater exploitation of waterways—inland and sea, and adequate consideration of the topography and geography of the country, both of which had significant implications for the environment. In this connection, it also looked at the possibility of interconnecting certain river systems of the country,[101] an idea which has been entertained from time to time by the successive governments since Independence but without any results.

A Critique

At the end of this discussion, one may, however, like to ask: What is the significance of the NPC exercise? Since it was only an exploratory and advisory body without any executive powers, did it really have any significant consequences—short- or long-term—for the environment and ecology of the country? The answer is definitely 'Yes'. First of all, the NPC enquiry exposed the poor conditions and state of affairs prevailing in different areas of environment and ecology in India, and the obvious responsibility of the colonial government in this regard. Its findings presented disturbing data, even at the minimum standard of international parameters, especially with regard to soil conservation and landmass use, public health and sanitation, and depletion of natural resources including minerals, flora and fauna. What it suggested in the circumstances was representative of the nationalist aspirations.

Equally important was the timing and nature of the NPC initiative. Its period—late 1930s and 1940s—was one of political and social upheavals which was made worse by a severe famine in the country and of a global war to which India was compelled to be a party. All these events were sure to disturb the ecology and environment of the Indian subcontinent. Of course, as the NPC laboured under subjugation, it could not do anything directly in this regard, but its indirect influences were unmistakable. We may recall that after the national leaders were sent to jail during the Quit India Movement, the agenda of national reconstruction of the Congress, including that of the NPC, were virtually taken over by Indian scientists and social scientists many of whom were members of the NPC, too. The Indian scientists in particular deliberated on the reconstruction agenda at their professional forums like the Science News Association and its mouthpiece, the famous journal *Science and Culture*.[102] The subject was discussed also at the National Institute of Sciences of India and the still larger all-India forum, the Science Congress Association.[103] Everywhere, while discussing the national reconstruction in their scientific and technical context, natural resources, environment and ecology always came up for discussion in a big way. Some of the most profound discourses on the subject appeared at these forums.[104]

This helped prepare public opinion on a range of subjects and garnered wide support for India's development and independence. Interestingly, such support came also from the intellectual fraternity in Britain.[105] In fact, local pressure, coupled with the exigencies of the World War, compelled the GoI to seek scientific advice from the Royal Society, London, on how to organize and promote science and technology for developing India, which culminated in the visit to India of A.V. Hill, one of its secretaries and a Nobel Laureate, in 1944. Unlike the colonial emphasis on industrialization in the past, Hill shifted top priority to agriculture, health, population, management and development of natural resources, and transport and communications in this connection.[106] This was widely welcomed by the Indian scientists and others concerned, adding weight to Hill's advice, who persuaded the GoI to speed up the officially sponsored reconstruction programme on a line closer to the local interest and welfare that was full of environmental and ecological components.

Soon, a Department of Planning and Development was created by the GoI to chart out and coordinate the reconstruction programme. This had both short- and long-term consequences for conservation and ecology. Meanwhile, Indian scientists, especially the Science and Culture Group which were closely associated with the NPC, pressurized the government in the same direction.[107] The Council of Scientific and Industrial Research (CSIR) had been created in 1942; under the increased exigencies of the war and pressure for post-war reconstruction, scores of its sub-committees enquired into various industries and natural resources, many of which had close relations with environment of the country.[108] The creation of the Damodar Valley Corporation (DVC) as an integrated river valley development project in 1949 was one of the first outcomes. Establishment of wildlife sanctuaries and national parks soon after Independence amply exhibited the environmental concerns of the national government.[109]

These reports of the CSIR panels and those of the NPC served as a base for the massive programme of national reconstruction after India became free. In the absence of any routine data on the subject, the NPC survey yielded a huge volume of information that must have been utilized by the national leadership in this exercise; more so, because many of the members of the NPC were engaged also in formulating the plans and policies of the interim government and, later, of the national government from 1950.[110] It is worth remembering that the chairman of the NPC, Nehru, was now the architect of national reconstruction, and M.N. Saha, once instrumental behind the constitution of the NPC and subsequently one of its most important members, was a moving force behind the reconstruction programme after the World War and Independence.[111]

Needless to say, the NPC reports came to serve as a guide and framework for the newly launched national reconstruction programme whose focus on the scientific management of natural resources of the country, industry, agriculture, health, and transport and communications was unmistakable. The constant attention to rural reconstruction and appeal for village planning as the lowest but crucial unit of the national life and environment by several of the NPC's sub-committees was soon manifested in the all-India Community Development Project initiated by the GoI after Independence.[112]

One is, however, disappointed at the failure of the NPC to make efforts to harness the indigenous knowledge and skill in the proposed reconstruction endeavour, for India did have great achievements in the past in the fields of healthcare, farming and animal husbandry, and water management, which was still being used in the 1930s and 1940s.[113] There was a traditional respect for nature and environment, not only as a social practice but also as a matter of philosophy of life in the country, which is amply demonstrated by the views and efforts of Gandhi and Rabindranath Tagore around this time.[114] The occasional references by some members of the sub-committee to subjects like indigenous system of medicine and absence of any serious deliberation in the report clearly demonstrates NPC's indifference in the matter.[115] Such indifference to indigenous knowledge and skill can be partly explained by the uprooting effects of imperialism on the Indian society and culture.

Likewise, the NPC is generally silent on the impact of the Second World War on India's ecology and environment. But this is probably mainly on account of absence of information and varieties of war-time restrictions.

Conclusion

NPC's concern for conservation and its views and recommendations in the matter must have been one of the earliest endeavours in this sphere in the world. It was also among the earliest attempts to comprehend and elaborate upon the consequences of imperialism and capitalism on environment and ecology. The effort coming from a subject nation, it showed how the colonized nations responded in the situation both to the consequences of subjugation and to the problems of environment at large. In that, it showed India's sensitivity to environmental issues and her concern for the depletion of her natural wealth and environment. It was all the more so, because India was traditionally and culturally inclined to respect nature and maintain a harmonious relation with environment. As a prelude to the NPC thinking, Gandhi's thoughts on politics, man and nature offered a new vision of progress that was all-inclusive and global in approach. As his views have survived over time with growing appreciation, it is difficult to believe that they did not contribute to the NPC's holistic approach in the matter. In that, while the NPC called for planning the Indian villages as the lowest units of the national life and environment, it also pleaded for redistribution of the natural resources of the earth among the nations in an equitable manner and a scientific reordering of the planet for the welfare of all living on it. It is indeed reassuring to note that a global concern on these lines is being realized through concrete measures in the recent years; but one feels dismayed at why, even after half-a-century since the NPC's call, India is yet to plan her villages for all-round progress!

NOTES

1. For the views of the Indian National Congress on science and of those closer to the theme of this inquiry, see Jagdish N. Sinha, 'Science and the Indian National Congress', in Deepak Kumar, *Science and Empire*, New Delhi, 1991, pp. 161-81.
2. M.K. Gandhi, *Hind Swaraj or Indian Home Rule, 1908*, Ahmedabad, 14th reprint 2001.
3. Ibid. Also see M.K. Gandhi, Anand T. Hingorani edited *Modern V. Ancient Civilization*, Bombay, 1970; idem, *Industrialize and Perish*, comp., R.K. Prabhu, Ahmedabad, 1966.
4. Jawaharlal Nehru, *The Discovery of India*, New Delhi, 1982, pp. 402-9.
5. 'Science and Culture', editorial in *Science and Culture*, vol. 1, no. 1, 1935, pp. 1-3.
6. Jag Mohan, *Anand K. Coomarswamy*, New Delhi, 1979.
7. Krishna Kriplani, *Tagore: A Life*, New Delhi, 1971.
8. Jagdish N. Sinha, 'Origin of India's Science Policy: M.L. Sirkar to M.K. Gandhi, 1875-1935', *Indian Journal of History of* Science, vol. 27, no. 2, April 1992.; also Amit Mishra, 'Public Health Issues and the

Freedom Movement: Gandhi on Nutrition, Sanitation, Infectious Diseases and Health Care', in Deepak Kumar (ed.), *Disease and Medicine in India: A Historical Overview*, New Delhi, 2001.

9. M. Visvesvaraya, *Reconstructing India*, London, 1920; idem, *Planned Economy for India, 1934*; Bangalore, 1936.
10. For the views of M.N. Saha, Santimay Chatterjee (ed.), *Collected Works of Meghnad Saha*, vols. 2-3, Calcutta, 1986-92.
11. Jawaharlal Nehru, Presidential Address to the Annual Congress Session, 1936; idem, Message to the Silver Jubilee of the Indian Science Congress, 1937, both quoted in Sinha, 1991, pp. 168-7; idem, 'The Progress of Science', Address to the National Academy of Sciences, Allahabad, 5 March 1938; idem, *The Discovery of India*, 1946; Bombay, 1977, pp. 395-402.
12. Ibid. Also NPC Series: *National Planning Committee (Being a Summary of National Planning Committee Booklet No. 1, 2, 3 & 4)*, complied by K.T. Shah, Bombay, 1946; idem, *Handbook of National Planning Committee*, compiled by K.T. Shah, Vora, Bombay, 1946. Reports of the National Planning Committee, edited by K.T. Shah, run into 25 volumes with different titles which are unnumbered.
13. NPC Series, *National Planning, Principles and Administration*, Bombay, 1948, pp. 91-2.
14. NPC Series, *Soil Conservation and Afforestation*, Bombay, 1948.
15. Reference details to the reports of these committees would be provided when we return to them for detailed discussion.
16. For working of the NPC and the contemporary situation, see *Handbook of National Planning Committee*, 1946.
17. *Soil Conservation*, 1948.
18. Ibid., p. 17.
19. Ibid., p. 26.
20. Ibid., p. 39.
21. Ibid., also p. 43.
22. Ibid., p. 38 and other pages.
23. Ibid., p. 187.
24. Ibid., pp. 187-8.
25. Ibid., p. 188.
26. Ibid.
27. Ibid.
28. Ibid., pp. 188-9.
29. Ibid., p. 189.
30. Ibid., p. 190.
31. Ibid., pp. 46-7.
32. NPC Series: *Animal Husbandry and Dairying, Horticulture and Fisheries*, Bombay, 1948.
33. Ibid., p. 17.

34. Ibid., pp. 48-53.
35. Ibid., pp. 37-42, 51-5.
36. Ibid., p. 23.
37. Jagdish N. Sinha, 'Science Policy of the British in India during the Second World War', Ph.D. Thesis, University of Delhi, 1994, chaps. II-III.
38. *Animal Husbandry and Dairying,* 1948, pp. 21-3, 55-6, 103-4.
39. Ibid., pp. 34-5, 38-9, 90, 102.
40. Ibid., pp. 63-70, 105.
41. Ibid., pp. 102-5.
42. Ibid., p. 104.
43. Ibid, pp. 115-48.
44. M. Afzal Husain, 'The Food Problems of India', Presidential Address, Indian Science Congress, 2-8 January 1946; and S.L. Hora, 'Food Crisis and Fisheries', *Science and Culture*, XI, no. 11, May 1946, pp. 396-9.
45. R.B. Seymour Sewell, 'Sea-Fisheries in Indian Waters', *Science and Culture*, vol. III, no. 4, October 1937, pp. 189-92.; and B. Sundararaj, 'Development of Indian Marine Fisheries', *Science and Culture*, vol. VIII, no. 11, May 1943, pp. 435-43.
46. G.C. Chatterjee, 'Ecology of Man in the Sundarbans.' *Science and Culture*, December 1935, pp. 372ff.
47. NPC Series: *Report of the Sub-Committee, River Training and Irrigation*, Bombay, 1947.
48. As early as 1922, he had written on the problems of flood in the *Modern* Review, vol. 32, 1922, p. 605, and which became a lifelong concern for him. For his views and ideas, see M.N. Saha, *Collected Works of Meghnad Saha*, vol. 2, 1986, pp. 3-181.
49. *River Training and Irrigation*, 1947.
50. Ibid., p. 115.
51. NPC Series: *Power and Fuel*, Bombay, 1947.
52. Ibid., pp. 128-30.
53. *River Training and Irrigation*, 1947, p. 120.
54. NPC Series, *Mining and Metallurgy*, Bombay, 1947. Ibid., p. 101.
55. Ibid., p. 102.
56. Ibid., p. 103.
57. *Power and Fuel*, 1947.
58. Ibid., p. 129.
59. *Mining and Metallurgy*, 1947.
60. Ibid., pp. 20-1; also see *Power and Fuel*, 1947.
61. Ramchandra Prasad, *Bihar*, New Delhi.
62. NPC Series: *Population*, Bombay, 1947.
63. NPC Series, *National Health*, Bombay, 1948.
64. NPC Series, *Education: General Education and Technical Education and Developmental Research*, Bombay, 1948.
65. *Population*, 1947.

66. For detailed discussion, refer to Jagdish N. Sinha, 'Population, Health and Development in Colonial India', *Social Science Probings*, March 1994-December 1995, pp. 88-96.
67. *Population*, 1947, pp. 32-9.
68. Ibid., pp. 32-4.
69. Ibid., pp. 40-52.
70. Ibid., pp. 50-52.
71. Ibid., esp., p. 52.
72. Ibid., pp. 144-5.
73. Ibid., pp. 66, 87-8, 133-5, 145.
74. Ibid.
75. Ibid., pp. 63-7, 129-31.
76. Ibid., also p. 145.
77. Ibid., pp. 68-78, 132.
78. Ibid., pp. 12-4.
79. Ibid., pp. 12-3.
80. Ibid., p. 14.
81. *National Health*, 1948, esp. pp. 119-47, and 193-200.
82. Ibid., pp. 224-6.
83. Ibid., for example, pp. 81-118, 176-89.
84. Ibid., pp. 17-36.
85. Ibid., pp. 47-9, Appendix II.
86. Ibid., Appendix III.
87. Ibid., pp. 218-23.
88. Ibid., Appendix IV.
89. Ibid., Appendix VII, X.
90. Ibid., Appendix IX.
91. See *Handbook of National Planning Committee*, 1946.
92. Joseph Bhore, *Report of the Health Survey Development Commiittee*, 4 vols., Delhi, 1946.
93. For the post-Independence developments refer to *India 1980*, Publication Dvn, Govt. of India, 1980, chap. 8.
94. NPC Series, *Education: General Education and Technical Education and Developmental Research*, Bombay, 1948.
95. Ibid., pp. 139-43.
96. For details, refer to Santimay Chatterjee (ed.), *Collected Works of Meghnad Saha*, vol. 2, 1986; and Santimay Chatterjee and Minakshi Chatterji, *Meghnad Saha*, New Delhi, 1984.
97. *Education*, 1948, p. 149.
98. NPC Series: *Transport*, Bombay, 1949.
99. *Report of the Committee Convened to Consider the Measure to be taken to Prevent the Creation of Condition Favourable to the Spread of Malaria during the Construction of Roads and Railways*, Simla, 1947.

100. *Transport*, 1949, pp. 28-9. *Kheda* is a traditional method of trapping elephants in India.
101. Ibid., pp. 77-8.
102. For scores of articles on the subject, see the contemporary issues of the *Science and Culture.*
103. See their *Proceedings*; also see Jagdish N. Sinha, 'Technology for National Reconstruction: The National Planning Committee, 1938-49', in Roy MacLeod and Deepak Kumar, *Technology and the Raj: Western Technology and Technical Transfers to India, 1700-1947*, New Delhi, 1995.
104. Ibid.; also see *Proceedings of the National Institute of Sciences of India*, especially on 'Symposium on Post-War Reconstruction of Scientific Research in India', 27-8 September 1943.
105. See A.V. Hill Papers at Royal Society, London, and at Churchill Archives Centre, Cambridge. Also refer to M.N. Saha Papers, at Nehru Memorial, Museum and Library, New Delhi.
106. A.V. Hill, *Scientific Research in India*, 1944; Simla, 1945.
107. For a detailed discussion, see Sinha, 1994, especially chap. IV.
108. As for example, *Report on the Panel on Sugar, Alcohol & Food Yeast Industries*, issued by the Dept. of Planning and Development, Govt. of India, 1946; *Report of the Panel on Paper, Pulp, Board and Chemical Cotton Industries*, issued by the Dept. of Industries and Supplies, Govt. of India, n.d.; *Report on the Panel on Wooden Industry*, Govt. of India, n.d.
109. For developments after Independence in these areas, see *India 1980*, Publication Divn., Govt. of India, 1980, esp. chapters 8, 9, 14, 15, 29ff. Also see R.S. Bisht, *National Parks of India*, New Delhi, 1995.
110. See *The Advisory Planning Board*, New Delhi, 1947 (a printed volume without much publication details, probably meant for official circulation); also see the Govt. of India proceedings on the Five Year Plans.
111. Later, he gradually fell out of Nehru's association and thus out of the planning for the national development, too. Also refer to Santimay Chatterjee, 1984; idem, 1986.
112. For example, in the NPC Series, *National Housing*, Bombay, 1948; *National Health*, 1948; *Population*, 1947; *Rural Marketing and Finance*; *Crops—Planning and Production*, Bombay, 1948.
113. D.P. Chatopadhyay (Gen. Ed.), *History of Science, Philosophy and Culture in Indian Civilization*, Delhi, 2000; and Zaheer Baber, *The Science of Empire*, New Delhi, 1998.
114. For a detailed discussion, refer to Jagdish N. Sinha, 'Science and Culture under Colonialism: India between the World Wars', *Indian Journal of History of science*, vol. 39, no. 1, March 2004.
115. *National Health*, 1948, pp. 190-2.

12. Genetic Change and Colonial Cotton Improvement in Nineteenth and Twentieth Century India*

Sumit Guha

In the last few years, the introduction of transgenic plant varieties has become a (sometimes literally) burning political issue in India and elsewhere in the world. Campaigners have targeted companies developing and distributing such varieties and presented these as immensely dangerous for 'traditional' farmers in Third World countries. These agitations have played on an image of 'traditional' Indian farming as a practice that evolved centuries ago and has existed unchanged ever since. It came as a rude shock to many campaigners (almost all of whom were upper-class literati) when it was discovered that farmers had actually secured and reproduced genetically modified crops—notably cotton—and were planting them in several Indian states. This was understandable if we know that boll-worm infestations have often proved ruinous for Indian farmers and that the insect has sometimes become resistant to pesticides. Ronald Herring provides a succinct account of how the secret diffusion of Bt technology was discovered in 2001:

> Sharad Joshi, leader of the largest farmer organization in India, the Shetkari Sanghatana summed up the phenomenon: 'It [2001] was a year of miseries for the cotton growers of Maharashtra. Neelkanth Mankar, a cotton grower in Yavatmal district, unable to face creditors, committed suicide.'

* I am deeply indebted to Ronald Herring for encouraging me to think about this aspect of environmental history, and permitting me to quote from his forthcoming article. An earlier version of this paper was read at Cornell University on 30 April 2005. I benefited from the discussion that followed. The usual disclaimer holds.

But in neighboring Gujarat, Joshi noted: 'Through a lucky stroke a nondescript seed company managed to play Robin Hood and smuggle into Gujarat one line of anti-bollworm gene. For three years nobody noticed the difference and then came the massive bollworm rampage of 2001.'
There was no way to distinguish transgenic lint or seeds from their opposites, but fields indicated the difference:
'Gujarat saw all its traditional hybrid cotton crop standing devastated, side-by-side the Bt-gene crops standing resplendent in their glorious bounty. The Government was upset and ordered destruction and burning of the bountiful crop.'

Government of India (GoI) promptly ordered a ban on the new cotton varieties and decreed that the standing crops should be seized and burned. This prompted farmer resistance that led the GoI to beat a speedy retreat, and silently abandon its universal claim to know best on all issues of public welfare.[1]

The experimental use and adaptation of a new crop by farmers—especially Gujarati farmers—should have come as no surprise. As we shall see the region has a century-old history of governments—beginning with the British colonial one—seeking to manipulate and control farmers' selection of plant varieties and seed strains, in an often disastrous and unproductive way. The farmers' skepticism of government officials and urban doom-sayers whose slogans are often riffs from Hollywood movies ('Staying Alive' from *Saturday Night Fever*; 'Terminator' from Schwarzenegger's *Terminator I)* has a long history. Its beginnings go back to at least the time when the leading transnational NGO working to improve the world was the Manchester Chamber of Commerce. On the other hand, peasant trials and experiments are in the long tradition of experiment from which practically all the modern agricultural crops have been genetically engineered. Human agency has both consciously and inadvertently caused massive genetic changes in human, animal and plant populations for thousands of years. The pace of change has accelerated dramatically since the fifteenth century, when the establishment of regular trans-oceanic exchanges between the Old World and the American continent made available the genetic resources perfected by hundreds of generations of American plant breeders to the farmers of other continents, even as the faunal resources of the New World were dramatically enriched by the domesticated fauna of Eurasia. An early global presentation of this has been in the work of Alfred W. Crosby, who sketched its impacts on both Worlds in his path-breaking *The Columbian Exchange: Biological and Cultural Consequences of 1492*. The work ended with a pessimistic prognosis of the long-run genetic effects of the changes that he so vividly described. 'The Columbian exchange has left us with not a richer, but a more impoverished gene pool. We, of all the life on this planet, as the less for Columbus, and the impoverishment will increase'.[2]

Many of the domesticated plants and animals that participated in the Columbian exchange were originally found in either the older three or in the new continent. Cotton is an interesting exception, in that lint-bearing sections of the *malvacea* were found in both Worlds, and had been independently selected and domesticated for textile production in each of them.

But American growers had at their disposal the infinite genetic riches of polyploid Mesoamerican cottons, whose 26 chromosome pairs (as contrasted to the 13 of Old World cottons) enabled extremely successful breeding and selection for desirable traits. *Gossypium hirsutum* and *G. Barbadense* are the two major commercial cotton species of New World origin; *herbaceum* and *arboreum* were probably developed as fibre crops in the Indian subcontinent, where the earliest evidence of cotton fabrics comes from the ancient Indus Valley Civilization.[3]

There is archaeological and literary evidence of the export of fine cotton textiles from India going back at least 2,000 years. European consumption was interrupted after the fall of Rome and resumed in the seventeenth century, as hot baths and fine fabrics came into vogue once again. The cost and style advantages of Indian producers were such as to seriously threaten local textile industries, and early efforts to compete relied not only on prohibitions but also on the import of spun yarn from India. Strenuous efforts to mechanize the most labour-intensive stage of cotton production—spinning—began to yield results in the late eighteenth century, and international trade in raw cotton took off. The English East India Company's participation was initiated when the Company sought to find something to sell the Chinese before they discovered the wonderful possibilities of the addictive drug opium. The cotton-growing districts of Gujarat were acquired early so as to extract raw cotton in lieu of taxes.[4]

Meanwhile, the explosive growth of cotton manufacturing in England from the end of the eighteenth century soon outstripped the initial supply from the Mediterranean littoral, and Indian and American cotton began to supply British manufacturers. Indian cotton was well known, but when 14 bales of American cotton were shipped to Liverpool in 1784, they were seized as contraband on the ground that they could not be American produce as America did not produce cotton! But American planters soon began to produce in quantity. Immense stretches of fertile land could be had cheaply by exterminating or expelling the native inhabitants, and African slaves provided a readily adaptable labour-force to replace them. In addition, the range of environments that Mesoamerican farmers inhabited had led to the creation of innumerable varieties well suited for particular niches and traits. These genetic riches were soon appropriated by American planters. Practically cost-free lands were seized from the native Americans, and preparatory processes began to be mechanized from the 1790s.

Indian raw cotton could not easily compete against these advantages, and at its high point in 1800, Indian cotton imported to England was only 6.6 million lbs., or about one-ninth of the total English imports.[5] American cotton soon began to bulk large in English consumption, but anxieties over its supply began as early as 1809. The East India Company was already functioning as an arm of the home government which was, in turn, feeling the pressure of the rising manufacturing interest in England. Alarmed at the trend of US policy in the run-up to the war of 1812, the Court of Directors wrote to their agents in India:

> The measures which have been lately adopted by the Legislature of the United States of America will, in their consequences, operate to very seriously harm some of the manufactures of this country, unless a liberal supply of cotton wool can be procured from other sources than these States, and it is to our territorial possessions in Asia that the hopes of the manufacturing classes are principally directed.[6]

Parcels of 'Bourbon'[7] (*barbadense?*) and 'Georgia Upland' (*hirsutum*) cotton seed were also procured and sent to India, the first in a series of efforts to introduce what were regarded as American varieties of cotton into India. In 1812, Mauritius cotton seed was sent to the district officers in south Gujarat with instructions to induce peasants to raise the crop on their own farms. At that time 'Bourbon' cotton sold at 2 shillings a pound and 'Surat' at 9 pence.[8] Efforts to get the peasants to raise the 'Bourbon' cotton failed; English officials were induced to try for themselves with little success: the plant often died before yielding any fibre, and what was produced 'possessed little of the natural qualities of its parent stock'.[9]

Occasionally tense relations with the USA notwithstanding, American cotton consistently out-competed that from all other sources, and the southern states soon became an agrarian appendage of British manufacturing. But the growth of the textile industry was achieved at the cost of a consistent lowering of prices and a shift in the terms of trade against textile manufacturers that persisted to the 1860s.[10] As manufacturers saw valueing-added and their margins declining, they turned not only to technological improvement and speed-up, but also made efforts to lower labour and raw material costs by indirect means, including free trade in foodstuffs and the repeal of the 'Corn Laws'. They also began to reduce the material content and compete with lower-cost producers by switching to finer spinning, which required cotton with longer staple length. A range of American varieties came to satisfy this requirement. But the manufacturers preferred to secure their supplies from areas under British control; and their free-trade ideas prejudiced them against the East India Company. The company's charter came up for renewal every 20 years after 1793 and each such renewal saw Parliamentary pressures on the administration in India. We shall see therefore a recurrent pattern in which coercion and persuasion were actively deployed in the years immediately preceding a Charter renewal. The results were poor, and the matter would be allowed to drop until another renewal was due. The Company therefore undertook a wide range of experiments in anticipation of the renewal due in 1832. Cotton seed from as far afield as Pernambuco in northern Brazil was raised on small plantations or distributed to local peasants from northern Mysore to Gujarat. The record was one of failure and in 1836 the experimental farms were wound up.[11]

But the pressure on profit margins in England continued

unabated, and commercial crises as well as the rise of Chartism led to renewed demands on India. One of these was consistent pressure on the British Indian administration to 'improve' Indian cotton to make it competitive with US supplies. Officialdom then began a campaign to teach the peasants how to farm. In 1840 twelve American planters were recruited to come to India in order to introduce both American seeds and agronomic techniques to the local farmers. This was not the first effort at technological enlightenment: in 1812 the Company had directed the translation of a tract on cotton farming originally intended for West Africa into Gujarati! American cotton planters were then recruited to persist with this enterprise and to introduce what were perceived as superior agricultural techniques to the benighted natives. But within a few years the experts admitted that they had nothing to teach. This was summed up in a report from north Karnataka in 1846:

> The impression in England was, when the American planters were sent out, that the system of cultivation in India was very defective, and that, by the diffusion of the experience and knowledge possessed by them among the ryots, the cultivation and the quality of the cotton might be greatly improved. This, however, by the admission of the American planters themselves, turns out not to be the case, but that the natives of India cultivate extremely well, and their system is better adapted to this country than that pursued in America.

Simpson, a planter who was sent to the Tapti valley in the north also came to the same conclusion:

> I have been informed by an American cotton planter (Mr. Simpson) who was sent out on purpose to introduce American cotton, and superintend its cultivation, that he could teach little or nothing to the cultivators of cotton in the plain of the Taptee in Khandeish; that, in fact, the husbandry was very good, and the yield of indigenous (not American) cotton in a good season very heavy.[12] Repeated efforts at transferring the seeds of cottons that produced superior staple were made. Experimental farms were run for several years with little effect on the surrounding peasants of south Gujarat. The Government of Bombay attributed it to native apathy: 'the people of the country evince no interest in the undertaking, and continue satisfied with producing a dirty and inferior staple.'

Why they did so became clear when an enterprising superintendent calculated comparative costs: the slightly superior experimental cotton yielded about 25 per cent more but at double the total cost of production.[13]

Such inconvenient facts were ignored and peasants were pressured to sow New Orleans seed by administrators eager to please their superiors in Bombay. Thus in the late 1840s, Alexander Elphinston, Collector of Khandesh (North Maharashtra), managed to get over 12,000 *bighas* (*c.* 3,600 ha.) planted with a seed that had a consistent record of failure. But Home authorities wanted rosy reports that could be presented to a critical Parliament, and these were duly generated by methods that bureaucrats are still known to deploy. The collector wrote to J.F. Royle in August 1850, boasting that American cotton had been grown before his own arrival in 1848, but now: 'The ryots are becoming well satisfied with the American seed, both on account of its greater yield of cotton, as well as its superior quality and its commanding a higher price; therefore, I feel no hesitation in saying, that in all the eastern districts of Candeish,... the American cotton seed may be considered established.'[14]

Peasant resistance was met with coercion by officials eager to impress their bosses with their successes in the field. As an Indian subordinate reported: 'To ensure good care being taken, circular orders are issued from time to time from the Hoozoor to the district officers, from the district officers to the village officers, and instructions are given verbally to the ryots ...' But he added that the peasants 'are destitute of any hope that this species of cotton will succeed in this country, and they state that Government should not saddle them with the seed; and they yield to the orders of Government because they are poor and cannot make a protest; that it is true that Government grants them remissions [of the land-tax], but only of the Government dues—their other profits are lost to them.' The collector actually provoked mass protests and in due course moved on. His successor described his farm extension methods with a bureaucratic circumlocution: 'unhealthy stimulus'.[15] No sooner was Elphinston transferred in consequence of peasant unrest than the area under exotic cottons shrank to nothing. But the

Company's Charter had been renewed for another 20 years. (It would be abrogated by the Crown after the uprising of 1857-8.)

The chromosomal differences between the diploid Afro-Asian and haploid American cottons were of course unknown at the time. Nor was it recognized that US cotton was itself undergoing varietal change in the early nineteenth century as *latifolium* types originating in the Yucatan region were replacing the earlier *barbadense* strains.[16] But the planting of a range of cotton types may have encouraged the mixing of different types in the same field. An English cotton merchant observed of cotton in north Maharashtra that it was 'found to degenerate in the course of a couple or three years and lose the characteristics of the American to gain those of the Indian plant'.[17] True viable hybridization under open field conditions would seem difficult given the differing chromosome numbers of Asian and American cottons. In fact, Hutchinson found in the 1930s that American (Upland, G. *Hirsutum*) cottons 'although comparatively poorly adapted to Indian conditions, have persisted as admixtures in unselected crops of G. *Arboreum* cottons in Central India for over a century.'[18] Thus I think it plausible that the so-called degeneration was, in fact, the result of local farmers mixing in local seeds so that they would still get some return for their labour after the foreign plants had failed. That however did not prevent a recurrent cycle in which each period of high cotton prices on the world market was followed by Manchester pressure upon the Government of India, usually followed by the peasants being coerced into some unsuccessful experiment.

The other major cotton-growing region with access to the ports of western India was northern Karnataka, then part of the Bombay Presidency. So a very similar story can be told for the southern cotton growing district of Dharwad (now in Karnataka). In the 1840s an official thirsting for distinction began to force the cultivation of a variety of American Upland ('New Orleans') cotton. Thus the late 1840s a seed imported from New Orleans was pushed in northern Karnataka, and the farmers coerced into planting it. When little was produced a newly arrived official enquired into the matter, and elicited responses such as that below:

Six ryots (peasants) of the village of Belwutgee: 'The American crop does not produce well in this country; if it is sown there is no profit, but loss. Last year and the year before, the *sircar's* people urgently desired (*juggada nuchidroo*) us to sow it; we, therefore sowed it. This year we were ordered to sow what we pleased; therefore because we suffered loss from sowing American cotton, we have not sown it, but sown other crops. No one is willing to sow American cotton.[19]

An unusually candid Assistant Collector summed up the situation:

As long as Government interferes about its cultivation it will be considered an exotic—as something which belongs to the '*sirkar*' and not the ryot, while the cultivator of it, being liable to be continually sent for to the *cutcherry* (district office) to answer queries regarding the state of his crop, and to receive cautions about picking, etc., all of which inconveniencies are included in the word '*upudrao*' (constantly applied to it by the ryots), have not a little tended to create a prejudice against it.[20]

Once this pressure was withdrawn local farmers soon limited the new variety to areas where the climate suited it and evolved a cross with local strains that flourished under the name of Dharwar-American.

Once this pressure was relaxed the area declined: but interestingly enough, local peasants continued smallscale experiments and produced a us able variety that later acquired the trade-name 'Dharwar-American'. This is one of the earliest instances of the acclimatization of a New World *hirsutum* cotton in India. A few years later another variety that has supposedly travelled from Mexico to Southeast Asia via the Philippines was successfully introduced in parts of southern India under the name 'Cambodian'.[21]

After various misadventures, mechanized gins were adapted to use on local cottons. Farmers also became aware of a demand in the emerging Bombay and Ahmedabad mills as well as in Europe, China and Japan for strong, short-staple cotton yarn. 'The introduction of power gins resulted in a premium being readily offered for high ginning percentage.... The *bengalensis* mixture was therefore favoured, and encroached on the southern (*indica*) area, and a great cotton growing tract, comprising the Central

Provinces, Berar, Khandesh and Nimar, changed over from medium staple to short staple.'[22]

The farmers conducted their own plant breeding and selection trials in defiance of colonial efforts. Their response came in the 1850s. In 1861 an officer posted at the large annual fair at Maheji in Khandesh district reported:

> I have had some trouble finding out how Khandesh became overrun of an inferior kind of cotton seed... a few years ago a Marwarree, named Seewa Lall Kissondass, resident of Paldi, brought a large quantity of Malwa cotton seed, and sold it to the ryots of all the surrounding villages, who finding it yielded a larger quantity, though of much inferior quality, than that formerly grown, generally adopted it, and it has now become the most prevailing staple in the province.[23]

We may note that the superintendent classified this as an inferior variety because it did not meet the requirements of English textile mills. Its evident suitability for local farmers were not even a concern.

This was recognized by local farmers as a new strain which they named 'Waradi' or 'from Varhad', a province to the east of Khandesh, despite having been imported from Malwa to the north. The story also offers a striking contrast to the peasant reluctance to use the New Orleans cotton seed. The strain spread rapidly, and dominated the local crop in a few years. But then came the American Civil War, and the British government was forced to address a virtual cotton famine, the possible collapse of its textile industry and potentially revolutionary unrest in urban Britain. Imperial policy makers immediately looked to India. The collector of Khandesh decided to coercively turn the peasantry to a realization of their own best interests. The older medium-staple cotton still grew in Varhad, and so 1,800 tons of seed were imported through the newly opened rail system and compulsorily distributed to farmers in the Khandesh District. Farmers and traders were harassed into raising and dealing in the new variety. The creation of a Cotton Frauds Department in 1866 gave additional administrative sanction to such measures. This department was supposed to protect the interests of cotton growers as well as industrialists by preventing false labelling and adulteration of cotton. That phenomenon was blamed impartially on the peasants and local merchants. A.T. Moore, a retired army officer whose Victoria Cross (V.C.) seems to have adequate evidence of agronomic competence, was appointed to head the department. But the colonial administration financed the Department by a small export duty on raw cotton, and this was resented by the powerful export merchant lobby in Bombay, whose margins were squeezed by the fall in cotton prices after 1867, and even more so by the depreciation of the silver rupee that began shortly thereafter. Business interests headed by the big trading firm of Gaddum and Co. were able to force a Commission of Enquiry into the working of the Act.[24] The campaign bore fruit a few years later, and the Department was abolished in 1882. Only after this did the Agriculture Department live up to its scientific pretensions by conducting experimental field trials of the two varieties. The result was that Varadi or *Neglectum roseum* mixture proved itself consistently superior in yield, resistance to climatic variation and ginning percentage.[25] Reflecting on the varietal history of the region, H.N. Bhalerao, 47, farmer and cotton trader from the Tapti valley town of Raver told the Indian Cotton Committee in 1918:

> The old Indian cotton seed was grown here 25 years ago. It is not used nowadays nor is it available now. Fibres of that cotton were longer than those of the N.R. (*roseum*) cotton. Flowers were yellow and leaves short and isolated. The plant had many branches. The harvest was later by a month. The cotton was softer than the N.R. sort and was dim white. Income accrued was less.[26]

We see therefore a long history of coercion in the 'best interests' of the farmers—which turn out to be the best interests of cotton mill-owners—initially in Britian and then in India itself. The consistent assumption was that farmers could not recognize their own interests. In an interesting parallel to some modern NGO discourse, this recalcitrance was attributed to either their ignorance or to their being manipulated by capitalist interests. Logically then, they needed a coercive emancipation from these local exploiters.

But throughout this period, the peasants were better guided by their own understanding of local conditions and market opportunities, and pursued a stealthy independent programme of seed diffusion and selection. Let us take up the case of the Waradi or *roseum* mixture of cottons. Hutchinson traces its origins to the eastern Bengal-Assam hills centre of diversity of Indian *arboreum* cotton. This centre generated the race *burmanicum*, from which originated *cernum, sinense* and *bengalense*. The cottons of eastern India encountered a range of habitats: from deltaic lands barely above sea-level to altitudes of several thousand feet, with corresponding variations in soil and cultivation practices. They developed a range of types, both annual and perennial, adapted to almost every ecological niche in which human action chose to lodge them. For instance, the famous Bengal muslins demanded a fine, long staple for which hand-spinners readily paid premium prices. Therefore, Hutchinson observes, that the 'strongest selective force encountered by these cottons was human selection for fine quality'. But when the specific demand for fine spinning collapsed, East Bengal cotton swiftly, in the space of a few decades, moved to focus on robust short-staple varieties that came to be called 'Comilla', from the district where they predominated.

On the south-east coast from Orissa to the Godavari delta a different selection of G. *arboreum* produced medium staple cottons of the *indicum* type that then spread westward into Central India, including Varhad and the Tamil-Telugu country. The diversity of the eastern strains then provided a ready reservoir of genetic variability when a market for strong, short-staple high-yielding cotton developed in India and abroad. The enterprising Kissondass (see p. 387 above) introduced the new seed even as the railroad line to Bombay and the world market was under construction. The variety spread from its home in the hills around the Ganges Delta in the nineteenth century, when it was introduced into northern and central India—as far and as the different environments as those of Sind and Punjab. This was in response to 'the demand of the cotton industry for high ginning percentage with little regard for quality'. In central India it took the name of the more delicate medium-staple cotton marketed from the town of Amraoti (colonialese: 'Oomrawattee') and came to called 'Oomra'.[27] But here also, by the early twentieth century two successive replacements had taken place. The old *bani* or Hinganghat variety that the collector of Khandesh sought to impose in 1865-6 was replaced in its home range by *jari*, a more robust short-staple, and that in turn replaced by *roseum* mixtures.[28]

Illegal pressure grew harder to sustain as rural people found leadership from gentry, lawyers and others influenced by the new urban politics of western India. It was only after the failure of 'coercive improvement' that the newly created Agriculture Department of Bombay Province began to work with the peasants to evolve commercially viable selections. This effort began to yield results in the 1930s and 1940s. In those decades the Indian Central Cotton Committee undertook the first scientific studies of the technical capacities of Indian cottons, and tried to develop a better classification than the subjective opinions of experts or the cruder trade practice of describing cottons solely by the name of the principal railroad station from where they were shipped. This was increasingly useless as a wholesale change in the character of Indian cottons began under pressure of selection for staple length even at the cost of yield. V.G. Panse summed up trends upto the early 1940s:

> In recent years cotton breeding in India has been directed primarily toward the improvement of quality.... An examination of over 150 replicated varietal trials, conducted at several centres over a period of three years from 1940-41 to 1942-43 ...brought out the fact that all the improved strains gave on an average 10 to 15 per cent lower yield than the local cotton.[29]

By the end of that decade the Nehruvian programme of autarkic economic development began to once again regulate peasant farming in ways eerily reminiscent of the colonial war economy. Partition had placed important cotton-growing areas in Pakistan and the object was to 'produce enough cotton in the country of the types comparable to Pakistan varieties so that India might become independent of the supplies from that country as early as possible.'[30] Export controls and price controls were then introduced to sustain the project of autarkic economic development. Coercive paternalism cut off the growers from their export markets and price controls compelled them to subsidize an increasingly inefficient mill industry. The mills themselves could not compete in cost or quality with foreign producers who had access to the much wider range of cottons available on the world market. Finally, seed selection came under government regulation in several states, with the governments of Bombay, Madhya Pradesh, Hyderabad and Punjab passing legislation that restricted trade in seeds and required farmers in particular tracts to grow only government-approved varieties of cotton. In Punjab, for example, the popular and hardy *desi* cotton could now only be legally grown in three submontane districts with the worst farming conditions.[31] The damage may not have been as serious as with the nineteenth century efforts at regulation, partly because many of the improved strains developed in the middle decades of the twentieth century were selections from locally raised strains rather than freshly landed imports from various parts of the world. In addition, of course, one wonders how far the famously softening post-colonial state could actually coerce millions of small farmers across rural India into growing entirely unsuitable varieties of crops.

CONCLUSION

It must be evident that farmers in India or China[32] who seek to acquire and replicate genetically modified crops are continuing a long tradition of peasant experimentation and seed selection, even if they apply those methods to unprecedentedly novel genetic materials. But as the story told here should warn us, farmers have good reason to distrust the sagacity of GOs and NGOs alike.

NOTES

1. These three paragraphs are entirely based on Ronald J. Herring, 'Stealth Seeds: Biosafety, Bioproperty, Biopolitics', *Journal of Development Studies* (forthcoming). The quote is from p. 4.
2. Westport CT: Greenwood Press, 1972. See especially Chapter 2 'Old World Plants and Animals in the New World', pp. 64-121 and; 'New World Foods and Old World Demography', pp. 165-207; the quote is from p. 219.
3. J.B. Hutchinson, R.A. Silow and S.G. Stephens, *The Evolution of Gossypium and the Differentiation of the Cultivated Cottons*, London and New York, 1947, pp. 32-51 and pp. 65-112.
4. Pamela Nightingale, *Trade and Empire in Western India*, Cambridge, 1972.

5. Walter R. Cassels, *Cotton–An Account of its Culture in the Bombay Presidency*, Bombay, 1862, pp. 4-6.
6. Cited in Cassels, *Cotton*, p. 9.
7. The name 'Bourbon' cotton derives from the Indian Ocean island successively held by the Portuguese and French, later named Reunion. It is not clear if this was a New World cotton or a superior Old World variety.
8. Cassels, ibid., p. 11.
9. Ibid., p. 14.
10. First documented by A.H. Imlah, *Economic Elements in the Pax Britannica*, Cambridge, 1958.
11. Cassels, ibid. pp. 28-9.
12. Cited in Cassels, ibid., pp. 246-8.
13. Ibid, pp. 52-4.
14. J. Forbes Royle, *The Culture and Commerce of Cotton in India and Elsewhere*, London, 1851, p. 392.
15. Cited in Cassels, ibid., pp. 97-8.
16. C.L. Brubaker et al., 'The Origin and Domestication of Cotton' and C. Wayne Smith et al., 'History of Cultivar Development in the United States' in C. Wayne Smith and J. Tom Cothren (eds.), *Cotton: Origins, History, Technology and Production* New York, 1999, pp. 3-29, 99-102.
17. Cited in Cassels, *Cotton*, p. 98.
18. J.B. Hutchinson, R.A. Silow and S.G. Stephens, *The Evolution of Gossypium and the Differentiation of the Cultivated Cottons*, London, 1947, p. 77.
19. British Parliamentary Papers, 1857, Session 2 Return of Measures to Promote Cotton Cultivation, Part III, Bombay, 507. The word transcribed as *juggada* is *tagada*, a term used to mean coercive pressure, which could include beating, confinement and other maltreatment. The translation clearly seeks to palliate the nature of the measures deployed.
20. Cited in Cassels, *Cotton*, p. 144. *Upadrava* is a lot stronger than 'inconvenience'. It can extend from 'harassment' to 'torment'.
21. S.M. Sikka and A.B. Joshi, Breeding, vol. 1, in B.L. Sethi et al. (eds.), Cotton in India: A Monograph, Bombay, 1960, pp. 137-335.
22. J.B. Hutchinson, 'The Distribution of *Gossypium* and the Evolution of the Commercial Cottons', in *First Conference of Scientific Research Workers on Cotton in India*, Indian Central Cotton Committee, Bombay, 1937, pp. 352-3.
23. Cited in Sumit Guha, *The Agrarian Economy of the Bombay Deccan 1818-1941*, Delhi, 1985, pp. 106-7.
24. *Report of the Commissioners Appointed to Inquire into the Working of the Cotton Frauds Act … with Minutes of Evidence and Other Appendices*, Bombay, 1875.

25. Guha, *Agrarian Economy*, pp. 107-9; *Annual Reports on the Working of the Dhulia Agricultural Station*, see relevant sections on varietal experiments in the reports for the years 1906-7 through 1912-13.
26. *Report of the Indian Cotton Committee* Bombay, 1919. Evidence volume 2, p. 18.
27. J.B. Hutchinson et al., *Evolution of Gossypium*, pp. 86-95; quotes from pp. 93-4.
28. Evidence of Bhaiyalal Dubey, Acting Deputy Director of Agriculture in the Central Provinces, *Report of the Cotton Committee*, 1919, vol. 2, p. 62.
29. V.G. Panse and V.B. Sahasrabudhe, 'Yield of Rainfed Cotton and Its Improvement', *Indian Cotton Growing Review*, 1,1, 1947, pp. 11-20, quote 15.
30. Sethi, *Cotton in India*, I, p. 31.
31. Ibid., III, pp. 266-70.
32. See 'China's Problem with "Anti-Pest" Rice', *Business Day*, *New York Times*, 16 April 2005, pp. 1- 3, for the unauthorized release and sale of transgenic pest-resistant varieties of rice in China.

SECTION IV
Beyond India

13. Shaping the Caribbean Environment: The Impact of India

Rita Pemberton

INTRODUCTION

Of major concern in the modern era is the state of the physical environment. Natural disasters are interpreted as warnings from nature for more careful human interaction with the physical environment. In fact, it is the possibility that mindless human action on the environment could precipitate disastrous consequences that underscores the current global interest in environmental issues. This interest has generated a number of specialist inquiries on different aspects of the environment, one of which is environmental history.[1] Broadly defined as 'the changing relations between people and nature', environmental history examines: 'how people have lived in natural systems of the planet and how they have perceived nature and reshaped it to suit their own idea of good living... [It] encompasses the investigation of how nature, now changed requires people to reshape their cultures, economies and politics to meet new realities... . And includes the history of environmental reform and politics.'[2]

There exist three major works on the history of the environment in the British Caribbean. In his seminal study of Caribbean environments, David Watts refers to the lush pristine vegetation of the islands, which impressed the early European visitors. He bemoans the subsequent environmental degradation of the region, which he deems 'a third trauma' along with the decimation of the indigenous population and the forced movement of people from Africa, to support slavery and the plantation system.[3]

Watts states that: 'It is interaction between, and the ramifications of these three major considerations which have molded much of West Indian history and geography.'[4] He argues that 'an objective assessment of the nature of such a potentially munificent environment, and of the ways it can change over time, is essential to any geographical interpretation of the consequences of human occupancy, in its several distinctive threads, within the region'.[5] Watts examines the geology and surface features, weather, climate, vegetation response, soils and fauna of the region as the backdrop for his discussion of the activities of the indigenous peoples and the Europeans and their impact on the island environments. His focus is on the impact of sugar and the plantation system on the Caribbean environments.

In a study of Caribbean societies in the 1800s, Bonham Richardson notes that the frequent use of buzz-words suggests a genuine preoccupation with things environmental but he argues that:

> ... if substance is to outdistance rhetoric and a true environmentalism set in motion.... That means focus and attention to real places and real problems because environmental knowledge, although subject to the laws of science and nature, really comes to life in particular localities, among rocks, trees, hillsides of different places and more and more physical features built or modified by human action.[6]

Richardson examines the environmental consequences of European colonization on the Eastern Caribbean from 1880 to 1900, with a focus on natural disasters, deforestation and economic distress.

A more recent work by Richardson examines the role of fire in British West Indian history through a discussion of the late nineteenth and early twentieth centuries.[7] Describing Caribbean colonial and environmental history as 'unique'[8] with an introduced 'native' population, he views fire as a catalyst rather than a determinant in Caribbean history and geography, a study of which 'emphasizes and underscores the material circumstances of lives lived there in the past'.[9] Noting that Caribbean history would have unfolded differently without the ways people have used fires, Richardson argues that 'The nature timing, and extent of, among other things, environmental transformations, agricultural regimens, and sociopolitical demonstrations in the region all have depended very heavily on the human use of fire.'[10]

While these three studies make valuable contributions to an understanding of the history of Caribbean environments, they all emphasize removal and destruction as the defining environmental change, omitting any discussion of other significant activities which modified the region's environments. While the term 'Caribbean environment' is commonly used with reference to forest cover and land formations and their adjustments, it ought not to be assumed that the colonial impact on the Caribbean environment was limited to reshaped landforms by removals. In fact, there is a growing body of literature which directs our attention to another dimension of imperial activity which had a great impact on the environments in the colonies—the migration of plants.

Alfred Crosby argues that perhaps the success of European imperialism has a biological, an ecological component.[11] He identifies three general kinds of life forms that usually prospered in the colonies 'not with but often without help and even despite European actions: weeds, feral animals and pathogens associated with humanity.'[12]

Imported weeds, which he said thrive on neglect, must have taken over extensive areas of the West Indies.[13] Crosby's study brings the impact of introductions into focus although his emphasis is mainly on those that were largely unintended and undesirable. The movement of plants is an area of inquiry which is meritorious of further study as an important dimension of Caribbean history. It provides the basis for a fuller understanding of the ways in which imperial actions reshaped Caribbean environments and the extensive trans-empire and global influences that were operational in this process.

Caribbean historians are indebted to Richard Grove for his enlightening study, which details the origins and development of this movement of plants into both the worlds of the colonizer and the colonized.[14] Grove directs attention to the role of colonies in the development of environmentalism. In so doing, he points to the development of natural history and the foundations of new botanical gardens as a part of the quest to expand European knowledge of the global environment. According to Grove:

The new botanical gardens were intended to bring together representative specimens from every part of the world. As such the gardens themselves acquired a meaning as symbols of an economic power capable of reaching and affecting the whole biological world. As landscape 'texts' they signified a particular type of ecological control that had not previously been available.[15] These gardens served as re-creations of paradise and the source of *materia medica*[16] and ultimately led to the development of botanical networks by the Dutch, French and British.[17]

Richard Drayton provides yet another valuable addition to this line of historiography in which he traces the history of the idea that the knowledge of nature would allow the best possible use of resources.[18] In his book, which focuses on the impact of European expansion on the science of plants, Drayton argues that the: '... sciences of collection and comparison—among which we may include botany, zoology, anthropology and geology—depended on Europeans becoming exposed to the planet's physical and organic diversity, and often to the scientific traditions of non-European people.'[19] He discusses how the idea of gardens developed in Britain, the growth of Kew Gardens and the empire gardens network, the applications of science to imperial activity and the resulting economic botany, which dictated the movement of plants across the empire. Both Grove and Drayton draw our attention to the movement of plants as a deliberate part of imperial activity, which, undoubtedly resulted in environmental altering. This activity was generated by the desire of the British to improve the quality of life in the metropole by environmental tinkering in the empire. That the British were not alone in this activity has been underscored by both scholars and in addition, Mathew has documented a similar activity conducted by the Portuguese between India and Brazil.[20]

Grove and Drayton both identify an important role for the botanic gardens in the British West Indies in this process, in particular, the St. Vincent Botanic Garden and later the garden at Jamaica. The issue of plant movement immediately raises the question of how much of our perceived floral and faunal heritage have in fact been introduced from other parts of the world. Hence it is essential to examine the impact of these introductions on the host societies.

The Nexus between the Caribbean and Asia

That the history of the Caribbean is deeply rooted in Africa and Asia, from which a significant part of the region's population originated, is well documented in the existing literature. Studies on the Asia-Caribbean connection generally focus on the experiences of indentured workers from India and their contributions to their host societies. There is a body of literature[21] which chronicles the plant introductions which were coterminous with immigration from India, including food and medicinal plants which became established as a part of the region's flora. It is to be noted however that the influence of Asia, and that of India in particular, was not restricted to the movements of indentured workers and the associated impact. There was an environmental impact which was distinct from and, in some instances, predated the movement of indentured workers into the region, which forms the subject of this paper.

The paper examines popular aspects of Caribbean life and identifies six ways in which India's impact on the region is evident. Building on the works of Grove and Drayton, the paper argues that through the network of botanic gardens, the Caribbean landscape was altered by a number of important introductions from India as well as by individuals who had worked in India. It must be indicated that there is a long list of floral introductions from India some of which came directly from India into the Caribbean while others entered through intermediaries. This examination centres around five introductions—one of the most popular fruits of the region, the mango; one of the most common species of flowers, the hibiscus: two important spices, the nutmeg and black pepper; and an animal that is now a common part of Caribbean fauna, the mongoose. The paper also discusses the initiation of forest services in the region by officers of the India Forest Service, which was itself an activity that generated further arboreal introductions into the region.

The paper is divided into four sections. Section 1 provides the justification for the study, offers a review of the pertinent literature and outlines the scope and organization of the work. Section 2 discusses the circumstances which led to the introduction of the new species of flora and fauna and how these introductions have impacted on the Caribbean. In this section reference is made to literary sources which reflect the impact of these introductions on Caribbean society. Section 3 discusses the role of officers from the Indian Forest Service in the establishment of the first forest conservation efforts in the region. Section 4, which concludes the study, assesses the overall impact of introductions from India on the Caribbean and comments on the value of environmental history for the Caribbean. It argues that environmental change in the region resulted from both plant and animal introductions and removals. It also argues that it is important that an assessment of the full impact of plant introductions into the region should be undertaken since colonial activity shaped the natural environment causing some of the common images of the Caribbean to reflect introduced, rather than truly indigenous elements.

I

Changing The Flora and Fauna of The Caribbean

European imperial activity in the Caribbean involved a search for profitable crops. After tobacco cultivation failed, the crop that was introduced was sugarcane, *saccharum officinarum*, a native of Southeast Asia and primarily India. Preparation of sugar from the stems of this plant first occurred in India and then spread to China, to Europe and then to the Caribbean.[22] Extensive sugarcane cultivation has had a permanent impact on the environments of the Caribbean and this impact has commonly been termed the sugar revolution. It resulted in the widespread removal of the forest cover that had characterized the region prior to the European presence, and was the cause of an unprecedented environmental change. Undoubtedly, this rapid deforestation resulted in untold irrecoverable biodiversity loss as well as soil erosion and climatic changes. However, although the impact of sugar cultivation is not a development that is specifically targeted in this study because it is already well documented, it is mentioned here since it is pertinent to other issues which would be raised later in the paper.

Despite the existence of a highly profitable enterprise in sugarcane cultivation, the imperial government was involved in the establishment of a botanic garden on the island of St. Vincent. Established in 1765,[23] this garden was intended to facilitate the movement of plants across the Empire in the quest for medicinal, and potentially profitable economic species and exotics. According to Dr. Alexander Anderson, the second superintendent of the Garden, its purpose was: 'of introducing into the English West Indian islands such plants as might be of advantage to them or to the nation as food, medicine or articles of commerce which would not grow in the northern colonies, for some of which the kingdom paid large sums of money to foreigners'.[24]

In this quest, plant species were moved to St. Vincent from other parts of the world. The St. Vincent Botanic Garden served as a botanical laboratory testing and experimenting with the new acquisitions in the attempt to foster new methods of cultivation of important crops and stimulate development of new ones. Thus, while the officers attached to the Garden catalogued and identified indigenous species, they also fostered the cultivation of imported crops which were then distributed throughout the region. Hence the Garden served as a veritable centre of plant exchanges in the British Empire and also maintained links with gardens established by other imperial powers and interested individuals and companies. Officers of the British Navy, government officials, and officials of the British trading companies were all engaged in the transfer of seeds and plants to and from the Garden. In addition, there was an element of rivalry among the imperial powers to acquire the most valuable species. Capture of enemy ships generally involved a search for valuable plant specimens that may have been on board.

From the onset of its activities, a premium was placed on the introduction of plants from Asia, particularly India and the East Indies. Even before a garden was established in Jamaica, a botanical enthusiast communicated to Sir Joseph Banks of his introduction of valuable plants from India.[25] The communication between botanists in the region and officials in England made frequent reference to plants from India. In a communication to Sir Joseph Banks in 1790, Sir George Yonge of the War Office mentioned that a shipment of plants from India had been sent to St. Vincent and Kew.[26] In a report on the progress of plants in the

Vincent Botanic Garden, Superintendent Anderson reported, with pleasure, that Indian teak plants had reproduced in the garden.[27]

The plants listed in the Garden's catalogue included several that were indigenous to India. These include, the mango (*Mangifera indica*), Jackfruit (*A. integrifolia)*, black pepper (*piper nigrum*), hibiscus (*hibiscus tiliaceus*), and the East India Palm, Gomertur.[28] This information provides an opportunity to examine more fully the nature of the intersection between the histories of India and the Caribbean outside of population movements. The discussion now turns to the introduction of plants and animals from India into the Caribbean.

The mango plant was introduced into the British Caribbean in 1782 when a shipment of plants from Mauritius, destined for the French West Indian islands, was captured by a British frigate, sent to Jamaica and then distributed to St. Vincent and other islands.[29] Subsequently, a range of varieties were introduced into the region. The reports indicate that emphasis was placed on the introduction and extension of mango cultivation in the Caribbean by the imperial authorities. There are constant references in Sir Banks' correspondence to receipts of mango plants in the region. In 1788 Yonge reported that a shipment containing a variety of plants, especially mango, had been dispatched to St. Vincent and Kew from the East.[30] Banks was informed that mango and other plants from India have been sent to the West Indies by the *HMS Excel* under the care of Captain Bowen who was a passenger.[31]

In 1790 Niles reported that mangoes from the East were thriving in Jamaica. Some were blooming and he promised to extend their cultivation.[32] In another report it was stated that although a ship taking plants from India to Jamaica was attacked, the mango plants arrived in a healthy condition.[33] Varieties of this fruit continued to be introduced across the nineteenth and twentieth centuries. In 1900 the Superintendent of the Trinidad Botanic Gardens thought it advisable to import additional species into the garden. He made an application to the Indian authorities to send the best varieties from all the provinces and plants were ordered from Mumbai (Bombay), Bengal and Chennai (Madras) to improve on the varieties then cultivated in the Caribbean.[34]

The plant became fully naturalized in the region. On some estates mango walks[35] were established, as the fruit was used to supplement slave food. During the latter part of the nineteenth century, the fruit was viewed as a potential export crop. The result was that this fruit became one of the most popular in the Caribbean. Its popularity is recorded in a lesson on fruits of the Caribbean in a book used extensively to teach reading to primary school children during the colonial and early post-colonial era. The description is as follows: 'Our commonest fruit is the mango. It came from India, but now grows wild. There are many kinds . . . mango vert, mango rose, zabricot and calabash. These, however are not the best kinds. They are known by such names as Julie, Peters and Gordon.'[36]

The mango season is among the happiest times for children in the Caribbean. School boys engage in the fine art of pelting mangoes which is captured in the story, 'The Mango Tree' by renownd Caribbean writer Samuel Selvon.[37] The fruit has become fully infused into Caribbean culture. It has fostered a wide range of culinary delights, not the least of which is mango chow—a pickle of green mangoes, salt, vinegar, seasonings and pepper—a perennial favourite of young and old alike. In a book named after a variety of mango that is popular in Guyana, Oonya Kempadoo, another Caribbean writer, describes the mango chow experience through the young girl narrator in the story. Of the mango tree located in the village on the east coast of Georgetown, she says: 'Everybody coming for two green mango to make curry, or a dozen to make chow. We'd eat chow until we couldn't eat dinner—tongues hanging out and noses running from blazing pepper, lips purple with vinegar. The juice at the bottom of the bowl was the best part—dipping the mango seed in and scraping till your teeth edged.'[38]

The popularity of the mango is also reflected in songs. One of the national songs of Trinidad and Tobago extols the virtues of different types of mangoes:

Mangoes, mangoes, mangoes,
Mango vert, mango teen,
Ah want a penny to buy mango vert mango teen,
Gimme a penny to buy mango vert mango teen,
Mango duodouce sousait matan,
Savez vous all for me.[39]

There is also a Jamaican folksong by the name 'Mango Walk'.[40] There is a definite mango culture in the Caribbean where the trees grow in profusion. The trees growing on Crown lands were seen as communal property and the fruits were accessible to all. For a long time people assumed that they could help themselves to mangoes from any tree, wherever it existed, as mangoes were not 'stealable'.[41]

India was also important in the development of the nutmeg industry in the Caribbean. When nutmeg was first introduced into the St. Vincent Botanic Garden, two trees were brought from Cayenne. One of these died and the other was a male. In order to facilitate propagation of this spice, two plants were brought from India to Trinidad in 1806 and sent to St. Vincent where they were successfully cultivated. From St. Vincent, plants were sent to other territories in the region and to the Society for the Encouragement of Arts in England. From the plants received from St. Vincent, a stock was created in the Trinidad Botanic Gardens in 1820 which, by 1828, produced 1,300 trees. These, together with a subsequent batch planted in 1824, provided the basis for an economic enterprise in the island.[42] The lessons acquired from the early introduction of this spice into the region were later beneficial, when nutmeg cultivation became a major enterprise in Grenada during the 1860s.

The black pepper plant, which is indigenous to Travancore and Malabar, was introduced into the garden at St. Vincent in the attempt to develop new sources of this highly prized item at a closer location. While the plant survived in the region, its cultivation never became as widespread as was hoped. Several attempts were made to cultivate it extensively including an attempt made at a convict settlement in Trinidad in 1894.[43] Despite limited success in widespread cultivation, however, its use became so popular that it was fully incorporated into the Caribbean culinary practices.

Once introduced, the hibiscus plant[44] also became fully domiciled throughout the region. Valued as a decorative and medicinal plant, the shrub has been used to create hedges and fences and new varieties have been introduced as ornamentals. Popular images of the Caribbean depicting yards with mango trees and hibiscus hedges can be seen in tourist brochures as well as in art, post cards, song, poetry, and prose of the region. These plants have become fully accepted as symbols of 'Caribbeanness'[45] as many people are oblivious to the fact that they are introduced species. As a result of these introductions, the Caribbean landscape has been changed to include a wide variety of mango and hibiscus with each island priding itself as the source of the best types. Apart from enhancing the range of fruit and flora available in the region, these additions have impacted on the culture of the region in a variety of ways. They have influenced culinary practices, art, literature and song and they form important elements in popular images of the Caribbean.

However, their impact on the environment has never been studied. In particular, the extent to which these introductions contributed to the vulnerability of the region's flora to particular pests and diseases and the extent to which their naturalization occurred at the expense of some indigenous species remains unknown.

Imperial activity also involved the introduction of fauna. After over 200 years of its cultivation in the region, the sugar industry experienced a number of problems, not the least of which was rat infestation. This infestation was a costly one in a period when the industry needed to reduce its costs and increase its efficiency. To deal with the problem, the mongoose was imported from India first to Jamaica in 1860, to Barbados in 1870, to St. Lucia in 1885 to deal with the menace of the fer-de-lance snake, and then to other territories in the region.[46] The reports on the impact of this animal introduction on the rat menace were initially positive in all the territories. In Barbados, where the annual value of canes destroyed by rats was said to be £ 20,000 sterling, it was felt necessary to protect the mongoose by law. The animals multiplied in their new location to the extent that within 10 years they were seen as pests which some individuals were anxious to get rid of. As the rat menace subsided, complaints increased about the destructive habits of the mongoose which consumed ground game, especially quail, birds, poultry and even young pigs in the region. The snake population of St. Lucia was said to have been reduced as a result of the presence of the mongoose.[47] But the depletion of both ground game and snake species and the uncontrolled population explosion of the mongoose, which thrived in an environment devoid of its natural predators, was environmentally unsound. Thus, the introduction of this new species resulted in a reduction of the population of some indigenous species although its presence brought benefits to the sugar industry by solving the problem of the rat menace.

THE CULTURE OF FOREST CONSERVATION IN THE CARIBBEAN

For centuries, European colonizing activity displayed little concern for the environment, with notable exceptions in the region.[48] This changed during the second half of the nineteenth century when concerns about the state of the Caribbean environment were voiced by a number of colonial officials. In the years after emancipation, planters joined the rising chorus arguing that the activities of the ex-slaves were destroying the environment. Moved to action, the Colonial Office appointed E.D.M. Hooper from the India Forest Service to report on the state of forests in the Caribbean in 1887.[49]

Hooper visited the islands of Antigua, Jamaica, St. Lucia, Tobago, Grenada, St. Vincent, and the mainland territory of Belize, noting the extensive environmental damage suffered over the period of colonial exploitation and recommending corrective measures. His report did not elicit immediate action in many of the territories, but the island of Trinidad, which had not been included in his agenda, requested a similar investigation. F.A. Lodge, also from the India Forest Service, was sent to Trinidad in 1899 to report on the forests there.[50] Lodge noted the impact of environmental degradation on the colony and recommended that forest reserves should be established on the island. The outcome of this investigation was the establishment of the first Department of Forestry in the British Caribbean and the appointment of a Forestry Officer from the India Forest Service.[51] The training and experience which these officers had acquired in India had been brought to bear on the Caribbean environment.

From this point onwards, the establishment of forest reserves, first in Trinidad and an extension of the one previously established in Tobago has shaped Caribbean environments. The imperial government became committed to a policy of forest conservation and environmental protection in the region and conservation policies were subsequently applied in Jamaica and other territories. The creation of these reserves has had a major impact on Caribbean societies. Firstly, they were introduced in the post-emancipation period when planters and freed people were competing for land resources in these small territories. They therefore constituted another limitation on the access of the freed population to land. In some instances, their existence permitted an extension of planter control over these resources as well as on the economic activities of the freed people. Thus, these reserves impacted on the dynamic relations between planters and freed people in the nineteenth and twentieth centuries Caribbean.

The conservation policies also involved reforestation in the most denuded and fragile areas. This process involved a study of the indigenous species and the implementation of silvicultural programmes. From these studies came a widening of imperial knowledge of the nature and value of existing forest species which permitted increase in utilization of local, lesser known species and the accompanying reduction of over-exploitation of the more popular species. But reforestation also involved the introduction of suitable and desirable species from other parts of the world. In this regard, the teak plant, which had previously been introduced into the region from India and tested at the St. Vincent Botanic Garden, was introduced from Burma and became a popular timber species in some islands. The experiments in St. Vincent had established the suitability of the plant to the region and identified the best conditions for its cultivation. In Trinidad and Tobago, teak introductions formed the basis of an industry which remains in existence even today. Several other species, from both within and without the region, were also introduced through the conservation programmes. Thus, as a result of the conservation movement in the region, a change in the arboreal cover occurred in those parts of the islands which were identified as forest reserves. The new species contributed to another change in the natural environment of the region by additions to the existing arboreal species.

CONCLUSION

This discussion of the Caribbean environment has demonstrated the existence of important links between India and the Caribbean, which began prior to and were separate from the movement of indentured workers in the region. These links developed around the migration of plants, an activity organized by the imperial government in the attempt to develop new branches of trade. The result was the introduction of a variety of plants from India into the British possessions in the Caribbean which have played an important role in shaping the latter's environment. These new plants enhanced the diversity of the flora of the region and in some instances provided the basis for economic enterprise. The provision of the nutmeg plants from India was critical to the development of a thriving nutmeg industry in Trinidad during the early nineteenth century. These introductions were used to test the response of the plants to the Caribbean environment. The results of these tests provided valuable information and experience for the development of a large-scale nutmeg industry in Grenada later in the nineteenth century.

These plants, which became fully naturalized, may have done so at the expense of some of the indigenous species of the region but the overall impact of these introductions is a changed Caribbean landscape. The new landscape, reshaped by imperial activity, included reflections of India. The impact was not limited to the natural environment for some of these introductions have also influenced the social environment. The mango tree has become so fully entrenched in Caribbean life that it is difficult to perceive of the region without it. It remains a dominant symbol of Caribbean life, found in the homes of people of all social levels and has made an impact on the creative element of our society. Representations of the mango are to be found in the poetry, prose, song, culinary preparations and artistic representations of the region. Pictures advertising the region commonly use the hibiscus with a humming bird hovering over it as a typical Caribbean scene, while Caribbean gastronomical delights include a variety of mango preparations, zesty food seasoned with black pepper or spiced with nutmeg. When the indentured workers arrived in the Caribbean, they encountered floral precursors in their host societies. It is important that the scope of Caribbean historiography be widened to include studies on the environmental impact of the introduction of flora from other parts of the world into the region. This would facilitate both a better understanding of the historical development of and the nature of imperial activity in the region.

Initially, the introduction of the mongoose had a beneficial effect. It resulted, as was intended, in the reduction of the rat population, which was a menace to the sugar industry. This introduction however was not without negative consequences. The mongoose proved to be also a predator of desirable indigenous species, much to the consternation of some of the very advocates of its introduction. Thus, while this introduction added a new element to the fauna of the Caribbean, there was an accompanying reduction of the population of some of the indigenous species. Finally, it was to India that the authorities turned during the era of the development of conservation policies, in their attempts to forge a forest protection and conservation policy for the Caribbean territories. In this instance, both the experience of India and that of colonial officers working in India, were brought to bear on the environment of the British Caribbean. As a result, the Caribbean environment was reshaped in the effort to replace the forest cover that was ill advisedly removed at an earlier period, and to establish forests where none previously existed.

Caribbean environments reflect a number of influences from India, which resulted from deliberate plant and animal introductions. These have become so naturalized in the region that they assume the appearance of, and in some instances are presumed to be, indigenous species. Overall it is true to say, that along with an imported 'native' population, the natural environment of the Caribbean is partly naturalized.

NOTES

1. Louis S. Warren (ed.), *American Environmental History*, Oxford, 2003, p. 1.
2. Ibid.
3. David Watts, *The West Indies: Patterns of Development, Culture and Change Since 1492*, Cambridge, 1987, pp. 2-3.
4. Ibid., p. 3.
5. Ibid.
6. Bonham C. Richardson, *Economy and Environment in the Caribbean: Barbados and the Windwards in the Late 1800s*, Kingston, 1997, p. xv.

7. Bonham C. Richardson, *Igniting the Caribbean's Past: Fire in British West Indian History*, Chapel Hill, 2004.
8. Ibid., p. 6.
9. Ibid., p. 4.
10. Ibid.
11. Alfred Crosby, *Ecological Imperialism: The Biological Expansion of Europe, 900-1900*, Cambridge, 1986, p. 7.
12. Ibid., p. 148.
13. Ibid., p. 151.
14. Richard Grove, *Green Imperialism: Colonial Expansion, Tropical Island Edens and the Origins of Environmentalism, 1600-1860*, Cambridge, 1995.
15. Ibid., p. 75.
16. Ibid., pp. 75-6.
17. Ibid., p. 91.
18. Richard Drayton, *Nature's Government: Science, Imperial Britain, and the 'Improvement' of the World*, New Haven, 2000, p. xv.
19. Ibid., p. xiv.
20. K.S. Mathew, 'The Impact of Trade and Globalisation: A Study of the Migration of Plants and Producers from India to Brazil during the Seventeenth Century' in S. Jeyaseela Stephen (ed.), *Trade and Globalisation: Europeans, Americans and Indians in the Bay of Bengal (1511-1819)*, Jaipur and New Delhi, 2003, pp. 191-204.
21. Kumar Mahabir has written on this subject. See especially 'Animals from India in the Caribbean', in *Indian Arrival Day Commemorative Magazine*, vol. 4, no. 1, May-June 2003.
22. Leslie S. Cobley, *An Introduction to the Botany of Tropical Crops*, London: Longmans, 1967, p. 38.
23. Rev. Landsdown Guilding, *An Account of the Island of St. Vincent from its First Establishment to the Present Time*, 1825, p. 5.
24. A. Richard and Elizabeth S. Howard (eds.), *Alexander Anderson's The St. Vincent Botanic Garden*, Cambridge, Massachusetts: President and Fellows of Harvard College and The Linnean Society of London, 1983, p. 5.
25. Poore to Banks, 22 November 1770 Bank Correspondence (hereafter cited as BC), No. 1, 78.
26. Yonge to Banks, 17 August 1790, BC 2. 17.
27. W0 40/4 Anderson to Yonge, 1 March 1791.
28. Guilding, *An Account of the Island of St. Vincent*, pp. 17, 25, 27.
29. Edgar Adams, *People on the Move: The Effects of Some Important Historical Events on the People of St.Vincent and the Grenadines*, Kingstown, 2002, p. 25.
30. Yonge to Banks, 16 July 1788, BC 1. 307.
31. Yonge to Banks, 23 September 1788, BC 2.17.

32. BM. Add. MS 33978, 6 May 1785, *The Banks Letters—Sir Joseph Banks Correspondence: A Calendar of the Manuscripts and Correspondence*, Warren R. Davies (ed.), London, 1958, pp. 11-12.
33. Yonge to Banks, 6 October 1790, BC 2. 19.
34. *Bulletin of Misc. Information of the Trinidad Royal Botanical Gardens*, no. 24, July 1900, p. 257.
35. Olive Lewin, *'Rock It Come Over': The Folk Music of Jamaica*, Kingston, Jamaica, 2000, p. 107. The song 'Mango Walk' makes reference to these walks that were established on plantations during the era of slavery.
36. *Nelson's West Indian Readers* Book II, Compiled by J.O. Cutteridge, London, 1966.
37. Samuel Selvon, *Ways of Sunlight*, London, 1957, p. 109.
38. Oonya Kempadoo, *Buxton Spice*, London, 1998.
39. Olive Walke (ed.), *Folk Songs of Trinidad and Tobago*, Surrey, England, 1970, song no. 14.
40. Olive Lewin, *The Folk Music of Jamaica*, p. 107.
41. Ibid., 108.
42. *Bulletin of Miscellaneous Information of the Trinidad Royal Botanic Gardens*, no. 21, March 1894, p. 235.
43. Ibid., no. 26, January 1901, pp. 307-8.
44. Nineteen varieties of the hibiscus species were listed in the Catalogue of the St. Vincent Botanic Garden's Holdings in 1806. Rev. L. Guilding, *An Account of the Island of St. Vincent from its First Establishment to the Present Time*, Glasgow, 1825, p. 42.
45. The dust cover of Oonya Kempadoo's book *Buxton Spice* features a large red hibiscus flower.
46. CO 295-356 Despatch 374. Governor Knollys to Secretary of State Chamberlain, 28 September 1895. Kumar Mahabir, 'Animals from India in the Caribbean', *Indian Arrival Day Commemorative Magazine*, vol. 4, no. 1, May-June 2003.
47. CO 295-356 Despatch 374, Governor Knollys to Secretary of State Chamberlain, 28 September 1895.
48. A forest reserve was established on the island of Tobago in 1764, which was said to be one of the first in the New World.
49. R. Pemberton, 'The Evolution of Agricultural Policy in Trinidad and Tobago, 1890-1945' Ph.D. Thesis, University of the West Indies, St. Augustine, Trinidad and Tobago, 1997, p. 217.
50. Ibid., p. 230.
51. Ibid., p. 232.

14. West Tennessee, Cotton Cultivation, and the Environment, 1820-60

Lawrence Gundersen

After the Revolutionary War and War of 1812 veteran land grants to West Tennessee were issued and settled. Following the Jackson Purchase in 1818,[1] most of the lands east of the Mississippi and west from the approaches to the Appalachian Trail were still lush forests with at least one to ten feet of topsoil.[2] When West Tennessee began the cotton or antebellum period, the area was ideally situated for agricultural production and expansion. There were plenty of water sources, rich and fertile land replete with plentiful topsoil, a plethora of river transportation networks, and a climate conducive to cotton agriculture.[3] As the West Tennessee cotton frontier and kingdom was established between the years 1818 and 1860, little environmental regard was shown to the land in the way of cultivation or usage. The repeated planting of row crops, especially cotton, without allowing fields to lay fallow, or by not planting in alternative years soil-restoring crops such as soybeans and clover, rapidly deteriorated the soil quality and nutrients.[4]

What has not been explained, and which this paper seeks to address, is the impact of intensive cotton cultivation on the environment and West Tennesseans between 1820 and 1860. In addition, my hope here is to convey to both the reader and historian the applicability and natural tendency to study 'man' in relation to the environment and vice-versa. However, to begin this exploration of the somewhat new field of environmental history, let us first establish the boundaries and territory of the field, as this historian views it from an agrarian perspective, and then examine the methods and bases from which this type of historical inquiry should be conducted.

In a recent memoir the noted American historian Forrest McDonald averred on page one that, 'The evolution of the animal kingdom, changes in climate, and the alterations of the surface of the earth...took place in the past and constitute what is sometimes called natural history, but these are outside the purview of conventional history, whose content is human affairs.' His endnote to the statement was as follows: 'The new field of environmental history has not yet shown that it is history rather than reinvigorated natural history, geology, paleontology, or expanded archaeology.'[5] I have profound respect and admiration for this historical giant, but his understanding of what environmental history has become seems misguided. Environmental history is but another brick, which we as historians use to build the historical wall of understanding and knowledge about the past.[6]

When Marc Bloch and company established and developed the Annales School of Historical Thought in the early 1900s, their focus was on the geographical, sociological, psychological, ecumenical, and cultural facets of the human past. What environmental history seeks to draw from, much as the Annales School strives to draw from the social sciences, is the science and hard data relative to the environment, that impacts 'man' and human affairs. It also seeks to show how 'man' and human affairs have impacted the environment. Furthermore, in the noble quest to better understand and interpret the human past, and to build upon our historical knowledge of the past, would it be sound to leave some of rocks unturned? Like the destruction of Carthage by the Romans, which was generational as well as environmental, nuclear, biological and chemical incidents are generational and environmental. More importantly, those forces significantly impact on man and human affairs by creating temporary, static, and permanent 'dead zones' for humans and much of the animal kingdom. Collectively, they can be called 'hot zones' because of their effects on human activities. The cause of a hot zone could be accidental, intentional, caused by an individual or collective act, state-sponsored, or corporate affiliated. As a historian, am I to forget Tacitus's dictate '...that evil words and deeds should fear an infamous reputation with posterity'? Of course this begs the question—should historians write about and document the history of a hot zone?

Each year, the livestock, agricultural, and industrial run-off flowing into the Mississippi River creates a chemical hot zone for marine life from 'as early as February and sometimes lasting until mid-fall' in an annually expanding area of the Gulf of Mexico.[7] And, although that history of aquatic death in itself is not the dominion of historians,[8] it is within the purview of the historian to document the human affairs that created this hot zone, and to document the hot zone's effect on people. Part of the contaminated run-off is agriculturally and chemically related from nitrates and some of it comes from West Tennessee. However, this is not the basis and foundation for my work here.

Expanding and intensive cotton production in West Tennessee between 1820 and 1860 changed the environment and the conduct of human affairs in the region. Cotton became 'king', slavery was fully institutionalized and ensconced, by both the yeoman farmer and planter, and the socio-economic and political patterns of the region became formalized. With this formalization emerged a philosophy of unlimited productivity of the soil, as evidenced by the repeated planting of cotton: a philosophy ruinous to the soil, which went unchecked until the mobile rail exhibits by the Department of Agriculture in the late 1800s showed farmers environmentally friendly ways of conducting cotton cultivation, and methods to combat soil erosion.[9] Most importantly, for our purpose of study here, the topsoil in West Tennessee diminished over time from repeated deep-plough tillage for cotton, and this had a social dimension as well as modern implication in land use.[10]

In an earlier work, I reviewed the settlement patterns on the West Tennessee cotton frontier after 1818,[11] following Gary Edwards' studious work reviewing the life of the yeoman farmer in the region.[12] However, the West Tennessee cotton-producing region by 1860 was no longer 'The Old Southwest'. From many of the accounts of the pioneers and early settlers,[13] the cotton frontier from 1820 to 1860 produced settlement patterns that gradually encouraged early settlers to move either further west or further into the wilderness from their existing hub of operations (often by the money the planter class could offer for their land). John Marshall, discussing early settlement in Tipton County, addressed this movement outward when he said, 'it appears that the first decade of settlement in Tipton was marked by disease and discouragement. Crop yields were poor. The onset of the 1830s brought better times with high cotton prices and a new wave of settlers more equipped with capital. Through their efforts the county began to prosper and develop.'[14] Unable to sustain the enormous expenses related to slave labour for the cultivation of this cash crop, and at times jealous of the slave labour they could not compete with, as Dr. Edwards indicated in his examination of the yeoman's political outlook,[15] the yeoman farmer eventually gave way to the planter class.

The planter still deforested, as was needed for his long-term economic growth, but generally he would consolidate several yeoman farmer landholdings when either buying into a region or enlarged their existing plantations, thus not really needing to immediately deforest for cotton cultivation. Their cash crop of choice was cotton when prices were high in New Orleans, and prices remained high between 1820 and 1860 with only a few disappointing years.[16] Slave labourers increasingly replaced yeoman labourers clearing the land in the off-season.[17] In short, the planter was not in the business of clearing land or creating an existence: he was concerned with cultivating as much of his farmable land with a single cash crop and cotton was king.[18] The yeoman farmer of West Tennessee could not invest that much of the financial future in one crop,[19] and between 1840 and 1860, the planters solidified their dominance over cotton agriculture. The planters could count on an array of factors, brokers and merchants, at Randolph Landing, Bolivar Landing, Alexandria (Jackson), and Memphis to relay and post their financial assets. By the late 1840s, Memphis had become the best internal port for cotton on the Mississippi River.[20]

West Tennessee has been endowed with significant wetlands and a rich river network between the Tennessee and Mississippi Rivers. From the early descriptions, West Tennessee was one vast forest, God ordained, and there for the many proud founding veterans who may not get the attention we give Washington, Jefferson, and Jackson. Settlements, towns, and cities emerged on the banks of the larger and smaller rivers, and into the interior the pioneers and settlers pushed, gradually deforesting large sections of land for homes, farms, and plantations. Although Native Americans set forest fires to flush game in preceding generations, their overall impact was insignificant ecologically and environmentally. However, the deliberate, permanent, and continued deforestation, increasingly for the sake of cotton cultivation, had a lasting impact on the environment.

The cotton frontier was settled as the towns and cities expanded their boundaries,[21] pushing yeoman and settlers outward to hack and saw. Rural towns and cities in the South were not really seen by the planter class and yeoman farmers as places to live and work in but rather as a place to conduct business on occasion. The towns and cities still grew, but it were the pioneers, settlers, and planters combined pushing outward that provided for most of the initial deforestation (for cropland) of West Tennessee. The totality of the destruction of the landscape of West Tennessee must have been complete to any viewer in 1865, had they been original settlers from the 1820s. With over forty years of constant deforestation and cultivation, and with four years of destructive Civil War, the landscape, ecosystem, and forests had been forever changed. The Civil War may have allowed the land to somewhat regenerate its topsoil as the lack of farm labour and output contributed to a decrease in cultivation.[22]

By 1850, Tennessee cotton amounted to 7.9 per cent of the total United States output, and the State's corn and tobacco production rates were at 8.8 and 10.1 per cent, respectively. Tennessee's percentage of the total United States output of cotton during 1860, 1870 and 1880 varied between 5.5 per cent and 6 per cent. And, from 1890 until 1920, Tennessee's contribution ranged between 2.5 and 2.7 per cent of total cotton output—even with the improved farming techniques taught by the Department of Agriculture. Interestingly, the number of acres in Tennessee farms was 18.9 million by 1850, but in almost every Federal census until 1950 the numbers of acres in farmland hovered between 18 and 20 million acres for Tennessee.[23] This can be interpreted to mean, without a clear survey of the exact original acreage of forest, that most of this total acreage was deforested between 1820 and 1850 for cropland, and since that time the agricultural base has not significantly increased (yield and erosion has). In addition, this static number of acres in farmland, with cotton production plateaus, provides further historical evidence of soil degradation over time from the repeated planting of cotton.[24] The 'Old Southwest' of West Tennessee, its wilderness and forests, had been conquered by 1840.[25] Finally, the decrease in the amount of Tennessee's cotton production as part of the national total, between 1850 and 1860, may represent either yield declines from soil exhaustion, expansion in cotton production in other states and countries, or a combination.

The most critical measurement of environmental impact from the repeated planting of cotton and other crops should be the loss of topsoil. Poor farming methods, as much as massive soil erosion, deteriorated the arable lands to begin with, but it was the repeated planting of cotton and other row crops that increased the rapidity of the deterioration. Although the historian is sometimes limited by the availability of sources concerning specific and measurable information, like annual topsoil erosion reports for a given set of years, in the case years 1820 to 1860, using more modern erosion reports can give the researcher an estimated projection of soil deterioration based upon agricultural production.

I have chosen to use a modern government report, and although possibly biased toward over-projection by my standards, it will suffice as a historical 'marker' for past soil erosion estimates. Given the farmer's or planter's lack of knowledge on curbing soil erosion between 1820 and 1860, it would be easier to assume otherwise. In 1980, the United States Department of Agriculture's 'Soil and Water Resources Conservation Act, Summary of Appraisal' shed light on topsoil loss associated with water erosion. The 'Summary' indicated Tennessee had one of the highest rates of topsoil loss from water averaging 14.1 tons of topsoil per acre of agricultural land.[26] Using a marker of 14 tons loss per acre, and coupling that with West Tennessee cotton production estimates between 1820 and 1860 yields interesting environmental history about repeated cotton cultivation (see Table 14.1). However, it should be noted that Tennessee, by acts of the state's legislature, founded a Tennessee State Agricultural Society in 1841 to provide for

TABLE 14.1: ESTIMATED WEST TENNESSEE TOPSOIL LOSS FOR COTTON IN GIVEN YEAR

Year	*West Tn Cotton**	*Est. Acreage+*	*Tons/Inches of Loss†*
1829	50,000 bales	45-50,000 acres	4,05,000/½
1830	75,000 bales	70-75,000 acres	6,30,000/½
1831	35,000 bales	30-35,000 acres	2,70,000/½
1833	62,500 bales	60,000 acres	5,40,000/½
1939	34,000 bales	30-35,000 acres	2,70,000/½
1840	42,000 bales	40,000 acres	3,60,000/½
1850	97,000 bales	100,000 acres	9,00,000/½
1860	1,48,000 bales	150,000 acres	13,50,000/½

Notes: * Bales (376 to 400 lbs) of cotton produced in West Tennessee taken from 'West Tennessee and the Cotton Frontier, 1818-1840.' The Federal census in 1850 started covering the amount of acreage in cotton. Today, cotton bales range from 486 to 500 pounds.

\+ Estimated acreage under cotton cultivation, until 1850, the author based on the amount of cotton produced.

† With a loss of 14 tons per acre, minus 5 tons of sustainability, the years in question reflect the author's estimation of topsoil loss in tons and inches for cotton base. With tobacco and corn added, the other 67 per cent of row crops, the trend in topsoil loss was obviously unsustainable.

an agricultural college,[27] and created a Bureau of Agriculture in 1853, to improve and exchange knowledge about crops statewide.[28]

If West Tennessee was losing 14 tons of topsoil per acre of cropland,[29] there was a steady and gradual decline in topsoil and overall soil condition between 1820 and 1860.[30] An unknown facing the historical analyst is how rapidly the excessive soil erosion ultimately reduced crop production. Table 14.1 reflects the estimated loss of topsoil based on cotton yields between 1820 and 1860[31] and where available, the amount of acreage under cotton cultivation during the year. From some earlier work on West Tennessee cotton cultivation estimates,[32] and from the estimated topsoil depletion rates,[33] this provides the foundation of an overall environmental assessment between 1820 and 1860. Furthermore, this frames an environmental research paradigm in agricultural history; an approach which seeks to use research for the purpose of explaining the historical implications and social impact of land use patterns.

Sumit Guha, in *The Agrarian Economy of the Bombay Deccan, 1818-1914*, noted agrarian cotton-based economies, in a very similar situation and time as was the cotton kingdom during the antebellum period, of which West Tennessee was part of the northern tier. According to Guha, repetitive cultivation led to 'stagnant agriculture'. This type of agriculture emerged when farmers were unable to increase either the area cultivated or the productivity of the land under cultivation. 'Cotton, for instance, was a profitable export crop, cultivated under superior environmental conditions, and a great deal of research effort was also invested in it. But its yield stagnated or declined. The grain crops must have fared worse.'[34] Corn, and later wheat, as the West Tennessee cotton frontier expanded, was a staple crop to all pioneers and settlers. The settlers, or yeoman farmers needed corn not only for themselves but also an ample supply for swine, which the pioneers brought with them—provided they had cleared and planted an area of corn before moving-in. The point being that repeated planting of corn and tobacco, and mainly cotton, three crops that leave large parts of the soil exposed to erosion, between 1820 and 1860, significantly decreased the availability of prime cotton base and pushed pioneers and settlers further into the frontier seeking fresh land.

Governor James K. Polk in his legislative address in late 1841 highlighted and defended the rights of property owners, especially farmers, when he said, 'Our (State) is essentially an agricultural State, Nineteen–twentieths of her population are cultivators of the earth, and the protection of their interests therefore, at the same time that the just rights of others shall not be impaired, should at all times be an object of paramount consideration.'[35] To further the interests of the farmers in the Tennessee, Governor James Chamberlain Jones (1841-5) signed into law and appropriations a bill incorporating a Tennessee State Agricultural Society capitalized with $1,00,000 dollars.[36] The first intimation of a revolt against the prevailing unlimited soil philosophy was issued in 1858, when Governor Isham G. Harris (1857-61), at the Fifth Annual State Fair said, 'The time has come when Tennesseans should learn the importance of a variety of crops and diversifying their labor, thereby improving, instead of impoverishing, a soil so generous and fertile as almost to tempt our people into a system of careless and slovenly farming.'[37] In 1859, Commander Matthew Fontaine Maury of the United States Navy, at the same event, called for a state committee or bureau to 'enable the planter to answer the merchant well and truly... till the cotton is all picked'.[38] His remarks seem intended to re-enforce the prevailing philosophy of the unlimited sustainability of the soil.

'The growth rate of agricultural output in the nineteenth century was high relative to that of the twentieth century. At the beginning of the nineteenth century, land, capital, and labor grew at similar rates, but as the century wore on the growth rate of labor started to lag behind that of land, leading to a rise in the land-labor ratio.' The social change that emerged after the yeoman farmer labour shifted to slave labour in the production of cotton, was a 'decline in the growth rate of labor relative to that of output' near the middle of the 1800s. This led to social change in agricultural communities and regions as labour was increasingly forced to migrate out of farm labour.[39] Many of those citizens that remained in the rural agricultural areas after the Civil War, especially in the South, became sharecroppers and tenant farmers and suffered the attending economic hardships.

By using what is referred to as the 'Russell Equation' (discounting the *T* value),[40] West Tennessee's estimated erosion between 1820 and 1860 was a half an inch a year. Assuming the farmers during that period knew little about the long-term impact of continuous and ruinous cultivation, eventually the complete and irreplaceable loss of topsoil, it would be easy to speculate that the loss was closer to two feet. This was not sustainable. What allowed for the resumption of cotton production on marginal land after the Civil War was the introduction of fertilizers, improved farming methods (mechanization), and anti-erosion techniques to enhance output. However, the topsoil still declined.

To further document this historical trend of loss of topsoil in West Tennessee, a 1999 article in the *Engineering & Technology for a Sustainable World,* entitled 'Researchers Help Preserve Soils' said, 'The Tennessee Valley . . . is very fertile, (but) the soils in this area are heavily eroded and heavily compacted, and plant roots don't extend very deep in the soil.'[41] Today, the continued erosion estimate is at 6.4 tons per acre of cropland (over the sustainable 5 tons per acre). The Water Erosion Prediction Project, using estimates from the 1992 National Resource Inventory, recommended the implementation of technological upgrades from soil erosion data to better manage unsustainable soil erosion.[42] India began those same efforts a few years before that.[43]

Currently, only one associate degree programme, also used for baccalaureate internships in agriculture technology, with emphasis on precision agriculture is offered in the Southeastern United States. Jackson State, one of the Tennessee Board of Regents' comprehensive community colleges within its governing system, provides the unique Associate of Applied Science in Agriculture Technology (Precision Concentration). The curriculum, developed in partnership with the region's agricultural industry, focuses 'on the new emerging technologies of the Global Positioning System (GPS) and Geographic Information System (GIS) integrated with an emphasis on Agronomy and Computer Science'.[44] The new satellite-based technology allows the modern farmer to conserve water, fertilizers, insecticides, and the controversial defoliants similar to Agent Orange, by using real-time analysis in the cab of a tractor or combine to automatically discharge a measured application of any of those substances.[45] The West Tennessee soils, mainly Loveland Loess, Roxana Silt and Peoria Loess,[46] which tend toward compaction with no-till plough methods and accelerated erosion from repeated deep-till planting methods, provide an ideal setting for the study and collection of data to monitor soil erosion.

The social impact from the introduction of cotton to the environment of West Tennessee can be found in the demographics. Bell Wiley's graduate thesis, 'Cotton and Slavery in the History of West Tennessee', clearly illustrated how the expansion of cotton was related to the growth of slave labour in the region.[47] Between 1820 and 1860, the number of slaves in Tennessee increased from about 80,000 to 2,75,000,[48] and West Tennessee had about 40 per cent of that total.[49] Before the Civil

War, whites and blacks lived in close proximity to one another throughout most of the South.[50]

With the end of slavery, the advances of agricultural mechanization, the decrease in the agricultural land-labour sustaining rate, and the need for labour in the emerging industrial capabilities of the towns and cities, the entire social dynamic of the antebellum period was forever changed. Segregation for African-Americans, especially in the towns and cities of the South, became the mainstay as local yeoman farmers, former yeoman farmers, tradesmen, and merchants were not about to provide equal social status to former slaves who were increasingly attracted to the urban centres for employment. The lot of those African-Americans, and poor whites, staying in agriculture as small farmers, sharecroppers, and tenant farmers was a never-ending cycle of perpetual debt and poverty.[51] It took one hundred years after the Civil War for the Federal Government, led by President Lyndon B. Johnson in his 'War on Poverty' campaign, to begin to seriously tackle the socio-economic problems related to the legacy of slavery and rural poverty in the South.

There is no need to further legitimize the epistemological foundations of environmental history. A pluralistic and converging methodology has begun to take shape, which addresses land use, chemical, biological and nuclear accidents and intentional usages, environmental determinants, and which seeks to better understand and interpret the impact of man's behaviour using the historical lens to snap a more complete and accurate picture of events and people in the context of the environment. Moreover, from a structural emphasis in garnering a theory towards a better understand of man and land use, especially row crops like cotton that diminish topsoil, again the environment determinant approach of measuring topsoil loss in the context of socio-economic and political change would only be natural for historical exploration and edification. Apropos, as historians we must guard against politicizing objectivity for the sake of vanity and present-mindedness when rendering environmental history. Anything less would be surrendering historical objectivity.

The continued emphasis on cotton yield rather than soil conservation has all the makings for environmental problems in

West Tennessee in the twenty-first century. In 2000, *Texas Agriculture* reported a cotton yield decline between 1970 and 1985, and between 1992 and 1998. The article went on to explain that new varieties should be 'developed that have the ability to better adapt to environmental stress'. The article concluded, 'A rise in the average land productivity is not a sufficient statistic for concluding that technical change is land augmenting'.[52] In 2005, the *Delta Farm Press* reported 'Mississippi Cotton Yields Set Record'. In the article, it was explained that the yield averaged 378 pounds of cotton per acre in 1953, and that a new record of 806 pounds per acre had been achieved.[53] With current yields high[54] and prices stable[55] there seems to be no respite for West Tennessee soil, and its continued erosion from the repeated planting of cotton and other row crops. The longitudinal impact of these decidedly human affairs on the existing ecosystem of West Tennessee might best be studied using precision agriculture technology to measure and improve soil quality rather than to increase yield and decrease fertilizer and nutrient waste.

NOTES

1. John S. Bassett (ed.), *Correspondence of Andrew Jackson*, vol. II, Washington, D.C., 1928, pp. 278-9.
2. Bob Moore, Interview by Lawrence Gundersen, 10 December 2004. Moore was Assistant Professor of Agriculture Technology and former agent of US Department of Agriculture.
3. Edward B. Espenshade (ed.), *Goode's World Atlas*, 15th ed., Chicago: Rand McNally, 1980, pp. 28, 120-1. The Wolf, Obion (North Fork and South), Loosahatchie, Hatchie, Forked Deer (North and South Fork), and Big Sandy Rivers provided the natural infrastructure to support cultivation and transportation.
4. Jeremy Atack, Fred Bateman, and William Parker, 'The Farm, the Farmer, and the Market', *Cambridge Economic History of the United States,* vol. II, New York, 2000, pp. 245-84.
5. Forrest McDonald, *Recovering the Past: A Historian's Memoir*, Kansas, 2004, p. 1.
6. C. Vann Woodward, 'Report on Current Research: American History', *Saturday Review of Literature*, 36, 4 April 1953, p. 16.
7. Janet Raloff, 'Dead Waters: Massive Oxygen-Starved Zones are Developing Along the World's Coasts', *Science News Online*, 5 June 2004, vol. 165, no. 23, accessed at www.sciencenews.org, on 19 January 2005.

8. McDonald, *Recovering the Past*, pp. 1-2.
9. The U.S. Department of Agriculture was founded by Abraham Lincoln in 1862, when about 58 per cent of Americans were farmers. Even the late 1800s production increase stabilized until the 1920s, when increases began again with electrification and the tractor, causing another decrease in demand for labour.
10. Yair Mundlak, 'Economic Growth: Lessons from Two Centuries of American Agriculture', Discussion Paper No. 2.03, revised May 2003, accessed at www.departments.agri.huji.ac.il/economics/indexe.html on 4 November 2004, p. 35. The work concluded, 'Another lesson is drawn from the changes in average labor productivity. Here the rate in the US exceeds somewhat the median of the country distribution. This is due to the changes in output and in labor. The agricultural sector in the US declined relatively fast, reflecting the rate of off-farm migration, and also the relatively low growth rate of the rural labor force. The rate of the off-farm migration has been affected favorably by the growth of the nonagricultural sector.'
11. Lawrence G. Gundersen, 'West Tennessee and the Cotton Frontier, 1818-1840', *The West Tennessee Historical Society Papers*, vol. LII, 1998, p. 26.
12. Gary Edwards, 'Venerate the Plow: Agricultural Life in Antebellum Fayette County, Tennessee', *The West Tennessee Historical Society Papers*, vol. LI, 1997, pp. 88-94.
13. Effie Meek Maiden, *Home in the Wilderness*, Norfolk, VA: Mouseterpiece, 2003; John Marshall, 'Settlement Patterns in Antebellum Tipton County', *The West Tennessee Historical Society Papers*, vol. LV, 2001, pp. 16, 22-7; Edwards, 'Venerate the Plow', pp. 88-9; and, Thomas Perkins Abernathy, *From Frontier to Plantation in Tennessee*, North Carolina, 1932, pp. 249-54.
14. Marshall, 'Settlement Patterns in Tipton County', 16, pp. 26-7.
15. Edwards, 'Venerate the Plow', p. 91.
16. Gundersen, 'West Tennessee and the Cotton Frontiers', p. 29. The year 1829 had over a 50 per cent price decline in New Orleans. In 1836, the lowest price for cotton was 15 cents a pound, but that price dropped to 5 cents a pound in 1837. In 1838, prices plummeted to 11/2 to 2 cents a pound—largely as a response to the Specie Circular issued by President Jackson.
17. Donald B. Dodd and Wynelle S. Dodd, *Historical Statistics of the South, 1790-1970*, Alabama, 1973, p. 50.
18. Ibid.
19. Edwards, 'Venerate the Plow', p. 89.
20. Joe Wojak, 'The Factors of Urban Development: Cotton Brokers and Merchants in Antebellum Memphis, 1850-1860', *The West Tennessee Historical Society Papers*, vol. L, 1996, p. 71.

21. Edward C. Banfield, *The Unheavenly City: Revisited*, New York, 1990.
22. U.S. Department of Commerce, Bureau of the Census, *Historical Statistics of the United States: Colonial Times to 1970*, part 1, Washington, D.C., 1975, p. 518. US cotton output was 4.49 million bales in 1861, 1.59 million in 1862, 0.45 million bales in 1863, 0.3 million bales in 1864, and 2.10 million bales in 1865.
23. Dodd, *Historical Statistics of the South*, pp. 50-3.
24. *Historical Statistics*, p. 518. Plateaus of production occurred between 1835 and 1841, and 1851 and 1857 (within a range 3,00,000 bales). Acreage in farms held steady until 1950, and then the total acreage beginning in 1960 started a continuous decline. Yield and erosion went up with an increasingly smaller agricultural base.
25. Gundersen, part of the thesis of earlier work.
26. U.S. Department of Agriculture, *Soil and Water Resources Conservation Act (RCA), Summary of Appraisal,* Parts 1 and 11, and *Program Review Draft, 1980*, Washington, D.C., 1980.
27. Robert H. White, *Messages of the Governors of Tennessee, 1835-1845*, vol. III, Tennessee, 1954, p. 486.
28. Ibid., vol. IV, pp. 603-4.
29. *RCA*, pp. 42-61.
30. U.S. Department of Agriculture, *National Agricultural Lands Study (NALS)*, Washington, D.C., 1981, pp. 184-221. The study indicated that under 5 tons a year loss was sustainable or replacement level.
31. Gundersen, 'West Tennessee and the Cotton Frontiers', p. 28.
32. Ibid.
33. *NALS*
34. Sumit Guha, *The Agrarian Economy of the Bombay Deccan, 1818-1941*, Delhi, 1985, op. cit.
35. White, *Messages the Governors of Tennessee*, vol. III., p. 427.
36. Ibid., 484-7.
37. Ibid., vol. V, pp. 244-5.
38. Ibid., p. 242.
39. Mundlak, 'Economic Growth: Lessons from Two Centuries', pp. 17, 33-4.
40. Moore.
41. 'Researchers Help Preserve Soils', *Engineering & Technology for a Sustainable World*, November 1999, vol. 6, issue 11, p. 4.
42. Hans Becker, 'WEPP: Spilling the Secrets of Water Erosion', *Agricultural Research*, vol. 45, no. 4, April 1997, pp. 4-5.
43. Gurmel Singh et al., 'Soil Erosion Rates in India', *Journal of Soil and Water Conservation*, 47, January-February 1992, pp. 3-6.
44. *2004-2005 College Catalog and Student Handbook* Jackson State Community College, Springfield, Illiniois, 2004, 62, pp. 97-9.
45. Moore.

46. Donald T. Rodbell, Steven Forman, James Pierson, and Warren C. Lynn, 'Stratigraphy and Chronology of Mississippi Valley Loess in Western Tennessee', *Geological Society of America Bulletin*, September 1997, vol. 109, no. 9, pp. 1134-9, 1146.
47. Bell I. Wiley, 'Cotton and Slavery in the History of West Tennessee' (M.A. thesis, Univ. of Kentucky, 1929), pp. 1-2, 36-40, 53.
48. Dodd, *Historical Statistics of the South*, p. 50.
49. Wiley, pp. 25-33.
50. C. Vann Woodward, *The Strange Career of Jim Crow*, New York, 1955.
51. Ibid., *The Burden of Southern History*, 3rd edn., Louisiana, 1993, pp. 89-107; *Origins of the New South, 1877-1913*, Louisiana, 1971, pp. 51-73 142-5, 175-84, 202-3, 321-39.
52. 'Blue Ribbon Committee Finds Cotton Yields Stagnant', *Texas Agriculture*, 3 March 2000, pp. 1-5.
53. Eva Ann Doris, 'Mississippi Cotton Yields Set Record', 21 January 2005, pp. 1-3.
54. Ibid.
55. *New York Times*. The weekly commodity (cotton) value assessment by the author over the past 10 years showed little price change with cost-of-living and inflation adjustments factored-in.

15. Fire, Fume and Haze: Environmental Disorder in Southeast Asia and ASEAN Response

Tridib Chakrabarti

The epidemic outburst of smoke due to forest fire in some parts of Southeast Asia in 1997 has emerged as a major issue in the ongoing debate relating to the perceived environmental problems in today's world. This smoke hazard which ultimately converted into a transboundary haze problem was due to smoke, dust, moisture and vapour suspended in air sufficient to impair visibility. The hazard originating from large-scale forest and land fires, has been the most crippling environmental problem facing the ASEAN countries in the post-Cold War years. These large-scale fires are often deliberately set off by large plantation companies and farmer settlers who come from the more densely populated provinces of Indonesia and are provided homesteads in Sumatra and Kalimantan and who have joined the traditional shifting cultivators living in this region for a long time, clearing small sites for planting crops until the soil's nutrients have been exhausted and then moving to other sites by using fire as the most economical way of clearing forest land for cultivation. This has resulted in several large-scale forest fires and haze incidents. Besides this, long-term climate variability (glacial vs. non-glacial climate) and short-term climate oscillations caused by the El Nino-Southern Oscillation (ENSO) events have repeatedly caused droughts and even made rain forests suffer from wild fires in many parts of the region. These fires often create severe smoke pollution that persists for a long period. Since the early eighties—particularly the dry seasons of 1982-3, 1987, 1991 and 1994—such fires have caused severe damage that has gone beyond the destruction of forest land and ecosystem. The 1997 and 1998 forest fires in Indonesia's Kalimantan and Sumatran provinces of Jambi, Riau and elsewhere caused a smoke haze that hung over the entire Southeast Asian region, wandering as far as Bangkok, Kuala Lumpur, Manila, Singapore and Irian Java.

The haze from forest fires took a heavy toll on travel, environment and human life. It also caused public health disasters in the region, with a sharp increase in the number of patients suffering from respiratory, lung and heart diseases and reduced fertility. It also caused damage to the nervous system, blood cells and kidneys. Such health concerns turned many Southeast Asians decidedly impatient with their political leaders.[1] Moreover, serious transport accidents appeared more than coincidental during this smog period: a Garuda Airbus rammed into a mountainside on the approach to Medan in Sumatra and killed all 256 passengers on board. In the unclear Straits of Malacca, a small Indian cargo vessel hit a supertanker and lost 20 crew members. Many accidents were exacerbated by the haze. In Indonesia's eastern most province of Irian Java, severe drought caused staple food crops to fail in the highlands, which resulted in minimum of 500 deaths from starvation.

The economic impact of this haze catastrophe was a sharp blow to Southeast Asian tourism. Tourism in the entire region declined considerably along with a stock market collapse. Hotel and holiday bookings were cancelled in Malaysia and Indonesia. Governments in Europe and North America issued advisories warning citizens against visiting countries hit by the polluted air, particularly Malaysia, Indonesia and Singapore. Many multinationals like Ericsson and General Electric evacuated expatriates from this region and caused economic losses to the tune of over US $9 billion.[2] Further, this smog crisis destroyed more than 20,000 hectares of land, laying to waste small holdings, national parks and commercial plantations, mostly in Kalimantan. It also ravaged more than 3,00,000 hectares on the islands of Borneo, Java, Sulawesi and Sumatra. The economic losses due to log and timber destruction is estimated at US $912 million. A range of unquantifiable damages such as decreased quality of life, loss of biodiversity and atmospheric impacts also occurred.

Fire-related smoke haze episodes have a social component too:

a large part of the population in Southeast Asia does not have the financial means to buy protective measures such as respiratory masks and airconditioning nor can it refrain from outdoor work when air pollution is high. The same applies to escalating medical treatment costs for haze-related ailments.

CAUSES FOR THE HAZE CATASTROPHE

The causes of the haze catastrophe and its severity have become a major subject of discord among governments, forestry interests and conservationists. From most of the literature and commentary on this issue, it appears that haze occur due to degradation of environment in the region. However, some believe that this is essentially a man-made problem. What is amply clear is that most of the burning of forests was done by people contracted by large Indonesian forest plantations and palm oil estates (backed by government), in areas designated for clearing. Secondly, it is widely agreed that an occurrence of ENSO produces dry conditions which makes fires in normally moist rainforest and former rainforest terrain possible. While there is evidence of periodical fires in the remote past, in recent years unprecedented level of human activities has been a major reason for frequent fire outbreaks. Those connected with large-scale timber extraction attribute the fires to the practice of swidden agriculture, which in dry years leads to deliberately set fires spreading out of control.[3] The third factor for fires is the logging companies which clear land for timber extraction. Fourthly, palm oil production and commercial forestry, which has received massive government support in Indonesia, have also been grave factors in the outbreak of fires. The draining of peat swamps for rice cultivation–most notoriously in the one million hectare project in Central Kalimantan—has been another human activity that has augmented the fire problem. Dried peat burns easily, and as the fires sometime extend to deposits deep underground, rainfall does not always extinguish them.[4] Long-lasting fires in coal seams extending to or near the surface in various rainforest sites in East Kalimantan has been another cause for wildfires spreading into the surrounding forests. It is assumed that all the 150 coal seam fires known to be burning in 1980s were ignited by the 1982-3 wildfires.[5] Small-scale shifting cultivators who seasonally burn small plots for their subsistence are also culpable. Finally, the important large plantation companies, many of which have close connection to the government, illegally use fire to clear the land. The fire spreads particularly to those areas that have been heavily logged.[6] Many logging companies occasionally use sub-contractors or 'illegal' loggers who have little interest in and knowledge of fire prevention. Thus, the dynamics of forest of fires in parts of Southeast Asia, has become a matter of environmental politics in international relations. The haze calamity has also resulted in many riots in Indonesia over rising food prices and shortages of basic goods, and turned out to be the greatest ecological disaster of the decade.

ASEAN'S REPARTEE BEFORE THE 1997 HAZE DISASTER

The regional smog events in the seasons of 1982-3, 1987, 1991 and 1994 in Indonesia disturbed the environmental condition of the Southeast Asian region. The crisis triggered a series of national and international initiatives towards cooperation in fire and smoke management. At the 1992, Bandung Conference, a 'Long-Term Integrated Forest Fire Management Strategy' for Indonesian haze episode was proposed. A Pan-Asian Fire Management Programme was proposed during this time to coordinate all national fire management systems in the region through the 'Asian Forest Fire Management Action Plan'. The Action Plan would also include various other initiatives in fire research and management.[7] The haze crisis of 1994 in Indonesia accelerated these regional initiatives. According to the Indonesian Ministry of Forestry, the 1994 forest fires and smoke destroyed over 5.1 million hectares of land and smoke caused large-scale health and safety problems not only in Indonesia, but also in Singapore and Malaysia. It impelled the ASEAN countries to take measures to overcome this calamity in the form of the 'ASEAN Cooperation Plan on Transboundary Pollution', which was agreed on in October 1994 at the ASEAN Ministerial Meeting on the Environment convened in Kuching, Malaysia. In this meeting, the ministers extensively discussed the work of the Commission on Sustainable Development, the results of the first conference of the parties of the Convention on Biological Diversity, the implementation of the Montreal Protocol and the Basel Convention on the Control of the Transboundary Movements of Hazardous Wastes and Their Disposal, and the activities for ASEAN Environment Year 1995.[8] In addition to this, in order to address the increasing periodicity and worsening impact of the haze problem in the Southeast Asian region, the ministers agreed that measures should be taken to control the problem and that a regional cooperative plan to build capacity should be prepared.[9] Further, this meeting recommended longer term 'zero burning practices' and 'awareness building' efforts to eliminate the use of fire in land clearing through economically sound and environmentally friendly methods in agriculture.

As a follow up to the decisions taken at the ministerial meeting and as a programme for the ASEAN Environment Year, the Government of Malaysia hosted an 'ASEAN Meeting on Transboundary Pollution' in June 1995 in Kuala Lumpur. In this meeting, it was agreed that there should be regional understanding on and appreciation of the impact of transboundary pollution/haze and the need for capacity building and cooperative efforts to combat transboundary pollution/haze. The members agreed to develop an Asian cooperative plan to address the transboundary pollution issue. The plan among others, contained:

(1) Comprehensive measures for prevention, management and control;
(2) Establishment of an early warning system including identification of focal points for information exchange;
(3) Building up of national and regional institutional capacity; and
(4) Establishing cooperative links with developed countries to assist ASEAN's efforts.[10]

What is most important to note in this meeting is the avoidance of any reference to promotion of forest conservation or protection as a means of minimizing the generation of smoke. Following this meeting, a 'Haze Technical Task Force' was established at the Sixth Meeting of the ASEAN Senior Officials on the Environment (ASOEN) held in September 1995. The task force was chaired by Indonesia and comprised senior officials from Brunei Darussalam, Indonesia, Malaysia and Singapore. The objectives the task force were to operationalize and implement the measures recommended in the Asian Cooperation Plan on Transboundary Pollution relating to atmospheric pollution, particularly the problem of fire and smoke. This meeting further iterated the aim of disseminating information on fire prevention and containment, including making available satellite data on actual fires. But despite these resolutions, there was no real progress as the countries were still not fully committed to solving the haze problem.

However, things have gone in a different direction, after the 1997 and 1998 epidemic outbursts of haze produced by forest fires in Indonesia's Kalimantan and Sumatra provinces. The haze engulfed entire Southeast Asia and posed a severe challenge to every aspect of ASEAN's structure and modalities. It confronted ASEAN for the first time with a serious multilateral problem and revealed the failure of environmental management programmes not just in Indonesia but ASEAN in the region as a whole. In fact, ASEAN for the first time was caught between rhetoric and reality, and the haze crisis brought the issue of environmental degradation to the top of the political agenda. Since the problem affected most countries of ASEAN, there was a big question mark about ASEAN's 'Principle of non-intervention in the affairs of another nation'.

Principle of Non-Intervention in Question Mark

The principle of non-intervention has always been a subject of contention in ASEAN affairs. On the one hand, the strict observance of this principle has helped to promote a stable environment of peace conducive to development. On the other, complete disregard of this principle has resulted in internal tensions. However, in the changed international and regional contexts, strict adherence to the principle in letter and spirit has tended to divide the ASEAN states. The founding members of the ASEAN, namely Indonesia, Malaysia, Singapore, Thailand and the Philippines had accepted non-interference in each other's affairs as a cardinal principle and characteristic of ASEAN amity. This principle was intended to apply not only for interferences by extra-regional powers, including United States, Russia and China, but also by Southeast Asian countries in the affairs of neighbours. The 1971 Kuala Lumpur Declaration on the Zone of Peace, Freedom and Neutrality (ZUPFAN) recognized the right of every state, large or small, to lead its national existence free from outside interference in its internal affairs, since this interference would adversely affect its freedom, independence and integrity. It also declared the neutralization of Southeast Asia as a desirable goal. Article 2 of the Treaty of Amity and Cooperation (TAC) adopted at ASEAN's first Heads of Government Summit in 1976 was aimed at promoting perpetual peace and ever lasting amity and cooperation among people, which would contribute to their strength, solidarity and closer relations. It stressed the principle of 'mutual respect for independence, sovereignty, equality, territorial integrity and national identity of all nations'. It also highlighted 'the right of every state to lead its national existence free from external interference, subversion or coersion'. Most prominently, it enshrined the principle of 'non-interference in the internal affairs of one another'.[11]

However, important changes in international relations has required a reassessment of these principles, especially when the domestic problems of one state have far-reaching effects on the neighbouring states. On many occasions, these domestic problems pose a serious threat to the peace and stability of the region. From Cold War to post-Cold War years, the genocidal acts of the Pol Pot regime during 1975-8; Vietnam's invasion of Cambodia in January 1979; the transboundary movement of insurgents; strained relations between Thailand and Malaysia over the activities of the Communist Party of Malaya (CPM) and the Muslim separatists in southern Thailand; Thailand's devaluation of the Baht; Myanmar's military repression; Cambodia's coup d'etat; and the sacking of Malaysian deputy prime minister Anwar Ibrahim in the 1990s have all generated critical comments from political leaders in the neighbouring countries and raised doubts about ASEAN's regionalism and its principles of non-interference and non-confrontation. Predictably, at the ASEAN foreign ministers' meeting in 1998,

Thailand's foreign minister Surin Pitsuan challenged the principle of non-intervention and called for a change: 'It is time that ASEAN's cherished principle of non-intervention is modified to allow it to play a constructive role in preventing or resolving domestic issues with regional implications.' Elaborating further, he said, 'When a matter of domestic concern poses a threat to regional stability, a dose of peer pressure or friendly advice at the right time can be helpful.'[12] He demanded that the ASEAN members be allowed to openly discuss each other's domestic affairs, if these issues have an impact outside their borders. In place of strict adherence to non-interference, as Pitsuan proposed the idea of 'flexible engagement', by which he meant that the members required more 'openness' in dealing with one another, and that they should not refrain from propounding on each other's domestic policies if such policies had regional connotations. His proposal however received only the support of the Philippines, and was firmly opposed by the rest of ASEAN members who advocated 'constructive interventions' in certain regional issues.[13] Thus, the debate over non-interference has raised serious questions about ASEAN's capacity to adopt to the changing domestic, regional and global circumstances and to move, in the foreseeable future at least, towards a deeper approach to regionalism characteristic of mature communities.[14]

The problem of forest fires and transboundary environmental pollution have focused attention on the ASEAN tradition of non-interference in domestic affairs vis-à-vis the rights of the regional community. The haze catastrophe has caused tensions and clearly divided the members of the ASEAN. Singapore and Malaysia are in support of the continuation of the norms of non-intervention, while Thailand and the Philippines are openly critical of these principles. The countries of Southeast Asia understand that the problem of haze is no longer an individual undertaking of the affected countries, but demands a coordinated and concerted response from the ASEAN members. This has resulted in the ASEAN taking a number of initiatives and not mentioning Indonesia as the source of the transboundary pollution. The ASEAN outlook on the haze episode is entirely based on dialogue, consultation, cooperation, engagement and mutual interaction.

It tackles the problem by regional consensus, known as 'the ASEAN Way', and avoids confrontation, without breaking away from the principle of non-intervention.

ASEAN Strategies to Overcome the Haze Calamity

The 1997-8 haze episodes resulted in an intensification of regional measures towards cooperation in fire and smoke management. The prolonged problem for the first time posed ASEAN with a serious multilateral problem. It compelled the members to take a bold step towards institutionalizing a regional environmental policy. It also created fear among the Southeast Asian countries of losing their decades old peace and stability. Against such background, in November 1997, senior officials of the ASEAN countries in a meeting agreed to a regional division of labour, with Singapore taking the lead in monitoring fire hazards, Malaysia concentrating on fire prevention measures, and Indonesia on strengthening fire fighting capability. Besides this, Malaysia also provided 1,200 fire fighters to Indonesia and sent three C-13 aircrafts to seed clouds to induce rain to douse the fires. Likewise, Indonesia identified 167 spots from fires across the sprawling archipelago.

Following this meeting, the ASEAN environment ministers met in Singapore on 22-23 December 1997 and adopted Regional Haze Action Plan (RHAP) to address problems of smoke haze in the Southeast Asian region caused by land and forest fires. The ministerial meeting was preceded by the Fourth Meeting of the ASEAN Haze Technical Task Force on 20-21 December 1997. At the environment ministers' meeting, the members extensively discussed the haze problem and noted the following objects:

(1) The smoke haze experienced by the region in 1997 was the most extensive in ASEAN's history, affecting millions of people in the region, particularly in Indonesia, Malaysia and Singapore;

(2) The members were pleased with the fact that the traditional ASEAN spirit of cooperation, solidarity and understanding had continued to prevail even during the most difficult haze period;

(3) The members agreed that the region's joint effort to combat fires and smoke haze had helped to bind ASEAN member countries closer;
(4) The ministers affirmed that ASEAN member countries would continue to protect the environment in their pursuit of economic development, while at the same time work closely to prepare for future environmental challenges, especially those arising from the effect of climate change; and
(5) The members noted that the convening of the ASEAN Ministerial Meeting on Haze, well-in-advance of the next dry season demonstrated the region's commitment and determination to work together to address the smoke haze problem.[15]

The RHAP identified three main objectives to develop better management and enforcement so as to prevent fires, to establish cooperative mechanisms to monitor fires, and to build fire-fighting capability. Thus, the signing of RHAP was a turning point in the region's effort to prevent and mitigate the damage from recurrent transboundary haze.

Meanwhile, in 1998, forest fires in the Indonesian province of East Kalimantan again resurfaced, due to prolonged drought caused by the El Nino phenomenon. To combat the haze, ministerial meeting was held on 25 February 1998 in Kuching, Malaysia. The members decided to take immediate action to combat forest fires and to prevent their spread and agreed to carry out the fire-fighting component of the RHAP. The action plan called for building up national and regional fire-fighting capabilities through a complete inventory of land and forest fire fighting abilities of each country and the identification of resources which could be used regionally. In view of the urgency of the situation, the ASEAN ministers urged Indonesia and Malaysia to work together on the basis of an existing bilateral arrangement on fires and haze prevention and control, with the other ASEAN partners contributing according to their capacities and the requirements of the situation.[16] In this meeting, most ASEAN members voluntarily submitted their national components of the RHAP.

On 4 April 1998, the Third ASEAN Ministerial Meeting on Haze took place in Brunei. In this meeting, the member countries agreed to encourage public reporting of violations and to provide incentive schemes to discourage burning for land clearance. The meeting also reviewed the progress of smoke haze in the region caused by land and forest fires, and decided that Indonesia would lay down the framework of an ASEAN Research and Training Centre for Land and Forest Management and that the centre would be established at the University of Palang Karaya in Central Kalimantan. It was also agreed in this meeting that the Haze Action Plan must focus on the provision of adequate fire fighting equipment and should emphasize more on strict enforcement agencies and personnel at the local level. This meeting further agreed that a Central Revolving Fund would be set up from both regional and international contributions, and welcomed the increasing role of the private sector and the non-government organizations, national and local, as well as outside international institutions to combat, prevent and mitigate fires.[17] Interestingly enough, Malaysia in this meeting donated US $2.5 million for the procurement of fire fighting equipment and also initiated official dialogue with its plantation owners. Further, while intensifying regional efforts, the ministers also launched an initiative to establish two Sub-Regional Fire Fighting Arrangements (SRFAs) for Borneo and Sumatra in order to incorporate mechanisms to rapidly activate and mobilize efforts to put out fires before they got out of control, and channel additional and complementary resources from regional and international sources.[18] Besides this, a landmark development of this meeting was that the Asian Development Bank (ADB) agreed to provide US $1 million to Indonesia for an advisory technical assistance programme and approved a US $1 million grant for the Regional Technical Assistance Programme (RTAP) to strengthen ASEAN's capacity in preventing and mitigating transboundary atmospheric pollution due to forest fires.[19]

On 19 June 1998, the Fourth ASEAN Ministerial Meeting on Haze took place in Indonesia. In this meeting, Indonesia agreed to coordinate an aerial surveillance programme with support from Malaysia (expertise and training) and Singapore (communication equipment). At the Sixth ASEAN Summit in Hanoi in December 1998, the members enunciated a comprehensive long-term vision having 15 major objectives for environmental protection and sustainable development with emphasis on transboundary haze control. At the end of this meeting, the ASEAN leaders declared:

> So as to ensure the sustainability of our nations' development, the protection of the environment shall be an essential part of our economic activities. We shall consolidate and expand our gains in the control and prevention of transboundary pollution, especially the haze arising from land and forest fires.[20]

Transboundary haze in late 1997 and 1998 saw the ASEAN members adopt the RHAP. On 15 April 1999, the ASEAN environment Ministers met in Brunei and reviewed the progress made in the implementation of the RHAP. One of the important decisions accepted by the ministers in this meeting was the policy of 'zero-burning' and promoting this policy among plantation owners and timber concessionaires, particularly in Brunei Darussalam, Indonesia, Malaysia and Singapore, which were most affected by the fire and haze episodes in 1997 and 1998. In this respect, the ministers agreed to use the presumptive clause in the law against open burning. They also committed themselves to the strict enforcement of zero-burning regulations and agreed to use the 'current burning activities in Central Sumatra to show that definite concrete action is taken on the ground to stop the fires'.[21] The members also agreed to launch the ASEAN Haze Action Online, which would include a public access website on fire and transboundary haze and restricted internet-based system for monitoring RHAP implementation. A RHAP Coordination and Support Unit within the ASEAN Secretariat was also to be up. Finally, the meeting appreciated the understanding and support of the international community in collaborating with the ASEAN on the transboundary pollution problem. Given the weak finances in the region because of the crisis, these assistances were particularly timely and important.[22]

In July 1999, the ASEAN environment ministers met in Singapore and endorsed the updated Implementation Plan for the RHAP. This plan identified priorities and actions to be carried out in the short term by the year 2000, and in the medium term by 2003. The plan also displayed a road map to show how far the

RHAP implementation had been activated, recorded its major achievements. These were:

(1) *Monitoring of Fire and Haze Pollution:* The centre piece of RHAP's monitoring activities is a network of national and regional institutions that include the ASEAN Specialized Meteorological Centre (ASMC), national meteorological agencies, and other related agencies in the region. The ASMC which is based in Singapore has been designated to play a lead role in long-range climatological forecasting, early warning activities and detection and monitoring of fire and haze in the region. Since April 2000, meteorological departments of Brunei, Indonesia, Malaysia and Singapore meet regularly to discuss regional climate forecasts and address issues related to fire and smoke haze. The Sub-Regional Climate Review (SRCR) has so far convened more than eight meetings.

The ASEAN Secretariat's RHAP Coordination and Support Unit continuously monitors the haze situation on a regular and region wide basis and shares information through its website. A technical officer has been recruited to look after the website and other information management functions of the unit. The website has been redesigned and upgraded, and provides, among others, daily updated information of hotspot and haze situation in the region with a direct link to the ASMC and a database of upcoming ASEAN events.[23]

(2) *Immediate Action Plans:* The Immediate Action Plans (IAPs) are designed to help local government units and communities in developing comprehensive action plans for forest fire and haze management. The IAP for West Kalimantan was completed with funding and technical support from Australia. The activities carried out were:

(a) Prevention, namely strengthening public awareness and education, training local extension motivators, formulating law enforcement guidelines and familiarizing the public about these;
(b) Monitoring, namely intensification of the application of the early warning system, strengthening early detection

system, and promotion of air quality monitoring system; and

(c) Mitigation, namely preparation of fire suppression mobilization plans (FSMPs) and field simulation exercise of FSMPs at provincial and district/local levels.

An IAP Phase 2 was also implemented for the Riau Province in Indonesia, with funding support from the ADB. The major activities included: (i) drafting and socialization of the governor's decree on land and fire management structure (PUSDALKARHUTLA); PUSDALKARHUTLA is the name of the provincial level agency or coordinating institution for fire management in the Riau province in Indonesia; (ii) development of a ten-year capacity building plan for effective functioning of the land and fire management structure and its relevant agencies; (iii) development of a Forest Fire Management Plan with standard operating procedures including a glossary of technical terms; and (iv) development of an integrated provincial FSMP for the Riau Province.[24] With technical support from the US Forest Service, FSMPs have also been developed for other fire-prone provinces in Indonesia, namely South Sumatra, Jambi, Lampung, Central Kalimantan, South Kalimantan, and East and West Kalimantan. These measures are part of ASEAN's efforts to develop long-term capability to suppress forest fires in other fire-prone areas in the region.

(3) *Law Enforcement Programmes:* Large-scale haze crises that caused transboundary pollution problem were often triggered either by small farmers or large plantation companies to clear land at nominal cost and effort. After the haze catastrophe of 1997-8, the ASEAN countries expressed serious concern about this regional environmental problem and warned the concerned companies about illegal burning. This resulted in the prosecution of a number of plantation companies (mainly in Sumatra and Kalimantan) accused of illegal open burning. Besides this, regional collaborative efforts to enhance the region's capacity for law enforcement actions were taken. These included establishing the SRFA Legal Group on Law and Enforcement in the Southeast Asian region.

(4) *Public Awareness Programmes:* In April 1999, the ASEAN members accepted the 'zero-burning' policy and urged all members to enforce laws and regulations to give effect to this policy. Following this decision, the ASEAN members convened a number of dialogue sessions with plantation companies and timber concessionaires to promote the zero-burning policy. The first dialogue was with plantation countries in Sumatra, held in January 2000 in Riau Province. The second dialogue session took place in Jakarta in July the same year. The third session involving local community, local government agencies, NGOs, plantation companies in West Kalimantan and the SRFA members took place in Pontianak on 22 May 2002. These dialogue sessions tried to raise awareness of zero-burning practices and techniques among plantation companies and attempted to establish a regular forum for maintaining the dialogue sessions with the plantation companies.

The ASEAN also encouraged the private sector, especially plantation companies, to undertake voluntary initiatives to control fire. It also implemented some public/community awareness programmes in fire-prone areas.[25] A workshop was conducted in March 2001 in West Kalimantan to explore the traditional values of Dayak and Melayu tribes in managing fire and haze in or surrounding their areas. This pilot activity was considered successful as the community leaders came to an agreement on the need to further strengthen their existing values applicable for fire and haze control.[26] Thus, with the establishment of the RHAP, the ASEAN laid out the cooperative framework and detailed operational plans to deal with transboundary haze pollution. This was also a proof of ASEAN's determination to actively tackle the problem.

Meanwhile, late February-early March 2000 saw a number of forest fires in three provinces of Sumatra, namely Riau, North Sumatra, West Sumatra, and in West and Central Kalimantan. The rapid spread of fire affected large as on the southern part of Indonesia. This sudden eruption of forest fires forced the Government of Indonesia to declare this problem a national disaster, and warn the concession holders and plantation companies that their licences could be revoked if they were found guilty of deliberately starting the fires. Responding to Singaporean Environment Minister Lee Yock Suan's letter, Indonesia's Environment Minister Sony Keraf assured that the government was taking comprehensive measures to address the situation, including strengthening of the national strategy on controlling land and forest fires and mobilizing resources in the areas where hotspots had been identified. Singapore, as the lead country for the monitoring component of RHAP, provided satellite pictures indicating hotspot locations to Indonesia. Similarly, ASEAN had put into operation its Fire Suppression Mobilization measures in Riau Province of Indonesia in order to contain the spread of forest fire and smoke haze. These mobilization measures were part of the broader Action Plan for the Prevention and Control of Land and Forest Fire and Haze in Sumatra and Kalimantan.[27] Fortunately, due to ASEAN's concerted efforts and sudden increase in rainfall in the second week of March 2000 at certain fire locations, the haze was temporarily cleared.

Immediately after this crisis, the Fifth Informal ASEAN Ministerial Meeting on Environment was held at Brunei Darussalam in April 2000. In this meeting, the ASEAN countries discussed the importance of keeping their commitment to environmental protection and sustainable development and expressed their conviction that the March 2000 haze episode was caused mainly by the plantation companies. The ministers jointly expressed strong objection to such irresponsible behaviour and agreed to take all possible measures to deal with the culprits and to enforce the zero-burning policy.[28]

Following this meeting, the Eighth ASEAN Ministerial Meeting on Environment took place on 6-7 October 2000 in Kota Kinabalu, Sabah, Malaysia. In this meeting, the ministers reviewed the progress of environment cooperation under the Strategic Action Plan and concluded that much progress was being made but the environmental issues were more complex and challenging than ever before. In order to meet these challenges, the ASEAN members needed to strengthen institutional and organizational capacity; promote technology transfer; speed up information networking; and deal with the negative impacts of globalization. The ministers also agreed that effective enforcement measures to tackle forest and plantation fires were needed.[29] Further, the environment ministers in this meeting agreed to 'synergize the ASEAN Strategic Plan of Action on the Environment with the Regional Action Plan for Environmentally Sound and Sustainable Development, 2001-2006 for Asia and the Pacific Region with a view to optimizing the utilization of limited resources in the implementation of the planned activities.'[30] The members also agreed to commence negotiations on an ASEAN Agreement on Transboundary Haze Pollution.

On 10 June 2002, all the 10 ASEAN member countries signed the ASEAN Agreement on Transboundary Haze Pollution. This agreement was signed in conjunction with the World Conference and Exhibition on Land and Forest Fire Hazards. It is the first such regional arrangement in the world that binds a group of neighbouring states to tackle transboundary haze pollution resulting from land and forest fires. The agreement contains provisions on monitoring, assessment and prevention; technical cooperation and scientific research; mechanisms for coordination; lines of communication; and simplified customs and immigration procedures for disaster relief. The agreement also provides for the establishment of an ASEAN Coordinating Centre for Transboundary Haze Pollution Control to undertake the various activities required under the agreement. The agreement entered into force on 25 November 2003.

The Haze Agreement provides a legal basis for the ongoing activities of the RHAP to deal with haze arising from land and forest fires in the region. These include timely and more accurate weather forecasts and early warning measures; strict enforcement of existing laws and enactment of new laws to regulate open burning; training of prosecution and law enforcement officers; development of preventive tools such as GIS database and fire danger rating systems; information management through the ASEAN Haze Action Online website; and mitigation efforts in member countries. Such a speedy conclusion of a regional legal instrument remains a clear testimony of the ASEAN's resolve to deal with regional problems constructively, no matter how complex they may be.[31] It is also an evidence of ASEAN's resolve to tackle land and forest fires and transboundary haze pollution comprehensively. The United Nations Environment Programme (UNEP) has recognized this agreement as a 'global role model' for tackling transboundary issues.[32]

Following the speedy adoption of the Agreement on Transboundary Haze Pollution, a preparatory meeting for the first meeting of the Conference of the Parties (COP) to the ASEAN Agreement on Transboundary Haze Pollution was held on 28-30 April 2004 in Kuala Lumpur, Malaysia. The meeting discussed preparations for the first meeting of the COP, and agreed to recommend the following to the COP: the rules of procedure for the meetings of the COP; the financial rules for the ASEAN Transboundary Haze Pollution Control Fund; the initial organizational structure of the ASEAN Coordinating Centre (ACC) for Transboundary Haze Pollution Control; and the agreement for the management and hosting of the ACC.[33]

The Ninth ASEAN Ministerial Meeting on Haze (AMMH) held on 11 June 2002 in Kuala Lumpur, in which the members decided on the actions to be taken for fire prevention and control in peatlands. The ASEAN Peatland Management Initiative (APMI) was developed with various partners and endorsed by the ASEAN Senior Officials on the Environment-Haze Technical Task Force (ASOEN-HTTF) in February 2003. On 25-26 October 2003, in Bogor, Indonesia, the international organization Global Environment together with the ASEAN Secretariat drafted a strategy document for action plan and sustainable management of peatlands in the ASEAN member countries. The strategy's primary focus was on the following four objectives:

(a) Enhance awareness and knowledge on peatlands;
(b) Address transboundary haze pollution and environmental degradation;
(c) Promote sustainable management of peatlands; and
(d) Enhance and promote collective regional cooperation on peatland issues.

This strategy also set out operational objectives that would contribute to the delivery of one or more of the areas above, which would serve as guidance to ASEAN Member Countries (AMC) and other implementing bodies and collaborating partners through specific action plans and the proposed time frame for these actions. Considering the increasing need for networking and regional and international cooperation to address issues of peatland fire and haze, conservation, sustainable management, and capacity building this strategy could play a key role in creating formal cooperation among AMC through technology and expertise transfer, technical and financial assistance in order to solve peat–related problems, which regularly caused smoke problems in the region.[34] In 1997-8, approximately 80 per cent of the haze was caused by fires in peatlands.

Finally, on 10 November 2004, the Eleventh ASEAN Ministerial Meeting on Haze took place in Hanoi, Vietnam. In this meeting, the ASEAN ministers reviewed the enhanced cooperation in addressing land and forest fires and the resulting transboundary haze pollution. The ministers noted the substantial progress in regional collaborative activities, such as the inventory of fire-fighting resources, the ASEAN Peatland Management Initiative, publication and dissemination of zero-burning and controlled burning practices, early warning information systems, standard operating procedures for monitoring assessment and joint emergency response.[35] These initiatives undertaken by the ASEAN countries to makes it clear that tackling the haze problem is no longer an individual undertaking of the ASEAN countries. It receives a coordinated and concerted response from all the members of ASEAN. The haze issue for the first time clearly formulated a collective response to a regional environmental problem in Southeast Asia.

Extra-Regional Institutions' Initiatives in Fire, Smoke and Haze Prevention

To control land and forest fire and haze, a number of international development partners (bilateral and multilateral), many of whom provided direct support to the implementation of ASEAN RHAP, took active part. To tackle the haze crisis, the ASEAN received the support of the ADB, Global Environment Facility (GEF), United Nations Environment Programme (UNEP), United Nations Development Programme, individual governments, and non-governmental organizations. To control land and forest fire and haze, the UNEP and the Australian government have extended technical assistance to ASEAN, amounting to US $50,000 and 1,73,000 respectively. Countries like Canada, Denmark, France, Finland, Japan, Germany, New Zealand, Nigeria, Norway, Spain, Russian Federation, UK and USA also wholeheartedly extended their support in combating and preventing land and forest fires.

The ADB has taken a proactive approach on many environmental issues to protect the ASEAN region's environment. One of the most pressing issues in the 1990s was the threat of forest fires affecting the Southeast Asian region. The raging fires forced the affected ASEAN countries to draw up strategies for coordinated action at national and regional levels. At the ASEAN level, the RHAP was formulated and endorsed by the ASEAN environment ministers in late 1997. This represented a turning point in the region's approach to the problem. The ADB responded by providing advisory technical assistance to Indonesia and regional technical assistance to ASEAN in order to strengthen capacity to put the plan into operation. It granted US$ 1 million to Indonesia for an advisory technical assistance programme and US$ 1 million grant to ASEAN for Regional Technical Assistance Programme (RTAP) to strengthen ASEAN's capacity in preventing and mitigating transboundary atmosphere pollution due to forest firest.[36]

Besides ADB, the UNEP, having the mandate from the United Nations Secretary General to monitor and coordinate the global assistance and expertise provided by the international community through the UN system, has been playing a catalytic role in soliciting and mobilizing resources from donor countries. The UNEP through the Global Environment Facility (GEF) funding is implementing the project 'Emergency Response to Combat Forest Fires in Indonesia to Prevent Regional Haze in Southeast Asia'. The main objective of the project is to contain forest fires in Indonesia and to combat regional haze in Southeast Asia. The main operation of the project has been the coordination of international and regional efforts on preventing and combating forest fires, establishment of an effective early warning system, establishment of GIs database, raising national, regional and global public awareness of the profound impacts of forest fires, and dissemination of lessons learned to other countries facing similar environmental disasters. One of the pertinent aspects of the UNEP-GEF project is to establish an early fire warning detection mechanism including local fire risk assessment, an aerial surveillance regime for Sumatra, and betterment of communication system. Following a request from the ASEAN members, the UNEP supported the 'Sumatra Fire Fighting Surveillance Pilot Project—Phase I and II', held from 27 July-8 August 1998 and 3-21 November 1998, respectively in the Riau Province of Sumatra. The main activities of this programme were early detection of fires using aircraft, near real-time remote and ground based information, photo documentation of fire sites, communication of fire information to ground fire stations, and rapid ground checking and fire suppression. The UNEP also raised the idea of using high-resolution remote-sensing data for early fire detection in the Southeast Asian region, and assisted the ASEAN members in preparing a spatial database consisting of elevation, hydrology, geology, settlements, land use and infrastructure which would be helpful in planning fire suppression activities and mobilizing resources.[37]

Further, outside the United Nations system, a number of international organizations like the World Bank, the World Wide Fund for Nature (WWF), the Centre for International Forestry Research (CIFOR), and the International Centre for Research in Agroforestry (ICRAF) have provided financial assistance and expertise to help ASEAN strengthen its capacity in preventing and mitigating transboundary atmosphere pollution caused due to forest fires.

Role of NGOs in Haze Prevention

The haze crisis in Southeast Asia brought the members of ASEAN to seek various international and foreign institutions and NGOs for aid, advice and funding. In Indonesia, the relation between NGOs and the State has always been bitter. There has been little love lost between Indonesia's NGOs and Suharto's 'New Order' government, which spurned non-governmental involvement in domestic and political matters. The NGOs on some environmental issues have categorically supported the rights of individuals and communities against the State and powerful interests. Accused of supporting workers' rights for their criticism of governmental policies, the NGOs frequently pressured the Suharto government for greater political pluralism. The Indonesian government, which treated these activities as 'political' never accepted the views of the NGOs. However, owing to international pressure and acknowledging the real need for pollution control and protection of environment, the Indonesian government in 1978 established the Ministry for Development Supervision and the Environment. The prime purpose of this ministry was to promote the idea of an efficient and economically and environmentally sound development that would utilize and manage resources for sustainable development and improve the quality of life. Unfortunately, the ministry failed to perform its desired functions due to the non-cooperative outlook of the Suharto government. This resulted in a number of environmental NGOs mushrooming all over Indonesia. Of these, SKEPHI (Sekretariat Kerjasama Palestarian Hutan Indonesia) and WAHLI (Wahana Lingkungan Hidup Indonesia) are the most important.

Established in 1980, WAHLI is a Jakarta-based network of local and regional NGOs located throughout the Indonesian archipelago. This NGO, an umbrella group for a number of NGOs, gained reputation for balancing advocacy and objective analysis in the 1980s, and it frequently put pressure on the Suharto government for larger political transparency. While openly disagreeing with the government issues ranging from endangered species management to indigenous peoples' rights and the granting of logging concessions over 'public' land, WAHLI openly called for a 'development process in which the people of Indonesia have a decisive voice in the formulation of policy about resource use in their areas.'[38] However, WAHLI's most dramatic challenge to President Suharto's development policies came in December 1988, when it sued PI Inti Indorayon Utama Ltd., a pulp and rayon factory based in northern Sumatra and backed by Suharto's eldest son and several government ministers, for compensation for damages caused by the factory's unchecked pollution and deforestation in the surrounding areas. Although WAHLI lost the suit against the government, it was seen as a moral victory for the NGOs and environmentalists of Indonesia.[39] Even in allowing the suit to proceed, the Indonesian courts had acknowledged for the first time that an agency could represent the environment, or a community, that was not the central government itself.[40] In fact, the WAHLI laid the ground work for future victories of the environment movement and the Indonesian people. As a result, in the 1980s and 1990s, the environmental NGOs of Indonesia played an active and influential role against the government's environment policy and put enormous pressure on Indonesian companies through international consumer campaigns.

The haze episodes in 1997 and 1998 brought many NGOs together and they (mainly WAHLI) pressed the Suharto government to police its own regulations. Activists in Kalimantan and elsewhere exposed the more flagrant violators and played a key role in delivering immediate relief measures, including the distribution of face masks and first-aid for respiratory complaints.[41] The outcry of various NGOs (mainly the WAHLI group) against the Suharto government, the exposure of military's involvement in timber companies (in 1980, 24 out of 34 companies had military involvement), and Suharto's sons' involvement in the International Timber Cooperation of Indonesia (34 per cent share) were reasons for the end of Suharto's rule in 1998.

Thus, the activities of NGOs and other interest groups in Indonesia posed a severe challenge to every aspect of ASEAN's character and modalities, since the Association sought to interpret the developments in Indonesia as intrinsic to the group-dynamics of the institution. The pressure from NGOs influenced ASEAN members to take a major step towards institutionalizing a regional environmental policy. The setting up of the ASEAN Cooperation Plan on Transboundary Pollution was no doubt a major achievement of the NGOs in the Southeast Asian region.

On 19 June 1998, the Fourth ASEAN Ministerial Meeting on the haze took place at Singapore. In this meeting, the ASEAN members finally accepted the role of NGOs in preventing transboundary haze pollution. The final communiqué clearly said: 'The Ministers also welcomed the increasing role of the Non-Governmental Organizations and the private sector in regional, national and local efforts to combat, prevent and mitigate fires. To this end, the Ministers welcomed regular dialogue between NGOs and the ASOEN Senior Officials on the forest fires and haze matters.'[42] Thus, acceptance of the role of the NGOs empowered the communities most affected threatened by forest fires to take up necessary preventive steps free from interference of the state machinery and from private interests. In other words, the endorsement of the positive role of NGOs has turned these organizations into key actors in Southeast Asia, ready to take strong measures[43] in the context of new world order, and being accepted as a major player in the ASEAN policy community. However, the acceptance of the positive role of NGOs also poses an additional problem for the newly enlarged ASEAN. The group presently incorporates countries in which civil society is either underdeveloped (as in the case of Laos) or is dominated by elites who contest or reject outright the legitimacy of autonomous agencies in civil society (as in the case of Cambodia, Vietnam and Myanmar). If ASEAN modalities are to be modified to recognize NGOs as an essential actor within the domestic and regional policy community, a major divide might crop up between the old and new ASEAN states in the coming days.

CONCLUSION

Having analysed the haze episode and its impact on Southeast Asia, it cannot be overemphasized that Southeast Asia remains a very important strategic region, both politically and ecologically. It is politically significant to the interests of the West, Japan and China. Its forest and other natural resources remain home to a significant level of biodiversity. Its forests act as potential sinks that have the capacity to absorb significant amounts of carbon in the atmosphere. Thus, any erosion in the quality of natural resources or political instability in any of the states can have significant impacts beyond the region. The land and forest fires in the 1990s (especially in 1997-8) in East Kalimantan and Sumatra and thus spill-over effects of transboundary air pollution in other countries of Southeast Asia came into international limelight due to their severity. This smoke-haze pollution virtually removed the boundaries of the countries of Southeast Asia without violating the principle of non-intervention. The crisis brought all the members of Southeast Asia on a single platform to develop and implement comprehensive regional strategies within the framework of a environment conservation strategy for the region.[44] It also displayed the importance of cooperative mechanism in the context of regional interaction and integration and enabled the region to fight any fires that do break out, and mitigate their effects. By making national plans an essential requirement for participating in the RHAP, the principle of non-intervention was respected, while simultaneously allowing room for negotiation and diplomatic persuation. This would help avoid any miscommunication and misunderstanding in the process of negotiations with one another and with the external donor community, and clearly display the growing importance of the doctrine of functional cooperation, which remains the pillar of ASEAN.

The success of ASEAN in resolving the haze crisis cannot be measured merely in terms of immediate gains of policy making. The most important achievement of ASEAN members in tackling transboundary haze crisis is their significant and concerted efforts towards institutionalizing a regional environmental policy and generating a broad consciousness among the actors at the local and regional levels. However, to resolve this haze catastrophe in its entirety, the ASEAN countries needs more time, more scientific plans, sustained commitment, firm determination and a broader regional outlook based on cooperation, interaction and integration. For a hazeless environment, the ASEAN members also need further change in the mindset of the governments, bureaucrats and the logging companies, whose careless attitudes have often resulted in uncontrolled forest fires in the past.

Notes

1. Tridib Chakrabarti, 'The Environment Battlefield in Southeast Asia: The Haze Catastrophe and Regional Responses', in Purusottam Bhattacharya and Sugata Hazra (eds.), *Environment and Human Security*, New Delhi, 2003, p. 180.
2. Ibid.
3. James Cotton, 'The Haze Over Southeast Asia: Challenging the Asian

Mode of Regional Engagement', *Pacific Affairs*, vol. 72, no. 3, Fall 1999, pp. 333-4.

4. 'Politics and Peat: The One Million Hectare Sawdh Project', *Inside Indonesia*, no. 48, October-December 1996, http://www.insideindonesia.org
5. Chakrabarti, 'The Environment Battlefield', p. 177.
6. Ibid., p. 182.
7. Ibid., p. 178.
8. Annual Report 1994-5, ASEAN Standing Committee, ASEAN Secretariat, Jakarta, 1995, p. 7.
9. Chakrabarti, 'The Environment Battlefield', p. 179.
10. Annual Report 1994-5, p. 41.
11. 'ASEAN: An Overview', ASEAN Secretariat, Jakarta, 1995, p. 56.
12. 'Surin Pushes "Peer Pressure"', *The Bangkok Post*, 13 June 1998.
13. Chakrabarti, 'The Environment Battlefield', p. 194.
14. Amitav Acharya, *Constructing a Security Community in Southeast Asia: ASEAN and the Problem of Regional Order*, London, 2001, p. 157.
15. Joint Press Statement, ASEAN Ministerial Meeting on Haze, 22-23 December 1997, Singapore.
16. James Cotton, 'The Haze Over Southeast Asia', pp. 343.
17. For details see http://www.gov.sg/env/psi/pad/rel–42–98.html (25 May 2004), p. 2.
18. Chakrabarti, 'The Environment Battlefield'; pp. 185-6.
19. David Rosenberg, 'Environmental Pollution Around the South China Sea: Developing a Regional Response', Contemporary Southeast Asia, vol. 21, no. 1, April 1999, p. 141.
20. *Vietnam*, Embassy of the Socialist Republic of Vietnam in India, New Delhi, January 1999, p. 21.
21. Joint Press Statement, Sixth ASEAN Ministerial Meeting on Haze, ASEAN Secretariat, Jakarta, 16 April 1999.
22. Chakrabarti, 'The Environment Battlefield', p. 188.
23. For details see www.haze-online.or.id/help/chronology.php (21 May 2005).
24. Ibid.
25. Chakrabarti, 'The Environment Battlefield', p. 190.
26. For details see www.haze-online.or.id/help/chronology.php (21 May 2005).
27. Chakrabarti, 'The Environment Battlefield', pp. 191-2.
28. For more information see www.haze-online.or.id/docs.php
29. http://www.arcbc.org.ph/Asian_environment_policy.html (15 March 2003).
30. Second ASEAN State of the Environment Report: 2000, Chapter 11, p. 168.
31. For details see www.haze-online.or.id/ (17 February 2005).

32. www.aseansec.org/ar04/CHAPTER%204.pdf (19 May 2005).
33. Ibid.
34. See www.pffsea.org/frames/friends/part.html (22 February 2005).
35. For details see www.haze-online.or.id (19 January 2005).
36. www.adb.org/documents/reports/regional cooperation/theme 400.asp (22 February 2005).
37. See www.rrcap.unep.org/issues/forestfi/UNEP initiatives.cfm (22 April 2005).
38. James F. Riker, 'Linking Development from Below to the International Environmental Movement: Sustainable Development and State–NGO Relations in Indonesia', *Journal of Business Administration*, January 1994, pp. 168-9.
39. Chakrabarti, 'The Environment Battlefield', p. 198.
40. Joshua Gordon, 'NGOs, the Environment and Political Pluralism in New Order Indonesia', www.hawaii.edu/cseas/pubs/explore/v2/ gordon. html (25 January 2005).
41. James Cotton, 'The Haze over Southeast Asia', p. 346.
42. Joint Press Statement, Fourth ASESN Ministerial Meeting on Haze, 19 June 1998, Singapore, http://www.aseansec.org/ function/prhaze4. html, p. 3 (25 June 2000).
43. Cotton, 'The Haze over Southeast Asia', p. 351.
44. Chakrabarti, 'The Environment Battlefield', p. 199.

Postscript: Recent Trends in Historiography

Ranjan Chakrabarti

Fernand Braudel, a well-known French historian and the front-runner of the Annales school, made a laudable effort to write a total history of the Mediterranean world giving sufficient importance to the role of geography and climate behind history in a *longue durée* context.[1] Regrettably, there is no such Braudelian history of South Asia yet, though there may be a few noteworthy exceptions at the regional or local level.[2] Historians who practiced history of India or colonial Bengal mostly preferred to steer history along the ideological and political lines. For example, many of them wrote hundreds of pages to identify the political forces that led to the Battles of Plassey (1757) and Buxar (1764) but did not show the carefulness to historicize the riverscape, waterscape, landscape, climate and the natural world in the heart of which all these political events were unfolding.[3]

Alfred Crosby, the author of *The Columbian Exchange: Biological and Cultural Consequences of 1492*, records a parallel development that transformed global ecology forever, the trans-Atlantic movement of plants and animals in which Europe transported staple crops like wheat, oats and fruits along with pigs, horses, and goats to the Americas, where they were not known, and sent back to Europe with the New World crops like maize, potatoes and beans.[4] The continents on the reverse side of the Atlantic, which were very different, began to become biologically and ecologically similar as a result of the discovery of America. Both Fernand Braudel and Alfred Crosby were able to raise new and fundamental questions, primarily because they conceived history, unlike many of us, in ecological, biological and cultural terms. The geographers and geologists have discovered how the Bengal Delta had been molded through the ages by the action of rivers. It was the historians' turn to determine how much Bengal's political economy, its production, crop pattern, inland and overseas trade, openness, demographic pattern, culture and economy, were designed by its river systems and hydrology. But, it is surprising enough to note that historians remained by and large unenthusiastic to be drawn into these essential questions. As a result, there is a grave slippage and silence in India's history relating to the ecological and historical significance of rivers. It is indeed necessary to reverse the trend and encourage young researchers to write Indian history from a fresh perspective. This is one of the important objectives of this revised edition of the book.

In the context of Indian history, I would prefer to argue along with Donald Worster[5] to make some space in history textbooks for the voice of nature to be heard distinctly. From the early Indus/Saraswati civilization, named after the river system in which it was located, through invasions from Asia and Europe to the division of India and Pakistan in 1947, and finally the human tragedy caused by the tsunami of December 2004, the people of South Asia have influenced, and been influenced by, their ecological surroundings in more ways than one.

The historiography of environmental history of India or South Asia is fast expanding, and at present there seems to be no dearth of books in this field. Since the first edition of *Situating Environmental History* was published in 2007, a large number of monographs and edited volumes have been published. However, out of these published works, very few endeavoured to address issues relating to the methodology or historiography of environmental history. Interestingly enough, the comprehensive accounts of the environmental history of India are even fewer. Much of these works are specific case studies harping upon the regional ecological or forest histories, histories of land use, natural calamities or environmental movements in the colonial or post-colonial contexts. A brief historiographical sketch is given here by reviewing a limited number of works published after 2007, the year of publication of the first edition of *Situating Environmental History*.[6] While this preface to the fresh edition of the book is sketchy and not comprehensive, it nonetheless, gives an idea of the different directions in which environmental history went after 2007.

Christopher Hill's 2008 book[7] made an attempt to present a total chronological history of India, Pakistan, Bangladesh, Nepal, and Sri Lanka from the perspective of the mutual relationship between humankind and the environment. Hill reveals how the civilizations of this geographically diverse region came into existence through their interactions with the physical environment – a relationship with particularly strong social and spiritual dimensions because of the interdependence of the predominantly agrarian population and the land. His focus swings from ancient irrigation techniques and adjustment of peasant societies to the environment, to the forceful thrust of British imperialism on the natural world, the effect of post-colonial technology, and the interaction of religion with ecological issues. But the scope of the work, though laudable, is too large and ambitious to handle in a single volume as attempted by the author.

Deepak Kumar, Vinita Damodaran and Rohan D'Souza who edited the 2011 anthology[8] is a follow-up account of the 1998 book titled *Nature and the Orient* (1998) edited by Richard Grove, Vinita Damodaran and Satpal Sangwan, which collected several dozen essays on the various aspects of environmental history of South Asia and for many years it helped scholars to open up new research frontiers. As such, it served a number of purposes and presented a broad overview of the historiography of environmental history of the region, to develop further on the research programme laid out by Grove, especially the ecological impact of colonialism and the colonial environmental knowledge systems, and, more broadly, to publicize the necessity of taking the empire as a useful scale of analysis in environmental history between the constraints of the local and the global histories. The volume emphasizes the empire-wide interconnections that fashioned South Asian environmental history from the eighteenth century onwards. It does this by classifying the subject into five cardinal themes, most of which were crucial to Grove's vision of the environmental history of South Asia. Richard Grove possessed the rare skill to draw these kinds of global linkages, and the editors overtly acknowledge that the collection reproduces only fragments of his broader vision.

Angela Mendonca et al. (eds), in *Natural Resources, Sustainability and Humanity: A Comprehensive View* (2011)[9] aims to study the mutual relationships of humans and the natural world through time and on diverse sites. It sees environmental history as consisting of three levels. The first deals with nature itself as it affects human history. The second shows how the human socio-economic structure interacts with the environment, causing reciprocal changes. The third is intellectual, showing how individuals and groups represent nature in the realms of literature, philosophy, religion and popular culture.

Sajal Nag's work, published in 2017,[10] argues that environmental history is not merely a history of forests or rivers, but also of agriculture, climate, economic practices and human culture. There is no aspect of environment which has not felt the impact of the presence of humans. Rivers have, thus, either dried up or are polluted with intoxicants. Seas and oceans have become the dumping ground of nuclear and other wastes. Streams have choked, rains reduced, forest covers depleted, wildlife has dwindled, concrete jungles have replaced green fields and natural water-bodies, desertification of landscapes has happened. It has had its own impact on human life as well. Droughts, floods, dust storms, landslides, water shortages, agricultural decline and food crises, starvation and epidemics followed. Planet earth and its inhabitants are currently in the throes of the most devastating human-made crisis for survival. In an attempt to enhance our understanding of the environmental crisis, this particular collection of essays focuses on a wide variety of environmental events ranging from understanding climate from the logbook of East India Company to the construction of the ideas relating to Himalayan tropics, the environmental cost of damning the Damodar river to water politics of south India, impact of the tsunami of the 1737 as well as of 2004-05, politics over earthquake rehabilitation and the Sarna movements of Eastern Indian tribals.

The recently published volume titled *Critical Themes in Environmental History of India* (2020) edited by the present author [11] addresses the fundamental questions of environmental concern in today's time and enquires into the complex patterns of the human–nature interaction within the discipline of environmental history in India. This book delves into history to address a number of critical themes in environmental history like rivers, water bodies and water, forest, land use, wildlife and the issue of the history of climate in India. It focuses on the methodological and historiographical aspects of environmental history and raises new questions to open up new windows leading to fresh research questions. This book argues that environmental history would serve as one of the important gateways to the history of the human-nature relationship such as, explore the role of water history in understanding the present context of water in Indian cities. It is a powerful reminder of the fact that in the context of Indian history it is now necessary to listen to the voice of nature more carefully.

As scholars from diverse disciplinary backgrounds are contributing to the field of environmental history – it has acquired an interdisciplinary character and remain an open-ended subject. Environmental history shares a very porous border with economic and social histories, history of science and technology, and with various other sub-fields of history. Environmental historians, historical geographers and historical ecologists are usually engaged with similar sorts of questions though their methodologies may vary.

> The choice of the subject of research is the unique autonomy of historians. Themes in environmental history like rivers, forest, land use and wildlife and the issue of climate are featuring frequently in recent researches on environmental history. Water history in particular is gaining popularity. Water is always a symbol of social, economic and political relationships – a barometer of the extent to which identity, power and resources are shared. In recent times we are witnessing a growing concern over water. The current environmental agenda, including the questions associated with climate change, are related to the question of sustainable management of water. [12]

Rivers and water resources have been central to the prosperity and survival of the human civilization in South Asia. For northeastern India and Bangladesh, the river is vital as it provides for sweet water and the annual gift of the fertile silt for farming.[13] Agriculture in this part of the world is heavily dependent on traditional 'overflow irrigation'.[14] Changes in the Indian monsoon over the past ten thousand years may explain the spread of agriculture in South Asia, as well as the rise and fall of the Harappan civilization.[15] Again, in different periods of Indian history, we have references to rulers dishing out to the peasants, hit by severe droughts, the package of exemption of land revenue. Human societies had found ways to adapt to the hydrological regimes and processes in South Asia – the variabilities, scarcities and excesses that occur over space and between seasons.[16]

Environmental science has established that water has a very complex relationship with soils, plants and human needs. Indian cultural heritage also endorses this. Resource-insensitive utilization of water may lead to rapid disruption of the essential ecological processes that recharge and renew water resources and make them available perennially for the generation of plant, animal and human life. Modern water management in capitalistic economies looks upon water as a stock to be tapped. Such an approach to water resource management that views water as stock and not as a flow in the water-cycle generates a misconception that through large man-made structures water resources can be augmented. However, water resource cannot be created. It can be stored, diverted, used, polluted, but its overall availability cannot be enhanced.[17]

There has been a great proliferation of interdisciplinary research in recent years in global environmental history with its thrust on environmental humanities.[18] Global environmental history is the historicized aspect of the lives of humans, societies and species, both human and non-human, as regards the various facets of their relationships with the physical and biological environment. Its intellectual origins, Richard Grove has argued, can be traced to the encounter of seventeenth and eighteenth-century western Europeans, especially naturalists, medical officers and administrators, with the unfamiliar natural world of the tropics, and to their realization of the damage being done to these environments in the course of resource extraction by European colonial empires.[19] Concern for environment among humans is not new. However, the present environmental crisis is unique in nature. The earth's protective layer of stratospheric ozone is no longer in a very healthy state. Until the first self-sustaining nuclear reaction in 1942, there was no nuclear waste anywhere on earth, but now things have fundamentally changed. The last century was a period of unusual environmental turbulence. Human activities, such as forest clearance, the use of fire and fossil fuel, fishing, farming, industrialization, use of advanced technology to extract natural resources in an unprecedented speed, have altered things. The fundamental question that has emerged on the surface is what a 'legitimate use' of the environment by humans should be. Global environmental history is rooted in environmentalism and historians are currently engaged in ascertaining the salient features of global environmentalism.[20] In global environmentalism, all local issues may become global issues and all global issues may become local issues. Both local and global problems have equal importance. It is on the basis of micro-studies on local ecosystems that macro-analysis can be made. This is precisely why global environmental history is increasingly assuming a *glocal* character.[21]

Interestingly, climate history is emerging as a crucial component of global environmental history. Climate history calls for an in-depth understanding of the inter-connection between water resources on the one hand and deforestation, rainfall, soil erosion, climatic change, global warming, drought, famine, and various natural calamities on the other. Another stimulating subfield relating to climate and political unrest has been opened up by scholars like Sam White (*The Climate of Rebellion in the Early Modern Ottoman Empire*)[22] and Zheng Jingyun and others (*How Climate change Impacted the Collapse of the Ming Dynasty*).[23]

Sam White explores the significant and far-reaching consequences of the 'Little Ice Age' in Ottoman lands. The author shows how extreme cold climate and drought sparked off the destructive Celali rebellions (1596-1610). This rebellion exerted an adverse effect on Ottoman fortunes and eventually led to their collapse. Based on the reconstructed temperatures, rainfall changes, and occurrences of extreme climate events, together with historical records on financial deterioration, food crises, and the frequencies of widespread unrest, rebellions and wars, Zheng Jingyun and his colleagues identified the principal ways in which climate change contributed to the collapse in the Ming Dynasty. The severe droughts occurring in 1627-1643 was a key factor behind the peasantry uprising. These droughts also played a weighty role to promote the peasantry uprising, especially reviving the peasantry troops by recruitment of famine victims when they were almost on the brink of perishing in 1633 and 1638, and severely unsettling the food supply for the government army, resulting in the final defeat of the government troops by the peasantry troops. This study contributes to an understanding of the climate-related mechanisms behind the collapse of the Ming Dynasty, and provides a historical case study that improves our understanding of the nature of interactions between climate change and social vulnerability.[24]

Climate has also made its way into another important sub-theme of environmental history in recent years, namely, health and epidemics. To cite just one example from the recent publications, Anthony McMichael (*Climate Change and the Health of Nations: Famines Fevers, and the Fate of Populations*, 2017),[25] an Australian epidemiologist, highlights the historical connections between environmental change and human health over the last 5000 years. The book discusses about societies gaining advancements in personal wealth and material comfort at the expense of natural resources. As the author looks back at the shifts in climate patterns and their effects on humans, he notes, for example, the decline of ancient Mayan cities. Desiccation in the eighth-century BC resulted in water shortage, decline in food production and stress on the social and political system. The book reveals how the break up of the Roman Empire, the bubonic plague at the time of Justinian, and the mysterious collapse of the Mayan or Harappan civilizations all have roots in climate change. [26]

Richard Grove has already shown the links between drought in South Asia and the institutional responses to it and the beginnings of modern scientific understandings of climatic connections between global scale tropical circulation and the strength of the Asian monsoon.[27] In colonial India, repeated droughts and famine sparked off institutional innovations and the Indian Famine Code (1883). It also triggered off a sharp debate about the connection between deforestation and rainfall change among the British officials.[28] It is necessary to historicize the debate in the light of the pre-colonial traditional perceptions of climate as it existed in India and South Asia. This may not be very well documented. But one has to understand that there are scattered and indirect references to climate and rainfall, pattern of tropical monsoon, and cyclonic depressions (which are important to quantify the available water resources and their historical role) in many ancient and medieval texts like the *Mahabharata* and *Ramayana*, the *Puranas*, *Arthasastra*, Kalidasa's works, several Chinese accounts and the writings of Mughal court historians. The ancient Greek sources relating to Alexander's invasion may be of some help too. Cultural representations of natural calamities or climate as found in literature or various visual arts are also worth looking into. It is high time to embark on projects of constructing comprehensive histories of water and climate change in South Asia.

NOTES

1. Fernand Braudel, *The Mediterranean and the Mediterranean World in the Age of Philip II*, Vol I, Berkeley: University of California Press, 1995 (1st pub. 1949 and revd. 1966).
2. Iftekhar Iqbal, *The Bengal Delta: Ecology, State and Social Change, 1840-1943*, London: Palgrave, 2010, see also Richard Eaton, *The Rise of Islam and the Bengal Frontier*, 1204-1760, Los Angeles: University of California Press, 1973, etc.
3. Cf. Rajat Kanta Ray, *Palasir Sarajantra O Sekaler Samaj* (in Bengali), Kolkata: Ananda Publishers, 1994; S. Chaudhary, *The Prelude to Empire: Plassey Revolution of 1757*, Delhi: Manohar, 2000, B.K. Gupta, *Sirajuddaulah and the East India Company*, Lieden: E.J. Brill, 1966, etc.
4. Alfred Crosby, *The Columbian Exchange: Biological and Cultural Consequences of 1492*, Westport (CT): Greenwood Publishing Group, 2003 (1st pub. 1972)
5. Donald Worster, *Nature's Economy: A History of Ecological Ideas*, Cambridge: Cambridge University Press, 1977 also Donald Worster (ed.), *The Ends of the Earth*, Cambridge: Cambridge University Press, 1988.
6. The list presented is far from exhaustive. The works mentioned and discussed here have been selected either because of their larger geographical sweep presenting an all India or global perspective or because of their significance from the point of view of their methodological perspectives. Books with grand narratives of regional or local environmental events, however, important but without a global perspectives/connections have been deliberately left out. This is precisely the reason why Sajal Nag's otherwise excellent works on environmental

history (*Pied Pipers in North-East India: Bamboo-Flowers, Rat Famine and the Politics of Philanthropy, 1881-2007*, Delhi: Manohar, 2008, or *Playing with Nature: History and Politics of Environment in North-East India*, Delhi: Manohar, 2017) have not been preferred in the context of the present discussion but his another book (*Force of Nature: Essays on History and Politics of Environment*, Delhi: Manohar, 2017) has been included in the discussion.

7. Christopher Hill, *South Asia: An Environmental History*, Santa Barbara: ABC-Clio, 2008
8. Deepak Kumar, Vinita Damodaran and Rohan D'Souza (eds.), *The British Empire and the Natural World: Environmental Encounters in South Asia*, Delhi: Oxford University Press, 2011.
9. Angela Mendonca, Ana Cunha and Ranjan Chakrabarti (eds.), *Natural Resources, Sustainability and Humanity: A Comprehensive View*, New York: Springer, 2012.
10. Sajal Nag, *Force of Nature: Essays on History and Politics of Environment*, Delhi: Manohar, 2017.
11. Ranjan Chakrabarti (ed.), *Critical Themes in Environmental History of India*, Los Angeles/London/Delhi: Sage, 2020
12. Ranjan Chakrabarti, *Critical Themes in Environmental History of India*, op. cit., pp. xi-xii.
13. The Brahmaputra river basin in India is most generously gifted with a fabulous water wealth that accounts for nearly 30% of the water resources and about 40% of the total hydropower potential of the country, Cf. Sutapa Sengupta et al. (eds.), *Rivers and Riverine Landscape in Northeastern India*, New Delhi: Concept, 2006, pp. 39-40, passim, also www.zeenews.com/news 575946.html.
14. Radhakamal Mukherjee and others attributed Bengal's social ecology to 'overflow irrigation' which once nourished Bengal's agricultural prosperity and held the colonial policy of construction of railroad and roadway embankments as the root cause of the decline of this prosperity. The decline of Bengal's economy has been also ascribed to the eastward shift of the Ganges. However, 'overflow irrigation' still remains the main plank of agriculture in modern northeastern India and Bangladesh; see Radhakamal Mukherji ,*Changing Face of Bengal, Kolkata: University of Calcutta*, 1938, S.C. Majumdar, *Rivers of Bengal Delta, Kolkata: Government of West Bengal, 2001;* The collapse of Bengal's prosperity in the 18th and especially in the 19th centuries came as the result of significant interference with delta's ecology. Central and western Bengal were especially hard hit. Murshidabad, and especially Burdwan impoverished and turned into malaria stricken tracts; see also Richard M. Eaton, *The Rise of Islam and the Bengal Frontier 1204-1760*, New Delhi: Oxford University Press, 1994, Iftekhar Iqbal, *The*

Bengal Delta: Ecology, State and Social Change, 1840-1943, London: Palgrave, 2010.

15. Ranjan Chakrabarti, History and Future of Water in South Asia, A Preliminary Probe, *From Exploitation to Sustainability: Global Perspectives on the History and Future of Resource Depletion*, Stuttgart: Nova Acta Leopoldina, 2013, pp. 81-90
16. Ranjan Chakrabarti, *Does Environmental History Matter?* Kolkata: Readers Service, 2006. p. xviii.
17. Vandana Shiva, *Ecology and the Politics of Survival*, London: Sage, pp. 183-8, has drawn our attention to the negative effects of the engineering bias in water management. It fails to perceive the natural river flows as critical to drainage, to recharge of groundwater, to the maintenance of the balance between fresh water and sea water. The engineering bias in water use results in large projects, which produce serious ecological instabilities and generate conflicts. The Bengal delta may be a case to track this case. The Gangetic delta covers a huge area in Bengal. The delta has been formed by the action of three great rivers, the Ganges, Brahmaputra and Meghna. The Ganges in particular has remarkable social, cultural and economic significance. Writing in the last quarter of the 18th century (between 1786-8), Ghulam Hussain Salim the author of *Riyazu-us-Salatin,* New Delhi: Idarah-I Adabiyat-i, 1975, (translated by Abdus Samad,) commented: 'Hindus have described volumes on the sanctity of this river. Considering the water sacred they fancy that bathing there washes the sins of a lifetime, especially bathing at certain *ghats*, like Benaras, Allahabad, Hardwar. 'The rich among the Hindus bring the water of the Ganges from long distance, take particular care of it, and on auspicious days, worship it. The truth of the matter is, that the water of the Ganges, in sweetness, lightness and tasteness has no equal, and the water of this river, however, long kept, does not stink.'
18. It is an interdisciplinary area of research, drawing on the many environmental sub-fields that have emerged in the humanities and social sciences over the past few decades, in particular environmental literature, environmental philosophy, history, feminist studies and science and technology studies, etc. Cf. http://environmental.humanities.ucla.edu.
19. Gabriella Corona (ed.), What is Global Environmental History? Conversation with Piero Bevilacqua, Guillermo Castro, Ranjan Chakrabarti, Kobus du Pisani, J.R. McNeill, Donald Worster, *Global Environment* 2 (2008), pp. 228-49, http://www.environmentandsociety.org/sites/default/files/key_docs/Forum-GE-2-2008_0.pdf, accessed on 17/11/20.
20. Ibid.
21. Ibid. Global environmental history also calls for the handling of the

problems created by Western hegemony in its production of knowledge. One of the ways to overcome this western centric bias is to de-westernise and de-colonise the knowledge systems, and place more emphasis on traditional or indigenous knowledge systems. The present environmental crisis has acted as an eye opener and convinced us of the need to retrieve these knowledge systems worldwide and substitute them for the westerncentric paradigms.

22. Sam White, *The Climate of Rebellion in the Early Modern Ottoman Empire*, Cambridge: Cambridge University Press, 2011.
23. Zheng Jingyun et al., 'How Climate Change Impacted the Collapse of the Ming Dynasty', *Climatic Change* (New York: Springer) November 2014, 127 (2), pp. 169-82.
24. Low temperature, aridification, and desertification during a cold period destroyed the military farm system, which was the main supply system for the provisioning of government troops on the northern frontiers; these impacts increased the military expenditure from 64% of total government expenditure in 1548-1569 to 76% in 1570-1589 and thus aggravated the national fiscal crisis that occurred during the late Ming dynasty. Secondly, climate deterioration (e.g. low temperature, aridification, and an increase in the frequencies of frost and drought-related disasters, etc.) led to a 20-50% reduction in the per capita production of raw grain in most areas of China, which resulted in widespread food crises and exacerbated the vulnerability of social structures during the last several decades of the Ming dynasty.
25. Anthony McMichael et al., *Climate Change and the Health of Nations: Famines, Fevers, and the Fate of Populations*, Oxford: Oxford University Press, 2017
26. The scholars are curious to know the relation, if any, between the ongoing pandemic of Covid-19 and global climate change. All viruses and bacteria are products of nature unless they are biotechnologically engineered or artificially invented in laboratories. There is no hard evidence of a direct link between climate change and the outbreak of Covid-19 yet. Climate change may indirectly affect the COVID-19 response, as like all other viruses it may thrive under specific weather conditions. Generally, most emerging infectious diseases, and almost all pandemics in history originate in wildlife, and there is evidence that increasing human encroachment on the natural environment may facilitate the emergence of new diseases. Consolidation of health infrastructure, surveillance of infectious disease in wildlife, livestock and humans, and protection of biodiversity and the natural world, reduce the risks of future outbreaks of other new diseases; Cf. https://www.who.int/news-room/q-a-detail/coronavirus-disease-covid-19-climate-change, accessed on 21/11/20.

27. Richard Grove and Vinita Damodaran, 'Imperialism and Environmental Change, Unearthing the Origins and Evolution of Global Environmental History from Edmond Halley to John Richards: 1676-2000', Ranjan Chakrabarti (ed.), *Does Environmental History Matter? Shikar, Subsistence, Sustenance and the Sciences*, Kolkata: Readers Service, 2006, pp. 35-86; also Richard Grove, *Green Imperialism: Colonial Expansion, Tropical Island Edens and the Origins of Environmentalism*, Cambridge: Cambridge University Press, 1995.
28. Ranjan Chakrabarti (ed.), *Does Environmental History Matter?*, op. cit.

Contributors

KARL JACOBY is Associate Professor in the Department of History, Brown University, USA.

ALOK KUMAR GHOSH is Research Associate with the Department of History, University of Kalyani, Kalyani, India.

ARUN BANDOPADHYAY is the Nurul Hasan Professor in the Department of History, University of Calcutta, Kolkata, India.

ARCHANA PRASAD is Reader in History at Jamia Milia University, Delhi, India.

VINITA DAMODARAN is Director at the Centre for World Environmental History, University of Sussex, UK.

RITAJYOTI BANDYOPADHYAY is Sylff Fellow at the Department of History, Jadavpur University, Kolkata, India.

KAUSHIK ROY is Lecturer at the Department of History, Presidency College, Kolkata, India.

ARABINDA SAMANTA is Reader in History at the University of Burdwan, Burdwan, India.

AMAL DAS is Professor at the Department of History, University of Kalyani, Kalyani, India.

SAHARA AHMED is Lecturer in History at the Rabindra Bharati University, Kolkata, India.

JAGDISH N. SINHA is Reader in History at Rajdhani College, Delhi.

SUMIT GUHA is Associate Professor at the Department of History, Rutgers University USA.

RITA PEMBERTON is Senior Lecturer in History, at The University of the West Indies, St. Augustine (West Indies).

LAWRENCE G. GUNDERSEN is Professor of History and Political Science at Jackson State Community College, Tennessee, USA.

TRIDIB CHAKRABARTI is Professor in the Department of International Relations, Jadavpur University, Kolkata, India.

Index